THE BIG LIE

Books by David Solway (a selection)

THE BIG LIE

ON TERROR, ANTISEMITISM, AND IDENTITY

David Solway

A COUNTERBLAST BOOK

First published in Canada in 2007 by
Lester, Mason & Begg
491 Davenport Road
Toronto M4V 1B7

Library and Archives Canada Cataloguing in Publication

Solway, David, 1941–
The big lie: on terror, antisemitism, and identity / David Solway.

"A counterblast book."
Includes bibliographical references.
ISBN 978-0-9781765-0-1

1. Terrorism. 2. Jihad. 3. Antisemitism. 4. Civilization, Western. 5. Liberalism.
I. Title.

HV6431.S645 2007   303.6'25   C2007-900090-8

Copy Editor: Andrea Knight
Book Design and Typesetting: Mark Goldstein

Printed and bound in Canada
07 08 09 5 4 3 2 1

for Karin and Hannah

Table of Contents

There she crouched, the old Uraka,
In the chimney-corner cowered,
Melting lead and casting bullets,
By her side her son Lascaro.

—HEINRICH HEINE, "Atta Troll"

Their very fund of strength,
Satan, bestrides the globe.
He stalks its breadth and length
And finds out even Job.

—ANTHONY HECHT
"It Out-Herods Herod. Pray You, Avoid It."

On the Left are grinning dogs, peering down into a solitude too deep to
*   fill with roses.*
On the Right are sensible sheep, gazing up at a pride where no dream
*   can grow.*

—W. H. AUDEN, "For the Time Being"

In the big lie there is always a certain force of credibility; because the
broad masses are always more easily corrupted in the deeper strata of
their emotional nature than consciously or voluntarily; and thus in the
primitive simplicity of their minds, they more readily fall victims to the
big lie than the small lie."

—ADOLF HITLER, *Mein Kampf*

Preface

"Fortunate boys!" said the Controller. "No pains have been spared to make your lives emotionally easy..."
"Ford's in his flivver," murmured the D.H.C. "All's well with the world."
—ALDOUS HUXLEY, *Brave New World*

In September 2001, I happened to be staying on the remote Greek island of Tilos, serenely oblivious to what was going on in the world and occupied mainly with my own work. The new book of poems was proceeding well, the letters from home were reassuring, my landlord's good-natured wife plied me daily with fruit and homemade pastries and saw to it that my writing table was redolent with cut flowers. The island itself was stunningly beautiful, all soaring mountain and lush, alluvial valley, home to several rare varieties of wild bird, and blessed with seascapes giving onto a glitter of small, circling isles. With a local population of only 350 inhabitants and limited tourism, the rhythm of daily life was relaxed and pleasant. The only practical issues one had to deal with, it seemed, were which *kafeneion* to take one's breakfast in, which beach to visit in the afternoon, and which restaurant to patronize in the evening. I had no trouble for the time being subscribing to Browning's sentimental hallelujah from *Pippa Passes*: "God's in his heaven, All's right with the world." It seemed apt.

On the morning of September 12, I was sipping my coffee in one of the portside *kafeneia*, scribbling in my notebook and trying to damp out the inevitable strains of "Zorba the Greek" on the perpetual audiotape when my attention was drawn to the television screen flickering over the counter. A knot of men had gathered around the set in almost complete silence, which struck me as odd given their usual excited volubility. At first I thought they were watching a B-grade war movie or CIA thriller as the camera tracked the flight of two passenger jets into

the World Trade Center, culminating in the typical Hollywood extravagance of leaping flames and billowing smoke, plummeting bodies, and
hysterical crowds panicking in the streets. But then something even
stranger than Greek silence occurred. The image was replayed, and
then replayed many times over again, as if the film had snarled in an
endless loop. The men still did not speak but remained riveted to the
set. Suddenly a commentator appeared on the screen and in solemn
tones explained that terrorists had attacked New York and that thousands of people were dead.

The pall of silence lasted a few minutes longer as we digested the
news, but soon everyone had an opinion to offer. The Greeks are no
friends of the Americans but they have never forgotten the 400-year
occupation they suffered under the Turks and their aversion to Islam
is universal. "We have another bloody Sultan on our hands," someone
said. It was then that I first heard the name Osama bin Laden, which
has now acquired the status of a proper noun. It fell from the lips of
the café proprietor as the Greek-inflected "Osama been London," causing me to react in surprise. Had there been a second attack in London
as well? "No, no," my interlocutor replied, "Osama *been London!*" The
enigma was resolved by an English tourist standing beside us, who
corrected the pronunciation and assured me that London had been
spared. But this prank of articulation struck me as somehow prophetic,
for it gradually dawned on me as we spoke that New York was only the
first act in what would be a prolonged, unofficial war and that other
cities in the West could expect to be targeted *sti sira*, as the Greeks say,
one after another. It is curious how in the midst of tragedy or disaster,
the mind begins to play facetiously. In the ensuing years, I thought, one
would say "Osama been London," "Osama been Paris," "Osama been
Rome," "Osama been everywhere." But the frivolity of the word game
soon faded into a profound intuition of present menace.

From that moment on, nothing was the same any longer. All the
usual concerns, pleasures, and preoccupations that filled the hours
vanished as the horror and magnitude of the event and the prospect of
a sanguinary future began to sink in. I spent the rest of the day wandering aimlessly about, sensing that the world had changed irrevocably
and that there were no more enclaves of safety and recreation, no more
"Greek islands" where one could enjoy time out of time, be leisurely and
unconcerned, admire the views, disregard the burdens and confusions

of the real world, write poems destined for slender audiences of literary sophisticates in Toronto and Montreal, and pretend that one was not implicated in history. When the shock had abated somewhat, I decided that I should return home immediately, but the travel agency informed me that all transatlantic flights had been cancelled and even local ferry traffic had been indefinitely suspended. No one knew what the coming days would bring, but there was a distinct possibility that, along with the modest cohort of tourists on the island, I might find myself marooned on Tilos for months.

As a young man living in Greece in the late 1960s, I had awakened one morning—it was April 21, 1967—to the sound of martial music spilling from the radios and the news that a military putsch had taken place. Over the next year and a half I counted my share of harrowing if predictable experiences, including the threat of imprisonment, constant surveillance by the *Asfalia* or security police, the loss of my teaching job for spouting anti-Junta sentiments, and one interesting episode when I found myself facing down a tank in the streets of Piraeus, the turret machine gun trained on my chest. But none of this had shaken my basic feeling of self-assurance. Being young and Canadian, I was presumably invulnerable. Despite the need to be vigilant and wary and ultimately to rely on the protection of the Canadian government, it had all seemed like a great adventure that would eventually issue in a rich store of anecdotes with which to regale my friends back home.

September 2001 was different. Although I was not personally threatened and had no reason to seek asylum again in the Canadian embassy, my self-assurance—the assumption of inviolability and non-involvement—had crumbled and been replaced by an unexpected feeling of responsibility coupled with a deep sense of intellectual insecurity. "No man is an island, entire of itself," John Donne had written in the 17th *Devotion*, "every man is a piece of the continent, a part of the main." Tilos, I understood, was a part of New York, and I, like my neighbour at the next table listening intently to his transistor, was united in catastrophe with my fellow man. As Donne had asked rhetorically in his meditation, "Who takes his eye from a comet when that breaks out?" An island is a good place on which to get some thinking done, especially as all the customary social props are unavailable, distractions kept to a minimum, and one is thrown back chiefly on one's own resources.

Tilos became for me a kind of stoa, an olive grove, a lyceum in which I had no alternative but to stroll back and forth, more or less solitary, to focus on the comet, as it were, and assess its impact.

During the next several weeks, I submitted myself, perhaps for the first time in my life, to a kind of Cartesian interrogation, a relentless scrutiny of the values and beliefs I accepted as gospel. What did I really *know*? How solidly grounded in authentic knowledge were the political convictions I habitually expressed with such negligent insouciance? What were the sources of my attitudes, ideas, and judgments? Why was I almost instinctively anti-American and, for that matter, anti-Israeli in my sentiments? Why did I wish to deny my kinship with Jewish thought, Jewish communion, Jewish antiquity? Why did I march in my thoughts with the Palestinians, the anti-globalists, the welfare socialists, the Peace Now movement? Why did I consistently vote Left as if no other option were even imaginable? Did such intellectual conformity make life emotionally easier for me, binding me to a coterie of the wise, the virtuous, and the just? Intellectually speaking, I had thought that I was pole-vaulting; was I instead merely doing the limbo? Was I in search of psychological shelter rather than political edification? Did my unquestioning compliance with the ideological axioms of the day have anything to do with tilling the ground for such terrorist atrocities as I had just witnessed? Was I in some way guilty? What did I *know*?

The answer I arrived at jarred me to the very foundations. When it came to my political beliefs, my state of mental preparedness, and what is called one's "world view," the truth was that I knew practically nothing. The sundry university degrees I had accumulated also meant next to nothing, mere alphabetical excrescences added to my name, not dependable signs of accomplishment or acuity. I felt and acted out of mere prejudice and fortuitous conjecture, out of an unexamined desire to think in accordance with the inferences and presuppositions of my friends and colleagues, my fellow poets, my intellectual contemporaries, who were all members in good standing of the approved Left and who, like me, had been educated, at least initially, in the roiling universities of the Student Revolution in the utopian 1960s. We had embraced the multicultural pieties of the era, were duly anti-colonialist, anti-corporatist, anti-Zionist, sabbatarian, and postmodern, and had grown convinced that imperial America had to be "brought to its knees." But the evidence for the credos I shared with my contemporaries did not emerge from a scrupulous cultivation of the relevant literature or a broad familiarity with primary documents. I had not consulted sound historians and the more trustworthy political analysts and philosophers—those who did not necessarily share my congenial opinions. Rather, the sources I—and we—relied on were the editorials of the *New York Times*, the *Guardian*, and the *Globe and Mail*, the news reports of the BBC and the CBC, the pages of the *Nation* and the *New Republic*, the popular accounts of American perfidy that crammed the shelves of the major book chains, and, most significantly, the smog of stock conceptions that were "in the air," pervasive but insubstantial as are all airy things. It had now become clear to me that this state of intellectual and psychological affairs was no longer tenable.

When, several weeks later, something like normality had been restored and the day came to leave the island, I had by then understood that I would have to remake my thinking, recalling Rainer Maria Rilke's famous conclusion to "The Bust of Apollo": "You must change your life." It was no longer possible to revert to the *status quo ante* and to continue mistaking reflex gestures for cognitive perspicuity, bias for insight, phobia for enlightenment. A fresh point of view was necessary. I would have to recognize that poring over books on prosody and poetic theory to the exclusion of politics and history would no longer do. I would have to give myself over to genuine study and to check my susceptibility to the infectious notions that percolated in the atmosphere of the times. I would have to remember anew that as a Jew I was and always would be at risk, and that it behooved me to acquire a deeper familiarity with my own tradition, with the subtle and not-so-subtle maneuverings of the antisemitic Left, and in particular with Islamic theology, if I were not to become just another ignorant and helpless victim of malice, revulsion, or violence. I would have to distrust my friends and mentors, learn to read critically, think independently and arrive at my own verdicts. I would have to ready myself for rejection from what I now regarded as the aristocracy of the like-minded, to which I was once proud to belong. In short, I had to become honest with myself or, should that turn out to be too fugitive a goal, at least to fail honourably in the effort. And the way in which I determined to set about my re-education was to write this book. The unexamined life, as Socrates told us, is not worth living.

But there is little doubt that the book I decided to write is in some ways a rather unusual one. It is not intended as a historical narrative or as a seamless development of a single political thesis. Instead, the plan I adopted, following the examples of Leo Strauss in such works as *Persecution and the Art of Writing* and *On Tyranny* and Alain Finkielkraut in *La Défaite de la pensée*, was to link together related yet discrete essays bound by a skein of interconnected motifs. Each would contribute in a different way to an overarching theme, tributaries to the same turbulent river. In the first essay, I chose Michel Houellebecq's recent polemical novel, *Platform*, as a starting point for my investigation of militant Islam and the left-liberal ethos that commands the intellectual life of the West. It furnished me, so to speak, with the platform on which to erect my general argument. Beginning as a survey of the critical reviews that met the novel's publication, the auditing method enabled me to work up my own critical review of the mindset that encourages so damning a response and to move from there into a dissection of the anatomy of the times. In the second essay, I embarked on a search for my long-neglected Jewish roots, which evolved into a personal meditation on the meaning of Judaism, the complex nature of Islam, the demonology of antisemitism as directed against both the Jewish diaspora—in Europe especially—and the Jewish state, the never-ending story of Middle Eastern conflict and the metamorphic concept of *adamat Israel*, the "land of Israel." In this portion of the text I finally became aware that antisemitism, in its occidental (or Christian) as well as its oriental (or Islamic) guise, did not only affect me privately or impinge only on the life of my family and my people. Penetrating its dynamic was also crucial to a grasp of the lengthy and troubled trajectory of Western civilization.

The essays in this book, then, seek to elaborate a composite and panoptic view of the central predicament confronting the world today: the onslaught of a theologically-inspired terrorist movement which, in the minds of most observers, cannot be dissevered from the conflict raging interminably in the Middle East and which thrives parasitically on the left-liberal belief-system that presently dominates the sensibility of the West. Although the tremors of this undeclared war have spread throughout the world, its perceived epicentre is the Israel/Palestine nexus. But as we will see, the Israeli/Palestinian conflict is by no means the most significant question for the West, despite the tenacity of our aberrant conviction. Palestine is the Trojan horse of the Islamic world—an analogy first used in the current context by Yasser Arafat and his cronies for whom the Oslo Accords were regarded as a means of destabilizing Israel. The real conflict in the Middle East is not over borders or Palestinian self-determination, but over the right of the Jewish people to exercise its sovereignty in its ancestral homeland. The major issue for the rest of us is the rise of a global jihad and the almost universal opprobrium in which America—and by extrapolation the historical endowment of Western civilization—is held by the official institutions of the international community and by a vast number of its own educated (and uneducated) citizenry. What Irshad Manji has called the "theocracy of tolerance" for militant Islam now on exhibit in the West is intimately connected to this internal condition of ambiguity and vacillation regarding the value of our own civilization.

These are questions that will need to be addressed directly and unsentimentally if we are to come to an understanding of the situation and an effective means of dealing with it, assuming that it is not already too late. The omnibus tendency in the world press and in such institutions as the United Nations, the International Court of Justice at The Hague, and the European Union to appease a mondial Islamic insurgency, stymie American efforts to combat the growing menace, and vilify Israel for any and every policy it adopts to defend itself against the threat to its very existence should not be allowed to sidetrack us from assessing the nature of our dilemma in the struggle against a determined and ruthless antagonist.

This is what I have attempted to do here. I am conscious, however, that many readers will reject my attitude throughout this work as unnecessarily dark and pessimistic. Like the yeshiva schoolmaster who ladled honey on the Hebrew letters so the learning would be sweet, I might have sought to make both my tone and my message more palatable to my readers, but I am afraid the truth—so far as it is determinable—remains, like most effective medicines, as bitter as it is necessary. I recall in this connection the poet Shelley's caution in *Hellas* regarding the apocalyptic turn of mind, "drain not to its dregs the urn/Of bitter prophecy." But such counsels of wisdom should not induce us to ignore the ominous previsions of another, twentieth-century poet, who sensed that:

Mere anarchy is loosed upon the world,
The blood-dimmed tide is loosed, and everywhere
The ceremony of innocence is drowned...

Yeats was thinking of the looming upheavals of his time, but his premonitions continue to apply and cannot be brushed off as mere poeticizing.

I am also aware that many readers will dismiss the tone of my argument as too irascible and personal, and go on to impugn its content as objectionable and inordinate. But I would maintain that, on the contrary, it is my detractors who err on the side of moral anemia and intellectual diffidence, the former masking as good taste and the latter as proper scholarly deportment. I readily grant that I have grown impatient of mannerly writing in the midst of the firestorm. Others will complain that my research is selectively chosen and presented for maximum effect or to score points against my ideological adversaries, but here I can only reiterate that before 9/11 I was solidly in the camp of those against whom I am now litigating. I read Chomsky with approval, harboured duly anti-American sentiments, abominated George W. Bush and Ariel Sharon, commiserated with the Palestinians, subscribed to the appropriate dailies, and agreed with the political slant taken by our major news networks. The truths I began to uncover in the process of a painful re-education left me disoriented for some considerable time but determined nevertheless to abide by my findings. For this book was written against the grain as I came to realize that I had been wrong about nearly everything—my research was conducted in a spirit of non-partisan inquiry and my conclusions did not derive from a preordained search for answers in the service of a prior commitment. And I have noticed, too, that many of those who may be said to support my general thesis flinch from expressing their convictions in plainspeak, that is, in language that may endanger their safety, offend their readers, imperil their professional credentials, or require them to enrol in sensitivity training sessions. They are willing to go out on a limb, but not so far as to fall from the tree. These two broad classes of readers and writers, the complicit virtuous who, whether they know it or not, work for the enemy and the conflicted tremulous who work against their friends, may be in for a rude awakening.

There are several salient facts that we must now acknowledge. We must recognize that terror and antisemitism are intimately related; in particular, the weakness of our response to the one and the waxing strength of the other are reciprocal indicators that we are living in a faltering society. We must come to terms with the fact that we are under sustained attack and that we will have to respond courageously and with open eyes. We need to see that our very civilization is threatened and that, for too many years now, we have practised the rites of evasion, craving asylum in blindness, conciliation, sophistry, and equivocation. There is no more pressing requirement for us today than the obligation to reconsider our ideological premises and to revise both the concepts and the vocabulary with which we react to the world.

Taken together, this is my subject.

I

Platform:
A Biography of the Occidental Tourist

I am not so anxious that we should note the horrible savagery of these acts as concerned that, whilst judging their faults so correctly, we should be blind to our own.

—MICHEL DE MONTAIGNE, "On Cannibals"

*In our city where all are besieged, each man and woman of us is
    invidiously and painfully beset.
The enemy has sundered all ways whereby we might transcend, even
    abjure this perfectly severed state;
We, our own enemies, permit few words to pass between us, fewer even
    with a weight of poetic joy.
The expert pigeon rises confidently over us freighted with our bemused
    injunctions...*

—HARRY MATHEWS, "Volusian Music"

And the West has not come to terms with the Arab, and I include the Palestinian, mentality. We project a Western approach—that if only we do this, they'll do that. We turn a blind eye to where they're coming from and what they're thinking.

—ARI JESNER, conversation reported in
DAVID HOROVITZ, *Still Life with Bombers*

1

Michel Houellebecq's *Platform* has been reviewed and discussed so often by now that it is scarcely necessary to recapitulate the plot of this complex and vexing novel. Suffice it to say that the various *pensées* and adventures of its feckless protagonist in a world devoid of meaning, his dismissal of the common values and assumptions that once governed everyday life, the ennui of a directionless existence, the sexual escapades in which this modern anti-hero at times vicariously and at times ravenously participates, his eventual discovery of an unlikely love and compatibility-in-unfaithfulness, the terrorist violence in which it comes to pieces, and the squalid denouement of a largely misspent life in the cold indifference of a barren solitude provide us with a vivid portrait of contemporary mores as repellant as it is convincing.

When they are not merely rehashing the story, the holier-than-thou attitude adopted by many if not most reviewers of *Platform*, prompts the inevitable question. Can this commentariat of the enlightened intent on merdifying both the author and his book all be wrong?[1] "Michel Houellebecq is an ugly writer, vulgar, silly, sex obsessed. His heroes are unprepossessing loners…and generally, egotistically, they are named Michel" is how Jenny Turner begins her *New York Times* review. (Though one of the reasons for the presence of "Michel" might be as a stylistic import from Hitchcock's filmic self-introductions, to which no one seems to object.) Variants of her condemnation are ubiquitous. "The characters in *Platform* are detestable," Max Winters piously intones in the *San Francisco Chronicle*. The *Independent*'s Boyd Tonkin wonders if, "Sooner or later, will we all be bored stiff by the internet homilies of Cardinal Houellebecq?" For Janet Maslin, reprinted in the *International Herald Tribune*, "the plot development [is] far too sentimental for the book's overriding contempt" and is "dangerously ambiguous" in its "casual racism and…scorn for the Muslim world."

Similarly, Alex Lefebvre, representing the French socialist outlook on the ICFI website, chides Houellebecq for "glorify[ing] the most depraved feelings" and goes on to sing a *Dies Irae* over "anti-Muslim racism or hysteria over 'security' issues." Julian Barnes writing in the *New Yorker*, albeit with approximate respect, nevertheless points out that the novel is somewhat flimsy in structure and consistency of tone, the narrative "unevenly paced" and the bouts of invective inadequately founded. And so it goes. The overall critical perspective on the book gives new meaning to the term "et cetera."

There are a few welcome exceptions to this wall-to-wall strain of media obloquy, like Charles Taylor's brilliant assessment in the *Boston Review* and Salman Rushdie's advocacy in the *Guardian Review*, but they are few and far between. Is there little, then, that redeems this work—and its attitude to the cultural "platform" of our era—apart from its weird, exotic flavour and the bracing if disturbing candour of its author? Are we dealing with another Céline whose racist musings and habitual spite must ultimately estrange the reader or with the depressive world view of a novel-writing Cioran giving us yet another short history of decay? Is novelist Will Self right when he dismisses Houellebecq as "just a little guy who can't get enough sex"? Or, on the contrary, are we confronting someone and something quite different, a fearlessly honest writer delivering a rigorous and imperturbable analysis of our time, laying out the age in cross-section?

Despite the torrent of objections, there can be little doubt that the book develops enormous torque and staying power in its pursuit of what it proposes as an important truth. Houellebecq's books work less through strict verisimilitude than in the mode of fable or parable, one story contained within or evincing another. He is, after all, a poet as well, plying the customary techniques of allusion and anagoge, whose oeuvre is haunted by the shade of Baudelaire, in particular, *Le Spleen de Paris*. (Michel at one point quotes pertinently from the poet.) The difference is that Baudelaire's Parisian microcosm morphs into Houellebecq's international macrocosm. But there is an epic component as well to his analogical structures. In some ways, *Platform* is like an ironic rewrite of Bunyan's *The Pilgrim's Progress From This World To That Which Is To Come*; in others, like a tourist excursion through Dante's *Inferno*. Most significantly, the personal account of the novel's anti-hero encloses within it the arc of a social world fast approaching terminal breakup. Michel's investments of emotion (such as they are), the damaging choices he tends to make, his larval inconsistencies, his gainful lassitude, and his predictable losses are also ours, irrespective of how numbed, unlovable, and alien he may strike the reader. What Houellebecq is giving us in the peregrinations of this cynical voluptuary through the circles of his private world is a kind of modern allegory, a public disclosure of the intrinsic meaning of events as "[h]umanity in all its different forms…creep[s] into the third millennium"—the story really gets under way on New Year's Day, 2001. As Dante explained, "literra gesta docet, quid credas, allegoria" (the literal sense teaches the fact, the allegory what you should believe). For Michel is an emblematic figure, an accurate and unflattering mirror whom the reader must learn to accept as *son semblable*.

Extrapolating from the reviews and the considerable roof-chatter the novel has generated, it is clear that *Platform* is seen as a more or less *interesting* if off-putting work, on the one hand morbidly incisive, on the other full of juicy episodes, chiefly sexual, that cannot but intrigue as much as they may offend, whether morally or representationally. But even faint praise, with which unfriendly reviewers and prunella-minded critics sometimes leaven their animadversions, is usually grudging. The critical response to the book likes to foreground issues of credibility—one thinks of the lawyer-wife Audrey subbing as an S & M dominatrix, an episode that tends toward the risible—but then what novel does not contain blemishes of realization or minor-character weaknesses? More to the point, the response, as we have seen, is almost always qualified by a perhaps understandable reluctance to empathize with the protagonist's disagreeable personality, his distressing convictions and problematic actions, the creepy itinerary he follows as he embarks on no less than a career of sexual entrepreneurship, and especially with what many deem as a gratuitous and over-the-top denunciation of the Islamic faith, which, in their estimation, steers uncomfortably close to actionable defamation.

The question is whether these exorbitant passages—arguably the most emotionally charged and socially volatile portions of the text—are a sign of the character's peculiar pathology or would be better placed against the backdrop of the author's own reflections on contemporary events. Considering that Michel is not the only character in the novel to express such opinions, and given the author's recent arraignment in the French courts for disseminating anti-Islamic asper-sions, the answer must be self-evident, despite Houellebecq's intermit-tent disclaimers, patently designed to keep reporters and journalists at arm's length and avoid further proscription. The man knows what he's doing and continues incorrigibly to do it. As Anita Brookner allows in her review of *Platform* for the *Spectator*, despite contriving to prudently avoid the Islamic question almost entirely, "Houellebecq ploughs a lonely furrow of political incorrectness." His publisher, Flammarion, apparently agrees, having proceeded to distance itself from its trouble-some author in the wake of the Grand Guignol spectacle of French judicial proceedings and the growing Islamic backlash—the same backlash, incidentally, that has recently resulted in Brigitte Bardot's daffy conviction on the charge of racism in a Paris court for protesting the Islamization of France in her new book, *Un cri dans le silence*. Bardot may be an intellectual lightweight but nevertheless had the *chutzpah* to accuse Muslims of being "invaders, barbaric and cruel, responsible for terrorist acts," in the words of the judgment brought down against her. (She does not, however, appear to have been abandoned by her publisher, Éditions du Rocher.) In the interim, the physical threat posed by a Houellebecq-hating Arab to the crew filming an interview with the author in Paris on September 6, 2002, forcing the interview to be conducted in the safety of the crew car, goes uninvestigated by the authorities. The policy of non-confrontation with an obvious threat is only inviting more trouble, which the future will provide in spades.

Platform is no mere fictional exercise or self-indulgent fancy. Houellebecq is not playing metaphorical paintball; he is, like the antag-onist he targets, playing for keeps. It is therefore important to recog-nize two things. First, that far too much is made of the supposedly prurient element; the sex merely lubricates the politics for readerly consumption. And second, that the "Islamic" tropes are not extrane-ous to the story, part incoherent rant and part adjectival insistence, but are central to its substantive theme and testimony. Houellebecq's anti-Islamic harangue exists at the very heart of his constatation and is meant to be construed as the other face of Western complicity and blindness. This is often not appreciated. James Buchan, for instance, in his *Guardian* put-down, objects to Michel's derogatory view of European culture as "lonely, demeaning, faithless" and reckons that Houellebecq has euchred himself by endorsing the Islamic account of the West: "Michel is the Muslims' friend." But Houellebecq is enunciating what is basically a warning, signalling the alarm, raising the ante. In other words, his message should rather be interpreted as, "Let us be advised; let us *not be* the Muslims' friend." Otherwise, to cite from his second book of poetry, *Le sens du combat*: "Je sens s'accumuler les prémices d'un désastre."

The burden of the story or at least one of its key thematic strands is that, for all its nihilistic decadence and uncontrolled individualism, the West is worth defending. There would be no reason for producing such a novel unless the author, a profoundly *serious* man, had a redemptive purpose in mind. The defence of one's society, however, does not rule out simultaneously adopting a pugnacious attitude toward it. In a provocative essay entitled "To Stay Alive: A Method," Houellebecq writes, with reference to the authentic intellectual and the farsighted writer, "The goal of the society where you live is to destroy you. You have the same goal with regard to society. The weapon that it will use is indifference. You cannot allow yourself to have the same attitude. Attack!" But this attack is a prosecution in the public interest, a remedial assault upon those aspects of our society that work against its best elements and would prevent it from surviving, not to mention flourishing. This is the register in which *Platform* as well as Houellebecq's earlier publications find their justification. What most reviewers refuse to see is that he is writing far more as *amicus curiae* than *in partibus infidelium*, and that he should be taken at his word when he confides in his 1998 essay collection *Interventions* that "la seule supériorité que je reconnaisse, c'est la bonté." (The only superiority that I acknowledge is kindness.) "Mais au fond," asks Michelle Levy in her spirited vindication of Houellebecq's work on her Paris website, "n'est-ce pas un appel pour une société aux rapports humains retrouvés, renouvelés?" (But at bottom, is it not an appeal for a society with rediscovered and renewed human values?) The evidence from Houellebecq's poetry is equally persuasive, as, for example, in this stanza from *Le sens du combat*:

> *Donnez-moi la paix, le bonheur,*
> *Libérez mon coeur de la haine.*
> *Je ne peux plus vivre dans la peur,*
> *Donnez-moi la mesure humaine.*

(Give me peace and happiness,
Release my heart from hatred.
I can no longer live in fear,
Give me the human scale.)

—his expansion of Baudelaire's famous lines from "L'invitation au voyage," "Là, tout n'est qu'ordre et beauté,/Luxe, calme et volupté." (There, all is order and beauty,/Profusion, calm and voluptuousness.)

But our world is now under siege, not only from radical Islam—"Something stirs in the East, a sleepless malice," says one of the characters in *The Lord of the Rings*—but from Western anomie and its blatant philistinism. Indeed the former preys relentlessly upon the latter as it does upon its ineluctable corollary, the presumably tolerant and progressive ethos of so-called liberal thinking for which Houellebecq has little sympathy. One can imagine Houellebecq's abhorrence of the type represented by some of the novel's ephemeral "intellectuals," cookieless browsers like the journalist who, in his appraisal of the carnage wrought by Islamic terrorists on the Eldorador Aphrodite nightclub in Krabi (a clairvoyant pre-run of Bali), opines that "the reaction of the Muslims was understandable," or the bituminous editorialist who, "pick[ing] up the theme in his weekly diary," proleptically sums up what has become the staple liberal reaction to the tragedy of 9/11 thus: "Faced with the hundreds of thousands of women who have been sullied, humiliated, and reduced to slavery throughout the world…what do the deaths of a few of the well-heeled matter?" (The book appeared two weeks before 9/11.)

These passages are uncannily prophetic of the Leftist response to 9/11 expressed in articles, conferences, and lectures in the very shadow of the event. Indeed, on September 12, 2001, while Ground Zero was still smouldering, influential "rights activist" and former head of the University of Colorado's Ethnic Studies Program, Ward Churchill, published an online essay, entitled "Some People Push Back: On the Justice of Roosting Chickens," praising the "gallant sacrifices" of the terrorist "combat teams" and referring to the victims of the attack as cellphone-toting "little Eichmanns" conducting America's business in the "sterile sanctuary of the Twin Towers." (The passengers on the ill-omened airliners were clearly too unimportant to mention.) One day later, Robert Jensen, a professor of journalism at the University of Texas at Austin and author of *Citizens of the Empire*, published an op-ed article in the *Houston Chronicle* in which he declared that "my primary anger is directed at the leaders of this country" and expressed his deep concern for those who might be on the receiving end of American retaliation. His great fear was not "the fear of where will the terrorists strike next" but of "when and where" the United States will inflict its reprisals and "which civilians will be unlucky enough to be in the way...." (Jensen has also come to Ward Churchill's defence, claiming that his essay was an attempt "to take love out of the realm of dreams and make it real in the world," and that in his central themes, "Ward Churchill is right.") On September 16, Edward Said published a comment in the *Observer* in which, while professing sympathy with the dead and injured, he went on to deprecate the American "superpower almost constantly at war...all over the Islamic world," the "ignorance of 'Islam' that takes new forms every day," and "the influence of oil, defence and Zionist lobbies." Advising his readers to avoid fictive constructions that only complicate the issue—this from Said!—he placed 9/11 in the context of "the Iraqi people's suffering under US-imposed sanctions" and, of course, the "Israeli occupation of Palestinian territories," concluding that the "roots of terror" lay in "injustice." No one seemed to notice that this was the rhetoric of the ideological scavenger, picking over the carcasses to feed his hatred and fatten his agenda. Shortly afterward, on September 24, Susan Sontag in an article for the *New Yorker* claimed that 9/11 "was not a 'cowardly' attack on 'civilization' or 'liberty' or 'humanity' or 'the free world' but an attack on the world's self-proclaimed [sic] super-power, undertaken as a consequence of specific American alliances and actions." Similarly, and on the same day, Peter Dale Scott, a transplanted Canadian and the author of several books of crepuscular verse, jumped on the anti-American bandwagon, proclaiming via telephone hookup to a class at the University of California at Berkeley that "what goes around comes around," and defending the terrorists who, we are assured, "aren't cowards, if nothing else, it surely isn't cowardly to ride the plane in for something you believe." Less than a month later, on October 10, Naomi Klein writing in the *Nation* responded to the bloodbath of 9/11 by considering that, "Now seems like a good time to challenge the forces of nihilism and nostalgia *within our own ranks* while making more room for the voices...showing that it is indeed possible to challenge imperialism..." (italics mine). In a speech delivered at

MIT on October 18, entitled "The New War Against Terror," Noam Chomsky, in a typical effort to manufacture dissent, asserted that the US was "apparently trying to murder 3 or 4 million people," that "plans are being made and programs implemented for the death of several million people in the next couple of weeks, not Taliban of course, their victims" and that the American retaliatory strike against the Taliban and Osama bin Laden should be understood as "some sort of silent genocide." The sheer nonsense of his ramblings somehow escaped his university auditors. In an article entitled "The Spirit of Terrorism" for *Le Monde* of November 2, 2001, the cynosure of the postmodern Left, French philosopher Jean Baudrillard, wrote of the "prodigious jubilation of seeing this global superpower destroyed"; he went on to explain that "this is the one which, in its unbearable power, has fomented all this violence that is innate the world over." On December 11, former attorney general Ramsey Clark, previously a member of Saddam Hussein's legal defence team, addressed a letter to the United Nations vehemently condemning, not the terrorist strike in New York or the Islamic states that harbour the terrorists, but the United States itself for having "violated the Genocide Convention" in Iraq, for conducting "a constant campaign of vilification in the international media it controls" [sic], and for attacking Afghanistan in order "to consolidate US domination over the Middle East, the Gulf region and central Asia"—accusations as ill-timed and manifestly absurd as they are brazenly false. Writing in the online political newsletter *Counterpunch* for December 17, 2001, William Blum, author of *Rogue State: A Guide to the World's Only Superpower,* justified the terrorists by describing their actions as "retaliation for decades of military, economic and political oppression imposed upon the Middle East by the American Empire." As for the thousands of murdered American civilians, well, "In the hijackers' view, these people could be seen as collateral damage." *These people*! That Muslims celebrated 9/11 worldwide is understandable if deplorable; but that highly educated Western intellectuals should blaspheme the memory of their own dead is almost beyond comprehension and surely beyond repentance. One wonders how they would have reacted had members of their own families been among those cremated in the World Trade Center or the incoming jetliners. The sympathy they so prodigally exhibit is almost never with their own people, the particular individuals murdered by the terrorists—office workers, firemen and policemen, passengers, pilots and flight attendants, mothers and young children facing the horror of their own approaching deaths—but with an abstract population of Afghanis and Iraqis to whom they gave scarcely a passing thought before the American counteraction.

The fact that these pundits were wrong or disingenuous *on every count* did not have the slightest inhibitory effect—and still doesn't—on left-wing marathon thinking. The claims and predictions made by such professional skeptics are nearly always exaggerated or meretricious, yet no adjustment to reality ever seems to occur and the next dire prediction or assessment sails forth on another voyage of collective delusion only to sink without remark and without regret or embarrassment. A little attention to Voltaire would not be out of keeping here: "Nul n'a le privilège de toujours se tromper." (No one has the privilege of always being wrong.) But what is most disconcerting is that many of these intellectuals, exploiting the rich terrain of conventional affront, are so divorced from the real world that they are more worried about the American president than the Islamic aggressor while others feel that the crisis can be defused by extending the hand of friendship to the jihadis. The range of responses runs between outright commiseration with the terrorists at the farther limit and a saccharine complacency at the nearer, that is, between palpable madness and ineffable foolishness—if they are not simply shilling for the enemy. But whatever the reaction, the consensus is that any terrorist atrocity visited upon America or its allies can be explained by Western corruption and consumerist exploitation and justified as legitimate payback.

While anatomizing the smug hypocrisy of Western intellectuals— those mentioned above would fit right into the world of *Platform*— Houellebecq threads a second theme into the loom of his novel, namely the phenomenon of mass tourism that exposes the "traveller" to the reductive commodification of fantasy and the (often legitimate) resentment of the "other." How the two braid together has become more and more visible not only in Egypt, Yemen, Algeria, Tunisia, and Bali, where terrorists have struck at will and must surely strike again, but, taking into account the maniacal and bloodthirsty sort of tourism practised by those with student passports, a predilection for take-out pizza, false diplomas, and pilots' licenses, in the cities of the West as well. (This is a variant of what Paul Berman in *Terror and Liberalism* has dubbed "revolutionary tourism," a term that applies to terrorist recruits who are familiar with or actually live in the West.) Sex and bombs, desire and resentment, the raising of expectations that can rarely be met and the levelling effects of mass travel, Western penetration and Oriental penis envy, guilt and retribution—the two terms of the relation can no longer be separated. The bruited future development of Osama bin Laden's Tora Bora mountain hideout as a tourist site illustrates the close link between terrorism and tourism, the former both repelling and attracting the latter in a strange symbiosis of differing yet related forms of exploitation.

But the situation is even more convoluted. In considering the Western slope of the divide, it is by no means a stretch to suggest that the hedonistic indifference and centripetal lifestyle that Michel exemplifies furnishes the *sine qua non* for both the ideological self-destructiveness of the neototalitarian Left—those stentorian pulpiteers whom Salman Rushdie has branded in his defence of Houellebecq as "the thin-skinned guardians of Islamic sanctities"—and the incendiary viciousness of a resurgent Islam. The former is the allotrope of the twinned latter. Houellebecq is not simply regaling us with a quasi-autobiographical *bilan* of his own predispositions, as many skeptical or unfavourable readers appear to think, but mounting a scathing critique of what may well be a sunset civilization (the Iranian media refer to the US as an *ofuli* [sunset] power), "an old bitch gone in the teeth," in Ezra Pound's telling phrase, a culture, as Jacques Barzun puts it in *From Dawn to Decadence*, that "is old and unravelling." This is the theme of Houellebecq's latest novel, *La possibilité d'une île*, which projects a moribund future devoid of love, a "neo-human" winding-down of civilization into a condition of benumbed and epidermal sterility—the sequel to the desolate finale of *Platform*. "Le futur était vide," the narrator concludes, "J'étais, je n'étais plus." (The future was empty...I was, I was no longer.) In Houellebecq's estimation, we have grown so deracinated from the ground and source of our own civilization that we have come to behave like a pack of tourists, not only abroad, but here in our own backyard, seeing things from an antiseptic distance, resisting authentic engagement, oblivious to troublesome facts, seeking distraction and forgetfulness. And when it comes to the chattering classes—those denizens of Michael Moore country, well-fed, self-righteous, and with a pseudo-documentary penchant for dissembling facts—the spectacle of capitulation they present is mortifying, as they crawl into their ideological coverts like ladybugs in the first days of winter.

2

Houellebecq's characters are often parented from elsewhere in the genealogical field of literature. It is unlikely that the half-brothers Michel and Bruno in *The Elementary Particles* would have made it to the page, at any rate in the semiotic tandem they present to us, had Joyce in *Finnegans Wake* not first given us the Earwicker twins, Shem and Shaun, the Penman and the Postman, Saint Kevin and runcible Jerry, the sundered halves of the creative life force. One wonders, too, about the extent to which Hanif Kureishi's *The Black Album* might have figured in the broad conception of *Platform*. Further, Michel's lover Valérie, who is described as a "radiant exception," owes much to Baudelaire's flamboyant and aphroditic mistress Jeanne Duval whose evenings, as the poet wrote in "Le balcon," were "illuminés par l'ardeur du charbon." The same is the case with Michel himself who, along with a soupçon of Albert Camus' queerly apathetic Meursault from *The Stranger* (Michel's surname is Renault; the two novels begin almost identically), is an updated version of another erotically driven egotist, André Gide's Michel from *The Immoralist*, himself fervently touched by the Arab world.

But the equation here is not so much with the source as with the reader. Like Gide's Michel, we broach the end of days in a state of malingering torpor and self-confusion. Like Houellebecq's Michel, we find ourselves living out the rest of our time in increasingly soulless and desolate surroundings as the world we knew or thought we knew atomizes around us. Our hectic self-preoccupation, our lack of connection with both the vectors of history and the underlying gradients of the present, the contradictions we blandly accept as we proceed to exploit what we at other times reprove, in short, our having permitted ourselves to shrink to the status of what Christopher Lasch famously called "the minimal self," have become the condition for the demise of a civilization at the hands of Islamic terror and internal ideological rot. Unless, improbable as this may be, we can belatedly come to our senses and pull up before we topple over the precipice.[2]

It is, of course, the noble—and politically correct—thing to say that the enemy at the gates is not Islam as such but fundamentalist jihadi Islam and that Houellebecq's blanket indictment is an unpardonable and invidious distortion. Many critics of negative stereotyping point to the definitive contribution of Islam to philosophy and science, forgetting that this was an eon ago and may therefore be considered an historical anomaly. The enlightened courts of Moorish Spain—the record of these celebrated regimes is actually quite spotty—quickly ceded to a millennium of stagnation, culminating in a vast cultural/religious community that translates fewer books in any given year than a small country like Greece, and whose main exports, apart from what just happens to be in the ground, are religious fundamentalism and promiscuous violence. Houellebecq's gist would seem to be that it is extremely difficult to separate the host from the parasite, the carrier from the virus that it carries. And if the two turn out to be indistinguishable from one another, to have merged identities, then the prognosis is bleak indeed. The Christian militias in the United States and the more radical settlers in Israel represent the uncountenanced extremes of mainly pacific faiths, but the same, unfortunately, cannot be said for Islam or for what Yossef Bodansky, in *Bin Laden: The Man Who Declared War on America*, identified as "the dominant trend in the Muslim world—the rise and spread of radical militant Islam."

"The borders of Islam are bloody," wrote Samuel Huntington in *The Clash of Civilizations*. "The underlying problem for the West is not Islamic fundamentalism. It is Islam...." (That it should take an absurd if sanguinary ruckus like the cartoon rampages of February 2006 to awaken journalists to the fact that, as some are now saying, there is indeed a "culture war" and a "clash of civilizations" going on, when it was perfectly obvious twenty years ago, does not say much for their alertness to the world.) Former Islamic zealot Ibn Warraq in *Why I Am Not a Muslim* has also emphasized that fundamentalist Islam *is* Islam and rebuked Western intellectuals and apologists for fudging the distinction, an act of conceptual amalgamation that he regards as nothing less than shameful. "Western scholars and Islamicists have totally failed in their duties as intellectuals," he declares. "They have betrayed their calling by abandoning their critical faculties when it comes to Islam. Some...have even abandoned any attempt to achieve objectivity, to aim at objective truth." In his view, the term "Islamic fundamentalism" is a kind of tautology and functions primarily as a "useful and face-saving device for those unable to confront the fact that Islam itself, and not just something we call 'Islamic fundamentalism,' is incompatible with democracy." The same idea is developed in Robert Spencer's *Islam Unveiled*, where he writes, "The problem is that for all its schisms, sects and multiplicity of voices, Islam's violent elements are rooted in its central texts." (Even that old Arabian tale, it occurs to me, *Ramonah of the Flashing Sword*, features among its tropology of effects an exploding flying carpet.) "It is unlikely," Spencer continues, "that the voices of moderation will ultimately silence the militants, because the militants will always be able to make the case that they are standing for the true expression of the faith." What our multiculturalists have failed abysmally to understand is that, since Muslims believe the Koran is the literal word of Allah that pronounces on matters both sacred and profane and governs their conduct in the world, it follows, as Spencer argues, that all genuine Muslims are by definition fundamentalists who, as Muslims, must consent to the indivisible unity of religion and politics. The distinction we like to make in the interests of political correctness between Islam and Islamism is a specious one; as Warraq says, it is "a distinction without any justification." In her recent book, *The Caged Virgin*, Ayaan Hirsi Ali makes the same point: "What, then, can Westerners do? At an international level, leaders such as Blair and Bush must stop saying that Islam is being held hostage by a terrorist minority. They are wrong. Islam is being held hostage by itself."

This is something that is hard for us to accept. It offends our multicultural sensibilities, our self-approved conviction of social virtue, personal magnanimity, and civic high-mindedness, but attests nonetheless to our ignorance and sentimentality. We regard it as an infringement of the rules of social decency, if not a moral trespass, to investigate the community that regularly grow-ops terrorists whose sole purpose is to kill and maim in the name of their faith, preferring rather to "understand" the perpetrators of these unspeakable deeds while exonerating their communal background, to take the burden of responsibility to a large extent upon ourselves, and under no circumstances to turn an unsparing searchlight upon that faith itself or to familiarize ourselves with its prescriptive texts. "There are many reasons why this matters," writes Diana West in the *Washington Times* for June 16, 2006, "not least of which is that without understanding the religious nature of jihad...there can be no triumph over jihad.... There can also be no understanding of the religiously rooted attitudes toward jihad movements among even non-violent Muslims, generally ranging from tacit ambivalence to wild adulation." We should perhaps consider Willie Sutton's reply to the question of why he robbed banks: "Because that's where the money is."

Houellebecq would surely agree, although the majority of our critics and commentators would not. In particular, many of our somnambulists object to the Islamophobic aspects of recent fiction, scholarship, and notably film. Jack Shaheen's *Reel Bad Arabs: How Hollywood Vilifies a People* is a prominent example of such unseasonable objections.[3] Shaheen, professor emeritus of Communications at Southern Illinois University, proposes as an experiment that we replace the Islamic baddies in Hollywood productions with Christian or Jewish villains and then check our reactions. The simple-mindedness—or is it bad faith—of this suggestion is arrant. The villain in the 2004 Hollywood remake *Starsky & Hutch* is a kippa-wearing Jewish gangster, but no one in the Jewish community seems bothered much. Indeed, Shaheen has no cause to fret. Hollywood of late, in a tremor of political correctness, has bent over backwards to de-Islamicize its villains. The Bruce Willis thriller, *The Siege*, makes a special point of staging the "good Arab" at the expense of the patriotic white American who is portrayed as one-dimensional and cold. The Sean Penn flick, *The Interpreter*, transfigures the original Islamic terrorists into Africans from an obscure country called Matobo, and the film of Tom Clancy's *The Sum of All Fears* has converted Muslims to neo-Nazis. Hollywood schlock is doing its job. In *State of the Union*, an upright and far-sighted John Kerryish president who wishes to tone down America's military posture and seek collaboration rather than confrontation on the international scene is abducted by a hardline Donald Rumsfeldish Defence Secretary organizing a putsch. There is not a whisper of an Islamic terrorist or an Islamic rogue state to be found anywhere in the film's reproduction of the contemporary world. The enemy is the neoconservative within. The Michael Douglas/Kiefer Sutherland vehicle, *The Sentinel*, based on the Gerald Petievich penny dreadful, gives us a shadowy group of post-Soviet KGB assassins who wish to eliminate the president of the United States for no discernible reason—except, perhaps, that he intends to ratify the Kyoto Accord. How September 10, as the saying goes. (The film's director, Clark Johnson, is no fan of the sitting president.) The recent *Syriana*, to take one more example, plays by the rules of the usual anti-American game, featuring a noble Arab prince, whose like is to be found nowhere in the Muslim world and who is assassinated by the CIA (naturally), the standard gang of ugly Americans, and the lustral consummation of a terrorist finale. Hollywood actors have also fallen in line with their directors, producers, and funding executives. Celebs like George Clooney, Jane Fonda, Richard Gere, Barbara Streisand, Sean Penn, and many others, histrionic, uninformed, always self-infatuated and often downright incoherent, are only the most visible of that troupe of entertainers who seem never to have entertained an original thought in their lives. It is precisely such friendly witnesses who should make Shaheen and his kind reconsider their positions. Meanwhile, taking a page from the European Film Academy, the thespian community is busy writing the script for *Reel Good Arabs Redevivus*: the Golden Globe Awards has selected *Paradise Now*, a film glorifying Palestinian suicide bombers and posing them as victims, as Best Foreign Language Film, and the Academy of Motion Picture Arts and Sciences followed with a nomination. Whither now, Shaheen? The ditz factor that prevails throughout the industry seems impregnable and the trend shows no sign of reversing itself anytime soon.

In the real world, where liberal rhetoric always seems to come up short of the facts, we note that of the nineteen 9/11 hijackers, all nineteen were Muslims, none were Christians or Jews. All the principals of the Madrid bombing were Muslims. All who were involved in the various Istanbul attacks were Muslims. The Beslan murderers were Muslims. The London Tube bombers were Muslims. The Heathrow airline plotters were Muslim. The rioters in France were chiefly Muslims. The shoe bomber was a Muslim convert. Those who slaughtered the Coptic Armanious family in Jersey City were Muslims. The killer of filmmaker Theo van Gogh, the Dutch producer of *Submission*, a film critical of Islam, was a Muslim. His accomplices were Muslims and the Amsterdam cell to which they belonged, the Hofstad Netwerk, is a Muslim organization. The leftist "militant" who murdered Dutch politician Pim Fortuyn claimed that he acted "to protect the rights of the Muslims." The massive bomb blast in Beirut that killed former Lebanese Prime Minister Rafik Hariri and sixteen others, wounded another 120, and destroyed a portion of the city's waterfront district was a Muslim family affair—indeed, the central figure appears to have been a Palestinian terrorist, Ahmed Abu Adas, who fled immediately afterward. It was another Muslim, a Taliban assassin, who murdered five members of Doctors Without Borders, thus forcing the organization to leave Afghanistan. The car-bomb that demolished a theater packed with Westerners in Doha, Qatar, and severely damaged a British school was Muslim-detonated. The 1997 Luxor massacre of tourists was a Muslim operation, as was the 2002 copycat attack on the Tunisian island of Djerba. The motorcycle bomber who blew up a crowded Cairo market was a member of a group identifying itself as the Islamic Pride. The Red Sea resort attacks were perpetrated by Muslims. The seventeen Canadians arrested for planning to bomb power plants, storm the parliament buildings, and behead the prime minister were Muslims. The two men who attempted to blow up commuter trains in Germany were Lebanese Muslims. The fifty-seven dead and 300 wounded in the Amman terrorist attack in November 2005 were victims of Muslim suicide bombers; in September 2006, at the Roman Amphitheater in Amman, a Muslim gunman killed a British tourist and wounded five more from other countries. The ongoing butchery in Iraq is the result of the Sunni Muslim "insurgency" and the Mahdi militia. The Darfur genocide is Muslim to the bone. Those who regularly strap explosive belts on their bodies and take scores of innocent bystanders with them, like the terrorist in the film *Executive Decision* to which Shaheen objects as negative stereotyping, are Muslims. This is not negative stereotyping; it is factual reporting.

Let us pursue this larger inquiry into both the nature of Islam and its relation to the West and, in so doing, try to determine whether Houellebecq, one of the lonely voices crying in the textual wilderness, is correct in his appraisal and judgment of the Islamic threat and Western shuffling. The source of Islamic violence is not simply a question of Wahabbi puritanical literalism, as many Muslims claim, or, alternately, of the much-publicized resentment of an Islamic world at the mercy of the bellicose West, but of the very structure of a faith that is out of step with the modern sensibility and refuses to acknowledge the distinction between the realms of the sacred and profane. One should be wary of setting up a straw man, but Islam would appear to have no effective mechanism to resist its own extremist tendencies and is therefore perforce defined by its most radical elements, which it is unwilling or unable to reabsorb and neutralize. As a result, it seems fair to suggest that a faith that is intrinsically hostile to everything the West stands (or stood) for, which can be so catastrophically perverted or put into political practice, which so readily tolerates Wahabbi sectarian fundamentalism, and which takes no significant action to counter the upsurge of violence through the many, ostensibly "moderate" social and charitable Islamic organizations found everywhere in the Orient and the West, is a faith that poses a devastating threat to the civilized world, particularly in the nuclear and chemical age. A significant body of people who give every indication of living mentally and emotionally in the twelfth century while deploying twenty-first century technology and weaponry will more than likely wreak some form of chiliastic havoc upon all of us. What Robert Kaplan has named "re-primitivized man" moves freely among us, using a cellphone and enjoying access to the Internet to further his terminal purposes. Such extremism feeds off mainstream support or lack of deterrent action as much as it does off Muslim backing, as well as European subsidies or business arrangements. (Houellebecq, as we have noted, comes down hard on the diverse forms of European connivance.) But the most important consideration, if we are to avoid a visitation that may engulf us all, is that the Muslim *umma* and its theologians, magistrates, and rulers will somehow have to get used to the fact, despite their facility with the appliances and techniques of the modern world, that we are now living neither in the desert nor the past. And they will have to realize that they cannot honourably continue to condemn the West while availing themselves of its scientific advancements, industrial benefits, military technology, and consumer goods—everything but the Western institutions themselves and their informing spirit of critical, analytic, and empirical inquiry that have made such advantages possible to begin with.

We might also remark that while Islam claims to be a universalist faith, it is not only divided turbulently down the middle on the issue of prophetic succession but is predicated on a tribalist perception of the world. Of course, tribalism and Islam *as such* are by no means identical phenomena, but the degree of mutual interpenetration over the millennia has made it impossible to separate them out as pure cultural constructs and distinct codes of behaviour. They are now, and have been over the long course of history, one. This is why many Muslims can feel a kind of family outrage at an al-Qaeda attack on an Arab housing compound in Riyadh in which women and children are among the victims, but remain silent or even jubilate when women and children of other faiths or nations are slaughtered by these same militant factions. It is only when they are hit themselves that they can be moved to forceful action or passionate condemnation against their own devotional kinsmen, who are otherwise protected and often admired. But even such *selective* outrage, implying a partial capacity for empathy, is effectively counteracted by the frequent and profuse expressions of euphoria and gratitude in much Islamic commentary on the decimations of the terrorists. Such people, shedding tears of joy over the suffering and destruction of 9/11 and offering thanks to Allah for having allowed them to behold so exhilarating a moment, cannot possibly be "reached out to" in the hope of establishing a "dialogue." I am tempted to say that they can scarcely be considered, in the vocabulary of Western humanism, as "ethical subjects," but remain in the service of an exclusionary universal and as such are inaccessible to us. Even those suddenly temperate editorialists of the Islamic newspapers who repudiate the Muslim butchers of the schoolchildren of Beslan and the roaming bands of Iraqi beheaders routinely refer to the errant "sons" of Islam—the terrorists are still part of the family—while continuing to blame an imperial America and the exploitative West for fueling "Muslim rage." Responsibility is cannily distributed rather than candidly accepted. There is no recognition of the fact that "Muslim rage"—which Christopher Hitchens calls " the rhetorical tropes of Muslim self-pity"—is little more than a political decoy since Muslims are almost always the victims of other Muslims carrying out their bloody vendettas, and that it is the Western powers, primarily the United States, that have intervened to save Muslims from the slaughter campaigns of tyrants like Saddam Hussein and Slobodan Milosevic. Nor does one detect the slightest gratitude for Western rescue efforts and emergency aid—again, mainly American—to alleviate the effects of natural disasters, as when the tsunami hit Muslim Indonesia.

But what of those moderate Muslims we hear so much about in the press and in the more reflective literature on the subject? Houellebecq, for one, would not concur with the distinction drawn by Daniel Pipes between militant Islam and moderate Islam, with the latter as the only meaningful deterrent to the former. "Moderate Islam" is either the

sugar pill of Western intellectuals who do not want to appear regressive or the sentimental hope of Muslims who do not wish to surrender
their faith. Moderate Muslims, insofar as they cling to the Faith, cannot
be relied upon to wrest their religion out of the hands of the extremists,
and to wait upon so improbable an event is only to hasten the devastation that is louring. But the fashionable theory now advanced by some
heads of government, taking their cue from political analysts like Pipes,
that the central struggle is within Islam—one between "moderates"
and "radicals"—is clearly preposterous and serves only as a licence to
shirk what is nothing less than a civilizational duty. The major fault
line is elsewhere.

Irshad Manji, who in *The Trouble with Islam* places her hopes in the
reconstructive energies of Muslim émigrés in the West—and in the
entrepreneurial power of Muslim womanhood engaging in a "God-
conscious, female-fueled capitalism"—is only indulging, if I may be
permitted, in a Pipes dream. Manji's attempt to distinguish a forward-
looking, acceptable Islam from "desert Islam" or "foundamentalism"
with its fixation on the past and its rigid interpretation of the scriptures
does not seem overly promising. In *The Caged Virgin*, Ayaan Hirsi Ali
takes exception to Manji's belief that Islam can be purified of its autocratic and patriarchal structure, carrying Manji's own doubts to their
logical conclusion. The efforts of mathematician Jeffrey Lang who,
in *Even Angels Ask*, strives to factor out the tribal and cultural appur-
tenances of his adopted Faith from a more progressive, Westernized
version of Islam, seem equally counterproductive. As Nonnie Darwish,
an Egyptian-born woman living in the US and founder of the website
arabsforisrael.com, has written, "reforming Islam is not going to be easy,
especially because the change must come from within. So far, Muslims
do not seem genuinely interested in reformation." Like Manji, Darwish
is nevertheless cautiously optimistic; but also like Manji, she seems
unwilling to recognize that Islam will not readily yield to the moral
suasion of a few scattered reformers and that a more plausible solution
to her dilemma as a practising Muslim is to refrain from practising.
Such rebels, of course, are fortunate to be living in the West, unlike,
for example, Bangladeshi journalist Shoaib Choudhury, editor of the
Weekly Blitz and a holder of similar views, who at the present time is
under arrest in a Dhaka jail for his efforts to foster interfaith dialogue.

In the light of current events and the savage oratory pouring from mosques and madrassas around the globe, the distinction frequently drawn between Islam, which is said to be moderate and peaceable, and Islamism, that is understood as a perversion of the cardinal tenets of the faith, is academic as well as unhelpful. A moment's reflection should make it obvious that there must be something inherent in Islam which allows for large numbers of believers to kill and maim without compunction while taking their own lives in the process—we do not see Christian or Jewish terrorists regularly blowing themselves up in crowded marketplaces. It is true, as many scholars have noted, that the earlier, Meccan portion of the Koran attests to a degree of tolerance, but the later, Medinese writings, for the most part, show little mercy to the unbeliever—and it is the Medinese scripture that forms the basis of much Islamic worship and most Islamic legislation. Though the issue remains vexed, there being no general agreement on the number of Koranic *ayaat* (messages) to which the rule of abrogation may be applied, contradictions between the various suras are frequently decided on the principle of *naskh*, according to which later revelations may cancel out earlier ones, giving doctrinal (if not temporal) priority to the Medinese section of the Koran. The earlier suras that speak of peace and harmony could thus be annulled (*mansukh*) by those that come afterward. The Koran itself permits such revision. Sura 2:106 reads, "We do not abrogate a verse or let it be forgotten without substituting a better or similar one." The fact that the rule of abrogation presumably applies only to certain *ayaat* (duties, prohibitions) and not to others (elucidations, information) does not impact the principle itself. But this is an old story and the problem has been studied as far back as the Christian Arab al-Kindi writing near the turn of the first millennium, who deprecated the internal contradictions in the pages of the Koran as well as the principle of abrogation.

Further, we cannot have failed to note that the so-called "moderate majority" of the world-wide Islamic community has done little to check the upsurge of violence committed under its aegis—though no doubt many live in fear of sectarian retribution, like barbers in Baghdad executed for shaving beards. Equally to the point, as Melanie Phillips writes in *Londonistan*, "moderation among the majority appears to be a highly relative concept considering their widespread hostility towards Israel and the Jews, for example, or the way in which the very concept of Islamic terrorism or other wrongdoing is automatically denied."

Putting all our eggs in the basket of moderation, waiting for amiable and inoffensive Muslims to neutralize the preachings and activities of their more muscular brethren or to revise some of their own hostile attitudes and conditioned reflexes, seems a Humpty-Dumpty solution—not only because this is unlikely to happen but because moderation is the close confederate of extremism and the condition that allows it to flourish. A "moderate" who does not loudly protest and energetically renounce the evil that is done in his name, even if this should demand personal sacrifice on his part, is not a "moderate" but an apologist for that which he presumably abhors. If he does not speak up—and emphatically—on behalf of the tolerant and pluralistic societies that have welcomed him, he has forfeited his right to our respect. Yet there is more to the matter than that. "Religious moderates," cautions Sam Harris in *The End of Faith*, "are, in large part, responsible for the religious conflict in our world, because their belief provides the context in which scriptural literalism and religious violence can never be adequately opposed." But the proportionate relation between moderates and extremists may not be the issue here. As former Muslim and Al-Azhar Cairo university professor "Mark Gabriel" suggests in *Islam and Terrorism*, echoing Ibn Warraq, extremism is not a deviation from the faith or a matter of relative percentages but authentic Islam itself. Corroboration comes from an unlikely but authoritative source. As reported in the London *Telegraph* for July 20, 2005, Anjem Choudary, head of the radical al-Muhajiroun ("the immigrants") movement in Britain, assures us that the division between moderates and extremists is a "classification [that] does not exist in Islam." The radical is only the shadow cast by the moderate. As things now stand, the fissile core of the faith is always ready to be activated.

"Militant Islam" will not be so easily tamed by an expatriate community or a caucus of new converts directed by leaders adept at playing the victimhood game, who have largely failed to publicly reject the electric call of the imperious muezzin or the firmans of a mufti-driven educational curriculum. Islamic scholar Eric Ormsby puts the question in an article for the *Wall Street Journal* (August 4, 2004): "Throughout the Muslim world, fatwas are issued every day on all conceivable subjects; where are the fatwas condemning such barbaric acts as the beheading of hostages or suicide-bombings?" As the terror escalates, we will surely hear desultory Muslim voices raised in protestation, but this will

be largely a laggard or rhetorical performance, motivated by self-interest and with little effect on the actual course of events. Petitions for
peace and disclaimers of responsibility, signed by councils of suddenly
edified imams, will no doubt circulate the morning after further
terrorist attacks on Western soil, yet no effort will be made to get to
the marrow of the trouble. Rather, such petitions will also warn of an
upsurge of Islamophobia, as if Muslims were in greater danger than
the unsuspecting targets of the terrorists' bombs. As we have seen in
Britain and Canada following the uncovering of new terrorist plots,
"moderate" Islamic organizations are striving to turn such incidents to
their advantage by arguing for political and social concessions—*shari'a*,
official holidays, a change in the direction of national foreign policy—
that would presumably strengthen their hand against their own radical
elements. Such tactical cardsharping may in the long run be far more
effective than the terrorist threat itself and discloses the peril for the
West inherent in the "moderate" project.

Additionally, the customary silence of the *soi-disant* "silent majority" of pacifist Muslims and their supposedly benignant symposiarchs
has been until most recently almost as deafening as the detonations
of their more explosive alter egos, and their putative moderation can
only be described as rather immoderate. As a character in Kureishi's
The Black Album says, "Our religion isn't something you can test out,
like trying out a suit to see if it fit! You gotta buy the whole outfit!"
There is, so to speak, no such thing as Islam Lite. Charles Moore asks
germanely in an article in the *Daily Telegraph* for December 18, 2004,
"How does a belief system founded, in part, on conquest, and preaching a virtual identity between religious and political power, live at ease
in plural, free, secular societies?"[4] Even super-tolerant Holland is now
having second thoughts: a Motivaction poll conducted in June 2006
found that 63 per cent of respondents believed that Islam was incompatible with modern Western values. The undoubted richness and
complexity of Islamic literature and the subtlety of ulemic commentary it has engendered have not muted the crude impetus of its horta-
tive interpreters whom the religion has manifestly accommodated.
Judging from the prolonged absence of spirited repudiation and practical action, aside from the occasional blips when the situation seems
to warrant a response, one can assume that the terrorist continues to
enjoy asylum in the larger Muslim community. Ditto for most of the

"moderate" Islamic regimes whose survival is contingent on indefatigably stoking anti-Americanism and fanning the Arab-Israeli conflict as well as exporting a corresponding ideology of sacerdotal violence. "Moderation," as I have argued, basically serves the interests of entrenched barbarisms.

What we have learned to call militant Islam seems here to stay. Its revival has been accounted for by many factors: the felt need to resist the incursion of what it sees as the polluted and godless West, the economic stagnation of the despotic Islamic backwaters, ecological and demographic convulsions, the primordial animus against individual assertion and thought, or even as the latest crescendo of those bizarro mass movements devoted to the cult of death that Norman Cohn has studied in *The Pursuit of the Millennium* and that have wrenched apart our own specific epoch from the tumultuous early decades of the last century to the present. Moreover, a faith that can promise seventy virgins in the afterlife for eruptive self-immolation on earth plainly offers the best warranty in the business. As Irshad Manji archly put it, the liturgical focus is now on babes, not books. Cordoba was once "home to seventy libraries. That's one for every virgin today's Muslim martyrs believe they're pledged. Libraries then, virgins now...." Even the slightly retarded adolescent suicide-bomber dispatched by Hamas in March 2004 was tempted by the promise of a celestial bacchanal. The heavenly seraglio, though, is merely an accessory or bonus for committed practice. More relevantly, death in the service of jihad offers direct and instantaneous access to the afterlife, without the postulant having to wait in the vestibule of the grave for Divine Judgment whose verdict is never assured. This explains its attraction to the terrorist "martyr."

However we construe the matter, then, Islam seems set in stone and Semtex. There is a bomb strapped to the body of a people, and it is a holy book. Like the Bible, which is also rife with contradictions and bloodshed, the Koran is a magnificent scripture, rich and various, that demands respect and study. But unlike the Bible, it has not been subject to literary archeology or demilitarized by textual scholarship. As Salim Mansur has written (*Western Standard*, July 2006), "Muslims of the first generation took the Koran and converted it from a pearl into an instrument for power and its glorification." It is moot whether Islam can be reformed without a thorough reconsideration of the Koran in which the more ambiguous or excessive passages are either expurgated or canonically reinterpreted. And such doctrinal amendment does not seem likely.[5] For one thing, it goes against the Islamic grain—the few dissenting voices that are occasionally raised are in real danger of being silenced. For another, the undeniably ravishing quality of its poetic and mellifluous recitations, or *tajwid*, tends, on the evidence, to hold the interrogative mind captive. Indeed, as Philip Hitti writes in his *History of the Arabs*, with respect to the influence of the Arabic language on the minds of its users, "the rhythm, the rhyme, the music, produce on them the effect of what they call 'lawful magic,'" especially "the resonant and electrifying cry," *La ilaha illa'-llah*—there is no god but Allah.

As well, Islam has been issued *carte blanche* by the influential clique of postmodern area specialists who argue that such concepts as progress, evolution, reformation, and Enlightenment are culture-specific and do not apply to the Islamic historical continuum. They appear to have forgotten the travesty of Lysenkoism—a false genetic theory adopted in the Soviet Union on ideological grounds—that demonstrated at great cost to the agricultural development of an entire country that the "nature of things" does not necessarily conform to political manipulation, theoretical caprice, or verbal redefinitions of stable entities. A thing is what it is irrespective of the conceptual glossolalia that would alter its definition to suit an *a priori* belief system. (In the words of Philip K. Dick, "Reality is that which, when you cease believing in it, doesn't go away.") You cannot have an anti-democratic democracy or retrogressive progress or evolution that does not evolve or a reformation that changes little or an Enlightenment that leaves systemic oppression, religious rule, gender inequalities, and stalled education programs where they always were—unless, of course, you are a Middle East specialist, a university liberal, a left-wing journalist, a State Department apparatchik, or an Arab dictator. It is curious to observe that the religious Islamic Right and the secular Western Left have joined forces in creating a post-Orwellian form of doublespeak—peace (surrender), resistance (terrorism), apartheid (self-defence), freedom of religion (Islamic privilege), anti-Zionism (antisemitism), international community (competitive dissensus), diplomacy (appeasement), justice (prejudice)—phrases used like flags of convenience under which to float an ideological agenda and to avoid the high cost of truth.

Finally, as W. R. Clement suggests in *Reforming the Prophet*, "The issue of human rights is not one that Islamic countries feel comfortable with…there is little incentive for a Muslim nation-state to even begin to nibble away at the human rights Pandora's box." (A similar point is made by Amir Taheri in *The Spirit of Allah: Khomeini and the Islamic Revolution*, where he recounts how the Iranian delegate to the United Nations stated categorically that, in the delegate's own words, the "concept of human rights was a Judeo-Christian invention and inadmissible in Islam.") The joke—and a rather caustic one—is that when Muslims are in the minority, they tend to be extremely vocal about human rights; when they form the majority, one or another instance of repressive *sharia* law takes over and the stranger in their midst is generally reduced to pariah status. Might it not be more appropriate to ask why these late arrivals to the West, who regularly go into paroxysms of resentment about their supposed marginalization and ill-treatment, and who are now suing in growing numbers for the installation of *sharia* in local Muslim communities, do not return to their homelands—or why they should have emigrated in the first place? But the fact is that in the bucolic valleys and pastures of Multiculti Land, they are doing very well and promise to do even better in the future. For they have powerful allies on their side: politicians investing in electoral futures, obsequious social agencies, dull-witted government bureaucrats, intellectuals, journalists, editors, and academics with no grip on the real world, and a deeply unread host population whose ignorance masquerades as open-mindedness.

When the seventeen homegrown Muslims were arrested in June 2006 for plotting to blow up buildings and landmarks in Toronto with three tonnes of ammonium nitrate, the Islamic Foundation of Toronto proclaimed that religion was in no way involved, the police chief of the city, Bill Blair, boasted that no mention had been made of religious affiliation, and the *Globe and Mail*, Canada's "national newspaper," headed its lead editorial with the front-page rubric "Let not fear destroy our great virtue of tolerance" and called for "perspective." Adam Radwanski, one of the press corp's vocational innocents who writes for the *National Post*, avoiding all reference to the obvious common denominator, dismissed the plot hatched by these local Muslims of mainly middle-class backgrounds as "involving, by all appearances, a small number of social outcasts," and Islamic authorities and their liberal sympathizers were more worried about a possible backlash against the Muslim community than about the lives and properties of Canadian citizens as a whole. A consensus began to develop, as during the earlier Paris riots, that the detainees were alienated young men with a social grievance that needed to be understood. "Why are they so angry?" wondered David Miller, the mayor of Toronto. In the same way, when the plot involving British-born Muslims and recent converts to the faith to bring down a fleet of airliners, which would have killed between 3,000 and 4,000 people, was uncovered in England in August 2006, police studiously avoided using the M-word, anti-terrorist experts stressed the "criminal" rather than the religious motivation of its perpetrators, and London mayor Ken Livingstone vigorously defended the country's Islamic community. One need not wonder what the author of *Platform* would have said.

Since Houellebecq does not develop a precise analysis of the social, political, and theological agencies active in the Islamic world, one may ask if Jenny Turner is right when she argues that "Houellebecq's ideas begin to unravel around the aspect of the novel that has attracted most attention—its lambasting of Islam"? Or is she simply expressing the conventional and pusillanimous reaction to an abrasive and unvarnished polemic unafraid to tackle the paramount political issue for our times? I suspect that Houellebecq is no more "constructing" Islam than he is fabricating an imaginary West. The thesis or "platform" he is developing resembles to some extent the anti-Islamist execrations of Oriana Fallaci in *The Rage and the Pride*, in which she deplores "the burkah in place of the miniskirt" and rejects the hypothesis that we are only dealing with extremist fringes and fanatical minorities. "They are millions and millions, the extremists," as she laconically remarks.[6] This goes counter to received wisdom. For example, in the aftermath to the June 2006 terrorist arrests in Canada, Sheema Khan, chair of the Council on American-Islamic Relations and a frequent contributor to the *Globe and Mail*, urged that "we must root out the terrorist fringes in Islamic society." Khan would clearly have no stomach for Fallaci's pummelling style. She should perhaps turn to the measured, scholarly prose of Efraim Karsh who, in *Islamic Imperialism: A History*, shows quite conclusively that the terrorist strikes around the globe are only "the most recent manifestations of the millenarian jihad for a universal Islamic empire" and that its "vision [is] by no means confined to an extremist fringe of Islam, as illustrated by the overwhelming support for the 9/11 attacks throughout the Arab and Islamic worlds." Indeed, how can we plausibly speak of "fringe elements" when entire Muslim countries and pseudo-countries are or were terrorist-sponsoring entities—Taliban Afghanistan, Saddamite Iraq, Syria, Iran, Saudi Arabia, the Palestinian Territories, and now, once again, Somalia—or when the network of cells, madrassas, and mosques they subsidize has become a worldwide enterprise, infiltrating every major Western nation and largely unopposed by Muslim immigrant communities? It is not the fringe elements we must root out; it is the belief that only such fringe elements are the source of the trouble rather than the texts, dogmas, traditions, communal incubations, and historical convictions that sustain the jihadi mentality.

Like Houellebecq, Fallaci has come in for much sanctimonious reproof. But whereas she focuses on "the monstrous darkness of a religion which produces only religion" and its offshoot, insensate brutality, Houellebecq trains his sights as well on a narrow, libertine culture whose self-indulgence renders it vulnerable to the machinations of those who would abolish it. In point of fact, ours is a society at war with itself, struggling with its dark interior double, its deep, unconscious desire and masochistic instinct to destroy itself. One is reminded of the character Rudi in Houellebecq's earlier novella *Lanzarote*, no paragon himself, who is partnered with a Muslim wife despite his detestation of "the monstrous hordes of Islam." (The fact that she deserts her abusive husband is merely a narrative twitch and in any case is soon to be cancelled, thematically, by the murder/funeral with which *Platform* opens.)

Houellebecq's fulminations may be as intemperate as Fallaci's and as corrosive as Ibn Warraq's in *Leaving Islam* and especially *Why I Am Not a Muslim* or Irshad Manji's in *The Trouble with Islam*.[7] But his real target—as in *The Elementary Particles*, as well as in his 1997 novel, *Extension du domaine de la lutte* (translated into English as *Whatever*), which pillories the ennui, anomie, and deprivations of contemporary life, his acid critique of modernity in *Interventions* and his projection of the torpid future that awaits us in *La possibilité d'une île*—is the effete and ideologically riven culture of the West, divided between the quest for sensual pleasure on one side and an amnesiac intellectualism on the other. Both tendencies come together in their refusal to read the past, to detect patterns and similitudes, to observe that certain causes invariably produce certain consequences, to prevent memory from falling victim to the facile occlusions of laziness, ignorance, and greed. It is a culture that has lost touch with the core of genuine feeling and civic solidarity and that has devalued its own reasoned and humanistic centre while refusing (with the partial and late exception of the United States) to garrison its outposts and protect its citadel. Such is the psychological condition arrived at by our character's predecessor, André Gide's Michel with his desire for "the afflux of a richer, hotter blood," his enthusiasm for "the crude morality of the Goths," his love affair with North Africa, his living exclusively in a Lethean and insular present, and his effort at "exalting and even justifying savagery," which culminates in his tardy acceptance of the fact that "I had sought and found what makes me what I am: a kind of persistence in the worst." The reader is implicated here as well. The "drama," as Gide attests, is "too general to remain circumscribed by his singular adventure." This is essentially Houellebecq's point. And so in our congenial myopia and jejune wilfulness we find ourselves inhabiting a culture that may soon be reduced to fragments, to the great rejoicing of its enemies. Muslim populations exulted when the shuttle burned up and disintegrated.

Aided by the penitential stance of the liberal West absorbed in ginning up support for the dedicated saboteur and linked with the monadic, isolating, self-preoccupied *lebenswelt* of a pleasure-seeking society, the enemy at the gates is now inside the gates, multiplying in sleeper cells and backed by media bellmen and university oracles who rush to surrender the cognitive Palladium upon which the safety of the city depends.[8] But this stripe of adversary should by no means be mistaken for the great Alexandrian-Greek poet Constantine Cavafy's barbarian, who promises to rejuvenate us. ("They were, those people, a kind of solution," intones the speaker of that famous poem, "Waiting for the Barbarians.") Far too many of us resemble Houellebecq's Michel in the epicurean solitude of our appetites and cupidities, our motives, ambitions, and inclinations, ending like the Sullen in the Fifth Circle of the *Inferno*, who sink beneath the "dry bank" of where they have arrived and the "putrid moat" of where they have been. Precisely Michel's fate.[9]

For Houellebecq, plainly, we are on the verge of succumbing to the depredations of that which, in an interview with the literary magazine *Lire*, he gleefully borked as "La religion la plus con…une religion dangereuse." Here he is following in the footsteps of his own illustrious predecessor, the nineteenth-century hermeneutic critic and religious historian Ernest Renan, who described Islam as "the heaviest chain that ever shackled humanity," though Houellebecq's rhetoric is rather saltier. We also find him echoing some of his own characters, the biologist Desplechin in *Particles*, who describes Islam as "by far the most stupid, false and obfuscating of all religions" and the narrator of *Platform* who states that "Muslims on the whole aren't worth much," going on to compare them to blood clots migrating through the veins of Europe. Curiously, according to Muslim tradition the angel Gabriel commanded Mohammed to commence the great work of the Koran thus: "Recite in the name of your Lord who created man from clots of blood," deriving no doubt from Koran 22:5. Houellebecq obviously did not have this tradition in mind when he penned his abusive phrase. Still, we must admit if we are sincere, despite what we may think of the stark incontinence of his phrasing, that the menace Houellebecq is documenting is tangible and imminent. One thinks as well of the TV documentary Michel is watching at the beginning of the story, entitled "The Silurid Demystified," about the sudden proliferation in the rivers of the country of mysterious giant fish "fond of the area around nuclear power plants" (an image trawled from *Whatever*, which introduces the meat of the story with a reference to the narrows of Bab-el-Mandel noted for "the extraordinary density of the shark population which characterizes this area of the Red Sea").[10]

But readers are more at home accusing writers like Houellebecq of extravagance and prejudice than heeding the burden of their message. To the contrary, despite the many warnings we have received and the gruesome parade of events we have witnessed, we sanction our literary imams and media mahdis to continue pontificating with impunity and mainlining the global data stream with social and ideological phantasms, doing little to discourage the bomb dispensers and bring down the Ringwraiths of Islam. That would be racial profiling. That would be infra dig. That would be contrary to the proud European "liberal-left" and social-democratic tradition that, solemnly fetishizing the "Other," welcomes an avowed and implacable theocratic antagonist into the heart of its complaisant polity. It would offend smug palatinates like the BBC (and its Canadian nephew). It would infuriate not only the Arab street but the Western boulevard. It would go against the deliberate tendencies, elevated to the dignity of official policy, of self-seeking

and craven ministerial bureaucracies embracing political fragmenta-
tion, rampant immigration and tacit acceptance of violence as earnest
of their own hypothetical benevolence and compassion. It is instructive that the United Nations revised its 1948 Declaration of Human
Rights to bring it into line with the 1981 Islamic Declaration of Human
Rights: Article 18 calling for the elimination of religious discrimination
was rendered toothless, rewritten to affirm only the right "to have" a
religion rather than "to adopt" or "change" one's religion, as stipulated
in the original document. It is equally instructive that in the funeral
orations made in Yasser Arafat's honour, French President Jacques
Chirac described the man who steered $6.5 billion of donor income
for the Palestinian cause into his private accounts and businesses as a
man of "conviction and courage" and the Vatican went part way toward
secular beatification, referring to the arch-terrorist as the "illustrious
deceased."

The various quangos, NGOs, and welfare organizations ramifying
around us come off no better. Thus the International Red Cross in a
typical access of humanitarian empathy visits the imprisoned Saddam
Hussein, a truly unspeakable sadist responsible for the death of
hundreds of thousands, to "see whether he is getting enough food and
water." Human Rights Watch frets that the videos released by the Iraqi
Interior Ministry showing captured terrorists as well as footage of their
crimes are inappropriate, raising the question of whether the abduc-
tors and beheaders of Iraqi and foreign civilians are subject to "abuse,
torture and mistreatment." Its military expert, Marc Garlasco, prominent in blaming Israel for the Jenin "massacre" that never happened,
quickly accepted the Palestinian version of the June 9, 2006, Gaza
beach explosion that implicated the Jewish state, despite important
evidence to the contrary and without hesitating to use the dignity of
his office to support the propaganda efforts of his Palestinian protégés.
(When the acquitting evidence could no longer be ignored, Garlasco
later opted for the theory of an unexploded Israeli ordnance lying on
the beach—the first thing, no doubt, that a picnicking family would
play with.) The same organization also objects to the rendition and
forceful interrogation of senior al-Qaeda leaders in "ghost prisons" in
Jordan and elsewhere, beyond the reach of US courts, as a violation
of their inalienable rights. That this may be the only way of extracting
information that could avert another terrorist attack with its hundreds

or thousands of civilian dead does not seem to enter the thinking of such altruistic organizations. The argument that the subtler of their proponents bring forward, namely, that coercive practices put the interrogator and the community he represents at moral risk, profaning their mutual adherence to the principles of human dignity and worth, must certainly be taken into consideration, if only as a check against excess. But sometimes we need to muster the courage to put ourselves in harm's way, not only physically but morally as well, and tempt what is most dear to us in order to save, not an abstraction, a doctrine, or a "system," but living human beings. This is the unavoidable constraint upon our idealism inherent in what is called "situational ethics." And yet, for many of these organizations, the killing of countless innocents does not weigh in the juridical scales, it seems, so long as the terrorist, who by his actions has forfeited his civil and conventional rights, is treated decently. What planet, we might ask, are such people living on?

Public individuals may also be expected to cooperate. Thus British MP Jenny Tonge, after professing that she might consider becoming a suicide bomber in the service of the Palestinians, is invited by the BBC to visit the families of these homicidal "martyrs," whom she then proceeds to exonerate. What choice do these poor folk have but to get at "civilian targets"—a happy euphemism. Cherie Blair agrees, condoning the suicide bombers who are only acting as they do because they have "no hope," as she remarked on the same day that nineteen Israeli civilians, including schoolchildren, were blown to bits in a Jerusalem bus bombing. Ken Livingstone, aka "Red Ken," has desecrated his mayoral office in receiving firebrand Islamic preachers as honoured guests, indulging his usual anti-Israeli vituperations and professing to understand the takers of innocent life in Israeli towns and cities. His indignation over the London terrorist attack, however, knew no bounds although, for Livingstone as for so many others, it is not only Israel but the West writ large that is judged responsible for Islamic terrorism, wherever it may decide to strike. Our own Liberal MP and former Parliamentary Secretary Colleen Beaumier, aka "Baghdad Beaumier," had no qualms about sipping tea with Tariq Aziz and Saddam Hussein and pronouncing Ba'athist Iraq a progressive state. Beaumier's colleague Carolyn Parrish and former Liberal Press Secretary Francoise Dubois overstepped the bounds of parliamentary decorum in openly reviling the American president, in this way also giving support to a common enemy. For such people, whose hatred of everything American seems almost psychopathic, it is primarily the United States that is the enemy in the war on terrorism. Thus the Reverend Bill Blaikie, as interim leader of the New Democratic Party, publicly accused George W. Bush of dreaming of killing babies, while glossing over the bloody track record of the murderous regimes in countries like Afghanistan and Iraq that the American president undertook to liberate.

Still others see the preoccupation with the horror of 9/11 as a presidential conspiracy to secure increased funding and power—the lunatic fringe goes so far as to accuse the present administration of allowing the tragedy to happen or even staging it in order to secure a pretext for attacking Afghanistan and Iraq in the interests of the oil cartel. (Though with respect to Afghanistan, no American company has yet to bid on a phantom pipeline and, with respect to Iraq, oil flows sluggishly through the sabotaged installations, as was easily foreseeable.) One need only glance through the pages of Thierry Meyssan's goofy *9/11: The Big Lie* to see what Reason is up against. Webster Tarpley's *9/11 Synthetic Terror: Made in USA* is no less dotty—Tarpley is the arch conspiracy theorist among a growing throng of cultic infatuates, waving his "false-flag" terror model (as he puts it, a strike is carried out by Party A, who assigns guilt to Party B), questioning the veracity of all the major terrorist attacks, contending that the media are controlled by "a worldwide Zionist network," and massaging evidence to fit his prior assumptions. Even more "respectable" productions like R. T. Naylor's *Satanic Purses*, filled with reams of presumably hard economic data that argues that the war on terror is largely deceptive and feeds of a hoodwinked public in order to advance various entrenched interests, are complicit with the real enemy—the atrocious titular pun on Salman Rushdie's major novel is enough to extradite the author's intellectual credibility.

Naylor deserves a sidebar to himself, for his book is potentially the most damaging in the long term. Once inured to the battery of "information," it requires only a few pages for the reader to recognize that the writing is vitiated by a sophomoric snideness, working in the vein of pseudo-mockery and referring tongue-in-cheek, to take just a couple of examples, to the "regime of brooding Islamic fanatics" in Sudan or the "gang of misanthropic miscreants" in Taliban Afghanistan. These groups, insofar as they harbour evil purposes, are meant to be understood as the inventions of unscrupulous neoconservative operators like George W. Bush and his Republican backers or of the "machinations of the pro-Israel lobby." It is the latter, we are given to understand, who are the brooding fanatics and misanthropic miscreants. But when Naylor goes on to define al-Qaeda as "largely a law-enforcement fable akin to the Mafia myth," we know we are witnessing a slick polemical shell game, for the Mafia is no myth and the global reach of its tentacles has been amply documented. But Naylor will have his target audience eating out of his hand—the United States is exposed as the real Evil Empire, Israel and its American-Jewish supporters are the devil's deputies, Hamas is a world-class charity, the Oslo Accords were sabotaged by the Israelis, radical Islam is basically innocent and is only reacting to "Western meddling in the Islamic world," jihad does not mean Holy War, the American government seeks "to demonize Muslims worldwide," the international banking infrastructure is "a global espionage apparatus," and so on *ad infinitum*.

Then there is A. K. Dewdney, a computer scientist at the University of Western Ontario, who has recently published a web article that attempts to give scientific backing to the 9/11 conspiracy theory. Dewdney introduces us to a blizzard of high-tech gizmos and devious manipulations involving transponder codes, "master" and "slave" aircraft, radar substitution, flight swaps in mid air, surreptitious television monitors equipped with Tinkertoy joysticks and so on, all purportedly showing that the entire event was a well-planned, superbly coordinated, and diabolically cynical plot hatched by the White House and carried out by Secret Service operatives. Dewdney, incidentally, is the author of a rather interesting fantasy book called *The Planiverse*, describing what he soberly assures us is a genuine two-dimensional universe, much like Edwin Abbott's flatland, in which he makes computer contact with a certain Yendred, an inhabitant of the planet Arde. I would suggest that when it comes to conspiracy theories, Yendred reigns supreme. Indeed, such theories belong more in the sterile, techno-perfect planiverse of Arde than in our own actual, messy, three-dimensional world.

Such works, whether absolute rubbish like Meyssan's or Tarpley's, or impressively detailed but casuistical performances like Naylor and Dewdney's, somehow manage to write off the thousands of dead and maimed at the hands of very real terrorists as a thesis deduction.

This is how the game is played. Undaunted by common sense, many conspiracy theorists are convinced of a secret collaboration between the Mossad and the CIA to inflame popular opinion against a benign and law-abiding Islamic community—although it cannot have been that secret since they seem to know all about it. Accrediting what has been called "rejected knowledge," that is, whatever has been disproved by competent investigation and official institutions, a growing constituency of facile skeptics has found a way of avoiding the rigour of critical thinking and substituting simplistic explanations and closed conceptual systems in its stead. They are wonderfully adept at constructing slanted interpretations of plain linearities, reading the facts backward, or fitting them on Procrustean beds to stretch or chop as their prejudices dictate. Having lost faith in the viability of a stable moral and psychological centre and unable to come to terms with a world verging on incoherence, the conspiracy theorist opts for a reductive simplicity that cannot be proven false. In doing so, he will even seize upon contradictory facts as evidence for the rightness of his claims, contending that such facts have been manufactured by a cabal of plotters who are *a priori* guilty. An obstinate fact is not an inconvenience but a godsend and, as if by sorcery, that which resists the theory is re-interpreted as endorsing it. Personal responsibility goes out the window, to be replaced by a belief in clandestine forces subtly controlling the course of events. Since whatever contrary information that comes in from elsewhere is already pre-judged as counterfeit, the conspiracy theorist is relieved of having to bear the burden of proof. But the system of adjudication he employs is self-referential, a closed circuit, a species of mystification if not of madness—and the madness, it appears, is spreading. Given the brisk trade in 9/11 conspiracy theories and the embarkation of so many scholars, bloggers, and commentators on this floating refuse barge, one suspects that the lunatic fringe is no longer a fringe.

Anything goes, it seems, but the truth or a sense of reality.

3

The unhealthy attitude of acquiescence and consent to the heinous and the primitive also underwrites the implicit program of the postcolonial *Schickeria* dominating the Humanities Departments of our universities, like renegade Shaolin monks trafficking in narcotics. For example, speculators like Homi Bhabha who, in his *The Location of Culture*, claims that "metropolitan histories of civitas cannot be conceived without evoking the savage colonial antecedents of the ideals of civility" and lobbies for a reinscription of "the cultural relations between spheres of social antagonism"—in other words, one way or another we had it coming. The same goes for the irresponsible babble of Jacques Derrida who, in Giovanna Borradori's interview volume *Philosophy in a Time of Terror*, refers to the date 9/11 as a "telegram of metonymy" that, according to his misbegotten logic, merely "points out the unqualifiable by recognizing that we do not recognize or even cognize that we do not yet know how to qualify"—in other words, we are too ignorant of the greater hermeneutic not to deserve what we got coming. As for that feverish and mendacious simplifier Noam Chomsky with his storyboard vision of the world, whose condition I can only diagnose as one of expository delirium, we got it coming for the sins of our corporate marauders and their political henchmen. (Chomsky is perhaps a special case: consumed by a furious hatred of America, he is the Bobby Fischer of the intellectual world, another brilliant, mentally over-specialized Jew gone round the bend.) It is equally hard to explain how educated intellectuals and area specialists could have bought so readily into Edward Said's ridiculous if convenient excuse in *Covering Islam* that the Islamist insurgents were merely "acting the part decreed for them" by the stereotypes engendered in the oppressive and imperialistic West—in other words, once again we got it coming for the terrorists are merely behaving in a reactive mode for which we ourselves are wholly to blame. (Said's *Culture and Imperialism* goes even further, throwing out not only the baby with the bathwater, but the bathtub too and finally the entire Western plumbing system, the very project to which the terrorists of Islam have covenanted themselves.) The doltishness of such analysis can only appall. These thinkers work in a climate of academic dementia which, in the words of Hannah Arendt from *Eichmann in Jerusalem*, derives from the "untrammelled inspiration of intellectuals who…are not in the least interested in facts but treat them merely as a springboard for 'ideas.'" Hatred of one's own, a proneness to delusion, and the seductive reverie of antirealism, moral evasiveness, and the habit of rejigging the past seem hardwired into the collective mindset of this strange human colony, so glibly eloquent and yet so morally inarticulate.

Indeed, for these iconoclasts, whose theories should long ago have been consigned to the dustbin of historiography, the past has been made the victim of radical theorizing about the past, about the indeterminacy of truth, about the "constructed" nature of fact, about the primacy of methodological issues over genuine substance—or even about the moral need, as Howard Zinn writes in the 1995 edition of his bestselling *A People's History of the United States,* to produce a "biased account" of significant events as a "counterforce" to standard historical scholarship. (The 1999 edition modifies these assertions, with Zinn merely conceding that his critically formative "experiences were hardly a recipe for neutrality in the teaching and writing of history.") This is done to further what he and his compeers regard as the good fight, the struggle to bring the "American empire" to its knees and—taking a page from Coleridge's *Kubla Khan,* labouring to build "that dome in air" and feed the planet on honeydew—usher in a classless, anti-capitalist Xanadu among the peoples of the world. They have no problem making false allegations, doctoring statistics, giving the most pejorative interpretation possible of pre-selected data, conscripting assumptions as facts, omitting unfavourable material, and teaching and writing about history that never happened. Our textual elites do not seem to understand that rewriting the historical muniments to conform to their ideals or prejudices only violates the cause to which they have attached themselves and that the world that has escaped their sagacity has done so because it is *outside the text.* This peculiar blindness has led to what Keith Windschuttle has called, in his book of that title, "the killing of history." In denying or revising the past, including the recent past, in practising the art of signal omission, and in viewing the world through an ideological astigmatism, that is, in killing history, these carriage-trade authors betray the present as well as the living memory of the dead. It is always those who have the greatest empathy for human suffering and surrender their practical consciousness to synoptic plans for human renovation who seem to end up shedding the most blood or being indifferent to the spillage. In so doing, they are utterly unmindful of the great lesson of history and notably of the twentieth century, namely, that the road to Heaven-on-Earth passes through Hell and never re-emerges.

In consequence, our intelligentsia, whose quest for truth has been aborted by an exaggerated regard for the clichés, mantras, and shibboleths *du jour*, have become the greatest internal threat to the integrity of the West, insofar as they refuse to understand that the West is now itself under threat—the kind of threat that must be met and dealt with in the Real if the world we live in and take for granted is not to founder. They bear a disquieting resemblance to the left-wing fellow-travellers from the 1930s to well on in the last century who supported the Soviet Union and regarded Joseph Stalin and his successors as heroes, humanists, and benefactors, having bought into what Arthur Koestler called the *grand mensonge*. Thus, regardless of his international acclaim, a self-preoccupied and vainglorious Leftist historian like Eric Hobsbawm can write a major autobiography, *Interesting Times*, in which, from the safety of his lifelong sinecure in Britain and the repose of his unexamined ideas, he glides serenely over the horrendous acts of the Soviet regime, the nonaggression pact with the Nazis, the gulags, the assassination and imprisonment of dissidents, the liquidation of Jewish intellectuals as "cosmopolitans," the show trials, the client dictatorships imposed on its constellation of satellite nations, the forced starvations, the crushing of popular revolts, the Potemkin Villages, the disastrous program of farm collectivizations, the microbial reign of lies lived on the level of daily life by hundreds of millions of people, the entire record of abominations, in order to preserve his communist sympathies from interrogation and the test of actual experience. Hobsbawm is what happens when you sell your soul to an Idea. A capacious mind is not necessarily a good one, and is certainly no defence against weakness of character, moral cowardice, and ideological obsession.

The chief hazard of the professional academic and university-bred paraclete is a resident, tenure-fed utopianism no amount of brute fact can evict. They are plainly susceptible to what Eric Voegelin in *The New Science of Politics* has called "theoretical illiteracy," which shows itself in "the form of various social idealisms" or an "axiological dream world" where the accent falls "on the state of perfection without clarity about the means that are required for its realization." The absence of a practical blueprint is no obstacle to the current neo-leftist romantic idealist whose energy goes into the projection of a civil Shangri-la without contour and substance to be constructed upon the ruins of the very liberal democracy that has provided him with life, livelihood, and professional honour. The world he lives in is a dream world because it meets the dangers that surround it, says Voegelin, not "by appropriate actions in the world of reality" but rather by magic incantations "such as disapproval, moral condemnation, declarations of intention, resolutions, appeals to the opinion of mankind…outlawing of war, propaganda for world peace and world government, etc.," so that in the course of time an entire society comes to be pervaded "with the weird, ghostly light of a lunatic asylum."

A good example of this elysian affliction, of this refusal to accept the structure of reality, is Martha Nussbaum's celebrated fantasia of "the community of human beings in the entire world" that she proposes in a widely circulated 1994 essay, "Patriotism and Cosmopolitanism." There is nothing novel and certainly nothing offensive in her recommendation that we learn more about other cultures and traditions and about our common problems as human beings. Such receptivity should be a part of any worthwhile system of education. Nor can we look askance at her very sensible suggestion that, while spending time on our own history and politics, we should "seriously consider the right of other human beings to life, liberty and the pursuit of happiness." These propositions are wholly unexceptionable and, indeed, are mere theoretical placebos. The trouble begins when we are instructed to give our "allegiance and respect" not primarily to the nation in which we live, but to humanity's "fundamental ingredients, reason and moral capacity," to "the moral community made up by the humanity of all human beings," and to the effort to transcend "a morally arbitrary boundary such as the boundary of a nation." These glorious schemes and abstractions, which are meant to serve "the formation of public policy," might be innocuous enough and even commendable in a time of extended peace that would allow us to indulge our prelapsarian hopes and aspirations. But when the nation whose borders are regarded as constricting and injurious to the soul is itself under siege by an adversary who does not recognize "the world community of justice and reason" and who is committed to our complete destruction, then the injunction to "join hands across these other barriers" and to become "citizens of the world" is a recipe for national suicide, the sign of a society that is progressively beheading itself, even without outside help. Such a program bespeaks the resurgence of a political romanticism wedded to motives rather than consequences, unachievable ideals rather than practical values. It consists largely of the cryogenized remnants of an antique crusade for unperturbed happiness and tranquility, actuated by a child-like desire for transcendence that is the curse of liberal political civilization, and that, in various spiritual and revolutionary forms, has caused untold harm and suffering in the past. As William Pfaff writes in *The Bullet's Song*, the effort to deny the tragic but inescapable limitations of human life, the "flight from the reality of the human predicament" and the search "for a revenge on life as it is" is also "among the fundamental factors responsible for what happened in the twentieth century. Utopianism defies tragedy—and fails."

In his scrupulously researched *Unholy Alliance: Radical Islam and the American Left*, American political historian David Horowitz explains that such Cinderella sentiments express "the anti-American voice of an 'internationalism' that goes back more than a century to Marx's idea that radicals should have no country, that their only loyalty should be to the revolutionary future and the forces presumed to embody it. The secessionists are heirs of Marxism and Communism who believe they are "citizens of the world" rather than of the nation that guarantees their survivals and freedoms." Under the rubric of "social justice," the Left is busy trying to dismantle the imperfect but still effective political and economic structure of the world's greatest democracy, the bulwark of what we know as civilization, in order to pursue a universalist program of salvation on earth that was discredited, once and for all, with the collapse of the Soviet empire. ("Social justice" is, of course, a stick-on label that can apply to anything one believes or any cause one serves; it is not only the Left's catch-all, it was also the name of Father Charles Coughlin's fascist and antisemitic newspaper that flourished in the 1930s and 1940s.) For today's intellectual orthodoxy, writes Melanie Phillips in *Londonistan*, "The nation and its values are despised; moral legitimacy resides instead in a vision of universal progressivism" that has created a society "so badly confused that even now it cannot grasp the danger that it is in." That one may be a loyal citizen and yet critical of one's country's policies and actions is by no means a contradiction, but censure of the nation that certifies one's right to live and the unstructured longing for an all-embracing brotherhood and sisterhood should not be allowed to short-circuit one's intelligence or to call one's commitment to the common ground of our political existence into question. For national sublimation subtends cultural vacancy and the historical nocturne. Patriotism may often be "the last refuge of a scoundrel," as Dr. Johnson remarked, but treason is the act that always bears his signature.

Should it not be obvious to even the most donnish of observers that a mawkish and unrealizable platitude, an empty generalization, the white flag of best intentions, an edifying phylactery like Nussbaum's "worldwide community of human beings" never stopped a determined killer and never will? Nor are the basic questions adequately addressed in her assumptions. How is the community of mankind—or, we might add, even a statist bureaucracy replacing autonomous nations of elected governments, as in present-day Eutopia—conceivable apart from the political articulation of civil and national society with all the tensions, compromises, trade-offs, hierarchical distinctions, defensive alignments, and institutional constraints that are inevitable in a world inhabited by real human beings? And how is this orphic community to be secured against the activist powers arrayed against it when the prevailing mood, to cite Voegelin's aniline critique again, is a sort of psychological lethargy that takes our survival as written, a spirit "of relaxation into the sweetness of existence…of a blindness to obvious dangers, and a reluctance to meet them with all seriousness…the mood of late, disintegrating societies that no longer are willing to fight for their existence?"[11]

The idea Nussbaum is championing is, of course, not new and is, indeed, pre-Marxist. We find it, as she indicates, in Diogenes and Marcus Aurelius. But there is no need to reach so far back. It is also Wilhelm von Humboldt warmed over who, in *The Limits of State Action*, dreamed of "mankind in its entirety…as a great family of brothers, marching toward one and the same end, the free development of its moral powers"—a notion put forward in all its formal grandeur by Immanuel Kant in his *Perpetual Peace: A Philosophical Sketch*, with its "Third Definitive Article" embracing the condition of universal hospitality and world citizenship. (Kant, of course, was merely elaborating Rousseau's teaching, in *On the Social Contract*, of a universal political constitution whose moral legitimacy was also understood to be universal.) It is an idea that has been most recently taken up by Anthony J. Hall, a modern and suitably tempered Fifth Monarchy man if ever there was one, with his vision of a new Golden Age and a New Model Army of intellectuals to bring it to pass. In *The American Empire and the Fourth World*, Hall trashes the post-Columbian American imperialists, rejecting "the cover of a self-righteous war on terrorism" while excoriating the "Bush regime" and the "inward-looking dynamic of [American] reactionary mentality." "Who knows," he wails, "how many other groups on the next frontiers of American power in both the Arab-speaking and Muslim worlds will find themselves demonized…." Weaving through his text is the pastoral concept of a new world that incorporates the "biodiversity" of all mankind in a process of "epistemological cross-fertilization" and "transcultural blending." Hall pins his hopes on an eclectic though intellectually unified mosaic of selfless ambassadors from the fourth world of supranational Enlighteners—a "bowl with one spoon," to use the wampum-belt image that serves as his emblematic principle. The fourth world relies not on pre-emptive power "against menaces *thought to be lurking* within and beyond the frontiers of the American Empire" but on "those narratives of renewal that are most essential to the equilibrium between continuity and adaptation in the perpetuation of all human cultures" (italics mine).

This latter is a pleasantly vanilla sentiment of little practical significance in itself, but when presented as the basis of foreign policy in a world about to explode, it is both childish and reckless, a throwing of sops to Cerberus. Such sententious commonplaces may have appealed to the ancient Stoics (one of Nussbaum's primary references) or nineteenth-century libertarians or to the revolutionary syndicalism of the twentieth-century European Left, but, put into circulation today, can only work to promote the terrorist's cause. Saul Singer, author of *Confronting Jihad*, is on the mark when he deplores what he calls "the seemingly inexorable march of a blind Kantian universalism" and points to the dubious careers of the League of Nations, the United Nations, the Arab League and the European Union as evidence of the ultimate frivolity of the notion. His conclusion is that "it doesn't work to fix the world all at once. It has to be done piecemeal, and the nation…is the key agent of change." (The idea clearly derives from Karl Popper's concept of "piecemeal social engineering" proposed in *The Open Society and Its Enemies*.) Saul's thesis is a necessary corrective to the starry-eyed somnambulism of his fellow Israeli, perennial minister Shimon Peres, who in *New Genesis* confidently asserts that "human nature will change" and that the world will soon leave behind "the demarcation lines of sovereignty"—an expansion of the key notion in an earlier book, *The New Middle East*, in which Peres, looking to Western

Europe as his guiding light but showing no awareness of the serious unrest simmering under the social surface, declares that "particularist nationalism is fading and the idea of a 'citizen of the world' is taking hold." It never fails to amaze how what passes for advanced social thinking may be little more than native puerility coupled with a type of intellectual cynicism, a mass sell-off of the "core values" of one's own country or civilization in exchange for a vapid but potentially harmful ideal—a distraction from the actual problems at hand and a dilution of the will to take a stand against a very real enemy who does not share these values. "Oh baby, baby," folksinger Cat Stevens once sang, "it's a wild world"—one to which Stevens, reborn as Yusuf Islam, is now contributing, along with our born-again Panglossians submitting their drafts for a best possible world and in so doing, merely adding oil to the flames.

The scenario being enacted is hardly believable. In the name of "the brotherhood of man," of human sympathy and an oceanic desire for peace, pragmatic democratic institutions and powers ready to entertain the prospect of conflict and sacrifice in the service of specific, empirical commitments to beneficial change or the preservation of authentic liberal values are slagged as aggressors, and courageous individuals unwilling to surrender themselves to the chants, slogans, and sentimentalities of the morally occulted are swept aside as vestiges of an archaic state of mind. This is a position that in today's world is urgently in need of refreshing. The issue must be faced, and those who seriously trade in the ideological sedatives and Disneyfied proposals of the day, busy imagineering a new world, are nothing less than enablers for a resolute belligerent who has our end at heart.[12] These are the modern descendants of those whom the Koran prophesies will go down to certain defeat, "for they are people devoid of understanding" (8:65). And some of them, I regret to say, seem to have interiorized the Leninist concept of "revolutionary defeatism," that is, giving one's allegiance to the enemy of one's country in order to hasten the destruction of the nation of which one is a citizen and replace it with a universal phalanstery. What *Jerusalem Post* columnist Caroline Glick says in the context of the Israeli debate with its own utopian and revisionist elements applies on a much larger scale. "The legacy of heroism of those who fought for freedom—whether of the entire world or just our tiny nation—is one of constant vigilance in the defence of our liberty, and not the embrace of childish, self-indulgent and naïve dreams."

An equally good example of the sheer drollery of the programmatic Left is provided in the writings of Ignacio Ramonet, the esteemed anti-globalist editor of the Paris monthly *Le Monde Diplomatique*, coiner of the theoretical abstraction *la pensée unique*—the "uniform think-ing" of the free-market world that he condemns, retreading Herbert Marcuse's concept of one-dimensional man—and considered by many as Europe's Noam Chomsky. In his article entitled *Résistances* in the May 2004 issue of the journal, all the world's problems are resolved through a long series of positive and negative apodictic utterances. He begins with the *nons*: "Non à l'exclusion...Non à la pauvreté. Non aux inégalités.... Non à l'oubli du Sud.... Non à l'hégémonie militaire d'une seule hyperpuissance. Non à la guerre préventive. Non aux guerres d'invasion. Non au terrorisme...," etc. Then comes a phalanx of *ouis*: "Oui à la solidarité entre les 6 milliards d'habitants de notre planète.... Oui à l'existence d'une ONU renouvelée.... Oui à une offensive interna-tionale contre la fracture digitale.... Oui à la préservation des cultures minoritaires. Oui aux droits des indigènes. Oui à la justice sociale et économique...," etc. "Résister," he concludes, "c'est rêver qu'un autre monde est possible." If Ramonet could have his way, America would be displaced as a superpower, pre-emptive strikes would be a thing of the past, the Taliban would still be hosting al-Qaeda's murderous septs, the unelected bureaucracy and "limousine intellectuals" (in Kenneth Timmerman's phrase) of the European Union would persevere in their flagship policy of Islamic propitiation while projecting their Kantian hallucination of universal peace upon a seething and refractory world, and 6 billion people would miraculously unite into one big happy Nussbaumian family while retaining their cultural identities. And presto! the wild world will have rasterized into the best possible one. More significantly, what has happened in this visionary process is that the sabbatical dream has been transmuted into an imaginary and oper-atic surreality via a chain of apostrophes and vocatives that adamantly refuses to take the world of mutinous facts and intractable forces into account or to examine where our true welfare lies in these distraught and tempestuous times.

As a counterweight to the Ramonets *et al.* of the multicultural, Coca-Cola ad world, one might be well advised to consult the work of French philosopher, Alain Finkielkraut. In *L'humanité perdue: Essai sur le XXe siècle*, Finkielkraut has thoroughly dissected the idea of the brotherhood of man, showing that it is not intrinsic to the human condition, but an intellectual artifact whose effects are generally barbarous. Finkielkraut understands that the philosophy of "realizing the unity of the human species" leads almost inevitably, as in the vast ideological movements of the previous century, to its proponents "releasing themselves from the bonds of humanity," exposing men "to limitless violence" and taking away "their ontological dignity." *Humanity*, as he intimates, is the higher value in the name of which so many crimes are committed. "Better to fight evil wherever it appears than to set one's sights on a hypothetical good and enter into the murderous dialectic of ends and means in the hopes of attaining it"—the history of the twentieth century. The new century begins where the last left off. "[T]he tradition of political romanticism, bas[ing] relations among humans on the mystical model of fusion," has led to the loss of freedom. The individual disappears into the community since freedom is now conceived in the mode of identity politics and the paradoxical integration of cultural specificities, that is, "as a collective attribute, never as an individual possession." Though Ramonet will have no truck with such chaste and unintoxicated thinking, it is encouraging, I suppose, to learn that he says *non* to terrorism. Perhaps the terrorists will now lay down their arms.

What European thinkers like Ramonet refuse to understand is that the triple platform of myopia, bad faith, and dependence on which their new world order is to be erected will not sustain the weight of reality. For Europe is trying to forge a socially advanced twenty-first century without seriously considering that a significant and growing immigrant population, as well as those who control much of its energy supply, still live in a medieval mental world, and forgetting as well that its military defense—and the large expenditure that goes with it—are met to a great extent by a country it affects to despise. It is American "barbarity" that has allowed Europe to dream on by permitting it to invest what otherwise would have been earmarked for defence into its social welfare programs, its generously paid work holidays, its munificent child-care allowances, its lavish agricultural subsidies. Europe is the ultimate parasite. This is why the much-lauded, dirigiste, Left-oriented "European project" is bound to fail. The brave new world cannot establish a new horizon of sensibility while incorporating the indigestible residue of an atavistic epoch into its body politic, nor can it hope to prosper if it is unwilling to defend itself against the forces that envision its ultimate downfall, or if it continues to disdain and reproach the very power that protects it—against itself.

Even those who march left—a little left of right, left—a little left of right in an effort to accommodate reality must inevitably stumble and fall executing so awkward a mental gait. A case in point is Canadian-born intellectual Michael Ignatieff, who in his latest book, *The Lesser Evil*, elaborates the general thesis that the right response to mass casualty terrorism, even if some of our civil liberties must be temporarily suspended, is to resist the national security state that necessarily restricts our liberty and increases distrust among citizens. Undeterred by the facts on the ground, he urges instead that we should strive to "strengthen open government" and to reinvigorate "the institutions of freedom"—a proposal that in ordinary circumstances should enlist our unreserved support but in the current situation seems a trifle lame considering the self-admitted prospect of a collapsed economy and "zones of devastation sealed off for years." If a liberal democracy must respect the rights of the enemy, as he contends, the fact that this enemy refuses as a matter of policy to do likewise, has rejected all international conventions governing the conduct of war, and is planning to inflict upon his target nothing short of the unthinkable, must qualify the argument if we are to survive its consequences. In articulating the classic liberal position that due process and basic dignity "are independent of conduct and irrevocable under any circumstance," Ignatieff comes precariously close to a form of purist Christianity of a Quaker or Amish stamp, a veritable godsend to the terrorists in our midst. It is precisely the degree of restraint that is in question here, as well as the moral fear of coming to resemble the enemy in the process of defeating him—but a ticking bomb is not defused by cerebral distinctions that address the future when there may not be one.

Ignatieff is especially slippery because in many ways he does seem to have a grip on the complex issues and hard realities of the day. He promotes the United States, acknowledges the necessity of the war on terror, and recognizes, as he writes in *The Lesser Evil*, that "defeating terrorism requires violence...and may require coercion, deception, secrecy and violation of rights," and that "liberal societies cannot be defended by herbivores. We need carnivores to save us." At the same time, his libertarian bias has the effect of ensuring that his Praetorian carnivores will come to behave like harmless, contemplative herbivores. For the democratic war on terror of which he appears to approve is made subject to a series of tests that can only cripple the resolve to fight it effectively, tests such as "the dignity test—do [coercive measures] violate individual rights"—that allow us to ensure that such procedures "preclude cruel and unusual punishment?"; and the "conservative test," that is, do coercive measures deprive detained individuals of judicial review? These are followed by a chain of further trials, including the test of "open adversarial review," the consultation of other nations and respect for international obligations, and the "last resort test," the latter defined as the question concerning whether "less coercive measures have been tried and failed." Another such constraint is the proposed dismissal "of the carnivores who disgrace the society they are charged to protect." But carnivores tend to behave in certain ways and this is precisely why we require their services in the first place. The only alternative, if we intend to be consistent, is to geld them at the start, which would defeat their obvious purpose. Ignatieff's conclusion is that, "If all this adds up to a series of constraints that tie the hands of our government, so be it." But of course such criteria in their stringency, number, and, not least, in the time required to apply them, would have exactly that effect and the war on terror will have been critically handicapped and possibly even lost.

The two central legal principles Ignatieff likes to tout—the twin towers, we might say, of "invariance" (laws are immutable) and "equality" (laws apply to all)—were damaged (though, fortunately, not irreparably) not by American legislators or a neoconservative presidency, but by the terrorists themselves. Commitments to minority rights should certainly, as he claims, "be maintained as far as possible, in times of danger." But how far is as far as possible? And how justified is it to favour the rights of a minority from whose ranks the enemy is drawn and in whose bosom he is too often sheltered? Let us not forget that this is the very enemy responsible for compelling the majority of the citizenry, or its elected representatives, to invoke the suspension of some of the rights Ignatieff is strenuously defending. Civil libertarians will condemn such revocation as a victory for the enemy and this is doubtlessly the case *up to a degree*. Nevertheless, the victory that might ensue in the absence of such measures is one that may well be total and surely far more non-revocable than the principles of invariance and equality sanctified by the liberal Left. This is not Milton's war in Heaven in which the Law need never be suspended or attuned to circumstance. This is what H. J. Simson, in his important study, *British Rule, and Rebellion*, has termed "sub-war," which "creates a situation that cannot be met by the laws and punishments of ordinary times." To be sure, Ignatieff does appear at one point to soften his stance, vacillating toward an acceptance of commonsensical flexibility. But his hastily cooked-up middle way between invariance and practical effectiveness—that "laws do derive some of their powers from being difficult to change, and yet if they are completely unresponsive to emergency situations, they may be ineffective"—is really a Baby Bear's Porridge position, an ambiguous and mainly verbal compromise, neither hot nor cold, in a world that does not grant us the luxury of tepid equivocations and that is always ready to strike in the chink between the self and its contradiction. And, as we have noted, Ignatieff has set up so many hedges and conditions against the agencies of revocation and operational efficiency as to render them pretty well edentulous.

Let us stay with Ignatieff a moment longer since he provides a good illustration of how even an ideological dove gradually evolving hawklet's talons—he originally approved of the American-led invasion of Iraq—manages to gain so little purchase on the current situation. Ignatieff writes, "If apocalyptic nihilism feeds on political despair, it is in the rational self-interest of wealthy states to invest in assistance to help authoritarian societies in the Arab world—societies that have failed their people—to move toward democracy, even if the denouement is likely to bring Islamic parties to power." We should see how tenuous if not preposterous such "liberal" pronunciamentos really are. First, it is by no means certain that what we are now encountering is "apocalyptic nihilism"; apocalyptic movements may well spring from eschatological religious principles and appear nihilistic only to those who observe from the outside, which is more than likely what is happening now. The war that has been unleashed today is an all-out theological jihad, rooted in the Islamic scriptures, against both the secular state and the founding religions of the Western world. In the words of Houellebecq's compatriot Jean-François Revel in his recent book *Anti-Americanism*, "Islamic terrorism in general is the offspring of a religious *idée fixe* and has nothing to do with theories about poverty.... On the contrary, Islamists utterly reject as incompatible with the Qur'an all measures that might contribute to improvement: democracy, secularism, intellectual freedom and critical thought, equality for women, pluralism and openness to other cultures." Further, how wealthy states, by which Ignatieff means the Western democracies—as if the Islamic tyrannies were not already obscenely wealthy—are to invest in the Arab world, whether materially or through digital technology, so as to actually reach the disadvantaged beneath the impermeable layers of autocratic state control is a predicament that no one has yet been able to resolve, except in the realm of the political fairy tale. The only way of effecting so revolutionary a goal that has any possibility of success is "regime change," although the outcome of such interventions is always problematic and runs counter to majoritarian liberal thinking.

Finally, if such assistance were to bring Islamist parties to power, the chaos that would ensue on the international scene would be catastrophic. Democracy is not a panacea that cures all ills merely by being introduced, but is contingent upon a host of keystone conditions—on entrenched safeguards, the separation of Church and State, the schooling of the electorate, a sound economic basis, a robust and solvent middle class, a functioning and responsive bureaucracy, the political will for the ballot box, and, in particular, guarantees of electoral repeatability. But the concept of the rotation of power is alien to Islam, except by the time-vetted methods of assassination, revolt, and consanguinity. If the democratic option serves only to put a terrorist regime in power, on the principle of "one man, one vote, one time," then democracy becomes the means whereby violence is institutionalized, as, for example, was the case in Palestine when Hamas emerged victorious—the Hamas Charter promises to "spread the spirit of Jihad among the *Umma*, clash with the enemies and join the ranks of the Jihad fighters"—or in Lebanon when Hizbullah assumed a lynchpin role in the establishment of a new national parliament. Worse, merely imagine a violence-prone Algeria, a militarily powerful Turkey, a nuclear Pakistan operating as full-fledged, radical Islamic regimes on the world stage—very real possibilities. Indeed it is Pakistan, with its nuclear arsenal and its fundamentalist parties threatening to assassinate the president and assume control of the government, that fuels the gravest nightmare scenario. And Iran, as we know, is well on its way to nuclear enrichment and is constantly ratcheting up its anti-Western rhetoric. According to a report filed by the Adnkronos News agency,

Hojatolislam Gholam Hasani, who represents the Iranian supreme leader Ayatollah Ali Khameini, delivered a sermon at a Tehran mosque in which he stressed that, "Freedom, democracy and stupidities of this type…are not in sync with the principles of Islam. Islam always spoke with a sword in hand, and I don't see why now we should change attitude and talk with other civilizations."

The Western belief that the accession to power of Islamist groups and parties through democratic means will lead to moderation, responsibility, and an end to terrorism by forcing them to "get real" in their dealings with the empirical world is completely without merit and contradicted by the facts—one look at Arafat's Palestine and Khomeini's Iran should have dispelled all illusions about so improbable an alternative. Add to this dismal scenario the multitude of terrorist organizations and states who might soon deploy their own nuclear and biological arsenal (or already have them) and it becomes nothing less than a type of lunacy to maintain that the mere sowing of the democratic seed among the Islamic peoples will produce a flourishing harvest. Islam will see to the burning of the fields. The educated innocence of Ignatieff-style academics can only do us inestimable harm and must be diligently countered by the straight-shooting, no-nonsense, aquiline realism of the handful of Houellebecqs and Revels among us if we are to survive our fateful appointment with the most pitiless of enemies.[13]

The spectacle of our suave and cosseted intellectuals, pronouncing with dulcet serenity and didactic conviction on questions of unquenchable violence and a savagery that gives no quarter, is as melancholy as they come. Such rostrum bloviators, lost in the whorls of their meerschaum meditations, seem completely out of touch with reality. This is nihilism with a vengeance. As Theodore Sampson has written in *Passing Through: Notations of an Old-Fashioned Humanist*, "The flip side of demonic nihilism [is] tolerance, understanding and *la belle aujourd'hui*." But in clinging to what they conceive as a noble option, the cause of (multi)cultural Otherness, they are like the frog riding the kangaroo's tail in the Edward Lear poem. It will be a bumpy ride and a tumbling destination.

But chewy-centred academics are not the only problem. Neither is the literary community, which bears a striking resemblance to the Monty Python soccer team of Long John Silver impersonators, exempt from the charge of occupational self-indulgence and binge soft-mindedness evinced by our intellectual gentry. To take just a few examples from numberless such instances. Harold Pinter, a critic of the Bush administration ("a dangerous monster out of control") and of British Prime Minister Tony Blair ("a deluded idiot"), has favoured us with the products of an overheated—and undernourished—poetic Muse in which the total absence of original imagery, lapidary diction, and crafted prosody is obviously no liability. The much-praised "God Bless America" begins, "Here they go again,/The Yanks in their armoured parade" and concludes with our noses sniffing "the pong of the dead" while "the dead air is alive/With the smell of America's God." The book pages of *Pravda* could have done no better. Another poem, "Democracy," is redeemed only by its brevity; four lines reduce the damage, though the reader may be pardoned for wondering whether "the big pricks" that will "fuck everything in sight" are not unintentionally self-referential. For bathos is Pinter's stock-in-trade. David Farr, director of a recent production of Christopher Marlowe's *Tamburlaine the Great*, deletes the famous Koran-burning scene from Part II, Scene V of the play, explaining that his "choices...had nothing to do with politics." Kirsten Harms, director of Berlin's *Deutsche Oper*, cancels a postmodern production of Mozart's *Idomeneo* for fear that a certain prop, the severed head of Mohammed, will touch off protests and riots among the Muslim community—the companion noggins of Poseidon, Jesus, and Buddha obviously pass muster, which at least says something commendable about Greeks, Christians, and Buddhists. Alistair Beaton writes a play called *We're Sending You A Cluster Bomb From Jesus* ridiculing the regime-change policy of George Bush and Tony Blair. As theater critic Mark Steyn comments, a better title (and play) might have been something like *We're Sending You A Schoolgirl Bomb From Allah*. The laughs that Beaton is drawing from approving audiences will soon be on them and are simply one more sign of the ignominious self-defeatism of a civilization in precipitous decline, pandering happily to the enemy. (One remembers the episode Lewis Mumford writes about in *The City in History*, in which the citizens of Augustine's city of Hippo were too busy attending the games in the local Forum to defend themselves against the Vandals at the walls, with the inevitable result that the city was razed and these distracted citizens put to the sword.) The same is true of Sam Hamill's cabaret-light and melodrama-heavy

Poets Against the War volume, perhaps the most embarrassingly weak and egomaniacal poetry anthology ever brought out by a reputable publisher—"war cries cries war war," (stutters Phyllis Webb), "war cries CRIES WAR CRIES there are there/are still still still still" is a typical specimen of the mindless maunderings to be found in it. Like lambs being led to the slaughter, our liberal peacelings must do everything in their power not to offend the butchers.

The problem, as Houellebecq intimates throughout the corpus of his work and especially in *Platform*, is thus compounded many times over. Islam is not only our "world-historical" antagonist. It is also an indication of what is wrong with *us*. How else explain how a crypto-Islamist like Tariq Ramadan, who passes himself off as a Muslim reformer but strongly implies in the pleonastic W*estern Muslims and the Future of Islam* that Islam will envelop and, so to speak, outperform Judaism and Christianity, and is the author of an arguably antisemitic tract entitled *Critique des (nouveaux) intellectuels communautaires*, can be celebrated by *Time* magazine as an intellectual innovator and invited by Notre Dame University to assume the Henry R. Luce Chair in its International Peace Studies program? Ramadan believes that Islam can infiltrate and conquer the West by initially peaceful means, continuing immigration, and the "duty for Muslims…to take Islam from the periphery of European culture to the centre" (interview in the *New Statesman* for June 21, 2004). The warrant here is clearly Koran 9:33, in which Allah sends forth his apostle "to make the true faith supreme over all religions"—a mandate that may be dissembled but cannot go unheeded. Ramadan coquettishly advances toward his goal of disarming resistance via the rhetoric of compatibility, ethical harmony, and doctrinal alignment between the two faith communities. He even goes so far as to refer to Islamic philosophers like Avicenna, Averroes, and Ibn Khaldun as "European Muslim thinkers…who…confidently accept[ed] their European identity"—a proposition as staggering as it is absurd. A cursory perusal of Robert Spencer's *The Politically Incorrect Guide to Islam*, a kind of *Islam for Dummies* (or Dhimmis), would quickly torpedo Ramadan's strange notion of cultural, religious, and jurisprudential consonance. (In her last book, *The Force of Reason*, Oriana Fallaci also calls attention to the new and concomitant Islamic "design based on gradual penetration rather than brutal and sudden aggression.") It is in this light that we should place Ramadan's agitating for unimpeded immigration in *Western Muslims*: "policies proposed to combat immigration are dreadful and assume that the 'clandestine immigrant' is a liar, a thief, even a bandit." But why stop there? Such policies might also assume that the "clandestine immigrant" is a misfit, a parasite, even a terrorist, as several European nations are now beginning to suspect. It is perhaps not without significance that Ramadan's father, Said, notwithstanding having received political asylum in Geneva, used the pages of his journal *El Mouslimoun* to promote ideological warfare against the West. In this regard, the son, playing the role of the "good cop," is far more sophisticated than the father in the prosecution of their common goal, and Western academics have fallen for this tactical combover. It would be more appropriate to ask why Hassan al-Turabi, the Sudanese host of Osama bin Laden, proclaimed Tariq Ramadan "the future of Islam" and why, for that matter, Ramadan continues to sit on the board of the Islamic Center in Geneva, which is directed by his brother Hari and which, according to reports, has come under suspicion by the Swiss Secret Service for connections to terrorist organizations and banks.

But there are moments when the mask drops. Ramadan wants Muslims who live in the West, as he writes in *Western Muslims and The Future of Islam*, to "become assured as people who know what they hold (a universal message)" and to bring into Western education "the overall philosophy of the Islamic message," blithely claiming that "there is in fact no confusion between the restraining authority of the religious and the civic independence of the individual, between the realm of dogma and that of reason." Islam, he continues, "is a Western religion in the full sense of the word" and that what should "be called into question" is not Islam in itself or the violence it is said to engender but "the immigration policies of Western countries and their social and urban policies," which give "rise to vexatious, discriminatory, and unjust administrative measures." One wonders whether Ramadan is living in the same world as the rest of us or is he just being shrewdly disingenuous? Ramadan does not stop there as he attempts to refute the well-known argument that the two realms of Church and State coalesce in Islam into a single entity. His contention that there is a "distinction" between the two spheres that "has not had to go as far as separation, even divorce, as in the Christian era," is simply not supported by the evidence pouring in from the international political arena or by the frequent legal suits against free expression mounted by Islamic organizations in our own societies. That a "distinction" between Church and State is as effective as a "separation" or a "divorce"—only subtler—or that it even exists, is a sophistry of the first order. When Ramadan goes on to develop his thesis on "the level of political involvement," we find that Muslims are expected to take "their Islamic frame of reference as the starting point" before "deciding on…strategies that make it possible to be faithful to both the essential principles and ethics." The "distinction" is not so subtle after all. And this is only the tip of the sand dune. Ramadan claims to be no Salafist or literalist (from Arabic *salaf* or "ancestor"), but his cassettes, made to appeal to Muslim youth, and some of his radio interviews suggest otherwise. These cassettes may be procured on the Internet or in specialized bookstores, and his more direct, unguarded utterances have been carefully referenced by Caroline Fourest in her recent *Frère Tariq*, the English translation of which is already overdue.

In one way or another, whether unwittingly or witlessly, we have become—to use Plutarch's term in his denunciation of Herodotus whom he thought too lenient toward the enemy—*philobarbaros*, a friend to the Persians, lovers of those who would annihilate us, human shields for the adversary, guarantors of the dysfunctional Muslim world from Mauritania to the Gulf States to Indonesia. This charge may be problematic with respect to Herodotus, but it certainly seems apposite with regard to our own version of recent events and to that genre of thinker that Mark Lilla in *The Reckless Mind* calls the "philotyrannical intellectual." Too many of us simply do not seem able to comprehend that the variety of terrorism now operating on the international stage is something completely unprecedented in the unrestricted nature of its scope, the global extent of its funding, the ordnance it is determined to acquire, the deep dye of theological pigmentation with which it is suffused, and its flaunting of the rules of engagement once acknowledged, at least in some degree, by its predecessors. Terrorism has turned its attention away from its earlier method of generally targeting selected individuals, usually men and women of fiscal or political influence, or representative national groups and official associations or institutions, to spreading fear and destruction among civilian populations at large and to disrupting the economies of nations.

Beginning with the tactics and policies of the *Ikhwan*, or Muslim

Brotherhood, founded in Egypt in 1928 (by Hassan al-Banna, the grandfather of Tariq Ramadan), perfected by the FLN in Algeria during the 1950s and inflamed by the writings of Said Qutb in the 1960s into a revolutionary terrorist vanguard, terrorism acquired its modern stamp, producing such notable exemplars of the trade as Yasser Arafat and Osama bin Laden. As Albert Camus wrote in "Preface to Algerian Reports," collected in his 1958 volume of essays and articles under the title *Actuelles III*, such practices are "a crime that can be neither excused nor allowed to develop. Under the form it has assumed, no revolutionary movement has ever accepted it, and the Russian terrorists of 1905, for instance, would have died (they proved this statement) rather than stoop to it." Admittedly, there were exceptions, such as the October 1883 Fenian dynamiting of two underground railways in London, but today this has become the norm. When the terrorist movement finally succeeds in acquiring WMD and decides to use them, with the intent of inflicting the greatest possible number of casualties and maximum material, psychological, and economic damage, it will have fulfilled the logic of its development. And the terrorists will have been aided in their purpose by our philotyrannical intellectuals plying their policy of compromise and reprieve, the political alchemists of our day labouring to turn gold into plutonium.

Terrorism has undergone a phase-change, vaulting into a completely new historical category. If our analysis of the threat is not grounded in recent historical events, from Cairo and Algiers and Jerusalem to New York and Madrid and London, anything we might say about it and our reaction to it, about "problematic" risk assessment, the tendency to exaggeration, the need for "balanced" response and so on, is no longer relevant or admissible. All bets are off. This generation of terrorists is retooling for Armageddon. If the mad mullahs of Iran succeed in developing a nuclear arsenal, they may well make good on Lear's empty threat: "I shall do such things—what they are yet I know not—but they shall be the terror of the earth." Except that they know quite well what they intend to do. We cannot reasonably expect that we will be able to treat with a nation ruled by a consistory of theocratic monomaniacs disposing of nuclear weapons and waiting for the return of the twelfth imam, or Mahdi, at the end of the world, whose advent they may be inclined to hasten. The paradigm of Cold War-style deterrence would be entirely ineffective here, if not suicidal.

Our reluctance to confront what we are incapable or unwilling to imagine is not uncommon. The universality of the inimical was not even foreseen by some of our most discerning Modern(ist) writers, such as Henry James in *The Princess Casamassima*, whose awareness of the "nearness (to all our apparently ordered life) of some sinister anarchic underworld heaving in its pain, its power and its hate" missed the essence of our slowly gestating predicament, Joseph Conrad in *The Secret Agent* (who came close, but not quite close enough), Gide again in *The Caves of the Vatican* with his theory of the gratuitous act, and André Malraux in *Man's Fate*, who postulated that anyone living in the twentieth century who has not killed is still a virgin. (And as Houellebecq says in *Lanzarote*, "we weren't likely to see the end of the twentieth century for some time.") Hannah Arendt, too, for all her acuity, could not extrapolate from the 1950s to the present. "Deadly danger to any civilization," she writes in *The Origins of Totalitarianism*, "is no longer likely to come from without. Nature has been mastered and no barbarians threaten to destroy what they cannot understand, as the Mongolians threatened Europe for centuries." She could not imagine the burgeoning Islamic menace, nor the deadly symbiosis of the *nomenklatura* who today would agitate for the civil rights of Genghis Khan.

Closer to the truth is the argument of the Egyptian scholar, Bat Ye'or, who has coined the term "Eurabia" to designate the political devolution of Europe through unbridled Islamic immigration (or what has been called "reverse colonization") and morally bankrupt foreign policy accommodations with the Muslim world—a transitional but accelerating condition that she denominates as "dhimmitude." (The Arabic word *dhimmi* refers to non-Muslim second-class citizens in the lands vanquished and colonized by Islam.) According to Ye'or's most recent book, *Eurabia: The Euro-Arab Axis*, Europe has now almost completely abdicated its oft-interrupted historical mission and compliantly entered the Islamic orbit of influence as it grows increasingly subservient to what she calls the "ratcheting method" of Islamic conversionary tactics—a destiny, we might add, that could well befall a still unyielding America if the chronic and quixotic course of appeasement exhibited by the liberal-left establishment is not parried and debunked. For, as I have tried to show, the liberal-left political creed, with its European origins, flaccid multiculturalism, and the antinomian view of America it shares with radical Islam, has become the secular Koran of our media elite and public intellectuals. One can perhaps understand European intellectuals who, having kept dry for two generations under the American umbrella, pay little attention to the rain. They are innocent of weather. But Europeanized Americans have less excuse to justify their aversion to the mundane and the painfully obvious. Even intelligent writers like the aforementioned William Pfaff, a Paris-based correspondent for the *International Herald Tribune* who considers the American-led war on terror "a postmodern parody of WW II," may live to regret their supercilious dismissal of the contemporary political environment.

In coming to grips with the contemporary challenge, Americans, Ye'or writes, "must discuss the tragic development of Eurabia," whose functionaries "are now well entrenched in each European parliament, and at the head of the European Commission," and whose citizens are "prisoners of a Eurabian totalitarianism that foments a culture of deadly lies about Western civilization." Indeed, deep in the warm, peaceable, social-democratic European soul, the egg of totalitarianism waits to be hatched again. Ye'or's warning is not to be lightly dismissed and has been taken up as well in David Horowitz's *Unholy Alliance*, where the danger represented by the American Left to the political integrity and homeland defence of the United States is soberly and factually documented. The effect is harrowing. What is required now is a refresher course in the *Federalist Papers*, with particular emphasis on Alexander Hamilton, who wrote in *The Federalist* (34), "We ought not to disable [the government] from guarding the community against the ambition or enmity of other nations." The Publius Principle remains in force today, especially when such "ambition or enmity" emanates from volatile states in contravention of international anti-nuclear proliferation agreements as well as from terrorist cells, jihadi inciters, and their intellectual collaborators operating more or less freely within our own borders.

It is no easy task to get one's mind around the fact that we live in a society whose intellectual vanguard and its numerous cohort of adherents have taken up the case for the lawless assailant and euphemized the terrorist into a "militant," a luetic society in which Taliban and al-Qaeda fighters sworn to the mutilation and killing of Western civilians are regarded as the unfortunate victims of illegal detention, a society swarming with a new breed of forensic parasites who earn their livings chasing after potential deportees, illegal immigrants, and suspected terrorists to defend chiefly at public expense, a society, in short, in which the juridical concept of human rights, however muddled, takes precedence over the reality of human existence, as if survival of the innocent were any less of a right than due process for mass murderers.[14] Bill Clinton's National Security Advisor Sandy Berger feared that should the US ever arrest Osama bin Laden, he would be acquitted in a court of law. Julian Benda would have been appalled, for the "treason of the intellectuals"—thinkers, scholars, politicians, professionals—has rarely been greater than it is today. And Raymond Aron would surely have added his voice to Benda's as well, if his landmark *The Opium of the Intellectuals* is anything to go by.[15] Obsessed with fine legal or moral distinctions even as disaster looms, our intellectuals are like those righteous drivers who, intent on sparing the chipmunk, hit the moose. As for the rest of us, we seem not to care—until the day we or those we love are reduced to body parts.

Thus some of us neglect to maintain the nest; others insist on fouling it. Some, like *Platform*'s Michel, take refuge in private pursuits; others take to the streets as peace marchers providing comfort for the enemy or flock to the journals and newspapers as fifth columnists. Blissfully unaware that a rigid edifice of civic legislation cannot compete with the prevailing form of Levantine suppleness that shelters under the very laws and traditions it seeks to do away with, our militant "social activists" and media experts are really the passive martyrs of their own credulity and the latest apotheosis of that category of Westerners whom Lenin tagged as "useful idiots" and Soviet propaganda czar Willi Münzenberg regarded as exploitable "innocents." As political analyst David Warren writes in the *Ottawa Citizen*, "I must say—without qualification—that our mainstream media are, despite their protestations of innocence and 'objectivity,' objectively working for the enemy." When even so sedate a commentator as William Watson refers in passing in a *National Post* column to that "demonic moron" George W. Bush, we know we are no longer in the world of responsible journalism, a world shrinking at a vertiginous rate. Another example of such a betrayal of responsibility is Charles Brooker's column in *The Guardian* for October 23, 2004, in which he calls for the assassination of President Bush: "John Wilkes Booth, Lee Harvey Oswald, John Hinckley Jr.—where are you now that we need you." Of course, the *Guardian* would object vociferously if master terrorists like Hamas's Ismail Haniyeh or Hizbullah's Sayyed Hassan Nasrallah were made to pay the price. Nor should it come as any surprise that the International Association of Journalists took very explicit sides in the Lebanese border war in the summer of 2006 by condemning Israel's attack on the Hizbullah propaganda tool, the Al-Manar television network, which the Association's general secretary, Aidan White, absurdly called a "free press." None of this is about to change in the foreseeable future.

There can be little doubt that the world press and international news media, while engaging in snidely personal attacks on some of our embattled leaders, have swallowed whole the European and Arab—and for that matter, the Palestinian—transcript of current and historical events, operating with slender contextual knowledge and, in far too many cases, overt prejudice in reporting or commenting on the global scene. Depicting Western political figures like Bush and Blair as nefarious manipulators while Stepfording the current crop of Arab and Islamist sympathizers, they have allowed themselves, whether willingly or heedlessly, to become the terrorists' propaganda mules. Setting aside the obvious bigots and those who frankly regard themselves as at war with their own country, their gullibility is almost beyond conceiving and wholly beyond condoning. The same goes, as I have indicated, for many of our high-profile intellectuals gesticulating in the mosh pit of the public forum. While superficially clever and articulate, they remain profoundly unintelligent. Filmographer Louise Wardle offers the following pithy description of a French TV *colloque* featuring Houellebecq and several "experts": "He is brighter than all of them and has seen the way we are more clearly than them. The crazier the hysteria around him, the more his ideas seem deadly correct."

These "experts" and their *coéquipiers* at large have yet to understand that the threat does not, as such, come from any particular country or terrorist organization—although these must certainly be dealt with as the carriers and manifestations of an underlying cause or force—but from Islam itself, a religion that does not temporize with its foe and for which there is no doctrinal alternative to universal conquest and domination, as enjoined by the Koran. This is made very clear in a popular book published by the Muslim Educational Trust entitled *Islam: Belief and Teachings*, where we read that, "Religion and politics are one and the same in Islam" and are reminded that *sharia* is to be imposed on believers and non-believers alike, wherever Islam is able to prevail. It is naïve to assume, as does our intellectual constabulary, that terrorism is only an instrument of nationalist causes; on the contrary, jihad is a far more primordial movement than nationalism and has penetrated many of the nationalist struggles in the world today to promote and spread its deadly message and objective, as happened in Afghanistan and is now the case in Palestine. Terrorism exploits nationalist fervour to advance its own purposes. Our "thinkers" have got their causes and effects in reverse order.

Thus, marshalling their exculpatory "root causes," casting the West as the guilty party, remaining shockingly ignorant of the long complexities of the historical record, and enslaved to an obsolete geopolitical paradigm that went out with the Cold War,[16] our elites have failed to recognize that we are now in the opening stages of the next World War—the very Islamic-inspired war that Albert Camus, in many ways among the most astute of twentieth century writers, warned us about in the *Actuelles III*. "The Arab empire," Camus wrote, "could not come about without world-wide upheavals that would mean the Third World War in a short time." We must, he urged, take a stand where we "refuse either to practice or to suffer terror." The enemy, thanks in part to what Camus stigmatized as "the follies...to be found in the habits and functioning of our intellectual and political society," now has the upper hand. In fact, from the subversive perspective of the intelligentsia, we are the enemy. Revel again: "they have caused roles to be reversed, attributing to the democracies the whole gamut of 'inspired,' megalomaniac, frenzied and homicidal tendencies that characterize Islamo-terrorism." The genus of cognitive dissonance we meet with here is almost breathtaking both in its scope and its wrongheadedness—"imbecility" would be the etymologically accurate word, deriving from Latin *imbecillus/imbellis* or "weak, helpless, unfit for war"—as our commentators, philosophers and academics do everything they possibly can to exclude reality from the figurations they prefer to deal with and to eviscerate conflicting data to conform with their cozy and formulaic worldview. Even Nostradamus was a more reliable interpreter of the historical drama than our contemporary elites. For the intellectuals patrolling the parapets are facing the wrong way, defending themselves against their defenders and yearning for the tented pavilions of a hoary Romantic illusion.

What could be more cringingly asinine, for example, than BBC2 in its three-part series, *The Power of Nightmares*, which sees global terrorism as a neoconservative myth intended to facilitate the Right's political takeover of the world? Our legionary paranoiacs haven't smelled the cordite yet.[17] They appear utterly incapable of realizing that the distance between Jihad and McWorld, between the minatory Islamic cleric and the urbane Western intellectual, is the unbridgeable span between the *minbar* (pulpit) and the minibar, between earnestness and dissipation. It is true that we are the enemy, but only in the sense that we are our own worst enemies. Bruce Bawer is only registering what should be obvious when he writes, in *While Europe Slept*, with particular reference to the frightened and envious "bureaucratic souls" of the European establishment, that "Europe's enemy is not Islam, or even radical Islam. Europe's enemy is itself—its self-destructive passivity, its softness toward tyranny, its reflexive inclination to appease, and its uncomprehending distaste for America's pride, courage, and resolve in the face of a deadly foe." (Bawer may have in mind the argument pressed by Pascal Bruckner in *The Tears of the White Man*, namely, that the United States has earned Europe's enmity "for having liberated [it] from the Nazi and fascist yokes.... America showed very clearly the life force that had once been alive in Europe.... It is hard to forgive assistance when it shows up such weakness. And so, the liberator of 1944 became the enemy of mankind.") But Europe, for all its hostility, has no monopoly on America-baiting.

One thinks of Ramakrishna's *baddha* or "bound souls," those who remain asleep and "do not come to their senses, even after receiving blow upon blow...." Liberal intellectuals bray nervously about a glorious and venerable faith having been temporarily hijacked by a small band of wacko extremists, a clutch of recidivists and sociopaths that the larger, peace-loving, circumventing faith will eventually reject if only we "reach out" to it.[18] The most we can say about such ideas, which are no longer relevant yet remain solidly in place, is that they are a form of sustainable rubble. To repeat, our patented intellectuals seem totally unable to perceive what they are up against: a vigorous and pandemic Islamic jihadi movement based on a strict interpretation of *sharia* law, bent on spreading its message by every means available including wanton destruction and indiscriminate death, with a view to establishing a universal Church, and deriving from a medieval

Weltanschauung from which both the iniquitous outsider and the corrupt insider have been ruthlessly expunged. Let us not be cavalier about reading the portents, recalling that the greatest scholar of his time, Pliny the Elder, dismissed the flames and smoke erupting from Mount Vesuvius as bonfires, went to bed unperturbed, and died next morning of asphyxiation.

In al-Qaeda's simplified worldview, based squarely in Muslim tradition, humankind is divided into two warring camps, *Dar ul-Islam* founded on the Koran and *Dar ul-Harb*, the degenerate remnant of the West, its dependencies and allies. (The intermediate realm, *Dar-ul-Sulh* or House of Truce, is only a temporary affair.) In the light of such ideological sclerosis, there are no shades in between and no compromise is possible.[19] It is not what we do that offends the Islamic enemy; it is who we are. "The Muslim theory of international relations," writes Elie Kedourie in *The Chatham House Version*, "recognises two possible situations only: war on the infidel or his subjugation to the faithful. Peace with him *de jure* is impossible; there can only be various grades of active or passive hostility until he recognises the authority of the Muslim ruler." For this reason, the battle will be one to the finish, regardless of whatever ill-advised concessions we might be disposed to make and which would only be used to our discomfiture. We should take Hamas' Gaza leader Mahmoud Zahar quite literally when he said, in the epilogue to another suicide bombing, "the march of resistance will continue until the Islamic flag is raised, not only over the minarets of Jerusalem but over the whole world."[20] This is no longer radical Islam; this is now dominant Islam in contemporary guise, rooted in what it regards as an immutable past, hallowed by the Prophet and his Companions and weaponized for the twenty-first century, an antiquated scimitar with a titanium edge. Of course, Muslims will have to learn that they too may occasionally have to experience collateral suffering. An Internet speech posted by al-Qaeda on May 18, 2005, explains that the killing of innocents is justified by the principle of *dharura* (extreme necessity)—the innocents in question are Muslim innocents; there are no others. When it comes to its struggle against the West, al-Qaeda is very frank about the fact that there is no such thing as collateral damage—despite, as we have seen earlier, what William Blum suggests.

Could we but open our eyes, we might then observe the doleful spectacle of a civilization in denial, a myopic civilization that in most of its cultural and political centres will not recognize it is under attack and that seems haplessly incapable of mounting meaningful resistance, let alone launching a counterattack against an apocalyptically inspired enemy to ensure its own preservation—what Paul Berman designates as "the self-absorbed delusions of the Eurocentric imagination" refusing to understand that "a liberal society must be, when challenged, a warlike society; or it will not endure."[21] Similarly, Neill Lochery warns in *Why Blame Israel? The Facts Behind the Headlines*, "In practical terms, if we are to protect Western-style democracy, then we must have the courage to actively defend ourselves," which implies, antipathetic as such measures may be, that we must accept the timely extension of police powers, curb the interpretive licence of an overly liberal judiciary, allow for the detention of dangerous suspects, and be prepared to attack the terrorists in their home bases. This is a war that cannot be fought in any other way no matter how unhappy we may be with the means that circumstance has forced us to employ.

Such is, of course, the core component of the Bush Doctrine, which, revising the Truman Doctrine for the new century, emphasizes the policy of pre-emption rather than Cold War deterrence or containment, a policy with which it is folly to disagree in the light of shadowy terrorist organizations tirelessly working to acquire WMD, embracing a first-strike agenda and cloistered politically and physically by rogue states. Unfortunately, the major weakness in the Bush Doctrine is its buoyant assumption that the Islamic world is amenable to democratization without touching the religious basis of state power or taking Arab duplicity into account (although, judging from its political accommodation with the demagogic regime in Uzbekistan, the US administration's belief in electoral portability is not entirely consistent). We ignore at our peril the admonition of Eric Voegelin who adverted to the mischief wrought by the "naïve endeavour of curing the evils of the world by spreading representative institutions in the elemental sense to areas where the existential conditions for their functioning were not given. Such provincialism [is] symptomatic of a massive resistance to face reality." The political culture in these regions is profoundly authoritarian and the democratic electoral process shipped Middle Eastward by the West will in many cases prove to be nothing more than a façade, a thin overlay that will eventually rupture or under which tyranny will continue to function even more efficiently—a fig leaf for the privileged rule of antidemocratic elites.

The electoral plank in the democratic platform, as I have suggested, is not some sort of magic wand that will somehow conjure liberty into existence. Let us not forget that Hitler and Mussolini came to power in free elections. Why this should be any different with the Arab regimes, which maintained close ties with Germany during World War II—the Arab countries declared war on the Axis in 1945, when the outcome was no longer in doubt—and have since adopted Nazi propaganda techniques wholesale, is a question we cannot afford to evade. And it is our own idealism, too, we should catechize, remembering that Alexis de Tocqueville, even as he lavished praise upon the democratic experiment in the United States, remarked on the American inclination to exalt "the scope of human perfectibility." (This is perhaps what unites the Left and the Right in America: the missionary passion.) A realistic view of history tells us that democracy comes at the end of a long social and political process when the ground has been adequately prepared; it is not a silver bullet. Introduced prematurely, it is the bullet that backfires, the disaster that follows from good intentions and bad judgment. The West seems to be confounding the ritual with the substance, as if the theater of elections could bring about a democratic reality in regions where there is no freedom of speech, no free or responsible press, no stable civil society, no rule of law, and which are torn apart by rival militant groups and warring religious factions. As Amin Maalouf writes in his *In the Name of Identity*, "what is sacred in a democracy is not mechanisms but values"; universal suffrage can result not in the establishment of a free society, but in "the abolition of democracy," in "tyranny, slavery and discrimination" if the appropriate cultural framework and political value-system are lacking.

With respect to the Middle East, we should keep in mind, for example, that semi-democratic Turkey is controlled by a secular-oriented army rooted in Kemalist tradition, the so-called "deep state," which has nevertheless been unable to block the gradual encroachment of the Islamic parties, that the Palestininian state-in-the-making is a mere plunderbund and terror-factory seeking electoral legitimacy whose democratic pretensions are a consummate farce, and that the recent elections in Iraq will not produce anything like a Western-style democracy. In Iraq, particularly, Islamic tradition prophesies that the

Antichrist (or *Dajjal*) will arise in that country—thus the widespread resistance to the American efforts at liberation and to the diabolism of an inclusive franchise. The profound tension between Islam, which does not recognize the independence of political institutions, and the Western principle of representative suffrage will remain a destabilizing factor. It is extremely doubtful, as Robert Spencer writes in *Islam Unveiled*, whether Islam can ever be wholly or even significantly secularized and "fit into place as another ingredient in a global multicultural society."

The record to date in all fifty-three Muslim states is not encouraging, and the growing effort by Muslim immigrant populations in Western Europe and parts of North America to introduce the rule of *sharia* is a potent danger sign of what we can expect from Muslim societies.[22] The fact that these locally embedded Muslim groups often lobby for "Islamist" causes through their Councils and bulletins, set up charities that are frequently used as conduits for the terrorist cash flow, and engage episodically in gangland-style killings backed by theological writ should also give us pause. But whether within our borders or without, this is not a culture that tolerates other points of view. And, on the global stage, these are not societies eager to assume the burden of freedom and its attendant responsibilities. Here we may locate the seemingly paradoxical but realistic adaptation that the Bush Doctrine will ultimately have to take on board if it is to be effective: containment is necessary, but it is only possible through unrelaxed vigilance, periodic pre-emption, and a critical attitude to the viability of its own sacrosanct principles.

The policy of pre-emption is associated with two focal assumptions that would appear to soften its militaristic impulse, namely, that all people yearn for freedom and that democracy is exportable. While I acknowledge that the ideal is a lofty one and may be applicable in many diverse circumstances, I cannot fully concur in the case of populations governed by a theocratic mindset and an archaic politics, and assuredly not when it comes to the repressive rule of conduct and worship imposed, as well as internalized, by the Islamic faith. Here the proponents of the Doctrine may be in for an unpleasant surprise, as the true Muslim communicant preoccupied with the salvation of his immortal soul does not resemble, for example, the oppressed citizen of the former Soviet empire hankering for personal autonomy.[23] Islam is not concerned with democracy but with doing what is understood as Allah's will. It is not committed to the temporal welfare of the human spirit but, very much like primitive Christianity, to the eternal profit of the human soul alone. The democratic state, the condition of political freedom and material prosperity on earth (at least for the multitudes) are no alternative to the Garden of Allah and the condition of heavenly bliss, where "reclining upon soft couches, they shall be ornamented with bracelets of gold and arrayed in garments of fine green silk and rich brocade" (Koran 18:33)—although the accoutrements of heavenly bliss are curiously earthly in nature. Nor is a Charter of Rights an acceptable substitute for the infallible Koran. The problem is not only the prevalence of corrupt and monocratic regimes, but the tenets and canons of a faith that cannot separate Mosque from State, God from Caesar, the soul from the spirit, eternity from time. Progressive movements like Process Theology are scarcely conceivable within the Islamic mindset.

It is thus a dangerous error to assume that the peoples of the Islamic world are oppressed only by tyrannical leaders and a police apparatus from which they yearn to be free. They are, in a far deeper sense, dominated by a holy book that is not readily subject to change or reevaluation and that is controlled by a heterogeneous rota of scholarly interpreters and fatwa-issuing clerics whose word is final and cannot be safely challenged. Until this situation is addressed, that is, until both the theological scaffolding and the internal predisposition to unquestioning belief are transformed, we should not expect the democratic option to produce the desired results. On the contrary, even as the balm of democracy is supposedly spreading throughout the Muslim world, we should expect ever more bloodshed, greater instability, and coups d'état carried out by radical Islamists and unscrupulous leaders wherever conditions are propitious. Indeed, Western political innovations frequently abet the spread of tyranny and disorder. As Elie Kedourie points out with his usual perspicacity, the tradition of oriental despotism is reinforced by modern techniques of organization, and such Western novelties "are all delivered over into the power of the legions of ill-will abroad in the world." Farhad Assad, a Hamas spokesman, said it openly in conversation with Thomas Friedman: "I thank the United States that they have given us this weapon of democracy" (*New York Times*, February 15, 2006). Here, perhaps, we should acknowledge that many on the Left do not support the forcible transfer of democracy to the Arab world—but at the same time they are ready to leave the Arab world in place *as it is*, out of a supposed respect for cultural differences and national autonomy that is really a timid retreat from the need to confront an avowed enemy. We have seen this before, in 1938.

The central question is how the rule of law, gender equality, free elections, impartial courts presiding over secular issues, the right of assembly, and freedom of the Press may be reconciled with the irreducible axioms and precepts of an absolutist religion of global reach. The so-called "Arab revolution"—the popular uprising in Lebanon, municipal voting in Saudi Arabia, the apparent recognition of presidential candidates in Egypt, the partial enfranchisement of women in Kuwait, the Iraqi elections—is in its earliest phases and we cannot predict how it will develop in the future. A long stretch of political time must elapse before we can pronounce with confidence. But we must recognize that Lebanon is not a monolithic Islamic collective but a multi-ethnic checkerwork, which alters the equation somewhat, and that its internal politics is dominated by Hizbullah; that antisemitism remains embedded in the cultural matrix of the Arab world; that Saudi Arabia and Iran have not relented in their sponsorship of international terrorism, the Iranians supplying weapons and know-how and the Saudis funding radical mosques, Islamic schools, and the Middle East Studies departments of Western universities; that Pakistan's Intelligence services actively collude with the jihadists; that the unstable economies, low literacy levels, tribal jockeying, sectarian conflict, inbuilt corruption, and authoritarian religious culture of these regressive regions militate against a successful democratic implant; and that concessions to the principle of democracy in certain states in the region may be little more than window dressing or political maquillage allowing dictatorial regimes to continue in place.

Modern Palestine in particular may be defined as an object lesson under a magnifying glass. The electoral victory of Hamas, which established a terrorist organization as a regional power broker, should reveal very clearly that the democratic process operating in an unprepared political and cultural environment can do far more harm than good. In such backwaters, electoral democracy complicates rather than simplifies, functioning as a handmaid to autocratic control, the resurgence of hidebound traditions and political mayhem rather than peaceable social arrangements and negotiating legitimacy. The Law of Unintended Consequences is the governing factor in these circumstances, fitting the terrorist engine with a pseudo-democratic turbocharger. David Pryce-Jones remarks in the conclusion to *The Closed Circle: An Interpretation of the Arabs* that, "At present, an Arab democrat is not even an idealization, but a contradiction in terms," a brusque distillation of his prefatory and more gracious suggestion that, "Perhaps Islam and representative democracy are two beautiful but incompatible ideals."

But even in a best-case scenario, it is prudent to allow that "Arab democracy" will not be based on national loyalties and liberal values, but on family, communal, and tribal affiliations, dependent on the backing of the largest, religious-controlled parties, and relying on the gun rather than the courts to enforce its policies. The result will not be anything like what even our most enlightened politicians and strategists envision. Arab nationalism has nothing in common with European or Western nationalism, but is essentially a platform for careerist adventures and conspiratorial takeovers. The lesson will be learned by Western powers, as usual, the hard way. And how they will extricate themselves from the contradiction of supporting a demo-cratic process that elects terrorist or demagogic regimes remains a great mystery. Democracy is supposed to produce democrats; when it throws up tyrants instead and empowers our enemies, it is time to rethink our premises.

But do we have the necessary fortitude to act in our own interests? One thinks of former British Foreign Secretary Jack Straw pursuing a policy of peaceful "engagement" with the Iranian ayatollahs, who in the meantime are jacking up their nuclear arsenal, developing and acquiring long-range missiles capable of reaching Europe, and, to show how little impressed they are by the country he represents, capture and proceed to humiliate British sailors on national TV. (But then, Straw represents the constituency of Blackburn, notable for its twenty-three mosques and 25,000 Muslim voters—his recent objection to the veil under certain circumstances scarcely qualifies as a serious critique of Islam.) Or of our own previous Minister of Foreign Affairs, Bill Graham, whose policy toward the Islamic world would have been better described as soft-handed rather than even-handed. (Canada, until recently, with its enfeebled military, inadequate immigration supervision, lack of port security, and toothless foreign policy fares even worse in the defence sweepstakes—consider its derisory protest to Iran over the state killing of Canadian photojournalist Zahra Kazeri. Hopefully, this pablum mentality will change under a Conservative administration.) Our postmodern governments, like our transnational bodies and organizations, have wambled into the never-never land of paper decrees and high-sounding principles minus the willingness to use or to sanction force to back them up, thus allowing terrorism to set the political agenda, dictate the course of events, and drive the results.

This is especially true of the European Union with its crowd of unaccountable bureaucrats in Brussels representing what has come to be known as the post-democratic "transnational progressives," or Tranzis, who control the political direction in which Europe is heading. The Liberals and NDP in Canada—a country that wants to dine at the American table but so far refuses to say grace—the Democratic Party in the US and the generic Western media may all be considered as honourary Tranzis too, envisioning a future, to quote John O'Sullivan writing in *The New Criterion* for October 2004, "of overlapping jurisdictions, multiple national identities, and governance by treaty obligation." This latter principle in particular was in evidence during the indecisive watch of the Clinton presidency that, pursuing the policies (or lack of such) of the disastrous Carter administration, allowed Iran and North Korea to secretly accelerate their nuclear progress and thus helped create the alarming situation we are in today.[24] It has not yet dawned upon our political and intellectual maniples that there can be no equivocating with terrorists or confrontation states. The EU's current rapprochement with totalitarian Cuba, while refusing to meet with Cuban dissidents and pro-democracy advocates, or its disposition toward lifting the arms embargo against China, are further indications of its increasing tilt to the disreputable and mongrel politics of the Left and its opportunistic embrace of anti-democratic regimes in the name of "peace," a sobriquet for "business." From the perspective of narrow self-interest, it is as if Cold War America and New Age Europe have simply changed places. Be that as it may, two generations of Western liberals, some well-educated and others merely passive imbibers of the "socialist" party line, seem entirely out of sync with reality. There might be something, after all, to the apothegm from Ecclesiastes 10:2: "A wise man's heart is at his right hand; but a fool's heart at his left."

This break from reality is even truer, perhaps, of those who merrily go along with the vogue ethos in order to safeguard their careers and maintain their peer networks, practising that species of dissimulation or internal vaudeville that Czeslaw Milosz in *The Captive Mind*, borrowing from the Arabic (and Arthur De Gobineau), called "Ketman," the false stance adopted by a person "in order to find himself at one with others, in order not to be alone." (The Arabic *kitman* refers to the art of tactical omission, telling only part of the truth.) Modern ketmaners in the West are oddly reminiscent of Livy's nitwit Romans who, as we learn in Book VI of his monumental *History of Rome*, in order to counteract the "fearful plague," that broke out in 364 BCE, "surrendered to superstitious practices [and] scenic entertainments, and made quite graceful movements in the Etruscan style." Needless to say, the deployment of the Etruscan style and its attendant performances, with their Fescennine verses and "medleys amplified with music," did nothing to dispel the plague but did provide much in the way of amusement. Surely, superstitious practices like sticking pins in presidential voodoo dolls and bobbleheads, scenic entertainments like Michael Moore's *Fahrenheit 9/11*, television clips of Shi'ite uprisings, Sunni car bombs and troupes of chanting demonstrators, and the Etruscan tournure of newspaper editorials and learned articles are equally ineffective against the plague that has broken out among us today, although filling the time divertingly enough. Ketman, which Milosz also defined as "social convention refracted through the individual temperament," has taken hold of an entire culture of political thought predicated on the evasion of difficult truths.[25]

Here we may point to another social convention issuing in the evasion of truths that are not in themselves that difficult, namely the common, politically correct response to the question of religion, especially as embraced by our immigrant populations, which is often used as a *passe-partout* for socially disruptive behaviour and is perfumed by the odour of sanctity. There is nothing in religion that entitles it to special dispensation from the secular authority when it poses a potential security risk or a threat to the orderly conduct of civil society, whether it is allowing Sikh students to wear the *kirpan*, or ceremonial dagger, on their persons or respecting the privileges of mosques where terrorist incitement proceeds largely unhindered. Most sane people would agree that when a religious sect refuses vaccination and rubella breaks out in the community at large, we have every right to insist on compulsory inoculation. In the same way, when an imam preaches hatred and violence at Friday evening services, we have a duty to revoke his licence and to consider shutting down the mosque for the rest of the week as well. Religion is or should be a private matter and belongs in the home or in the temple when the temple remains a house of prayer. But there is no good reason why it should be sheltered from criticism or defended against challenge. The Western propensity to stand in awe of the religious sensibility (except, perhaps, in a climate of otiose multicultural bromides, its own) and to accept or extenuate its interference in public affairs on the grounds of the individual's or the community's right to freedom of worship, puts everyone else at risk and safeguards only the public rites of sentimentality and the shirking of responsibility. Religion in its social and institutional manifestations is a cultural product like any other and does not merit exemption from censure or legislation. (The same is true of our unseemly rush to hallow the cultural folkway or the social custom. Ritual is *non disputandem*. Thus, for example the debasement of civilized people, including much of the feminist sorority, winking at the monstrous usage of labial infibulation.)

"The greatest problem confronting civilization," writes Sam Harris in *The End of Faith*, "is not merely religious extremism: rather, it is the larger set of cultural and intellectual accommodations we have made to faith itself." In our indulgent multicultural society, it has become a rule of conduct that one must neither insult nor restrict the expression of another's religion even if the price we pay for our overweening tolerance is individual suffering and cultural upheaval. The faith that has been the greatest beneficiary of such relaxed and self-destructive attitudes is, of course, Islam, although few will admit this in official and public discourse. The tabernacle retains its aura of sanctity even if it has been transformed into a launching pad. Once again Harris is precisely on message: "criticizing a person's faith is currently taboo in every corner of our culture.... And so it is that when a Muslim suicide bomber obliterates himself along with a score of innocents on a Jerusalem street, the role that faith has played in his actions is invariably discounted. His motives must have been political, economic, or entirely personal." Surely one must have noticed how Palestinian terrorism is almost never linked with Islam *per se*, which is nevertheless the ground from which it springs, in the same way as the wider terrorist phenomenon is explained by "root causes" and not by the faith that promotes it. Or, alternately, as springing from a set of cultural *moeurs* that are not in themselves evil or vicious, merely different, when it is far more plausible to assume that we are dealing with a culture which is still bound to the practice of human sacrifice.

This nerveless posture also explains why terrorism is often regarded merely as a social problem that can be handled by the police and the judiciary. Those who dismiss warnings like Berman's and Lochery's as apocalpytic scare-mongering and argue, on the British/IRA model, that it is a mistake to treat terrorism as a political/military issue rather than, as they recommend, a criminal/civil or law enforcement matter have completely misconceived the far-ranging virulence and ferocity as well as the very nature of the force they are up against. The courts as presently constituted in many if not most democratic nations are only another umbrella under which terrorist cells, funded and patronized by Islamic states and local organizations and draping themselves in the trappings of religion, can take shelter. Despite the fury, indignation, and admonitory counsels provoked, among those who pride themselves on their social conscience, by the dissenting opinion of Justice Robert Jackson in the well-known Supreme Court reference *Terminiello v. City of Chicago* (1949), his words must now be taken to heart. Jackson wrote, "There is a danger that, if the court does not temper its doctrinaire logic with a little practical wisdom, it will convert the constitutional Bill of Rights into a suicide pact."

As Malise Ruthven convincingly shows in *A Fury for God*, citing amply from Laura Mylroie's *The War against America* and other authoritative sources, "Criminalizing terrorism…tends to evade the question of [state] sponsorship by focusing on the evidential requirements for individual prosecutions to the exclusion of wider issues." You do not read terrorists their Miranda rights. Terrorism is injusticiable.[26] This is war, not civil disturbance or social mischief, and it cannot be effectively fought by relying on the courts, muzzling the executive power or refusing to confront, with all the means at our disposal, the source nations that offer immunity and sanctuary to terrorist organizations.[27] Absent the at times wavering policies of the United States—attacking the Taliban and the Iraqi Ba'athists but, up to this point in time, sparing the Saudis, the Iranians, and the Syrians—it would be game over. But we can perhaps take comfort that it is at long last atoning for its flagrant Cold War error of fostering and arming the *mujahidin* against the Soviets in Afghanistan, perhaps the most costly of its political miscalculations, including Vietnam. The Cold War blunders of the United States, and above all its support of the Islamic fundamentalists as a bulwark against the Communists, have become common knowledge, thanks in part to Robert Dreyfuss's exposé, *Devil's Game*, which documents the "blowback" effect from which America is now suffering. But we should be grateful that the Americans under the Bush administration are redeeming, at least to some extent, the earlier failures and misjudgments of a misguided foreign policy and have begun to man the walls against our contemporary Vandals so that Europe (and Canada) can continue playing and living vicariously under the protection of the international bully we love to hate.

Perhaps the most troubling element in the current situation is that the Bush administration has not gone far enough in prosecuting the "war against terror." The president's enemies consider him trigger-happy, but he has grown increasingly content of late to fire blanks. Indeed, in his second term Bush has clearly suffered a failure of nerve, going back on the virile commitment post 9/11 to confront international terrorism head-on, blunting his own Doctrine and turning the presidential office into what looks more and more like a Democrat holding company. Nevertheless, a partial effort has been made to face up to the inevitable, an effort still far more robust than that of any other Western nation. Though no responsible critic ever thought of America as the world's apostolic choirboy, it is a gross exaggeration to place it in the same category as its enemies. In doing so, the America-bashing Left has become Islamofascism's most valuable ally and its internal *mujahidin* in the war against Western civilization. Facetious as this may seem, we might recall that it takes a blast of good old traditional American country music and the values it enshrines to reduce Jack Nicholson's nemesis Martians to smithereens. The 1996 film *Mars Attacks!* that early (and rather uncannily) introduces a shot of the World Trade Center, traces a misguided official policy of appeasement and "cultural understanding," dwells on the dove-releasing antics of the peace constituency that provoke immediate slaughter, and concludes in near-universal disaster is a prescient cinematic transposition of what is now our 9/11 world.[28]

But why—omitting for the moment the indifferent majority—so many of us have embraced the Martians in our midst, that is, the *mustashhidin* and the regimes that support them, remains, aside from sordid mercantile considerations,[29] in some degree an enigmatic matter. This issue, what Houellebecq has called "the suicide of the West," is one of the fundamental questions posed by his novel, reprising the obiter dictum of Arnold Toynbee that, "Civilizations die from suicide, not by murder." Is it that we errantly believe they will supply us with the energy we intuit we are lacking, petroleum for an idling spirit? Or that we have simply grown weary of sustaining the elaborate and demanding social structure we—or our predecessors, rather—have so laboriously built over time and wish nothing more than to retire, hopefully on full pension—supine collaborators, according to Jean-Luc Bitton's ambivalent summary of Houellebecq's novel for *Routard Mag*, in "la déliquescence du monde occidental causée par l'ultra-libéralisme" (the decay of the Western world caused by ultra-liberalism)? Or is it that, in a protracted spasm of self-laceration, we have turned against a civilization that has spent too heavily in the bureaucratization of social relations and find ourselves envying an adversary that husbands the benefits of group feeling (Arabic: *asabiyah*)? Do we admire the other side so much for the sense of conviction we know we do not have and the communal solidarity it enjoys that we are willing to prostrate ourselves before it? Or was the reactionary Carl Schmitt regrettably correct when he wrote in *The Concept of the Political* that liberalism fears a decision more than it fears the enemy? Do we continue to believe with a kind of quaint liberal insouciance or as Hegel's befuddled heirs that the world is a fundamentally rational place and that the deranged will eventually return to sanity? Is it absolution we crave for our supposed "hegemonic" transgressions in a final, morally inevitable *Götterdämmerung*? Have we absorbed our principles and beliefs at so impressionable and formative a stage in our development, as students in the revolutionary 1960s, that we now act from rote behaviour rather than critical reflection, bearing witness to the truth of Jonathan Swift's apothegm that "what a man has not been reasoned into, he will not be reasoned out of"? Do we live in such profound fear of the future that we must do everything in our power to stave off recognition and direct our attention elsewhere—snicker at American rusticity or crass opportunism, gang up on Israel, join peace marches, prattle on talk shows and phone-ins, write letters to the editor, cluck disparagingly on bulletin boards and blogs, in chat rooms, and at parties, gatherings and colloquies, like children dozing in the comfort of the night light while knowing "deep down" that, in case of trouble, Uncle Sam will come, look under the bed and put the monsters to flight? Or are we merely hoping for clemency from an indebted foe who will spare us for our collusion? Perhaps we are trusting to statistical probabilities favouring the individual, like that ill-fated colony of rabbits in *Watership Down*, living the good life while slowly being culled, one by one, for the table? Is Victor Davis Hanson right when he declares that our present generation "is on the brink of moral insanity," victims of lazy thinking, unable to distinguish between the terrorist and his quarry, and subject to the clichés "of postmodernism, cultural relativism, utopian pacifism, and moral equivalence"?

The most damning explanation of all would be that we are facing the irrevocable and foreordained, casualties of inexorable historical forces that thinkers and historians like Polybius, Ibn Khaldun, Vico, Spengler, and Toynbee spelled out for us. Spengler's notion of historical "contemporaneity" as involving not present contiguity or synchronicity among civilizations sharing the calendar, but as a function of "corresponding phases" and "chronological parallels" may be appropriate here. In this sense we would be contemporary with late-fourth-century and early-fifth-century Rome, a civilization "los[ing] its desire to be, and…wish[ing] itself out of the overlong daylight and back into the darkness…."[30] There is a disturbing poem by Gottfried Benn, entitled *Gesänge* ("Songs"), written on the eve of World War I, which expresses this pivotal moment in the cultural life of a people when it feels itself overwhelmed by the struggle of existence and craves instead the palliative of ease, forgetfulness, and indifference, the surrendering of will and ego:

> *O dass wir Ururahnen wären.*
> *Ein Klümpchen Schleim in einem warmen Moor.*
> *Leben und Tod, Befruchten und Gebären*
> *glitte aus unseren stummen Säften vor.*

> (O that we were our primal ancestors.
> A little clump of slime in a warm moor.

Then life and death, insemination and birth
would glide out of our dumb lymph.)

For Benn, in this frame of mind, even a leaf, a gull's wing or the head of a dragonfly would be felt as too burdensome to sustain in the face of existence; such evolutionary designs "wäre zu weit und litte schon zu sehr" (would be too developed and already suffer too much). It is difficult to disentangle the psychological and historical salients at work in these orgies of renunciation, but it is also hard to repress the suspicion that, at the barometric levels of the cultural sensibility, *we really do want to die* and that the Islamists are right in believing that the West is ripe for the plucking. The data at our disposal are manifold and conflicting and as one of Houellebecq's characters affirms, "The world is equal to the sum of the information we have of it." But one thing is certain in our own historical moment, which may not be all that different from Benn's and may in fact be the same moment, protracted: the news is not good. Some trust the corsairs will have a sudden change of heart and others think that it is, after all, only a kind of Reality TV we are watching. But—and this is what is most unsettling—vast numbers of people, both among the illuminati and the general public, appear to be doing everything they can to arrange for their own demise, using Islam as the weapon they are turning against themselves and their own civilization.

Michel's interpreting the flight of a flock of birds as "heralds of an apocalypse" is no mere conceit.[31] Europe's so-called 3/11 nightmare, the Madrid bombing with its 191 dead and 1,500 injured, signaled only a beginning, the initial transference of the American and Bali strikes to another, woefully unprepared continent. The soulful rendition of Bach's *Sarabande Suite No. 2* to mark the first anniversary of the Spanish calamity will have done little to prevent further attacks in European cities, which grow increasingly likely as Europe grows ever more complacent and dhimmified. (Tourist resorts and population centres in the Middle East, aside from Baghdad, will also be at risk.) And when these strikes do occur, we can also expect the usual chorale of self-incrimination. What Elie Kedourie says about the "shrill and clamant voice of English radicalism" is true of Western intellectuals in general, "thrilling with self-accusatory and joyful lamentation." The other common tack is to shunt the blame onto national governments supporting the American presence in Iraq. (Indeed, terrorist operations are regularly blamed on the American involvement in that country, as if people had forgotten that 9/11 predated this adventure and that the World Trade Center was also bombed in 1993, with six fatalities and over 1,000 injured.) This hollow dodge will eventually reveal its bankruptcy as the terror begins to spread from city to city and nation to nation regardless of political affiliation or military alliance. It is enough that they are part of the occidental world. Spain's faint-hearted surrender to the terrorist threat, the voting in of a Left government and the withdrawal of its troops from Iraq, did nothing to prevent four more attempted bombings, luckily foiled by the security establishment. This time! As the pre-Michellian narrator of *Lanzarote* reflects, "no one was safe anymore. No social status, no relationship could any longer be considered certain. We were living in a time in which any Advent, any Armageddon was possible." And such an Advent is only brought closer as our communities of apologists continue to multiply and the pathology they have embraced tightens its hold.

The passion for self-destruction works on the level of the unconscious, manifesting in observable form as indifference, disbelief, or what passes for enlightened sympathy for those who wish to dispossess us of all we have been bequeathed. Thus—and it cannot be reiterated often enough—what both our intellectual provosts and the general populace seem unwilling consciously to absorb is that the enemy we are confronting is for real and absolutely committed—an enemy that will neither negotiate nor capitulate and that will fight on to the last suicide bomber, hijacked airliner, canister of sarin gas, and suitcase bomb. This is an enemy who has elevated the conflict to the level of a cosmic jihad that does not admit of nuances and who cannot modify his loyalties in the direction of arbitration and compromise. This is an enemy who cannot be bought off or seduced by incentives. This is an enemy who designates civilians in all the ordinary walks of life as "hostiles" and regards everything from the taking of innocent hostages as a legitimate means of enforcing his demands to the slaughter of entire populations as a primary war aim. (It may be a relief to know, however, that Ranzi bin al-Shibh, one of the masterminds behind 9/11, advises his compatriots that in killing Americans, "Muslims should not exceed four million non-combatants or render more than ten million of them homeless.")[32] We still have not understood—and this cannot bear too much repeating—that the very nature of warfare has changed in our time, or regressed to the dark ages of unlimited butchery when women, children, the aged and, indeed, civilians in general were swept up in the general hecatomb as a matter of course—except that it has now become a matter of calculated policy and enacted on a vastly larger geographic scale.

Meanwhile these new barbarians, the Shaitans and Ifrits of Terrorland, take cover among their own civilian populations, who are also co-religionists, or work out *sub rosa* agreements with their host nations, thus making them difficult to find and almost impossible to attack and root out—unless we suspend the provisions of the Geneva Convention and adopt the same tactics they have espoused. Rule-based warfare is no longer a feasible procedure in the same way that the fight against terrorism is not a micromanagerial or law enforcement operation. "The problem is," writes Haim Harari, former President of the Weizmann Institute of Science, "that the civilized world is still having illusions about the rule of law in a totally lawless environment…international law does not address killers shooting from hospitals, mosques and ambulances, while being protected by their Government or society."[33] We need to see what kind of enemy we are fighting—an enemy that uses civilians as human shields, that stores munitions in places of worship and in homes, which are also used as launching pads and sniper bolts, that burrows into the residential populations of towns and cities, that dispatches suicide bombers to wreak carnage among non-combatants, that relies on holy scripture as sanctification for unimaginable barbarity, that indulges shamelessly in the strategy of supposed victimhood to facilitate real aggression, and that does not subscribe to the principles of "game theory" with its balancing of options and payoffs, as in the West, thus transforming the rational political calculus we assume as a norm of human behaviour into a weapon that is turned against us. For this is an enemy that does not "play by the rules" we expect to be in place as a regulative framework for reciprocal action, or to put it more succinctly, this is an enemy that does not "play." And this is why liberal civilization cannot win this war without itself altering the "classical" definition of war, reinterpreting international conventions and acting accordingly.[34] Conversely, the enemy cannot lose: either we will cease to exist or, in order to exist, we will have to become less than what we are, more like the adversary, at least for some considerable time. We will have to avoid what Sam Harris tersely calls "asymmetrical warfare"—"when your enemy has no scruples, your own scruples become another weapon in his hand."

To complicate matters, the culture of liberal values we affect to cherish may need to be defended on several fronts. There is always the danger, in Europe especially with its long history of submission to totalitarian movements, that should we awaken too late from our post-Kantian dogmatic slumber, it will be only to face the growing strength of a far-Right racist ideology that will turn our multicultural clichés completely on their head, harrying or driving out the strangers in our midst rather than subsidizing them. We can no longer afford to live in a multicultural rhapsody with its formulaic notion of the sacred equivalence of all cultural values—except, of course, our own—if we are to prevent the double danger of the resurgence of the reactionary Right with its blood-hatred of our non-Western guests, and the invasion of so-called radical Islam with its blood-hatred of its Western host. There is only one way to defeat the fascist Right as it rises to its own version of the defence of the West, and that is to disarm the common enemy and, by so doing, deprive a nascent fascism of its populist fuel. Which is another way of saying we will have to become less Left in order not to become too Right, that is, less tolerant of the Other that refuses to recognize *our* values if we are to avoid the political pendulum swing toward a vicious intolerance of all perceived outsiders. Even as we assent to the multicultural expansion of what we like to call "civil liberties—which is to say, legislation that works to the advantage of special interest groups—the presence of a clamorous and growing Muslim minority will have the paradoxical effect of forcing us to become less liberal and tolerant in our attitudes. Religious symbols will be progressively banned (as in France), the veil or *niqab* will come to be regarded as "a mark of difference and separation" (as in England and Italy), "suspicious" individuals will be hounded off airplanes by nervous passengers and acquiescent pilots (as in the United States and elsewhere), and popular resentment will increase at such a rate as to outstrip the tentative proscriptions of a timorous and often incoherent political elite. In the absence of common sense and the consequent protection of *core* liberties, excessive tolerance has a way of ushering in the spectre of social repression.

Our authorities now have the duty to discard the policy convenience of institutionalized woolly-mindedness, to learn the apparently demanding art of calling a spade a spade, and to act decisively
and comprehensively if they are to forestall the upsurge of an extremist populist movement. It is the cherubs of political correctness, the
discourse-apologists quailing before unpalatable facts, who present the greatest danger to our wellbeing, for in recoiling from plain
speech and effective action they supply the means for *both* the jihadis
and the populists to pursue their respective agendas. In the words of
Albert Camus, "Mal nommer les choses ajoute au malheur du monde."
(Misnaming things adds to the misery of the world.) We will, in short,
have to rethink the premises of that species of demagogic preferential-
ism we call multiculturalism and its attendant language of obfuscation
that is threatening to undo us all. It is a grave error to conceive of a
nation as a sort of gigantic Noah's Ark in which every creature without exception is welcomed and given sanctuary, even those engaged in
boring holes in the timber, throwing their bunkmates overboard, and
blowing up the wheelhouse. This is the multicultural model currently
in vogue and in the long run it doesn't work. Admission must be strict
and those who may pose a significant threat, whether individually
or communally, must be carefully screened and, if necessary, refused
their boarding cards. A viable society does not resemble the interplan-
etary tavern in *Star Wars* serving all the weird and wonderful but also
rowdy and uncontrollable denizens hailing from every quadrant of
the known universe. We need not retreat behind the mountains of a
Swiss-like protectionism, but we will certainly have to become more
responsible and less maudlin in determining what array of behaviours
qualifies as good citizenship and how to prevent the self-ghettoizing
of immigrant communities. But all this, of course, presumes that it is
not already too late, for, *in the present environment*, even if Islamic terror
should be countered, the Islamic baby carriage is hard at work and
the issue that must be joined may likely have been decided, at least for
Western Europe.

It is never easy to cease indulging in anodynes and mirages.
Intellectuals in particular seem compulsively prone to kiting aerial
scenarios, often described as "a third way" or "a responsible alternative"
to the frictions and antinomies of the practical world. For in the dominion of ideas, reality is not necessarily an issue. "This is why," Norman

Podhoretz explains in *Ex-Friends*, "intellectuals are so often drawn to 'the third way' or 'the third force'—that is, some currently non-existent or utopian future alternative to the choices that are actually on offer in the here and now." But the world does not go away. Nor did we ask to be forced to perceive the world through a reductive, Manichaean lens; the "Other" has demonized itself and given us little room as well as little time for options.[35] There should be no doubt about this. Islam as currently practised is a faith that will neither accommodate nor allow itself to be merely accommodated, and those of our leaders and politicians who, whether for reasons of state, electoral expedience, or, in some cases, misplaced ethical conviction, have up to now refused to make the proper distinctions and to face up to the storm bearing down upon us, are only facilitating the debacle. Generally speaking, they are so caught up with the idea of power they have forgotten the power of ideas—of both the ideas they must combat and the ideas they must defend. Opportunism, appeasement, and willful short-sightedness are, to put it mildly, irresponsible acts, as is callow moral sentiment. To quote from Edmund Burke's *Letter to a Member of the National Assembly* (1791), but applied to our contemporary political actors, these are "men engaged in desperate designs with feeble minds. They are not honest; they are only ineffectual...." In this way our political and intellectual classes as well as the judiciary have failed us: years of blind-eye legislation, professional incompetence, the sway of personal interests, and unreflected tolerance have bred a network of efficient and clandestine terrorist covens on our own soil that are being activated in country after country even as I write. Europe primarily (but also endomorphic countries like Canada and many jurisdictions in the United States) would be far better off deporting its imams without legalistic hesitation and taking out the propaganda and incitement pillboxes before there is dramatically more to regret than there is at present. At the same time, the influence of the leftist establishment which controls the media, the universities, and significant strata of the legal system will have to be decisively challenged. Eventually the authorities will need to act, though when they do, now that a generation of subversives is already in place, it will be lamentably after the fact.

But neither does the public at large seem aware of the nature of the threat before us, which is interpreted as of our own making. It is precisely those very few leaders who have actually moved, albeit belatedly, against that threat—one that has been building for the last twenty years and more—who are condemned for bringing terror to our doors today and for violating our civil liberties. The general misunderstanding of the situation is so widespread as to insult both logic and imagination. Those who rail against the West and reach out to the enemy have not studied the Koran, read the relevant literature, absorbed the *hadith* (sayings of Mohammed) and the *sunnah* (deeds of Mohammed), numbered the links of the *isnad* (chain of tradition), followed the historical crescent of the terrorist project, or digested the fatwas and proclamations of the captains of terror who have devoted themselves to establishing a new, worldwide Caliphate by whatever means available to them. Western ignorance is perhaps the most powerful weapon in the terrorist arsenal. Here we find ourselves the accidental martyrs of a substandard educational system that has not only omitted to provide us with the knowledge we need in order to arrive at rational appraisals and defensible conclusions; it has also failed to create in us that inner *historical faculty*, that feeling for temporality, the intuition that there is always more than meets the eye, that realizes the necessity for *establishing context* before issuing judgments, deductions, inferences, and verdicts.

Worse, there may be a sense in which those who regard themselves as "free moral agents" are not as free as they think, but are rather like dummies ventriloquized by the age—their autonomy is compromised by the times in which they live and they speak with the voice of the *zeitgeist* more than they do *in propria persona*. But one way or another, misguided indignation and cultivated ignorance are not helpful, and the psychological ramparts of a moated illusion will not protect us against reality. The reality is that we have been put into the position of having to make a Hobson's Choice as the price of our survival. Lord help us.[36]

4

Platform may not be a great novel, but it is surely an accurate map of the future, recasting for the days to come the themes of two major prototype novels, Daniel Defoe's *A Journal of the Plague Year* and Albert Camus' *The Plague*. The pestilence, as we have seen, takes many forms, not the least of which is a slackening of the will to live, whether of the individual in the present or the collective in the future. Perhaps the most poignant moment in the story occurs when Michel, shortly before the terrorist attack in Thailand that brings his "second chance at life" to an end, reflects on the question of having children and concludes that with Valérie it might indeed be possible, even "unavoidable."[37]

This passage looks to the future and should be placed in the context of the fraying social and demographic fabric in the contemporary West, in which the plummeting birthrate may be plausibly interpreted as a sign of a civilization rapidly losing vigour, confidence, and clarity of purpose. The other side of the graph has to do with the sharp and ever-ascending spike in reproduction of the Islamic immigrant populations, both in Houellebecq's France, where a significant percentage of *les jeunes* are now of Muslim origin and in other EU countries, specifically the Netherlands where the Muslim population curve is especially steep. According to the 2002 census, nearly half of the residents of Amsterdam are Islamic. Meanwhile, middle-class emigration from the country has risen alarmingly since the slaying of Theo van Gogh. A recent survey suggests that one out of three respondents is contemplating the possibility of flight. (A Netherlander on the move might be tempted to ponder a sentence from Dutch novelist Harry Mulisch's *The Discovery of Heaven*: "After a few days Holland was so far away that it was as if he had never been there.")[38] Indeed, Holland—a nether land in more than one sense—is the harbinger of Europe's troubled future. In the larger, historical frame, continuing Muslim emigration to the West may be seen as a kind of modern *ghazw*, or desert raid, a vast, ongoing *razzia* upon a sedentary population that tries to shield itself by buying protection in the form of political concessions, outreach, welfare subsidies, and special treatment. Bernard Lewis, basing his calculations on immigration patterns and birthrate statistics, has predicted that Europe will have been Islamicized by the end of the century—others have advanced the date.[39] But time is on the side of Islam. As Koran 8:46 assures, "Have patience. Allah is with those that are patient."

One remembers Fallaci's thesis that a war is being waged not only with guns and bombs but with boats and babies. European politicos and newspaper editorialists constantly lament Europe's failure to integrate its Muslim populations, citing social and economic exclusion as the primary cause of Muslim disaffection and proclivity toward violence.

But the facts seem to suggest otherwise. Even Tariq Ramadan speaks of "numerous evidences for this quasi seclusion…their way of organizing themselves," including the need to "protect oneself" against an environment "that was considered morally and culturally dangerous." With few exceptions (e.g., to a certain degree, Germany's Turkish diaspora), it is principally these Muslim communities that refuse to integrate into the pluralist societies of the West, taking disproportionate advantage of generous social security and family reunification programs, a variety of available subventions, state housing, and a soft judiciary to advance the gradual Islamic penetration of the European Union. This is not to downplay the strategy of guns and bombs, notably in its vaunted plutonium casing, for a radiological strike will not only inflict numberless casualties but would also attack the next, unborn generation in its very genes—an ironic, real-world reversal of that blasphemous medieval calumny about Jews poisoning the wells of Europe.[40]

But a society in the process of legitimizing same-sex marriages while heterosexual unions are drying up stands little chance of long-term survival anyway. Same-sex unions have been a fact of mutual existence from earliest times, but same-sex marriages violate the premise of the institution of matrimony, which is reproduction. Homoeroticism may or may not be *contra naturam*—the concept is inherently ambiguous, and, after all, human beings have taken to the skies and the seas though nature has not provided them with wings and fins—but same-sex marriages are plainly *contra societam*.[41] As such they are a clear portent of a civilization very close to free-fall. Could we take a step back and refocus our cultural-historical perception of, say, Rome in its last days, we would see that this is exactly the pattern of decadence and excess we associate with a civilization coming to its end. Such practices are no less a mockery of the social dimension of our existence than Caligula vesting his horse with a consulship is a caricature of the political. The institutions that keep a society intact and ensure its prolongation are redefined in such a way as to cancel their fundamental intention. With regard to matrimony, the redefinition proceeds in the name of either compatibility, which is a welcome component of marriage but, from a societal point of view, is not the sole or even essential reason for marrying, or of untrammeled desire, often specified as a right or an entitlement. *La Dolce Vita* all over again. *The Satyricon* redivivus. Homosexual matrimony is, in more ways than one, a non-starter. Indeed, it is heterosexual matrimony that should be the object of our concern since it is teetering increasingly toward dysfunctionality. The situation has grown almost farcical, considering that it is now the gay community among the secular population that appears to have become the most outspoken upholder of the institution of marriage.

No matter. There is little future in an empty crèche—the satiric message of *La possibilité d'une île* with its dreary, clonal *beau monde*. Pregnancy in the developed world has tended to become something of a fashion statement and marriage a ritual performance to validate the barren. As Claire Berlinski writes in her dirge for a civilization, *Menace in Europe*, "Not since the Great Plague has Europe's population been so dramatically gutted," the reproductive replacement rate plunging sharply below the magic number of 2.1. (Only in those Western nations still committed to preserving their historical and cultural lineage do the numbers resist erosion: the United States, which maintains the ratio, and Israel, which exceeds it.) It is truly as if we no longer wish to perpetuate ourselves and to take custodial responsibility for the future, but instead prefer to knit our energies and loyalties to a convergent present, the acquisition of ancillaries, career, and sensations, immediate remunerations, the cult of private pleasure, and political infatuations that cater to our easy sense of righteousness and our emotional autism.[42] The Western individual has "progressively" tended to become a pure consumer, preoccupied chiefly with self, a Deleuze-and-Guattari "desiring machine" or a Lipovetskian "floating space, with no attachment, no reference, pure availability."[43] He brings to mind the pre-suicidal tourist animator Houellebecq cites in *Interventions*, who concludes that "Aujourd'hui, il n'y a vraiment plus aucun sens à donner à notre vie." (Today, there is really no longer any sense to give to our lives.)

In the language of our time, this condition of intellectual phlegmatism and unfettered emotivity constitutes, as much as anything else, a "clear and present danger." "Hazmat" may be defined in many different ways, including the psychological disinclination to propagate, economic exigencies that work against the progenitive family, and the social redefinition of marriage in terms of the couple rather than in terms of the children. Western infertility is no match for the Islamic birthing machine. We have simply moved the adversary's clock forward. This form of continental drift, both theological and demographic, should not come as a great surprise. Ottoman thinker Said Nursi prophesied nearly a century ago, in his famous *Damascus Sermon*, that "Europe and America are pregnant with Islam. One day they will give birth to an Islamic state."[44] As Allan Bloom (despite his own sexual leanings) cogently argued in *The Closing of the American Mind*, since the family must be understood as both the nucleus and reflection of the larger civilization, the fate of the latter cannot be separated from that of the former. The self-encapsulated and childless Michel we take leave of at the end of the story may well represent the future of modern Europe and, by implication, of a civilization wedded to sterility and on the brink of implosion. Indeed, the plight of contemporary Europe has become the mirror parody of Africa's. Ravaged by AIDS, the dark continent faces a future with a vast population of children and few adults to teach them; subject to a rapidly declining birthrate, the dying continent faces a future with an aging population and few children to teach anything to. "The future is not what it used to be," said the French poet Paul Valéry, surveying the human wreckage of World War I. The sentiment is truer now than it ever was.

Whatever the reason or reasons for the impending chaos, Houellebecq's conclusion would seem to go something like this: "It is not I alone who am Michel; we are Michel. This is the biography of our time. This is the peril we have brought upon ourselves."

II

On Being a Jew

Angels flew back to the caves of the firmament.
From his couch, God rose sadly and turned off the light for us.
                              —ASHER REICH, "The Book"

Spilled blood is not the roots of trees
but it's the closest thing to roots
we have.

                              —YEHUDA AMICHAI,
                                "Jews in the Land of Israel"

Antisemite: The Jews are responsible for the war.
Jew: Yes, the Jews and the bicyclists.
Antisemite: Why the bicyclists?
Jew: Why the Jews?
                              —Jewish joke

1

When I was five years old I was dragged off the street by our Catholic neighbour, stood before a picture of the suffering Christ that hung on her living room wall, and accused of killing the Saviour of the World. I assured her as best I could that the man I had apparently murdered was a complete stranger to me. I was under the vague impression that he was a close relative, perhaps her uncle, who had undergone a horrible fate at the hands of some vicious neighbourhood bully she had evidently mistaken for me. Her fury increased with each subsequent denial and so did my terror until the Lord God personally intervened by causing the chicken roasting in her oven to catch fire. I made my escape through plumes of black smoke and I can still recall her face, etched in the window as I fled past, glowering over the charred bird, which I later came to see as an avatar of the Holy Ghost.

Growing up ghettoized in a small French-Canadian town was not like trying to survive in Gdansk or Vilna, but it still wasn't much fun. When I was six 'Ti-Paul Parent, a midget who lived directly across the street, stepped out on his balcony, loaded his slingshot, and, in a bizarre parody of the David and Goliath story, put a stone right between my eyes. A direct hit that, to my great good fortune, was also a near miss. I came to some hours later still in the dark. Illumination arrived when I was eight. I was stopped on the street one afternoon by a large muscular boy of fourteen or so whom I had never seen before. He merely asked me if I was a Jew, nothing more. When I said yes, he promptly delivered a roundhouse right that loosened my teeth and sent me into another mini-coma. The raw taste I carried around with me for days was my deferred revelation of the bitterness of being a Jew. And when, at the age of ten, I was detained at the police station and threatened with a spell in the *seau à glace* for defending myself against a pack of determined assailants—the ambush on the way to school was an entrenched social ritual—I learned all I needed to know about the world's vaunted justice and its (now classic) "moral equivalency" evasion. No doubt in fighting back, I was contributing to the "cycle of violence."

There were other troubling episodes that supplemented my early education. Why was I the only one among a group of young bathers to be turned away from the beach of the German-owned Laurentide Hotel? This taught me the meaning of the previously cryptic word "Restricted" black-lettered prominently on a stake planted on the lawn of the hotel entrance. It did not take me long to figure out why I was one of two elementary school students forbidden access to the local Catholic church during a school visit arranged to promote greater understanding between the various communities of the town. I soon got used to the fact that the word *juif* rarely appeared in public discourse without being prefaced by the modifier *maudit*—damned—so that these two words eventually stuck in my consciousness as a single term, *mauditjuif*, the noun subsuming the adjective as a unified descriptor. One could not be a Jew without being damned. And when at the age of twelve I was viciously assaulted as a *mauditjuif* by my longtime neighbour and closest friend, a French-Canadian boy named Yvon Guindon, who banded together with the hated Pagé brothers living down the road to carry out a premeditated attack, the psychic trauma, the sense of betrayal, was so great that I gradually lost the ability to speak French. It was only in my thirties that I painfully began to relearn the language and I have never managed to regain my fluency.

My family, too, provided an initially inscrutable but eventually limpid educational milieu—though it was only with the passage of years that I came to understand the vestigial basis for the eccentric behaviour of those around me. At first I could make nothing of the sporadic visits of my uncle Snetzi, who would suddenly rush into the house, clamber up the stairs to the sleeping level and fling himself under a bed, whimpering, "They're after me, they're after me." It was an effort of hours to dislodge him, pale and trembling, from his bolt-hole. My auntie Fannie dressed as a dowager in sombre, flowing robes and went about embracing Jewish children in the parks and playgrounds of Montreal as if to protect them from some lurking child-molester. I derived a guilty pleasure spying on my auntie Rosie who, during her occasional descents upon our hospitality, would install herself in the bathroom and spend long, devoted hours rinsing out her lingerie, over and over again, like a working-class Lady Macbeth fascinated by invisible spots. My auntie Ida passed her entire adult life barricaded inside a small Montreal apartment looking after my great-*zeyda*, who himself rarely emerged from his dark, backroom genizah where he poured over the Torah and conversed with the prophet Elijah. My auntie Esther perfected the art of astral travelling. My uncle Aby raised two parallel families, one Jewish and the other Gentile, each serving as a domestic backup to the other, where he could take oscillating refuge in times of discord. Sadly, I never got to study my uncle Morrie since he was murdered in Israel by an Arab a few years before I was born; he was, it seems, the only member of the family who was reasonably normal and devoid of coping idiosyncrasies, which strikes me now as a cruel irony. My grandmother, like the Wife of Bath, married five, progressively wealthier husbands to pad her bank account against the fear of insolvency—as a young woman she had been stripped of all her possessions by the Russian muzhiks and fled with her children into the steppes before making good her escape to Canada—and in her declining years communicated with the pigeons roosting on her window ledge whom she was convinced bore secret tidings of advancing armies. My father kept two pistols and several boxes of cartridges hidden in a clothes drawer and hired a towering bodyguard named Bernard to patrol the borders of our property. My mother developed an uncanny ability to anticipate danger, which announced itself in the form of a black silhouette whose warnings were astoundingly accurate. It was only with time that I gradually realized that my relatives and parents had unconsciously adopted a posture of self-defence or systematic evasion, their lives shaped by the after-effects of their early experience of the Ukrainian and Georgian pogroms and the Jew-hunts of the White Russian irregulars. Suspicion of the world around them, the sense of contamination and menace, was the dominant force in their lives. Given the instruction they had received in their tender years, their behaviour no longer seemed aberrant to me but an intelligible response to the atmosphere of threat in which they had come of age and that, in truth, never entirely receded.

These are the people and events, my significant teachers and my prerequisite lessons, that prepared me for the future. For, although I did not have a Jewish upbringing, the world can always be counted on to supply the deficit. The fact is that a Jew simply cannot help being educated. He is the perpetual scholarship student, the prodigy who receives his doctorate before puberty, whose fabled intelligence is not a consummation of angels in the blood but the ambiguous gift the world bestows on him and resents. He goes to the head of the class to answer the question and be punished for it. Under rare and favourable circumstances, his intelligence and eccentricity can lead to world-class accomplishments and unpredictable solutions to pressing dilemmas, even to "paradigm changes," in Thomas Kuhn's coinage; in the majority of cases, his adaptations to the world are far more quotidian and, to put it gently, not altogether momentous or inspiring.

My Portuguese grocer, who claims a racial grandmother, is convinced that so-called Jewish intelligence is the result of abstention from pork, which he regards as a thickening or clotting agent. Pork clogs the mental pores, as it were, and obstructs sensitivity. He chuckles as he formulates the paradox: you have to stop eating pork to stop eating pork. (That this advantage is also shared by Muslims does not occur to him, possibly because he is fond of pork.) A Hasid I once knew informed me that Jewish smarts were the product of a mystical substance the Jew harboured within him, like an invisible pacemaker or an alien gene. A farmer I met many years ago in northern Quebec fingered the cognitive reinforcement of the Jewish nose, the repository of cranial surplus.

It seems as if being a Jew is like being born with six fingers (or, for Isaiah Berlin, with a hump). It is the kind of fact there is just no way around. Even the most skillful of surgical operations must leave a telltale stump or scar—like the cicatrix I still bear between my eyes, the memory of stone—as Braille for blind antisemites. Being a Jew is forever. The peculiar sourness of the apostate is ample testimony here: forgotten by his own, he is sure to be remembered by the others. The Nazis would not have spared Noam Chomsky for all his twisted, ideological blather and a lionized intellectual like Susan Sontag would have experienced a long-overdue awakening from the fugue of sectarian declamation and pharisaical moralism into which her work had increasingly subsided. At the very least, as the great Zionist visionary Theodor Herzl came to believe, the Jew is defined by his enemies. However else he may understand himself, a Jew is also a Jew by negative definition, in the same way that Hans Meyer (aka Jean Améry), as he recounts in *At The Mind's Limits*, discovered he was a Jew with the passing of the Nuremburg Laws in 1935. A Jew remains a Jew even without positive determinants. And his putative intelligence is the wound he brings with him, the brand that renders him both conspicuous and resilient—the mark of Cain on the forehead of Abel.

G. E. Lessing, in his play *Nathan the Wise*, proposed that the adherents of the three monotheistic faiths were all, as people, very much alike. I too wonder what all the fuss is about. My own experience tells me that most Jews are, on the whole, about as stupid as everybody else—except, perhaps, in those cases in which intelligence, whether practical or theoretical, is necessary for survival or distinction and in which a genuine historical percipience is produced by millennia of gratuitous suffering—the particular instantiations of collective memory. This has nothing to do with the sartorial ostentation of the Hasid who buttons his coat from left to right to affirm his difference from the rest of humanity (the reason Tacitus gives for circumcision) or with the fatuous conceit of that patrician caste who, as conveyors of the Shekhinah through the desert of time, feel superior to the goyim because of their supposed chosenness.

My relatives, for all their parabolical gravity, reeked of fish and mothballs. We lied, grovelled, swindled, and scrambled for the buck as did the disinherited majority we affected to disdain. The values that we lived by, the deceit of business affairs, the ostentation of having made it, the indiscriminate worship of material success, were identical in almost every way to those of our Gentile neighbours. Our attitudes and beliefs were neither hidden nor transmuted by the sacred vestments, the *tallisim* (prayer shawls) and *tefillin* (arm bands and frontlets) that the Torah enjoined upon us. These fringed, knotted, and elaborate garments and amulets did not conceal the fact that we were naked emperors. The best part of the Haskalah, or Jewish Enlightenment, seemed to have passed us by almost completely. Our contempt for the inferior part of humanity was equalled only by our lack of esteem for scholarship unless it led to social and economic advancement and by our lack of interest in anything that smacked of moral rectitude or magnanimity. Even the question of Israel did not loom especially large on our parochial horizon except as a sort of biblical emanation, a fabulous land populated by prophets, kings, and giants. Rather, we tended to sample our way through life, as if moving through a series of dissociated experiences imbrued with a lingering quality of peril and vulnerability that no doubt had something to do with both our psychological abnormalities and our cramping pragmatism.

This was true of all our Jewish landsmen in the town as well. Though many kept kosher kitchens, almost none had read Leviticus. The major ambition of the sons of our village patriarchs was to drive a Chrysler convertible or a Studebaker Golden Hawk once they had come of age. The daughters were groomed to marry doctors, an outcome deemed to justify the cost of university attendance. Rabbi Klinger hired Gentile boys to switch on the Sabbath lights since they were already damned. His rhyming successor, the crusty Rabbi Singer, administered a thorough tongue-lashing when, visiting his home one day, I methodically penciled in the missing "o" in the oft-repeated locution "G-d" that adorned the monthly synagogue bulletins stacked on the coffee table. When, smarting from his rebuke, I inquired why this superstitious practice did not, for example, retain the vowel and skip the consonants, or simply leave a resonating, aural blank in the text, I gained the rabbi's perpetual contempt. "A Spinoza in the making," he sniffed pedantically, and cautioned my mother to rein in her errant son if he was not to bring G-d's wrath down upon our family—which, he assured us, would not be prudent housekeeping. (When my mother, a rabbi's daughter, asked why he did not simply use the traditional evasion "Hashem" ["The Name"], he replied, "Because no one in the community knows who that is.") Indeed, as I grew up, I had more and more trouble distinguishing my Jewish friends in their habitual outlook on life from the offspring of the *vieille souche* (old stock) and the French-Indian Métis we shared the street with—with the important difference that we did not go around beating up people. The English minority were insufferably snooty but possessed a certain style and reticence that I at first envied and later recognized as simply a more tolerable form of insidiousness. But I could see nothing special about the Jew except a sense of esoteric pre-eminence caused by a history of oppression and segregation that eventually and to some extent became willed and deliberately assumed.

So unflattering a perception may have had something to do with the limited cross-section I had to work with growing up, and clearly belied the disproportionate intellectual achievement of this small segment of the human bandwidth. Statistical studies have revealed an asymmetrically high ratio of accomplishment and talent in the literary, critical, musical and mathematical fields among Ashkenazi Jews, which geneticists working in the International Haplotype Project associated with the Human Genome Project have ascribed to evolutionary pressures over millennia selecting for genetic traits related to intelligence. Yet little in my subsequent personal experience has led me to revise my estimation. My attitude, which was formed in the hamlet of Ste. Agathe des Monts in the Laurentians in the province of Quebec, might be compared to that of Israeli film director Amos Gitai, who in his extraordinary film *Alila*—based on Israeli novelist Yehoshua Kenaz' *Returning Lost Loves*—which is set in a rundown neighbourhood of Tel Aviv and focuses on the dishevelled lives of its denizens, arrived at conclusions no less ambiguous than mine. Nor could I help feeling, despite the absence of a Jewish education and no doubt erroneously, that my judgments were more or less authoritative, since I descended on my father's side of the family from the Ashkenazi strain and on my mother's from the Sephardi, presumably giving me a stereoscopic view of the follies and complexities of the community to which I nevertheless belonged.

In the course of the years, what I learned to admire in my people was something very different from that which earned them the grudging, double-edged credit of mankind. The Jews were the only "nation" chronically disposed to self-ridicule as a way of deflating its own pretensions to spiritual supremacy. Poles do not make Polish jokes. Muslims are not keen on kebabing themselves or their faith. But the Jew makes himself his own butt and motty, not to forestall the world's animosity, but to try and keep himself approximately and occasionally honest (which is saying quite a lot for any human being) and to practice up on that humility that saves him in the end—from himself. Not every Jew, of course, and perhaps not even most Jews, but the cultural tendency definitely exists toward a kind of prophylaxis against the dangers of both self-pity and self-election. Self-deprecation is the ark that keeps the Jew afloat in the flood of his own turbulent destiny. One recalls Pascal's praise for a people who assembled, preserved, and defended a Holy Book in which they were often portrayed unfavourably. The Jewish God also comes in for some berating by His people, from the hard and unanswerable questions of the book of Job to the baffled humour and teasing asides of the anecdotal literature.

The real and most unsettling question is one of definition. What is a Jew anyway? Jewishness obviously has nothing to do with race, as the Nazis believed, since there are Jews of every colour and physical type. To define a Jew according to rabbinic law as someone born to a Jewish mother only begs the question and involves us in a *regressus*—what makes a Jewish mother, apart from excessive nagging and the artful manipulation of guilt, Jewish? Some regard territorial on-siteness as the fingerprint of identity, but the saga of repeated population displacements, miscegenation following upon invasion and conquest, and waves of successive immigration over the centuries make for a high degree of tribal inconclusiveness—although, it is true, there are degrees of inconclusiveness. Moreover, territorial presence may generate a feeling of belonging, but does not resolve the conundrum of identity, or psychical self-definition. Is it the thirteen articles of faith articulated by Maimonides? But not all Jews are capable of abiding by every one of these, and the last article asserting belief in the resurrection of the dead is hardly substantiated in the Hebrew Bible, in which there are, depending on how one counts, only six references to the afterlife. Rabbi Akiva proposed that knowledge of the Torah is the essential touchstone of Jewishness, in which case the majority of the world's Jews are not really Jewish at all and a certain number of Gentiles are. Others put forward the accident of group conversion as a partial criterion. For example, Hillel Halkin in *Across the Sabbath River* tells the story of the Mizo people living in the Indian states of Mizoram and Manipur, allegedly descendants of the lost tribe of Menasseh (eighth century BCE), who are preparing for formal conversion to Judaism. In an earlier book, *The Thirteenth Tribe*, Arthur Koestler argues that the Ashkenazi branch of the Jewish people are eighth century (CE) converts to the faith. According to Koestler, a substantial number of us may have been evangelized Khazars who crossed the Volga and not the Jordan, a people of East European and Caucasian origin whose affiliations to the Middle East are more a political and psychological matter than a historical and racial one. It is only fair to say that Koestler's thesis is peppered with inconsistencies, and has been seriously challenged by genetic testing, and that many reputable scholars dismiss his argument out of hand, as does Bernard Lewis, for whom the issue is an ethnographic trifle, in *Semites & Anti-Semites*. Besides, the results of proselytization, whether on the level of the group or the individual, no more address the question of "essence" than does a mixed and shifting territorial provenance. Further, although we sponsor planting trees in Israel and cheer for the good guys in the wars that convulse the region, most of us are also not Israelis. And mainstream Israelis have their own problems pacifying not only the enemy but the ultra-Orthodox (who wear medieval *streimels* under the hot sun and stone their own soldiers mobilizing on the Sabbath), or controlling Lubavitcher interference in local political life, or curtailing the incommensurate power of the Haredi sects or reining in the right-wing squad that assassinates its own prime minister. In return, these fundamentalist Jews regard their Reform-minded or secular-oriented cousins as, for all intents and purposes, communitarian impostors.

Who is a Jew? Is a Jew by definition a stateless creature, one whose spiritual essence precludes a political embodiment or national realization, as many Jewish intellectuals, Hermann Cohen and Martin Buber among the most prominent, believed? Of course, Buber's convictions did not prevent him from taking shelter in the comparative safety of the Holy Land in 1938 nor did they compel him to return to Europe after the war in order, as we say today, "to make a statement" consistent with his principles. The same is true of the anti-Zionist Gershom Scholem who, the later softening of his position notwithstanding, suffered no crisis of conscience in retaining his sinecure as Professor of Jewish Mysticism at the Hebrew University in Jerusalem—currently the breeding ground for the subversive school of New Historians committed to dismantling the Jewish state or immersing it in a binational union with the Palestinians, as if, in Yoram Hazony's phrase, "the addition of the crescent moon to the Israeli flag" would not lead to the eclipse of the star of David.

And I would suggest that modern Hebrew-speaking sabras—who are in any case gradually being submerged by the waves of new immigrants—are Jews as much by accident as by necessity. And they are not particularly hospitable to American Jews eager to practise reverse assimilation, outsiders who, depending on their degree of commitment, either hunker down in the settlements or return to Brooklyn, addled and resentful. And what does an Ethiopian Falasha have to do with a Russian émigré or a Chinese votary or an ultra-conservative rabbi from Galicia? How could Gush Emunim messianists like Yuval Neeman ever be expected to rub shoulders with Labor Party fixtures like Yakov Shabtai, both equally "Jewish"? (As Thomas Friedman wryly observes in *From Beirut to Jerusalem*, Shabtai's widow had to threaten a lawsuit against the pro-settlement Tehiya Party for inducting her husband as an ultra-nationalist symbol.) Jean-Paul Sartre may not have been far off the mark when he said "a Jew is someone who is called a Jew" and "it is the anti-semite who creates the Jew." This is not the whole story, of course, but it is an important chapter.

So a Jew is not necessarily an Israeli and may have been a Khazar. Here and there a rare and tenuous bloodline may connect a given individual to incorrigible Habiru ancestors even the patriarchs and the prophets despaired of ever civilizing. They cannot be more than a handful and must remain undetectable. And it is far from clear whether even these originals may be considered "Jews," a designation that came appreciably later, rather than "proto-Palestinians" (or Judeans or Samarians or displaced Mesopotamians) whom the tides of history beached elsewhere. As the Koran rightly suggests, neither Abraham nor Moses were Jews; it appears that Mordecai of the book of Esther was the first to be called a Jew. But such considerations, it should be realized, do not imply that Israel is dispensable, for it has become the last refuge and haven of a persecuted people whose foundational texts derive from the area in dispute and whose checkered history cannot be oppugned. This means that the Holy Land will always remain the cadastral address of the diaspora, what the twelfth-century Hebrew-Andalusian poet Yehuda Halevi hymned as "the royal house, the Lord's throne," wondering "who will fashion me wings that I might fly far off,/ brokenhearted, to your mountain clefts?", and contemporary Israeli poet Admiel Kosman refers to as "the infant homeland, and longing, its mother." In support of these lyrical paeans, there is the recently discovered fact that tribes and confederations of indigenous Israelite settlers, despite their shrouded genealogy, seem "always" to have been there. Israel is mentioned on the Merneptah stele of 1207 BCE, which suggests it must have existed as far back as the Egyptian New Kingdom and even earlier. As well, archeological evidence has persuasively confirmed its existence in the thirteenth century BCE, forcing us to rewrite the standard biblical stories of exodus and conquest.

These findings were recently supported by an international archeo-logical team that, using high-precision radiocarbon-dating methods, has placed the battle between the Israelites and the Edomites in the tenth century BCE, thus attesting to the historical existence of the united kingdom of Israel and Judah ruled over by David and Solomon. Moreover, even during the Babylonian exile dating from 586 to 538 BCE, textual and archeological evidence indicates that up to 75 per cent of the total population of Judah may have remained on the land. The *Biluim* (early settlers) were a factor from the very beginning.[1] The so-called "minimalist" argument, dating "state formation" in the area to the Assyrian empire of the eighth century BCE, which is often taken as weakening Israel's claim to Palestine, seems to have been decisively countered. The world must be prepared to recognize that Israel will not go away, for it lives not only in the historical record but in the depths of the Jewish soul and Jewish memory, despite even the betrayals of Jewish dissenters and apostates. In the words of the poet Simcha Simchovich:

> *The heart is heavy and the eyes in tears*
> *for the ravages of not long ago,*
> *but my soul is still uplifted*
> *by the eternal Sinaitic glow.*

Which brings us inexorably to the Middle East imbroglio, where the issue would *appear* to be paradoxically simplified into one involving not Judaism but Zionism. For there can be no pursuing the question I am posing in these pages without a thorough consideration of the "Palestinian problem" and its intimate link to the unsolved riddle of Jewish identity.

2

The enmity of the Arab world is a complex phenomenon, based on a tradition of shared assumptions about the pre-eminence of the "Book," a monotheistic dispensation and a shared line of derivation presumably going back to Abraham, but the Arab surround will likely continue to regard the Jewish state as a regional interloper and the Holy Land as exclusive Islamic property. As will be elaborated in due course, the UN has worsened the situation by reformulating its definition of the refugee in favour of the Palestinians to apply to anyone who spent only two years in what eventually became modern Israel—a *temporal* criterion from which no other refugee in the world has benefitted. Adding to the demonic brew, as Bernard Lewis points out in *What Went Wrong*, is the "intolerable humiliation" felt after the 1948 defeat of five Arab armies "at the hands of a contemptible gang of Jews," but the hostility, as Muslim scripture makes clear, is ancestral. "Had the People of the Book accepted Islam, it would have been better for them…. Most of them are evil-doers. Do not be deceived by the activities of the unbelievers in this land. Their prosperity is brief for Allah has smitten them in their sinfulness. Hell shall be their home, a dismal resting-place" (Koran, 3:8). Sura 59:3, set in the context of the expulsion of the Jewish tribe of Banu al-Nabir and the confiscation of their property, is equally unequivocal: "Had Allah not decreed exile for them He would have surely punished them in this world. But in the world to come they shall be punished in Hell-fire…." In fact, they were massacred two years later at Khaybar. The source of much Arab/Palestinian hate-mongering and terrorist commination is plainly not far to seek. From the suras of the Koran and the Charter of Omar, who succeeded Mohammed as Caliph and instituted the twelve laws under which Jews were to suffer throughout Islamic history, it persists right into the present day in the UN General Assembly, where the Arab voting bloc has neutralized an Israeli resolution calling for the UN to recognize the right to life of Israeli children—a resolution worded identically to a Palestinian document carried the week before.

And this despite the existence of a kind of subliminal kinship recognized in Sherif Hussein's extended welcome to Chaim Weizmann and the Zionist Commission to Palestine at the end of World War I, as well as in the document signed by Emir Faisal Hussein, later king of Iraq, guaranteeing the Balfour Declaration of November 2, 1917, that provided for the establishment of a Jewish state; and despite the more sweeping fact that the conquering Muslim armies of the seventh century had even less title to Palestine than many of the Jewish immigrants of the twentieth, some of whom at any rate could plead continuity with the clans of peninsular Arabia crushed and expelled by Mohammed in the early seventh century, with the 3,000-year sojourn in Hebron (punctuated in modern times by the Arab massacre of 1929, a repeat of the Ottoman bloodbath of 1518), with the Jewish communities in the holy cities of Tiberias and Safed (sacked by the Arabs in 1610 and then again by the Turks in 1799), with the Spanish exiles of 1492 who found their way to the Holy Land, with the impoverished Chalukah community in nineteenth-century Jerusalem, or with the Zionist settlers of the first and second aliyahs (waves of immigration) who legally purchased land from Arab tribal overlords eager to make a profit. The indigenous population, however we struggle to define it and whatever its relation may be to its European successors, goes back a long way in the Middle East and peninsular Arabia. Israel was already a nation twelve centuries before the birth of Christ and, as the Reverend James Parkes spells out for us in *Whose Land? A History of the Peoples of Palestine*—even before the archeological data began pouring in—the Jewish connection with the land "has been continuous from the second millennium BCE up to modern times." It may be surprising to learn that even "Medina" is not an Arab word but a Jewish usage from Aramaic—*medinta*, or "the city"—which was later Arabized as *al-madina*, a term that came to replace the original name of the city, Yathrib. As Michael Cook points out in his biographical study, *Muhammad*, an ancient Jewish population predated the Arab settlement there. Israel is not a garrison kingdom, as its detractors in the West and its enemies in the Muslim world insist; it is an orchard kingdom, much of which was uprooted and felled over the ages but which never ceased entirely from blossoming and has now been replanted.

An episode involving the chief of the Tsimshian tribe in northwest British Columbia may help us to understand the Jewish feeling of proprietorship in the Holy Land. Rejecting the land claims of Canadian government officials, the chief posed the representatives from Ottawa a question they could not answer. "If this is your land," he asked, "where are your stories?" The land we call Israel is replete with the stories of the Jewish people from pre-Biblical times to this very moment of writing—stories that in fact spill over the present borders and establish what we might call the saturation of presence. But this is of no account in the Palestinian and Arab narrative, founded in the Koran, the annals of conquest and, as we will see, in the more recent rewriting of history.

At bottom, the hatred of the Palestinian for the Jew is theologically rooted. Sura 60:8 instructs the faithful that "Allah forbids you to make friends with those who have…driven you from your homes." Palestinians believe they have been driven from their home by an army of Jewish outsiders, although the historical muniments show that the majority of Palestinians are not Palestinian at all, their ancestors having emigrated from the surrounding Muslim countries in great numbers, primarily during the period of the British Mandate. Jews believe their people have lived in the land since 1200 BCE and that, despite conquest and expulsion, a remnant has always remained in place—a claim that is objectively indisputable. But the tenure of the Jews in the Holy Land, however indefeasible, has always been precarious and, certainly since the scourge of Islamic conquest, they have rarely ceased to hear or to anticipate—to use the language of the scripture—"the snorting war steeds which strike fire with their hoofs as they gallop to the raid at dawn." (Koran, 100:1)

The issue is even further bedevilled by another definitional quandary—namely, what is the current civic and political status of the "Palestinian"?—since the so-called "occupied territories" were part of Egypt and Jordan, captured by Israel as the spoils of a defensive war, and never constituted an independent nation or *official* Palestinian "homeland" in the first place—although a recognized Jewish state did exist in the Fertile Crescent before it was demolished by the Romans in 70 CE. As Dana Barnett, a correspondent to the *Democracy for the Middle East* website, reminds us in her discussion of the Palestinian cause, "Similarly, the people of Sinai were not Sinaians and did not form a particular collective." *Palestine was never regarded as an independent political state or entity, neither by those who lived there nor by the surrounding Arab nations.* Gaza was the creation of the Egyptian army following the United Nations' partition resolution of 1947; the West Bank was annexed by Jordan after the 1948 war. Thus, Gazan Arabs were until recently Egyptian; West Bank Arabs were Jordanian. Territorial citizenship and strong family ties bind them still to these countries and, as we have seen with respect to Gaza, the Israeli withdrawal led predictably to border chaos and a mass flux of family reunions. Former Fatah terrorist Walid Shoebat, in an interview he gave to Israeli national news on January 27, 2004, made no bones about this internal dynamic. "We considered ourselves Jordanian until the Jews returned to Jerusalem. Then all of a sudden we were Palestinian." He continues, "Never in history was there a Palestinian state, we never wanted a Palestinian state."

Whether the United Nations partition resolution of November 29, 1947, to establish a Palestinian state was frustrated by collusion between Israel and Jordan, as seems unlikely given the archival evidence as well as the hostility that erupted between them, or whether the Arabs themselves must take full responsibility for rejecting the partition plan and launching a disastrous war continues to be debated among "New" and "Old" Israeli historians without closure in sight. The New Revisionism (not to be confounded with the "Revisionist Zionism" of Vladimir Jabotinsky) has opted for the former explanation of these events in its intensive campaign to undermine the foundations of the state that affirms and secures the very existence of its practitioners. Fortunately, the latter-day revisionist perspective has been emphatically discredited by Yoram Hazony in *The Jewish State: The Struggle for Israel's Soul* and Efraim Karsh in *Fabricating Israeli History*, perhaps the two most important books on the subject.[2] Associated with Jewish New Historians like Avi Shlaim, Ilan Pappe, Menahem Brinker, Adi Ophir, Eliezer Schweid, Tom Segev, and Benny Morris, this "progressive" movement espouses, among other distortions, a postmodern recklessness with source documents, favours the brazen and monochromatic Palestinian chronicle, generates atrocity fabrications and inflated casualty statistics to condemn Israel, places Zionism in the prisoner's dock and stresses Israeli chicanery in the hotly disputed population transfer issue. It is hard to resist the feeling that the current intellectual scene in Israel is almost laughable and comes straight out of the Theater of the Absurd. But one is chastened by the spectacle of an intellectual movement that slanders and arraigns its own, like a modern edition of the sociopathic Frankist sect of the eighteenth century which charged its own people with blood libel. One is also saddened by the utter disregard in which the concept of truth is held. As Francis Bacon put it in his famous essay on the subject, "What is truth? said jesting Pilate, and would not stay for an answer."

While the avant-garde of left-wing savants, leading academics, and postmodern historians, known as the *branja*, natters on about problematizing foundational discourse, demystifying homogenous narratives (but only insofar as these apply to Israel), relativizing shared identities, repatriating multi-ethnic peripheries, interrogating the givenness of the prior and the normative, displacing organic and totalizing constructions of thought into the area of disclosive performativity by relocating multiplicity at the centre and siting new dimensions of freedom (translation: forming a single Palestinian state with a Jewish minority), encouraging a self-ironizing intellectual culture and foregrounding the necessity for open, pluralizing public spaces hospitable to nonrepressive political action (translation: remove the checkpoints, even if this means giving the terrorists the key to the city)—while all these ludicrous notions are being foisted upon a diminishing intellectual culture, the Palestinian opposite numbers are engaging in sophisticated enterprises of their own: assembling bombs, building rockets, pirating weapons across international borders, perfecting techniques of infiltration, and laundering charitable donations through complex banking networks or transferring money via the traditional *halawa* method of bypassing banks altogether in order to provide terrorism with the funds it needs to continue operating. The situation would be comical were it not potentially tragic.

As for the Jordanian question, contrary to the revisionist movement's *parti pris*, it seems legitimate to suggest that, despite the political slapstick following the so-called London Agreement of 1987 in which Jordan disclaimed all title to the West Bank, proper restitution would appear to require the treatied restoration of these lands to Jordan, as was the case with the Sinai Peninsula to Egypt in 1979, if the cartographical miracle that historian Raphael Israeli (who coined the term "Islamikaze") calls "squaring the triangle" between the three implicated litigants is ever to be negotiated. James Parkes was of the same opinion, pressing for permanent membership of the area and its people in the kingdom of Jordan, "which would lead to a natural independent entity, as homogeneous as any Arab country is, and viable if it lived in harmonious relations with Israel." No matter how much we try to suppress the recent political history of the contested arena in the interests of popular simplifications, the Palestinian question remains as much a Jordanian as it is an Israeli issue, even though Jordan's King Abdullah, in a press announcement on June 7, 2006, ran for cover, casting the Palestinians in the role of "a foreign people" with no right of return and, in an address the following day to a military academy, declared that Jordan would never become "a substitute homeland" for its own former citizens.[3] Yet Jordan, although it renounced its claims to Judea and Samaria, had no objection to accepting the reversion of a portion of land in the Arava region south and east of the Dead Sea (and then renting it back to Israel). Further, its paper cession of the West Bank to the PLO in 1988 does not have the force of international law since the territory in question had been illegally annexed by Jordan during Israel's War of Independence. And yet, since this is the Middle

East, who is who and what is what often remain wrapped in clouds of inveterate unknowing. And, we might add, in a mantle of environing madness as well. There is an old joke about the Arab scorpion who hails a Jewish carp to ferry it across the Jordan river. "But you will sting me," the carp protests. "Why would I do that," the scorpion counters, "since it would cost me my life?" The carp agrees and is duly stung in the middle of the river. As they are about to sink for the third time, the carp asks, "Why then have you stung me?" "It's the Middle East," the scorpion replies. The joke suggests probably the only paradigm of Middle Eastern Studies that can still pretend to be serviceable.

Koestler argues in one of the more fascinating books on the subject, *Promise and Fulfilment*, that "historic justice cannot be measured by absolute standards" since "the process of history is irreversible [and] all judgment becomes a function of time. Yesterday's act of violence is today's *fait accompli* and tomorrow's legal *status quo.*" (Analogously, Texas is no longer considered part of Mexico, Alsace-Lorraine is now French—the question has universal ramifications.) So the problem involves deciding where to locate the zero hour for Israel, where to make the "cut": the biblical crossing into Canaan, the return from Babylonian exile, settlement during the rule of the Ottomans, the first wave of European immigration in the 1880s, the Balfour Declaration of 1917, the battle for the Negev, or the decisive event for Jewish consciousness in our time, the *Churban* (destruction) in the killing fields of Europe? For the Palestinians, I would infer that the zero hour is simply the vague intuition of, in the British and Arab misuse of the phrase, "from time immemorial." Koestler allows that an injustice has been done to the Palestinians but rightly contends that the *effendi* class that sold tracts of land (mainly marsh and desert) to Jewish settlers over the heads of the *fellahin* and then decamped to Cairo or Beirut, if they were not already *in absentia*, were also responsible for the debacle, and that, compared with historical precedents, the injustice was a mild one, "the methods of Jewish colonization [being] relatively fair and humane." The simple truth, to quote Melvin Konner from his *Unsettled: An Anthropology of the Jews,* is that "from the outset the Jews acquired land from Arabs by legal purchase, and all the kibbutzim and other early settlements were made on such legally and voluntarily transferred lands. Until 1948, there was no transfer of land by force, in contrast to the Americas, Australia and New Zealand." And in historically more recent terms, what for Palestinians is remembered as *al-Naqba* (the Catastrophe) of 1948 may with at least equal justice be countered by Israelis, in their experience of the Sephardic and Mizrahic expulsions from their Arab homelands and the horror of subsequent events, as the *sitra achra* (the monstrous realm of evil). Ironically, had Israel not been created as an independent state in 1948, there would have been almost no chance of a Palestinian nation coming into existence. The Arab peoples of the region would now be citizens of Jordan, Syria, or Egypt. The idea of Palestine as a nation is, as we have noted, a modern invention, scarcely half a century old. In any case, there is no such thing as an allodial territory, or absolute estate, to be found anywhere in the settled world. But in the case of Israel, rooted in the long register of time, even a historic claim to regional partnership has now come to be regarded with suspicion, if not internationally discounted in the face of earlier official motions, resolutions, and declarations in support of the Israeli state. To dispute the legitimacy of modern Israel, in the light of the events that led to its formation and the fact that other subject peoples of the Ottoman Empire (under whose yoke the Jews also languished) acquired statehood through struggle and suffering, is to negate the historical process entirely.

Certainly, as the Peel Commission of 1937 recognized, *none* of the parties to the dispute can boast of incontestable beginnings, rights or prerogatives. Israel's lien is both reinforced and hidden by time. Jordan is the bootleg creation of British diplomacy that lopped off nearly 80 per cent of Ottoman Palestine (known as "South Syria" and originally earmarked by the League of Nations for the Jewish "National Home") to establish the Hashemite emirate of Transjordan, which thus incorporated Jewish (and "Palestinian") land into its hegemony. "Palestine" is even more problematic. Infested with terrorist organizations and militant factions, wholly reliant on immense infusions of foreign aid, lacking a functioning social infrastructure as well as reliable control over the instruments of violence, given to summary executions, prone to the extremes of mob pathology, and without genuine historical legitimacy founded in *veridical* memory, it is moot whether what we call "Palestine" may be considered as even a *potential* state, let alone a tenable economic and political entity.

One cannot quell a certain cynicism, given that the Palestinian leadership has been little more than a terrorist kleptocracy. While

Palestinian society has received proportionately more donor aid from the international community than any other group in all of recorded history—which it takes *as a right* owing to them by the world—80 per cent of Gazans live below the poverty line. Yet the Palestinian Legislative Council recently budgeted for each of its twenty-six members to acquire a $76,000 luxury car and its eighty-six legislators lesser-mark vehicles worth (merely) $45,000 apiece—the package includes chauffeurs, maintenance disbursements, and insurance premiums. Another thirty or so directors and deputies will also profit from such munificence. Even the spear-carriers will be doing very well for themselves and there are more spear-carriers in the Palestinian administration than in *Aida*. When one considers as well the billions in foreign aid stolen by the Palestinian leaders for their own personal enrichment and the billions diverted from development programs into the terrorist infrastructure, it is no less delusional to credit the sincerity of *any* Palestinian administration than it is to believe in the parsimony of African dictators. Even Muhammad Dahlan, Gaza's Fatah security chief, has admitted that fully half of international monetary aid disbursed over the last decade or so cannot be accounted for. The amount of good money, siphoned directly from the pockets of Western taxpayers and poured down the sinkhole of the Palestinian "economy," defies calculation.

Further, with the gradual closing of the Israeli job market to Palestinians, who are being replaced by immigrants and foreign workers, the economic future looks even bleaker. Israel has announced that it intends to shut its borders completely to Palestinian labourers by the year 2008. Hamas has released plans to develop an independent economy, but when one considers that the Palestinians use Israeli currency in their transactions and that Israel is by far and away the most important market for Palestinian goods and produce, it is clear that the new government is trading in propaganda rather than in products. A violent demonstration of 2,500 unemployed Palestinians in Gaza City on March 12, 2005, who stormed the parliamentary building and fought with police, is only a symptom of what lies in store for a restive quasi-state on international life-support. This nigh-irresolvable situation, along with the proliferation of extremist groups that have no other means of livelihood and no other expertise than violence, is Yasser Arafat's legacy to Palestine and the Middle East—an inheritance that poisons any imaginable future, at least in the short term. Arafat is like the horror-flick mummy who emerges from the tomb to trouble the world, accompanied by his loyal minions who wish only to restore his reign.

There is, on any candid analysis of the matter, something fiendish operating in Palestinian society. The level of lawlessness, civil disturbance, and clan rivalry, and the gun culture in general, may without exaggeration be described as Somalian in extent and rootedness. Car thieves run rampant throughout the West Bank in what has become, after suicide bombing, a major Palestinian industry; local gangs, when they are not killing Israelis, are busy shooting one another in turf feuds; competing factions in the PA police forces regularly exchange fire; suspected "collaborators" are shot in the street; assassinations are part of the political playbook. The violence has even spread to the centres of learning. Objecting to the difficulty of a physics exam, high-school students in Hebron broke out in a riot, burning tires and hurling stones at the Education Department. Student supporters of Hamas and Fatah clashed at Hebron University and had to be separated by other students associated with Islamic Jihad, and Fatah-affiliated students forced the closure of Al-Azhar University in Gaza City when they tried to lynch the newly appointed rector. Reacting to a continuous spate of violent acts, the Palestinian Center for Human Rights has called for immediate action on the part of the PA to ensure "the safety and security of Palestinian civilians"—not from Israel, be it noted, but from themselves. Meanwhile, the only potential source of effective resistance to Palestinian corruption and repression, the Press corps, is tightly muzzled by the PLO executive, and journalists are regularly beaten or imprisoned; the more compliant have been on the PA payroll for years. It would seem that the chances for the emergence and development of *authentic* democratic institutions and a durable peace culture, even after Arafat's death, upon which any successful "peace process" depends, are doubtful at this time and for the foreseeable future. The Palestinian Authority remains a tribal institution, whether it is controlled by Fatah or Hamas, which, whatever their disagreements, are united in documentation. The Fatah "young guard," which opposes "old guard" corruption, is no better and probably worse, openly calling for a "two-track" policy that, in their language, means supplementing diplomacy by continuing "resistance," aka, terrorism. Fundamentally, this is no different from the policy of Hamas, which is willing to negotiate Israeli territorial withdrawals with the very country it refuses to recognize while continuing to promote the terrorist option. Moreover, there can be little doubt that the growing conflict between the old and young guards in Fatah will add yet another destabilizing element to the political maelstrom that is Palestine.

Nor is it, I believe, an exaggeration to say that Palestinian society is not only corrupt and violent to the core, but also irredeemably infantile in the way it imagines itself and seeks to achieve its aspirations. Just examine the strutting grandiosity of the average communiqué issued *ad nauseam* by the terror groups: "The US-Zionist enemy is sending its criminal warplanes to attack the Front's position, in a bid to undermine its national role in protecting the Palestinian people." Then there is the usual crock of hyperboles—"heroic national resistance," "Israeli massacre," "the Zionist aggressor," "corrupt powers of the criminal US and the Zionists," the lot. Can one respond in any other way than with groans and incredulous laughter—unless one happens to be a Palestinian or a member of the liberal-left? Incurably refusing to acknowledge reality, this juvenile mindset assumes that the threat and practice of violence will bring Israel to its knees or, as many factions tirelessly affirm, will one day serve to establish a Muslim nation from the banks of the Jordan to the shores of the Mediterranean. But this is a dream world fed by hatred, lies, self-deception, a merely notional past and a fixation on an unrealizable future—a culture of dependency that has abdicated all responsibility for consequences as well as for its own proper development in a real-world setting. It is this lack of social and political maturity that is perhaps the most troubling element of all. Thirteen-year-old Anjad Abu Seedo, Gaza's "wonder boy" preacher, delivers regular Friday sermons focusing on the question of death and, in his own words, on "the way a good Muslim woman should behave"—subjects obviously within the purview of his vast experience of life and his comprehensive mastery of Islamic theology. Gushed schoolteacher Ahmed Khalil, "This small sheikh is God's gift to Hamas and all Muslims." Despite the Lord's bounty, there is a sense in which the Palestinians, for all their shrewdness in the propaganda wars and their skill in extorting financial contributions from the West, remain perpetually stuck at the age of thirteen.

That being said, my skepticism must be alloyed at least to the following extent. While I maintain that the Palestinian claim to historical title is shaky if not apocryphal, and that, despite the stridency of Palestinian spokesmen and the ignorance of their Western backers, the territory in question was never licitly "Palestinian" to begin with, I must also acknowledge that sixty years of collective suffering, economic mendicancy, and political displacement have created a feeling of both resentment and solidarity that cannot be easily overlooked. Along with this feeling go the presumption of historical empowerment and the belief in a homeland that inevitably transform themselves into a deep political conviction that can no longer be rationalized away or scumbled out of the picture. As a result, whether or not the Palestinians may be construed as constituting a legitimate nation—and the historical documentation makes it clear that they cannot—they have nevertheless in the course of the last two generations developed the *conviction of nationhood* that, as such, is now a "fact on the ground" there is no way of circumventing. They have, so to speak, established squatter's rights. Whether the Palestinians should have a state or not, there is an even chance that they will eventually get one, but what kind of state it would be is an open question. It remains to be seen whether Palestine would become another rogue nation or terrorist haven, persist in its condition as an ungovernable political adolescent, develop into a political hologram, or devolve into an economic basket case dependent indefinitely on foreign aid—or whether, with time, good will, farsightedness, the rooting out of corruption, the long-delayed dismantling of the terrorist infrastructure, and territorial concessions not only from Israel but from their Muslim neighbours as well, Palestine would metamorphose into a peaceful, cohesive, and self-subsistent country. But if my sense of fairness demands that I recognize the minimal possibility of felicitous conclusions, my sense of reality tells me to be prepared for a completely different *mise en scène*. It is hard to resist the impression that when a Palestinian is presented with a ploughshare, he will promptly turn it into a sword. As has been said more than once, give the Palestinians Switzerland to govern and they would run it into the ground in no time flat.

Any sober analysis of the Palestinian situation must take into consideration the very real likelihood of prolonged anarchy at worst or sporadic conflict at best following the Israeli pullout from the Territories, as the various political parties and their terrorist offshoots vie for local supremacy. We might also expect, given the internecine tensions between the Gaza and West Bank leaders and the trenchant differences in cultural sensibility between the two regions, that "Palestine" may one day fragment into *two* competing and turmoil-ridden states—let us call them Hamastan and Fatahland—with capitals in Gaza City and East Jerusalem (or Ramallah). Indeed, Gaza itself may disintegrate into a myriad of clan-based fiefdoms with power coming to rest with the hetmen of the various tribal militias and extended families, not to mention the gangs of gunmen who roam the streets and countryside pretty much unchecked. The evidence is already in. The Israeli withdrawal from Gaza led to a mass debauch of arson, rioting, and looting, so that the valuable infrastructure and physical plant left behind by the settlers, including its state-of-the-art greenhouses, which could have been used to buttress the nascent Gazan economy, were in large part demolished. Nor is the West Bank, though a more coherent entity than the Gaza Strip, immune from the chaos produced by political factionalism, local power struggles and the settling-in of terrorist subsidiaries from outside. We will also have to take into account the possibility of a civil war waged between Fatah and Hamas. Conversely, we can expect publicized efforts to form a government of national unity between the two factions since the anti-Israeli platform is shared by both, but this is like applying fresh paint to old plywood. It could even work for a time, but in the long run, a lowest common denominator would not be enough to resolve the rivalry between Hamas and Fatah for power, prestige, and perquisites. There is, of course, another ingredient in the mix. As Fatah official Hussein al-Sheikh has admitted, his party's desire to promote national unity is motivated not by a deep understanding between the two groups but mainly by "pragmatic" considerations, "to end the current financial crisis." There is nothing else, apart from a basic anti-Israelism, that could possibly serve as a binding agent. Once the budgetary constriction dissipates, the merger would be subject to dissolution. The situation could go either way, toward fragile unity or intestinal strife, or even the dismissal of the Hamas government by Mahmoud Abbas, who holds this trump card in his Presidential hands. However this latest farce works itself out, the likelihood is for increased anarchy. Further, there cannot be much hope for a "country" in which there are mainly two career paths open to its youth: the trade of guerrilla fighter and the rather shorter vocation of suicide bomber. Productive labour and professional achievement, as we have seen, fall by the wayside in an economy predicated upon foreign subsidies and local self-immolation.

I am afraid that anyone who believes in the Palestinian ability to form a stable and mature state is simply raving—although, politically speaking, we have no choice but to allow the scene to unfold, or unravel, as it will. And naturally, we must also expect that Israel will be held wholly or partially responsible, both by the PA and the international community, for whatever failures the Palestinians bring upon themselves. This is inevitable. Although if we looked more closely, what we would see is the unmasking of Palestinian terror that until now has used the so-called Israeli "occupation" to conceal its real intentions and practices. The overwhelming electoral victory of Hamas is far more than the result of a "protest vote" against Fatah corruption, as the Western press so ingenuously claims; it is the expression of the will of the Palestinian people itself, endorsing the public program of a terrorist organization. There should be no confusion about this. Most recently, a poll conducted shortly after the cross-border kidnapping of an Israeli soldier, Gilad Shalit, on June 25, 2006, revealed that 77 per cent of the respondents supported the abduction and 66 per cent backed the lobbing of rockets at Israeli population centres. The poll also found that support for Hamas had increased despite renewed violence and economic hardship. It is clear that the huge majority that put Hamas in power has knowingly cast its vote for a terrorist party whose central and oft-proclaimed creed is the physical eradication of Israel. Its stated policy and *raison d'être* is what we might call "kraticide," the killing of a country. Whatever "humanitarian aid" may find its way into Palestine, whether through direct or indirect channels and despite the current embargo, will only confirm its people in that choice and drape Hamas in the mantle of legitimacy, whether it remains in power or not. But, as noted, even financial hardship will only serve to strengthen loyalty to Hamas among many defiant Palestinians, a fact that regional surveys have verified.

Everything considered, the expectation of new initiatives in the negotiation process, such as they are at this time of writing, strikes me as unfounded, given the continued preoccupation of the Palestinians, some sixty or so years after the Arab offensive against the new Israeli state, with the "right of return" of millions of *artificially constituted* refugees, the refusal or inability of the Palestinian leadership to put a stop to terrorist attacks and paramilitary operations, the undiminished vigour of what David Pryce-Jones in *The Closed Circle* calls "the power-challenge dialectic" that has consistently vitiated the development of Arab and Islamic societies toward genuine representative institutions and a functioning electorate, the dogged misreading of the situation by the Europeans as well as its political exploitation by the Russians, and, most crucially, the ingrained contumacy of the Palestinians themselves. "Compromise" is not a word often used or heard in the Arab/Palestinian lexicon, as the Oslo fiasco clearly revealed. One can plausibly assume that Islamic Jihad, the Aqsa Martyrs Brigades, Hamas, and the rest will regard any brokered ceasefire as only a tactical entr'acte, a *tahdiah* or "period of calmness," in an ongoing war and will once again resort to violence when it suits them to do so, that the Palestinian Authority, regardless of which faction occupies the seat of power, will continue to regard its long-entrenched policy positions (to quote one of its spokesmen) as a "red line…that cannot be trespassed," and that the Gaza Strip—and possibly the West Bank—may eventually deteriorate into full-fledged terrorist demes, backed by Syria and Iran. There is no doubt that Gaza is being Talibanized even as we continue to debate on its future. In a region filled with jobless young men whose politics are driven by testosterone, poor education, religious brainwashing, militant propaganda, kinship loyalties, and ever-declining prospects, the future seems grimly Hobbesian. It should be obvious that a significant proportion of the population running around in ski masks and spending their time firing AK-47s and Kassams does not contribute much to the GNP.

It is true that we must wait upon events, but we should do so prudently. As former Israeli Foreign Minister Abba Eban famously remarked, the Palestinians never miss an opportunity to miss an opportunity. Thus unlike Israel in 1948, and despite the manufactured euphoria surrounding the election of Mahmoud Abbas (aka Abu Mazen, his *kunya* or honorific name from his terrorist days) as chairman of the PLO following the death of Yasser Arafat, or the subsequent hope that Hamas will moderate its hardline stance toward Israel, the conditions for democratic state-making in anything but a nominal sense appear to be absent. Robert Kaplan explains in *The Coming Anarchy* that "multiparty systems are best suited to nations that already have efficient bureaucracies and a middle class that pays income tax, and where primary issues such as borders and power sharing have already been resolved." As none of these provisos may be found in Palestinian society, the prognosis appears almost inevitable.

And unlike Israel, the general will to coexistence is absent as well. There are hawks and doves on both sides, but the proportions are staggeringly lopsided. May 15, 2004: a massive peace rally in Tel Aviv called for a new understanding between the two peoples and resoundingly backed Ariel Sharon's plan for disengagement as Shimon Peres eloquently proclaimed hope for a shared future; at the very same moment, an even more massive demonstration on the West Bank protesting the creation of Israel was addressed by Yasser Arafat who, quoting from the Koran, exhorted the cheering multitudes to "continue terrorizing our enemies." Readers can draw their own conclusions as to who was playing a zero-sum game.[4] Even though certain conditions have changed, let us, for once, look to the reality of the situation. The majority of Israelis have long accepted the Palestinian right to a state; the majority of Palestinians have not even acknowledged Israel's right to exist. To repeat, the electoral triumph of Hamas is a clear sign of the will of the Palestinian people, who are perfectly aware of the Hamas program to annihilate Israel. The country is not even depicted in Palestinian textbooks and maps—the space where Israel should be represented is referred to as "Occupied Palestine," which should make us reconsider what the Palestinians really mean by the term "occupation."

Obvious questions suggest themselves. How long will it take to detoxify the minds of generations of Palestinian children who have been injected with an unwavering hatred for Israel and Jews, assuming this is even possible? When one reflects that the new generation of Palestinians is already tainted from the cradle, that anti-Jewish and anti-Israel indoctrination commences in the early, formative years, continues through the various tiers of primary and secondary education, and culminates in a synthetic view of history that stresses the necessity of regional conflict, it only makes sense to temper unrealistic hopes for imminent accommodation. How plausible is it to suppose that a genuine and enduring peace is thinkable without a thoroughly revamped educational curriculum, starting in the home, and that its beneficial, long-term effects would require anything less than the slow development of another and more enlightened generation? In the current circumstances, the opposite is more likely to happen: the strategy of the Hamas government is to ensure that both the home environment and the educational system will raise a new generation of citizens committed to the destruction of Israel. "It is necessary to instill the spirit of jihad in the nation," declares the Hamas Covenant. While Israeli leaders must do everything they reasonably can to advance the "peace process"—irrespective of how certain aspects of that process may put Israel at a disadvantage—they must remain wary and guarded, keep whatever assets they must yield to a commonsensical minimum, and be prepared to drive the hardest of bargains, if they are to avoid another Oslovian miscarriage.

As for the standard dogmas of presumably "enlightened" Muslims, we must remain skeptical and vigilant. Mazen Chouaib, Director of the National Council on Canada-Arab relations, is one of these laundered zealots who throng the anti-Israeli forum. In a combative article in the *National Post*, Chouaib asserts that "a Jewish-only democracy is not a true democracy," a charge rebutted by Israel Asper in his facing response, who points out that this "Jewish-only democracy" contains over 1 million Arabs, enfranchised citizens with elected delegates in the Knesset. As Neill Lochery writes in *Why Blame Israel?*, the anti-democratic charge needs "to be viewed within the context of the permanent state of hostilities that Israel has found itself in…[I]t is a wonderful testament to Israeli democracy that…the treatment of minorities in the state remains good, particularly given the context of the ongoing conflict with the wider Arab world." Needless to say, nothing comparable exists in that wider Arab world—neither emancipated Jewish citizens in good standing nor Arab nationals with similar, unimpeded, or unthreatened rights of representation. (Ben-Gurion himself affirmed in an important speech delivered in late 1947 that, "In our state there will be non-Jews as well—and all of them will be equal citizens…without any exception.")

The strange fact that Chouaib is so intensely concerned with Israeli democracy when there is not a single genuinely democratic state in the rest of the Middle East (Turkey is problematic and Iraq is still in the making or breaking) suggests that he has got his priorities wrong and might be better advised to hew closer to home in his remonstrances and admonitions. Chouaib should know that Israeli Arabs enjoy freedom of speech, religion, and assembly as well as the right to vote, form political parties, and hold elective office. Concurrently, one would be hard put to imagine any Muslim country or territory that could pass what Natan Sharansky in *The Case for Democracy* called "the town square test," defined as follows: "Can a person walk into the middle of the town square and express his or her views without fear of arrest, imprisonment, or physical harm? If he can, then that person is living in a free society. If not, it's a fear society." The "town square test," however, is a test that Israel passes every day of the year. Nor is Chouaib, a public exponent of the fear society and the failed state, willing to recognize that his "Jewish-only democracy" (which happens not to be that), considering the unspeakable events of the last century, is the last possible redoubt of salvation for a decimated people in a legitimately constituted nation with demonstrable historical justification.

One wonders, too, what Chouaib might conceivably mean by the "numerous examples of Arab governments repeatedly extending the olive branch to Israel." The premeditated attacks of 1948? The coordinated, multi-nation offensive threat of 1967? The invasion of 1973? The years of Palestinian shelling from Lebanese soil of northern Israeli villages, kibbutzim, and moshavim (which led to the retaliatory incursion of 1982)? The recurrent terrorist attacks both abroad and at home? The scuttling of the Camp David peace negotiations by Arafat? The intifadas? The suicide bombings (which, it is worth remembering, date from as early as 1994)? The attempts to bring down passenger jets? And should we consider the Arab accusation of Israeli recalcitrance, we might ask where was Israel's negotiating partner? How could Israel have unilaterally created a Palestinian state when, in fact, there was for many years no statutory body to transact with after Jordan washed its hands of the affair and, subsequently, *every* Palestinian engagement in a peace initiative, including Oslo, was always conducted in bad faith, with the aim of extracting impossible or unrealistic accommodations, while keeping the terrorist heat up?

The promulgation of sophistries is quite extraordinary. The Arab lie has become a palpable and ubiquitous public institution. One thinks of Goebbels' dictum: "If you tell a lie big enough and keep repeating it, people will eventually come to believe it." But as David Pryce-Jones has pointed out, lying and cheating in the Arab world is not to be judged by a moral yardstick, but is an organizing principle of behaviour validated by the culture, a way of furthering one's career, propping up one's community status, or of acquiring and holding on to power and advantage. Those among us who for whatever reasons are too diffident to challenge so transparent a form of partisan mendacity are collusive—not only in the dissemination of urban legends but in the murder of innocents. Indeed, the lie has gone so deep that it is embraced even at the expense of national security and prosperity—e.g., Egypt initially implicating Israel in the October 2004 bombings in Taba when they were clearly the work of an al-Qaeda affiliate (the Abdullah Azzam Brigades later assumed responsibility for the carnage). And where Israelis do not happen to be among the victims, the blame will often fall on the Mossad. Such evasions can only facilitate further terrorist attacks as preventive measures will be misdirected and public awareness thinned out or deflected. As for the Palestinian lie, it is now so ingrained that any public statement that proves to be true is either a lucky inadvertence or a statistical necessity.[5]

Such tactical mendacity clings as well to those organizations that enthusiastically support the Palestinian cause. National Public Radio in the US, for example, whose interview schedule is heavily weighted toward the Palestinians and their supporters, dwells uniformly on presumed Israeli atrocities and airs unfounded claims and duplicitous assertions as if they were undisputed fact. Shrill Palestinian falsehoods are almost never challenged and the climate of controlled disinformation is pervasive. NPR reporter Robert Siegel describes the contentious security barrier being constructed by Israel as "it sure is a wall," neglecting to mention that 95 per cent of the structure is fence. Siegel, who was in Israel recently, filing at least fourteen stories, did not report on the Tel Aviv bombing of February 25, 2005. One of NPR's most frequently consulted interviewees, Palestinian journalist Rami Khouri, is allowed to get away with praising Hizbullah as "a very impressive, legitimate, even heroic resistance movement." Another guest, Patrick Seale, author of *The Struggle for Syria*, is an outspoken apologist for the late Syrian dictator Hafez al-Assad. I have only touched the surface.

Another example of phoney impartiality covering a Machiavellian agenda is provided by the influential public affairs group, Network 20/20. Calling itself an "apolitical educational organization," it is clearly anti-Zionist in its mission, sponsoring speakers like Tony Judt (whom we will hear of further along) and Javed Zarif, Iran's ambassa-dor to the UN. When the Polish consulate in New York cancelled one of its events, Network 20/20 president, Patricia Huntington, wasted no time blaming the ever-convenient Jewish lobby, under the guise of the Anti-Defamation League, for exercising censorship—an allegation just as quickly rebutted by Poland's deputy consul general in New York.

The *New York Times*, the unofficial organ of the Democratic Party, comes off no better, its well-known editorial policy that opposes the validity of the Jewish state embracing even the counterfactual. See, for example, PLO legal advisor Michael Tarazi's prevaricating op-ed piece for October 4, 2004, in which he claims that Christians and Muslims living in Israel are deprived of political and civil rights, or the *Times'* running of an Associated Press photo after the Temple Mount affair in September 2000 that captioned a Jewish law student, Tuvia Grossman, beaten nearly to death by a Palestinian mob, as a Palestinian demon-strator clubbed by Israeli soldiers. The same Gray Lady disingenuous-ness pertains to the myriad Islamic websites, hatcheries of misinforma-tion. One also notes a stock difference in the reporting of the conflict by the media in general, which trims the news to fit its ideological priori-ties. Not only are Palestinians given substantially more "clip time" in the boilerplate coverage of events,[6] the Palestinian casualty is almost always implicitly rued, the Israeli almost never. The first is accorded the tragic dignity of the human, becoming a resonant symbol, the second is an anonymous cipher, a faceless creature barely recognized as a member of the human community. Twelve-year-old Muhammad al-Dura, reportedly killed in a shootout between Israeli forces and Palestinian gunmen near Netzarim, becomes an international *cause célèbre*; four-year-old Afik Zahavi killed in Sderot by a Kassam rocket barely makes it to public attention. With respect to al-Dura, there is mounting evidence that the episode was almost certainly rehearsed, directed, and staged with the collusion of French TV and Palestinian stringers and cameramen. The Kassam rocket, however, was the real thing. (The proviso here, of course, is that the Palestinian child must be the victim, or the presumed victim, of Israeli fire; if he is killed by Palestinian infighting, as has often been the case in Gaza—the most recent instance being the clash between rival factions over stalled unity talks and unpaid salaries—he is scarcely mentioned, and almost never by name. Our Palestinian sympathizers are clearly motivated by other concerns.)

As for the "peaceful" advocacy of such people—the journalists, the broadcasters, the *bien pensants*, the instapundits, the weathervane commentators, the talking heads and plodding Teledontosauri, the frequently consulted Arab plenipotentiaries—this amounts to little more than a subtle technique of persuasion intended to promote the bloody agenda of Arab leaders like the late Yasser Arafat and Hizbullah fanatic Sayyed Hassan Nasrallah. Those few Arab public figures, like Egyptian sociologist Sa'ad al-Din Ibrahim and playwright Ali Salem or Palestinian banker Omar Ibrahim Karsou, who offer proposals for genuine political change are either imprisoned, harassed, or ignored. Ibrahim, who is chairman of the Ibn Khaldun Center for Development Studies in Cairo, spent nearly two years in an Egyptian jail from July 2000 to February 2002 (although it is sad to note that he has lately reversed course, lauding "Hizbullah's courageous resistance" in the war of summer 2006 and accusing Israel of "enjoy[ing] the killing and destruction"). Salem was prevented from visiting Israel as late as May 2005, during the "thaw" between the two countries, to receive a peace award from Ben Gurion University. Karsou, founder of the movement for Democracy in Palestine, put it on the money when he wrote in the *Daily Telegraph* in July 2000 that dwelling in the past "is part of our victimhood game: it seems always somebody else's fault." And that somebody else's fault is always Israel's aided, naturally, by its intimate ally, the Great Satan. (The 2004 Arab Human Development Report, released on April 5, 2005, once again blames Israel first and the United States second for the lack of economic progress and political freedom in the Arab world.) This kind of thinking applies even to natural disasters. Sheik Ibrahim Mudeiris, preaching on Palestinian Authority TV, accounted for the uncomfortable fact that the tsunami of December 2004 also struck Muslim Indonesia by citing "Zionist and American investments" in the country.

No matter what evidence advocates for Israel or knowledgeable scholars adduce to justify the existence and legitimacy of the Jewish state, and no matter how reliable and conclusive that evidence may be, antisemites both homegrown and exotic will continue seeding the media with their packages of propaganda and disinformation. Some perceptions never seem to change, irrespective of the facts. As Jean-François Revel says of garden variety "anti-Americanism" in his book of that title, but which applies across the entire field of political prejudice, "the mystery…is not the disinformation…but people's willingness to be disinformed." And the media are deeply complicit, using what in business lingo is aptly called a "peering function" to set up a network effect or "centralized platform" for "traffic exchange," in which an array of identical items—spurious "facts," hypotheses, figures, and assumptions—circulate freely and serve to corroborate one another, substituting a dictionary of received opinions for the truth. In this way our news networks establish and extend a corporate monopoly of information and its distribution in the globalization of a single point of view and the institutionalizing of non-debatable propositions: it's all about oil, President Bush is mentally defective,[7] Islam is essentially a peaceable religion, terrorism is the product of Western oppression, Ariel Sharon is a war criminal, Israel is a colonial aggressor and so on. As Hillel Halkin reminds us in *Commentary* (February 2006), reviewing Stephanie Gutman's *The Other War*, this process is abetted by the lazy incompetence of journalists and foreign correspondents who are generally unfamiliar with the areas and issues they report upon, have little or no knowledge of the languages of the regions to which they have been posted, rely on "fixers" and second-hand or biased sources of information, come to the job with their own set of prejudices, and are, for the most part, profoundly uneducated in politics and history— notably with respect to the Middle East. Add to this witches' broth the ingredients of intellectual dishonesty, left-liberal politics, and an antisemitism that bubbles just under the surface, and we have a fairly accurate portrait of the average contemporary journalist. But in the competitive world of the media, with its need to grind out news at an accelerated pace, such ineptitude and unscrupulousness plays into the hands of editorial chauvinism and its attempt to control public opinion.

That such a corporate monopoly of opinion disguised as news along with its practical irrefutability by dint of excessive repetition—the Nazi technique of the Big Lie all over again—is itself a form of intellectual terrorism, the tenebrous aspect of the globalization process, naturally tends to escape our attention. Israel, of course (followed closely by the US or its neoconservative stratum), is the primary victim of the innumerable franchises of the McMedia empire in its campaign to colonize the public mind. *This*—the manipulation of the international news market and the dismantling of editorial barriers and stringent tariffs against the worldwide spread of disinformation—is what the anti-globalization movement should be demonstrating against. But it is obviously incapable of doing so since it is the secret beneficiary of a globalization process whose operational strategy it is ostensibly protesting. That the news is often kneaded rather than reported has drawn little comment or attention. And that it is "news" that in this case is globalized and not goods and markets does not alter the fact or excuse the anti-globalist forces.

The American media at least adhere intermittently to standards of journalistic fidelity—the resignations of CBS anchor Dan Rather and CNN executive vice president Eason Jordan, implicated in their respective scandals, are encouraging if only exceptional signs. From time to time the American media are exposed and forced to acknowledge their mutilation of the news, as did *Newsweek* in the famous Koran-flushing perjury, CNN admitting that its journalists were shepherded and vetted by Hizbullah minders in Lebanon to present carefully selected footage implicating Israel, and the *New York Times* on more than one occasion. (The *Times* is a special case; its frequent divulging of leaked classified information has seriously harmed American counter-terrorism efforts and is, arguably, treasonable.) But large sections of the European media seem committed to the fabrication, omission, or misrepresentation of the facts without apology, small-print *errata* or subsequent non-committal admission—as, for example, France's *Nouvel Observateur* that in a 2001 story accused Israeli soldiers of raping Palestinian women but provided not a single iota of evidence, or the government-owned France-2 TV network that circulated and possibly collaborated in the calumny of the al-Dura affair, or Italy's national TV station RTI that in a letter of October 16, 2000, assured the Palestinian Authority that it would never air footage detrimental to its goals and actions and bleatingly concluded, "Please accept our dear blessings." The influential London *Guardian* with its pro-Palestinian slant is no less disgraceful, going so far as to employ among its staff of journalists a member of the radical Muslim organization Hizb ut-Tahrir (Party of Liberation)—which is committed to re-establishing the Caliphate and considers suicide bombing acceptable—and suggesting in a column that Israel and not Syria was responsible for the assassination of former Lebanese Prime Minister Rafik Hariri. (Not surprisingly, the author of the offending item was Patrick Seale.) The *London Times* compared the Israeli operation against the terrorist nests headquartered in Jenin to Bosnia and Kosovo, and the BBC, making the same comparison, offered an analogical figure of "tens of thousands" dead, although it was later shown by a UN mission to the city that no "massacre" had occurred—the casualty count was fifty-two Palestinians, mainly terrorists, and twenty-three Israelis. (The BBC is so demonstrably biased in its coverage that it must surely qualify as the jakes of international broadcasting.) The BBC and the *Times'* false reportage was seconded by Germany's *Sueddeutsche Zeitung* and France's *Libération*. Denmark's *Horsen Volkesblad*, Greece's *Ta Nea* and *Eleftherotypia*, France's *Le Monde*, Italy's *Il Corriere della Sera* and *La Stampa*, Germany's *Frankfurter Allgemeine Zeitung*, Austria's *Kleine Zeitung*, Ireland's NewsTalk radio, Britain's *The Independent* and *Daily Mirror*, Spain's *El Pais*, Norway's *Dagbladet*, to name only a few from a multitude of European dailies and media outlets, have run articles and editorial commentaries filled with misleading statistics or printed venomous anti-Israeli cartoons, thus contributing to the blacklisting of the Jewish state.

Another example of the poison pen at work involved the deaths of eight Palestinian civilians on a Gaza beach on June 9, 2006. Many newspapers around the world, including the *Washington Post*, the *New York Times*, the *Guardian*, the *Independent*, the *London Times*, and innumerable others immediately ran with the Palestinian narrative that Israeli artillery fire was responsible for the disaster. (One newspaper, however, seems to have acted responsibly, if tardily. After having first incriminated Israel, the *Sueddeutsche Zeitung* conducted its own investigation, carefully reviewing the evidence and suggesting in its June 18, 2006, edition that the event may well have been staged.) The fact that the Palestinians refused to cooperate with an IDF investigation into this tragic event and, moreover, had three days in which to compromise the scene by planting and/or removing evidence was never given a thought. But the evidence that does remain seems pretty conclusive. The absence of a shell crater, the fact that the six IDF shells fired on that day against rocket launching sites were all accounted for, and that shrapnel fragments removed from the bodies of the injured treated in an Israeli hospital were not made in Israel point to the likelihood that the explosion was caused by a mine buried on the Al-Soudanyia beach in a Palestinian defensive perimeter against Israeli naval commandos or to protect their launch sites. The Big Lie keeps circulating in one form or another. Indeed, even it were shown that the detonation was caused by an errant shell, Israel would still be accused of targeting civilians while the rockets deliberately aimed by Palestinian terrorist squads at Israeli civilian communities and directly responsible for Israeli preventive measures—it is estimated that to this date over a thousand Kassams have fallen on southern Israel since the Gaza pullout—would be largely ignored or extenuated by the international media. It is also most curious that a Palestinian cameraman from Ramattan Studios television was on the spot to capture film footage of another suffering Palestinian poster child, which was instantly beamed around the world and avidly picked up by Western news networks. Where have we seen this before?

More recently, in treating of the July 2006 eruption of hostilities in the Middle East, *Le Monde* condemned Israel for being "in violation of international law" in striking back forcefully at the Hizbullah aggressors; the Parisian daily *Liberation* blamed the US for vetting Israeli policy decisions; the *Guardian* deplored Israel's "collective punishment of Lebanon's fragile economy" without the slightest concern for the damaged Israeli economy or the bombs and missiles falling on Israeli communities, paralyzing one quarter of the country's population; the *Sueddeutsche Zeitung* labelled the Israeli offensive a diplomatic error; the *Toronto Star*, Canada's largest circulation newspaper, stressed Israel's "relentless bombing" of Lebanon but somehow skipped Hizbullah's relentless rocketing of Israel, up to 250 missiles in a single day; the CBC displayed excessive coverage of Lebanese suffering and featured lengthy, ingratiating interviews with Lebanon's pro-Syria President Emile Lahoud and a member of Hizbullah's "political wing"; Mexico's *El Economista* and South Africa's *Sunday Times* printed viperous anti-Israeli caricatures. The point will be taken. Radio and TV focused almost entirely on disaster scenes from Beirut and dwelt lovingly on the horrific experiences of the Lebanese evacuees—one would scarcely have known from their coverage that dozens of Israeli towns and cities, along with kibbutzim and moshavim, had been bombed daily and that Israeli hospitals were working overtime. Or that Israel's northern forests, set ablaze by Hizbullah rockets, will require fifty to sixty years to regenerate. Plainly, for the world media the only acceptable Israeli response to naked aggression is to allow itself to be pulverized.

We should also expect that atrocities will continue to be manufactured by a cynical enemy and disseminated by an equally cynical world press to impugn the Jewish state and render its pariah status even more pronounced, like Pluto banished from the planetary family. We have examined the fabrications of the al-Dura affair and the Gaza beach explosion. It should thus come as no surprise that Israel was blamed, not only by the media but by the UN Secretary General himself, for *intentionally* striking a UN observation post in Lebanon—a post that had no business being in the middle of a war zone in the first place and proximity to which was a deliberate tactic adopted by Hizbullah rocket launchers, not to mention that such a design by the Israeli high command would be obviously counterproductive and self-defeating. When, twelve days later, another UN post was hit by Hizbullah rockets, not a word of reproof was uttered. It should not astonish us that Israel was vehemently condemned by the worldwide media (in concert with the "international community") for war crimes when it targeted an apartment building in the Lebanese town of Kafr Kana. The fact that 140 missiles had been fired at Israeli communities from this particular building compound and environs, that residents had been leafletted for several days to abandon the premises, that—most suspiciously—there were no men in the building, that it was hit at midnight on July 29 but collapsed at 7 a.m. the following day, that cadavers were trucked in to increase the impression of carnage, and that Lebanese ambulance personnel only appeared on the scene several hours after that in a move precisely timed to the arrival of journalists and video crews, is almost never reported. And the fact that the casualty count, which was pegged at over sixty, was suddenly reduced to twenty-eight was also little noted. Shortly afterward, Lebanese Prime Minister Fuad Saniora claimed that forty people had died in an Israeli air strike on the village of Houla, but later had to revise his numbers to one fatality, an item largely ignored by the media.

Human Rights Watch also got into the act, claiming that Israel deliberately targets civilians. Nor was this organization able to find a *single instance* of Hizbullah fighters firing from residential neighbourhoods, mosques, and hospitals although eyewitness accounts proliferated and several newspapers and media outlets, in a rare display of objectivity, actually documented such cases—even those otherwise unfavourable to Israel such as the *New York Times* and *al-Jazeera*. (Sometimes an exception does prove the rule.) Similarly, as various reputable blogs keeping tabs on the media have shown, the Lebanese Red Cross staged an Israeli strike on an ambulance, which was then "reported" by a slew of newspapers and TV stations, and Reuters news service did likewise with an obviously fake Israeli missile attack on one of its press vehicles in Gaza. There is more here than meets the eye for an eye. Meanwhile, when fifteen people were killed and 200 wounded in rocket attacks on Haifa in one incident among many, there was no international outcry, no photos of mangled corpses flashed around the world, and no sermonizing editorials. (Of course, Jews do not flaunt the bodies of their dead as do their Islamic enemies to punch up the propaganda effect, but it is moot whether the international media would have been interested in any event.)

It cannot reasonably be doubted that the international press, tailoring its actions to those of Hizbullah and Hamas, is mainly interested in devising media ambushes in which Israelis are shot with cameras. A recent example involves Reuters once again, which posted a tainted photo incriminating Israel—the photo of a bombing in Beirut was doctored by one of its journalists, a certain Adnan Hajj, a Lebanese national, who was later found to have tampered with *nine hundred* such photos. Web logs have uncovered many instances of such adulteration—the same woman crying over the destruction of two different homes (*Associated Press*), a man shown dead in one photo walking about in another (the *New York Times*), the notorious "Green Helmet" rushing about carrying dead children out of the ubiquitous rubble, from April 18, 1996, to July 31, 2006, (*Reuters*, the *Guardian*, the *New York Times*, the *Telegraph*, *Gulf News*, *Arab News*), etc. The general *modus operandi* is simple: jump to premature conclusions, accept orchestrated events as veridical and interpretation as fact, accentuate negative images and coverage *when not actually concocting them*, ignore confuting or problematic data, and suppress or play down countervailing intel when the truth eventually emerges. The blueprint that the plurality of our media outlets and networks are following is frankly despicable. In any case, there is now little that may serve to distinguish our notable news organs from, let us say, the Palestinian daily *Al-Hayat al-Jadida* or the Arabic television channel *Al Jazeera*. Nor does the printing of the Mohammed cartoons in several European newspapers, which touched off a firestorm in the Muslim world, in any way diminish their responsibility for the Herodizing of the Jewish state where, in the years-long barrage of defamatory anti-Jewish cartoons and outright slander launched by the Arab world with the collaboration of the European media, no riots erupted, no embassies were trashed, no flags were burned, and no one was killed or hurt.

Sadly, the Israeli far-Left media are equally complicit with their foreign compatriots. A particularly distasteful instance was the libelous report and concocted film footage on the TV news magazine *Fact* in October 2004 of Israeli soldiers falsely accused of intentionally shooting a Palestinian girl and celebrating over the "kill." The journalist involved, Ilana Dayan, was not so much as reprimanded even though her star witness admitted in court that he had lied and the subterfuge, accepted without hesitation by the international press, did Israel irreparable harm. But all this is now standard fare. Robert Kaplan has justly written in *Policy Review* for December 2004 that "the ongoing centralization of major media outlets, the magnification of the media's influence through various electronic means and satellite printing, and the increasing intensity of the viewing experience in an age of big, flat television screens has created new realms of authority akin to the emergence of a superpower with similarly profound geopolitical consequences." This "superpower" has, for the most part, invaded the public mind with an army of reporters, columnists, think-tankers, and editors engaged in the diffusion of fables and distortions. For what we used to call "journalistic integrity" is a *rara avis* and news reporting has come increasingly to reflect editorial policy—even the headline will often brandish a compressed editorial opinion—making it difficult for the interested reader or viewer to arrive at a reasonable approximation of the truth. The Fourth Estate has become the Fifth Column. A basic trust has been broken.

Probity would demand that our journalists and anchormen, our commentators and academics, break from the doxological cotillion in which they dance so subserviently, and consult recognized and learned authorities who write without ideological bias or anterior commitment, so far as this is possible—scholars like Martin Gilbert (*Exile and Return: The Struggle for a Jewish Homeland* and, more recently, *Dearest Auntie Fori*), James Parkes (*A History of the Jewish People* and *Whose Land? A History of the Peoples of Palestine*), Paul Johnson (*A History of the Jews*) and Joan Peters (*From Time Immemorial*). Peters, especially, expanding on H. J. Simson's *British Rule, and Rebellion*, has produced a magisterial if controversial work in her strenuous effort to disinter the buried truth. Embarking on her seven-year project as an attempt to understand the Palestinian cause—"The book," she informs us, "was originally meant to be solely an investigation of the current plight of the 'Arab refugees'"—Peters' methodical and comprehensive study of the question led to a 180-degree turn in her prior assumptions and premises. Making many trips to the region, conducting first-hand interviews, and sifting through mountains of data, census statistics, official reports, travellers' narratives and archival material, she arrived at the conclusion that it was not the Jews who dispossessed the Arabs but vice versa. "[I]t was the Jews who were displaced by the Arabs—the Arab immigrant flocks would migrate into the Jewish areas of development…on land designated at that very time as the mandated 'Jewish Homeland.'" Moreover, Jewish immigration was severely restricted by the Ottomans, Arabs, and British, each in their turn, while the Arab immigrant population went on growing without statutory limit.

The popular history of Palestine may well be one of the biggest political and propaganda scams of all time as the veritable lies of yesterday become the counterfeit truths of today. As for the day before yesterday, it has been lost to sight. To adopt the metaphor of anthropologist Grant McCracken, the true history of the Middle East has become the "sunken ship" around which "new species and populations establish themselves"—only these later encrustations are now taken for the ship itself. The nebula of falsehoods in which the Palestinians have lived and which the world has accepted—even many Israelis, mainly those associated with the peace movement and the academic Left, have fallen prey to the Big Lie—is now almost impossible to dispel, but the task must still be undertaken. This has become nothing less than an intellectual duty and a moral obligation. As Peters makes clear, with reference to the question of the biblical title deed that has caused so many problems, "The Jewish presence in 'the Holy Land'…does not depend on a two-thousand-year-old-promise…. Buried beneath the propaganda…is the bald fact that the Jews are indigenous people on that land who never left…. It was only *'politically'* that the Jews lost their land. They never abandoned it physically, nor did they renounce their claim to their nation." (James Parkes makes the same point: "But it is only *politically* that the defeat by Rome, and the scattering of the Jewish population, made a decisive change in the history of The Land. That which had been created by more than a thousand years of Jewish history remained....") Peters' documentation, demonstrating that a Jewish population had always remained in place as indigenous stakeholders, that the number of Jews returning to their ancestral homeland was kept to a minimum by the occupying powers, and that *the Palestinians were to a great extent a society of immigrants to the area in dispute*, is unassailable. The argument is underscored by Melvin Konner, who points out that the Jews "did not come to Israel from anywhere else at any time. They have been there from time immemorial. They became a coherent people there, discovered God there, built a kingdom there, created the Torah there, and composed much of the Talmud there. Attempts to evict them partially succeeded, but their presence there has always been significant. Wherever they were in exile, they longed to go back there, and in every generation some did. Their presence there is permanent, and future attempts to evict them will incur a huge cost." Konner's use of the phrase "from time immemorial" is warranted in context. Further, as Jane Gerber has detailed in *The Jews of Spain*, although Ashkenazi Jews were cut off from the Holy Land during the extended period of exile, Sephardic Jews "have lived in Palestine for centuries while others continued to migrate there over the past 1,000 years"; the relationship of the Sephardim with Israel was "intimate, long-standing, and concrete." It has been justly said that the Jewish right to Israel is inherent, not conditional. It derives its legitimacy neither from its acceptance by the Arabs nor by an assize of Western nations, but in virtue of the historical incumbency of the Jewish people, a right which needs to be seen as irrescindable. Diplomatic recognition may be necessary and is certainly desirable in the world arena of political and military affairs, but does not in itself confer legitimacy; it can only help establish what is already the case in the realm of morality and justice.

The evidence assembled for the Jewish claim to national peoplehood by studies like the above leaves little room for motivated denial or paltering rebuttal, such as that evinced by revisionist Norman Finkelstein, who contends that Peters has been "debunked." But Finkelstein, as a student of Noam Chomsky and a defender of Holocaust-denier David Irving, is among the most rabid of Jewish Jew-haters and his docket must be put in the context of his frenetic anti-Zionism. Though Peters' findings have been vigorously contested by the academic Left and the book has been drenched in controversy, her major thesis, despite a tendency to overstatement—owing, perhaps, to a marked enthusiasm for her subject—has not been refuted. It is her detractors, rather, who have gone overboard in their attempt to discredit her scholarship—Albert Hourani's dismissal of her book in an *Observer* review as "ludicrous and worthless" and his claim, according to Mohamed Nanabhay, in his online essay *One Narrative*, that her over 1,800 footnotes have been "proved worthless in one way or another," is a typical example. Generally speaking, the standard mode of discreditation is to pick and snipe, to cite a number of factual errors here, some stylistic blemishes there, a couple of dubious amplifications somewhere else, perhaps a few omissions or misinterpretations or neglected attributions in between, the latter leading to an additional charge of plagiarism—thus succeeding, apparently, in demolishing an entire work, as if a mass of authentic and corroborating material did not exist. No scholarly text, no matter how painstakingly researched, is without warts, but to prescind from a cluster of warts to galloping leprosy is the method of the scholar-quack.

Peters' book is far from perfect, yet notwithstanding what even favourable readers regard as flaws in the work, namely overwriting and faulty presentation, *From Time Immemorial* is a *tour de force* and represents a valiant effort to redress the polemical balance, countering the prevalent scribal and journalistic tendency toward *presentism*, that is, the tendency to refer to the past as if it were part of the framework of the present. But in this case, the past is precisely that which most of us do not know and perhaps do not want to know since it would deprive us of our cherished illusions and force us to rethink our prejudices. The past that has entered the present is either an abridged past that never existed in the form it has acquired or a past that has been freshly invented to suit the political occasion. The modern and broadly accepted history of Palestine is a cunningly devised palimpsest, on which the original text has been written over and left unread. Our knowledge of the "Palestinian question" derives from the accreditation of a kind of second-layer history. What is required is a process that in painting is called pentimento—the reappearance of an underlying work that has been painted over. For the claim that all of Israel is Palestinian land is a historical howler—the truth is that almost none of it is. Indeed, much of non-Israeli territory is actually part of the Jewish national home, and much of what the Palestinians, many of whom were *comparatively* late arrivals to the Holy Land, assert as their own, across the entire map of the region, certifiably is not.

Nor should it escape our attention that most of the recommendations and solutions proposed to resolve the Palestinian/Israeli embroilment by veteran antisemites and Islamist stalwarts like Chouaib (and their Western backers) are remarkably cavalier when it comes to the issue of Israeli security, as if a series of crippling military concessions and a surrender of assets on one side and, on the other, a verbal promise or paper signature would stem the tide of Arab belligerence. Such proposals disregard the basic facts of the situation: mosque-fueled comminations, a legacied anti-Jewish school curriculum right across the regional spectrum supplemented by the worldwide Saudi-funded madrassa programs and bogus "charities," stage-managed General Assembly resolutions and international conferences meant to blockade and peripheralize the Jewish state, various national television mini-series in the Muslim nations promoting a phony and malevolent view of history accompanied by a feral anti-Jewishness, and the revanchist program of the various Palestinian terrorist organizations for whom the phrase "Israeli occupation" is merely cryptograph, as everyone knows, for the existence of Israel itself. When Walid Shoebat was asked in the above-cited interview what the Palestinians really want, he replied, "They want the destruction of the Jews, period"—a sentiment buttressed by a particular *hadith* and recently reaffirmed by Palestinian clerics, that all Jews must be killed and that the Hour of Resurrection cannot occur until every last Jew has been eliminated. (The *hadith* in question, framed in the voice of an oblatory tree, concludes, "O Muslim, O Abdullah, here is a Jew hiding behind me, come and kill him.")

Israel is also perfectly within its rights not to credit the guarantees and promises of the international community in arranging for a stable peace—the principle of *rebus sic stantibus* (i.e., circumstances have changed) has been invoked too often in the past to promote assurance, for example, by Richard Nixon and Henry Kissinger in 1974 and Jimmy Carter in 1976, among a host of such breaches of trust. Nor can it rely on the good offices of United Nations crisis management. UN peacekeepers on the frontier between Israel and Lebanon have regularly looked the other way during Hizbullah incursions, kidnappings, and

violations of the ceasefire—when, that is, they are not actively partici-
pating in such episodes. UN collaboration with Syria in the capture
of a five-man IDF squad on the Golan Heights on December 8, 1954,
culminating in the death of Golani soldier Uri Ilan in a Syrian prison,
is now an open secret. "Everyone knew that the UN collaborated with
the Arabs," said Ilan's brother Shimon to the *Jerusalem Post*, "Even today
they help them." Indeed. It has also become clear that the October
2000 Hizbullah abduction and murder of three Israeli soldiers was
condoned if not facilitated by UN "peacekeepers"; the attack was filmed
and the footage eventually found its way into the hands of Lebanese
TV producers, who aired the documentary on September 5, 2006.
The UN censored Israel for reconnaissance overflights in Lebanon but
kept silent on the reason for these maneuvers, the sort of Hizbullah
activities listed above. Hizbullah drones penetrating Israeli airspace
also went unremarked by the UN. The major Hizbullah rocket barrage
and kidnapping operation in July 2006, which Israel rightly defined as
an act of war, drew UN (and international) pleas for a "measured and
proportionate" Israeli response. The beat goes on.

A UN interim force, whether in Lebanon or Gaza, would only
insure that the traffic in illegal weapons would continue undetected,
remain tacitly ignored, or be actively abetted. Members of Hamas,
for example, are employed by UNRWA, the United Nations Relief
and Works Agency, as its former director, Peter Hansen, admitted to
CBC television on October 3, 2004, insisting that he had the backing of UN Secretary General Kofi Annan; and Hamas operatives have
also confessed to using UNRWA facilities—the May 20, 2005, attack
on Israeli troops policing disengagement near Rafah was carried out
from the shelter of an UNRWA building—and appropriating vehicles, including ambulances, for storing and delivering weapons and
convoying fighters from one destination to another. This is an attested
fact. Ambulance driver Islam Jabril, a member of Fatah Tanzim, was
stopped on March 27, 2002, while attempting to pass a roadblock
near Ramallah in an ambulance containing bombs and an explosive
belt hidden under a stretcher on which a young girl lay. Members of
Islamic Jihad and Hamas cells were arrested in October 2004 as they
were planning to smuggle an ambulance rigged with explosives into
Jerusalem. Moreover, during the past two years, something like 100 of
the 550 Magen David Adom (the Israeli "Red Cross") ambulances have

been destroyed, stolen, or repainted as Red Crescent ambulances, not all of which are used for medical purposes. The sordid story continues, in clear violation of international law. Shin Bet, the Israeli Security Service, has compiled a dossier of such infractions, replete with names, dates, and localities, which UNRWA has so far refused to investigate and act upon.

Given such revelations, it is clear that every concession that Israel may agree to along the route toward what has been so far an ever-receding peace will only lead to further turbulence unless such compromises and trade-offs are backed by solid reciprocations over which Israel maintains effective control and that some sort of security envelope remains in place. Whether land is ceded through disengagement or negotiation, policing measures would continue to be necessary. For what Neill Lochery calls the "disastrous land for peace formula" as pursued by the various Labour administrations, inflamed by "the problem of signing peace deals with non-democratic parties," entailed, he concludes, concessions that might well have led to the self-destruction of the state. Ehud Barak in particular just about gave away the store, including East Jerusalem, the sacred site of the Temple Mount and portions of the Negev, and Shimon Peres would have thrown in the title deed. The lessons of the past must not go unheeded in planning the peace curriculum of the future. No pragmatic dividend is otherwise forthcoming. The same thinking applies particularly to the process of disengagement, whether unilateral or coordinated, as in Gaza where Israel would have to maintain some sort of control over the land crossings, coastlines, and air space, despite the legal problems this would bring in its train, if the territory is not to turn into another south Lebanon. Failing this, Israel's major port, industrial installations, and oil refineries in Ashdod and Ashkelon, to take just one example, would be vulnerable to rocket and mortar attacks from Gaza, as the community of Sderot has been. But if the current situation is allowed to continue, the spectre of mutual destruction looms large. One can only hope that the prophet Zephaniah need not be taken at his word when he foresaw that "Gaza shall be forsaken, and Ashkelon a devastation."

In this context, despite the unofficial "Geneva Initiative" signed by Israeli peace activists like Amos Oz and Yossi Beilin and their Palestinian counterparts, it makes little sense to regard the two-state solution to the Israeli/Palestinian dilemma, *in the form proposed by recent American administrations and enthusiastically adopted by the EU,* as intrinsically workable. For one thing, Israel's pre-1967 borders are scarcely defensible in today's high-tech military world. And indeed, it is a good bet that *no borders*, however reduced, will ever be accepted by the Palestinians who, dredging up the pre-1947 partition proposals making for a thumbnail Israel, will continue to insist that they are suffering under Israeli occupation. This is why the "land for peace" formula was and will continue to be a dismal failure—the long-term Palestinian plan, as is clear from Arafat's maneuverings and the Hamas Charter, is *all the land*, peace be damned. For another thing, aside from the question of the West Bank acquifer, the new "accord" offered the Palestinians little that Arafat had not already spurned when he walked away from Camp David, a fact that seems to have been forgotten. More significantly, Mahmoud Zahar, a senior Hamas leader, has flatly rejected the Geneva Initiative. "Our position is clear," he said at a rally in Gaza City on November 13, 2003, "all of Palestine, every inch of Palestine belongs to the Muslims." Recent Hamas proclamations have only reconfirmed his stand. When Egyptian/British novelist Ahdaf Soueif stated in her *Guardian* report from the West Bank (November 24, 2003) that every Palestinian she met, as well as many Israelis, said the same thing, namely, that "What Israel wants is a Palestine as free of Arabs as possible," she was no doubt telling it like she heard it, but she was simultaneously turning the truth of the situation inside out for international consumption. It would be more candid to assert that what just about every Arab wants is a Palestine as free of Jews as possible. How is it, one may be permitted to wonder in the light of so manifestly skewed a public dynamic, that Palestinian journalists like Daoud Kuttab, Walid Awad, and Khaled Abu Toameh are regularly invited to write op-ed columns for the *Jerusalem Post*, where they are given complete freedom to express their views, which often take Israel to task, while an Israeli reporter is ejected from the Francophonie Conference in Beirut and the Israeli point of view is *never* represented in the Arab and Palestinian press?

For Zahar and his ilk, a Palestinian state would be only a preliminary stage in a movement of conquest and liquidation that may yet take years of subterfuge to achieve and this is the only reason the terrorist organizations, as was the case with the Palestinian Authority under Arafat, would be willing to accept a temporary *hudna* or ceasefire. As political analyst Uri Elitzur has written, "if the PA has been a swamp of terrorism, corruption and incitement, then the Palestinian state will be a whole lake." Nor does it take much imagination to conceive of the new Palestine as a Lebanon-waiting-to-happen, the willing client or vassal of Syria, Iran, and Hizbullah and a cantilever for renewed violence. Hizbullah has now assumed complete control over Fatah's Tanzim and is penetrating ever more deeply into the warren of Palestinian terror groups, running some forty-five cells in the territories whose members receive much of their training in Syria, as well as recruiting individual terrorists who are willing to act on their own. Hamas has gone on record that the West Bank will be the next staging ground for Kassam rocket attacks against Israeli towns and cities.

Let us pause for a moment and take a brief overview of the situation as it presented itself in the first half of 2005, if only to regain our bearings and to get some sense of what the future bodes. In the week after Mahmoud Abbas' election to succeed Yasser Arafat, Islamic Jihad, the Aqsa Martyrs Brigades, and Hamas renewed their terrorist offensive, killing seven Israelis and wounding eight in separate attacks. Shortly thereafter, even as the four-year intifada was in the process of being terminated by the PA leadership, fifteen mortar and rocket attacks were launched against the Israeli settlement at Gush Katif, six Israeli soldiers were wounded in two more separate attacks, a Palestinian youth was captured at a checkpoint carrying an explosive device, another terrorist was shot wearing an explosive belt, and a 40-kilogram bomb was found and detonated by sappers near the Sufa crossing in the Gaza Strip, among a continuing series of such incidents. In the week after the peace conference at Sharm el-Sheikh in which the second intifada was pronounced over, mortar shells and Kassam rockets continued to rain down on Israeli settlements and suicide attacks planned by Hamas and the Popular Front for the Liberation of Palestine in the French Hill district of Jerusalem were alertly thwarted by Israeli security forces. And a week after that, two more terrorists—one a former security prisoner released in the January 2004 deal struck with Hizbullah—were caught while attempting to carry out a suicide mission against the town of Har Bracha. A few days later, a female terrorist was apprehended on the outskirts of Har Bracha. On February 25, three more Palestinians were prevented from crossing the security barrier between the Sufa and Kafem Shalom crossings in Gaza. On the same day, two mortars fell near Netzarim and Neve Dekalim. On the next evening, a suicide bomber blew himself up in a Tel Aviv nightclub, killing five people and injuring over fifty, many critically.[8] (According to intercepted telephone transcripts, the bomber, Abdullah Badram from the West Bank city of Tulkarm, a member of both Islamic Jihad and Abbas' Fatah, was acting under instructions from Syria via a Hizbullah operative.)

There seemed to be no end to the violations of the ceasefire. Despite the well-publicized Palestinian peace overtures, it was still business as usual for Hamas, Islamic Jihad, Tanzim, the Popular Front for the Liberation of Palestine, and the al-Aqsa Martyrs Brigades, the latter receiving its orders and funding from Hizbullah.[9] On the weekend of the Tel Aviv bombing, Israeli Security registered thirty-five warnings of planned attacks, although it failed to stop this one. Fortunately, Israeli forces patrolling near Jenin on February 28 discovered a van with a cargo of several hundred kilograms of explosives, which the same Islamic Jihad cell that claimed responsibility for the Tel Aviv blast intended to infiltrate into Israel. On March 2 a car bomb exploded at Joseph's Tomb where Jewish worshippers were being escorted from prayer. On the same day a fully operational Hamas bomb factory was discovered in the village of Yamoun on the West Bank. On March 7, two Israelis at the holy shrine of the Cave of the Patriarchs in Hebron, a city with a long Jewish history, were wounded in a shooting attack. Also on March 7, it was revealed that an Arab-Israeli had been arrested for planning to carry out a bomb attack in the Knesset. Blowing up the parliament buildings is certainly an effective way of making a political statement and the Palestinians have their share of Guy Fawkes aspirants. Shortly afterward, five Arab men were indicted for assembling the terror cell responsible for planning the Knesset attack as well as engaging to kill members of the Druze community to inflame interfaith tensions. On March 14, another Palestinian terrorist, among the 500 released by Israeli Security on February 21 as a goodwill gesture, was arrested transporting weapons near the city of Kalkilya. On March 20, three soldiers and a policeman were wounded in a shooting attack south of Ramallah while searching for stolen cars. On March 28, eight Islamic Jihad fugitives—two of whom were recently freed terrorist prisoners—were apprehended in Jenin and the nearby village of Fahame attempting to manufacture Kassam-like rockets in preparation for attacks against Israeli targets. On April 9, over seventy mortar rounds and several Kassams fell on the community of Gush Katif. On the eve of the Passover, sixty-seven security warnings were recorded, several more shooting attacks occurred and another suicide bomber was apprehended. On June 20, a young Palestinian woman, Wafa Samir Ibrahim al-Biss, was captured en route to carry out a suicide attack at an Israeli hospital where she was being treated for burns sustained during a cooking accident, her mission to kill as many Jewish patients, medical personnel, and (in her own words) as many youngsters as possible. On June 24, a drive-by shooting attack perpetrated by Fatah's al-Aqsa Martyrs' Brigade, a wing of Mahmoud Abbas' own party, killed and maimed several Israeli teenagers between the ages of fourteen and seventeen. Indeed, Israeli soldiers capture would-be suicide bombers trying to slip into Israel on an almost daily basis, yet it is the check-points and roadblocks that are condemned by Palestinian spokesmen and the Western press, not the potential killers with civilian targets in mind. The terrorists, who are always perfecting their means and now specialize in ticking teenagers and boy bombers, cannot be expected to go on holiday—two more Palestinian youngsters, aged fifteen and sixteen, were captured on April 27 with eleven bombs in their posses-sions. In point of sobering fact, the month of April saw a 54 per cent rise in terrorist incidents. The actual figures for February to late spring 2005—the ceasefire period—show 812 attacks carried out and thou-sands more foiled, strengthening the argument of those who insist that the pullout constitutes a greater threat to Israeli security than the *status quo ante*.

This catalogue of incidents should not be interpreted as the inevi-table birth-pangs accompanying a new accord or dispensation, the mark of a society in painful gestation. They are symptoms of an ongo-ing malaise and signs of a violent and ideological recidivism that will in all likelihood persist far into the future. The list of such attacks and infiltrations grows daily. We have now entered the sphere of the Palestinian etcetera, dominated by the terrorist combines but also swarming with wildcat terrorist cells. After every such incident, the Palestinian Authority will issue a statement of regret or condemnation but will do nothing to prevent the next attack—while rendering such episodes even more likely in virtue of its vitriolic negotiating rheto-ric and facilitating measures. Though what I have provided here is only a sort of monthly tally, there can be little doubt that, despite their protestations of innocence, the terrorists' efforts to derail the "peace process" and the flagrant violations that are their stock in trade will continue, however spasmodically, and without any significant effort on the part of the Palestinian Authority, irrespective of which party dominates its proceedings, to intervene—and that such "low intensity" episodes will for the most part go unreported in the Western media. At the very moment that Mahmoud Abbas during his visit to Washington was assuring the Americans that the "suicide bomb era" may now be over, Israeli security apprehended several aspiring suicide bombers at the checkpoints—Abbas' words were duly highlighted in the Western press, the attempted infiltrations were not. Or if untoward events are not unreported, then they are often misreported. When three Palestinian teenagers were shot by an IDF patrol near the Philadelphi Route between the Gaza Strip and Egyptian Sinai on April 9, CBC-TV's the *National* claimed they were only playing soccer; shortly afterward, it was admitted by Palestinian security officials themselves that the three youths had been involved in arms smuggling.

From the perspective of the rest of the world, Israel should not respond in kind or take decisive action against its attackers, but absorb these assaults upon its citizens in order to keep the hopes of a prospective peace alive, even at the cost of many dead and many more crippled for life. Israeli lives, after all, are dispensable and cheap. Yet there is not another nation on earth that would rest inactive in the face of such ongoing carnage. Regrettably, in the wake of these latest provocations, Israeli MK Zevulun Orlev of the National Religious Party had history on his side when he stated in the Knesset that "every peace festival ends in fireworks and every summit results in bloodshed." Similarly, MK Uri Ariel of the National Union Party warned that the Palestinians were taking advantage of the "euphoria of peace" and that, in the final analysis, Israel "must trust only itself." Of course, not everyone shares such views. Uri Savir, former Israeli negotiator with Syria during the Oslo period and president of the Peres Center for Peace, cautions that Israel should "not miss this window of opportunity." But given his credentials, one has a duty to remain skeptical.

Prospects are unlikely to improve. Abbas was never a reliable "partner for peace"—the name "Mahmoud Abbas" sounds moderate to Western ears, but he is still "Abu Mazen," leader of a party that insists on the "right of return," underwrites summer camps in which children are indoctrinated to become "martyrs," presides over a religious and educational system that promotes the murder of Jews, and controls the propagandist Ministry of Culture (whose latest publication honours Hanadi Jaradat, the killer of twenty-one Israelis in a Haifa restaurant). Abbas wrote his own political epitaph when, rather than fight to disarm, arrest or extradite the terrorists, he chose instead to pursue a policy of mollification, negotiating with some and integrating others into the Palestinian Security Services, mainly gunmen from Hamas and Islamic Jihad, the two groups responsible for most of the suicide and rocket attacks over the last four years. These "rehabilitated" thugs and killers carried on their seditious activities from within the relative protection of their new billeting, incubating civil unrest and actively contributing to the tensions in the region, as Prime Minister Ahmed Qureia himself had to admit at a PA cabinet meeting on June 14, 2005. Hamas and Islamic Jihad, as we all know, should have been forcibly dismantled years ago, since the suppression of these terrorist groups was stipulated in the Oslo Accords, as was the demilitarization of the territories from which Israel withdrew. Naturally, the resolution was never implemented and no objection was made by Western diplomats. As for the arrest of terrorists by the PA, this was a flagrant burlesque, the famous "revolving door," since the detainees were usually let go or their escape arranged within a few hours, a few days, or a few weeks at most. A recent instance of this practice involved Shafik Abdul A'ani, a senior Islamic Jihad operative who planned the February 25, 2005, Tel Aviv bombing, and who "escaped" under the eyes of the PA from his Tulkarm jail cell—he was later killed by the IDF; following on the heels of this event, on May 3 the PA released a Hamas rocket specialist the day after having arrested him; on June 9, two of the Tel Aviv terror suspects were freed by the PA. More recently, Hamas announced its intention to release the assassins of Israeli Minister of Tourism, Rehavan Zeevi, leading to Israeli intervention. These same terrorists have made the release of thousands of their fellows from Israeli detention a condition of their apparent willingness to negotiate. And their propaganda efforts, focusing on "women and children" who have been incarcerated in Israeli prisons, are meant to obscure the fact that these "women" are full-fledged terrorists and these "children" are teenaged would-be suicide bombers.

Upon reflection, it is by no means far-fetched to deduce that an ostensible peace, as many still envisage it, may well be only a strategic means of conducting a more effective campaign in a war of extermination that has not yet succeeded. Mahmoud Zahar, in another speech delivered on the weekend of March 19–20, 2005, reaffirmed Hamas' position that all historic Palestine belongs to the Muslims. "If the present generations are unable to liberate Palestine," he vowed, "this does not mean that we have given it up. Even if the conflict is not solved militarily now, it should remain open for the future generations." The new Hamas "government" has not altered this position. And this is also why the so-called "right of return" of, and reclamation of property by, millions of Palestinians *born after* the calamities of the 1940s—many of whom were only distantly related to the original refugees—while withheld from the successors of the between 850,000 to 960,000 Jews expelled from the Arab nations, who now with their descendants form half the population of Israel, has become such a sticking-point.[10]

When looked at realistically, adopting the principle of the "right of return" would rule out the need to establish an autonomous Palestinian state alongside Israel right at the outset since Israel would in the course of events shortly cease to exist as an independent nation. The so-called road map would become irrelevant and the process of official negotiations between "partners" would be exposed as eyewash. The "right of return" means, effectively, a *de facto* Palestinian state occupying the stretch of territory between "the river and the sea." Indeed, the Palestinians have now come out of the closet to reveal their true intentions and the unfeigned nature of their project. This has been made plain in Michael Tarazi's above-cited *New York Times* article in which, speaking as a proxy for the PLO, he develops the proposal, not for two adjoining independent states as per the road map, but for a *single state* embracing the two peoples, that would entail the political and demographic subversion of Israel. Why, then, continue the current charade of diplomatic arbitration with the goal of attaining a negotiated settlement? None of this ultimately matters in the context of a "right of return" that would abolish one of the signatories to the proceedings partly intended to confirm its "right of existence." Egyptian President Gamal Nasser said it openly in 1967: "Return of the refugees means the end of Israel." And even should the claim be modified in the course of official negotiations, it is doubtful whether the terrorists will ever truly accept such diplomatic adjustments or whether the "right of return" will recede entirely from the Palestinian agenda and psyche. Meanwhile, the issue shows no sign of being defused. In a London rally on May 21, 2005, the Palestinian representative to the United Kingdom, Husam Zomlot, declared, "I say there will absolutely be no peace without the right of return. The right of return is non-negotiable." To put it candidly if indelicately: Palestinian rejectionists will not rest content unless and until what is now the legitimate, progressive, multi-ethnic, democratic, scientifically advanced, and modern state of Israel becomes another Arab wasteland of social repression, political and economic backwardness, dogmatic religiosity, and systemic corruption.

Rashid Khalidi, appointed to the anonymously endowed (which will doubtlessly prove to be Arab-endowed) Edward Said Chair at Columbia University, has introduced the distinction between "absolute justice" and "attainable justice," centred on a return of the refugees to a "national soil" rather than to their 1948 homes. But such a compromise is largely nugatory. It accepts the reality principle of Israeli *force majeure* preventing the implementation of what he calls "absolute justice," yet his notion of the latter precludes any consideration of an equally absolute justice with respect to the Israeli position and, with regard to the historical facts, the Jewish *right of habitation*. For, in Martin Gilbert's succinct formulation, "Palestine was not merely a haven, but the true centre of Jewish political and spiritual regeneration." Nor does Khalidi recognize that a large proportion of Palestinians were actually post-1918 immigrants from the surrounding Arab countries—Yemen, Lebanon, Egypt, Saudi Arabia, Transjordan, and Iraq, but also from as far away as Nigeria, Sudan, and Algeria—and that many others seeking employment were actively "allowed" into Palestine from Syria during the time of the British Mandate and afterward. As both Mark Twain and the Reverend Samuel Manning observed during their visits to the Holy Land in 1867 and 1874 respectively, the region was practically deserted and the soil gone to waste. And General Allenby, who conquered Palestine in 1917, found a desolate and sparsely populated "country" comprising only 600,000 to 700,000 Arabs thinly spread throughout the entire extent of the territory he surveyed. What Arab propaganda and the terrorist cartels now claim was a thriving, luxuriant, and densely populated Muslim homeland was in truth an Ottoman dust bowl. As for Jerusalem, Jews outnumbered Muslims by a factor of two. There is no getting around the fact that the Arab population in the area in the early part of the twentieth century was only a sliver of what it is today and what we call Palestinian society is basically a society of Arab migrants, itinerant workers, and illegal immigrants, ethnically indistinguishable from their congeners in the surrounding lands. But these facts are stringently suppressed in the present controversy over the "right of return" issue.

The United Nations, as we have noted, has further muddied the waters, in particular by creating a special department, the afore-mentioned United Nations Relief and Works Agency (UNRWA), specifically designed to redefine the Palestinian refugee, *whose status then differed from that of any other refugee in the world*, including Jews displaced from their homes in Arab countries—these latter were never considered refugees at all although their condition was originally at least as critical as that of their Palestinian doppelgängers. As Albert Memmi wrote in *Jews and Arabs*, "the Palestinian Arabs' misfortune is having been moved about thirty miles within one vast nation.... Our own misfortune, as Jews from the Arab countries, is much greater for we have been moved thousands of miles away, after having lost every-thing." Indeed, no one speaks of these Jewish refugees *whose communi-ties in many cases dated back thousands of years in the countries from which they were expelled* and who lost not only their homes, livelihood, and citizenship, but property valued in the billions of dollars that went to swell the coffers of their dispossessors.

But for UNRWA, the Palestinian refugee has not only been recog-nized to the exclusion of his Jewish semblable, he has been reinscribed *as anyone who had lived in Israel for only two years* prior to 1948 (even if that person had later returned to a village in which he had previ-ously made his home), and anyone who has descended from a refugee so defined. This unique category, which violates the remit of its sister organization, the United Nations High Commissioner for Refugees (UNHCR), applies nowhere else in the world and explains why the Palestinian refugee count has swelled to almost 5 million today. No one, it seems, is willing to admit the truth, namely, that the unsettled refu-gee problem is owing directly to the war aims of the Arab nations and their UN collaborators who, instead of integrating people displaced during the 1947–1949 war, as happened in Israel with its own inunda-tion of refugees, have together built and maintained an artificial "camp society," really UN internment camps—many of which can no longer be described as "camps" but as actual functioning towns with modern amenities—as a weapon in a sixty-year campaign against the Jewish state.

Meanwhile UNRWA is progressively bolstered by its Arab and European backers. (Not to mention Canada, which renewed its $10 million annual contribution in 2005.) The Swiss-funded donors conference for UNRWA held in Geneva in June 2004 pointedly excluded Israeli participation while featuring a series of grisly propaganda films in which Israel was portrayed as a nation of conquistadors. (The Swiss are no doubt smarting from having to restore a chunk of World War II Jewish loot cached by the Nazis in their secret vaults and from having to make financial restitution to Jewish families defrauded by Swiss banks in the latter's effort to curry favour with the Third Reich.) This prejudicial tendency is only journalism by other means. We cannot have failed to notice that any untoward incident in which Israel may be involved, from the slightest mistake to the most discernible blunder, is tenaciously seized upon by the press and the "international community" as incontrovertible evidence of Israeli treachery and aggression. Israeli action against its own dissident elements is emphatically approved, but when directed against the terrorists, is inevitably condemned as "unhelpful." Israel is then urged to show "restraint." A Palestinian atrocity by contrast is generally passed off as an unavoidable circumstance of war—a war increasingly regarded as legitimate whether it is being fought in the hospitals, buses, cafeterias, nightclubs, hotels, and pizza parlours of Israeli cities or within the carefully furnished prosceniums of the Western media and the General Assembly of the United Nations. The double standard is deeply entrenched. When the UN headquarters in Baghdad was bombed, killing twenty-two people including Sergio Vieira de Mello, Kofi Annan's heir apparent, the UN simply suspended operations and abjectly withdrew, issuing no stern condemnation of Sunni Islam or any of the Muslim nations from which the terrorists were recruited; when, as I have pointed out, the Israeli airforce mistakenly struck a UN observation post in south Lebanon, causing four fatalities, Annan immediately claimed that the attack was "apparently deliberate" and Israel was tarred and feathered in the international press. In this frame of reference, one should not be perplexed at the international consensus for a Palestinian state when those who have a far more straightforward claim to independent statehood, such as the Tibetans or the Iraqi Kurds, are ignored by the rest of the world. Terrorism, it seems, works.

3

Conor Cruise O'Brien has argued in *The Siege: The Saga of Israel and Zionism*, that Arabs would never be anti-Zionist; in real-world terms, he was dead wrong. Certainly, there is no antisemitism in the etymological or commensal sense in the political labyrinth known as the Middle East—how could there be between Ishmael and Isaac, neither of them eaters of pork? Yet Islam has imported the hate literature of the Christian world into its cultural bibliography (in the same way as Western-educated Muslim thinkers of a revolutionary stamp drew their seminal paradigms of collective identity structures from Fichte and Marx), thus becoming a natural ally of the Christian *Weltanschauung* and targeting a blurred, polysemous identity as if it were a unified concept. The new and distinctive alliance between the Arab and European strains of Jew-hating was formed and cemented rather earlier than the present time, if one remembers the British-appointed Mufti Haj Amin al-Husseini's politically active sojourn in Hitler's Berlin from where he contributed to the Axis war effort and pursued his deadly antisemitic program in furthering Hitler's *Endlösung*, or "final solution" by organizing three SS units, the Muslim Hanjar division, the Skanderbeg brigade of Croats and Muslims who collaborated with the infamous Ustashi militia, and the Kama division of Albanian Muslims; or Johann von Leers, Goebbels' partner in crime, receiving asylum in Egypt during the 1950s and churning out anti-Jewish propaganda for Nasser. Indeed, Muslim writers regularly repine that Hitler failed to complete the job of extermination, the only blot on his record. Whenever the unholy pact was sealed, it is real people regardless of their pedigree, not historical abstractions or a "Zionist entity"—or what the powerful Iranian cleric Ayatollah Hashemi Rafsanjani calls "extraneous matter"—who suffer and die.

It seems obvious to me that antisemitism is encoded ineradicably in the DNA of Christianity—I sometimes suspect there may be something like an antisemitism gene at work here—dating from the time of the gospel of St. John and the early church fathers to the present. The patristic writings alone are enough to turn one's hair, from the vile spewings of the patron saint of preachers John Chrysostom in his *Homilies Against the Jews* (Jews are "lustful, rapacious, greedy, perfidious...inveterate murderers, destroyers, men possessed by the devil... impure and impious," etc.) to the rantings of St. Jerome to the scourgings of St. Augustine and beyond. There was certainly no spirit of Reformation in Martin Luther's "little book," *On the Jews and their Lies*, in which he warns his readers "to be on guard against the Jews, knowing that wherever they have their synagogues, nothing is found but a den of devils," encourages them to "drive out the Jews like mad dogs," laments this "great vermin of human ordinances," and confesses that "We are at fault for not slaying them." (For a pictorial illustration of this attitude, shocking in its vividness, one need only glance at Hieronymus Bosch's *Christ Carrying the Cross*: apart from the noble visages of the Christ and the Virgin, Luther's contemporary left no doubt, in his jostling montage of twisted and vulpine faces, as to who were the Jews.) The chronicle of merciless inhumanity, of forced conversions, expulsions, and massacres of Jews by Christians throughout the ages is unrelieved and almost beyond the limits of historical credence. That such vindictiveness should continue, however mitigated, in this enlightened era only reveals how deep the unreconstructed bestiality of Christian and post-Christian Europe runs. This bent of mind is handily summarized in one of our great literary documents, Chaucer's *Canterbury Tales*, in which "The Prioress's Tale" still makes for edifying reading—the Christian anthem of hatred is always accompanied by the strains of *O Alma Redemptoris*, symbolizing the righteousness of the oppressor. The sentiment persists, if somewhat etiolated, into the modern world, as in the Anglo-Catholic T. S. Eliot's defamatory verses:

> *The rats are underneath the piles.*
> *The Jew is underneath the lot.*
> *Money in furs.*

Indeed, the secular West retains the Christian historical outlook, its world-view structured by the Church's eschatological preoccupations. This is especially the case with regard to the antisemitic Left which, with its reservoir of millenarian passions and its salvific vision of the heavenly city on earth, has coagulated into a profane Church promulgating its hatred of the hindering Jew in the form of a poisonous anti-Israelism. Western agnostics who reject or deprecate the Christian faith are themselves driven by the same primordial complex of resentments and ideals: the commutation of sins, the end of history, the society of the redeemed, the selective turning of the other cheek, the loathing of the Jew—sentiments transposed from the theological kingdom to the sociopolitical arena. The *entente* between the two sides continues to hold in the general atmospherics of the time. Just as the laic West has sanctified its Chomskys and Finkelsteins, its two Tariqs (Ramadan and Ali), and many others of like persuasion, it is no coincidence that the late Pope, Karol Wojtyla, beatified a corps of saintly antisemites such as Anna Katerina Emmenek, who perpetuated the blood libel myth and whose visions allegedly influenced the screenplay of Mel Gibson's *The Passion of the Christ*; Josemaria Escriva de Balaguer, who claimed that Hitler had been misrepresented since he could not have killed more than 4 million Jews, *at most*; Maximillian Kolbe, who promoted the *Protocols of the Elders of Zion*; Alojzjie Stepinac, archbishop of Zagreb, who supported the pro-Nazi puppet regime in Croatia; and Pope Pius IX, who confined Rome's Jews to the ghetto and forbade them to own property, teach in schools, or receive medical care, dismissing them as "dogs." One is tempted to propose that the Church take a *desanctification* process under advisement, placing Heaven off limits to those who have no right to be there—and revoking the credentials of some who have already been canonized. More realistically, in the course of time the new Pope may perhaps revise the beatification schedule, but the Catholic Church has yet to come to terms with its barbaric past and with its failure to adequately confront the Holocaust, both while the genocide was happening and in the Church's later assessments of its position. The much-publicized Vatican II Council was little more than a preface to a new text that has yet to be written. (Two subsequent ecclesiastical documents, *We Remember: A Reflection on the Shoah* and *Memory and Reconciliation*, acquitted the Church of wrongdoing, placing blame only on individual sinners.) What all such people who are given to commuting the past and compromising the future, whether they be eminent or laic, practicing or nominal, fail to recognize is that those who harbour antisemitic sentiments participate retroactively in the Holocaust or in the causes and events that led up to it. They are genocidal murderers by association, after the fact accomplices. Antisemitism is not just another whimsical attitude or social predisposition that is innocent of consequences. The antisemite has stamped himself in his very personhood. As Sartre has written in *Anti-Semite and Jew*, "In espousing anti-Semitism, he chooses himself as a person." More, he chooses hatred and falsehood as determinants of his being. Even armchair antisemites are implicated in a racial bloodletting that has gone on for millennia and continues into the modern world. There is no evading the austerity of this logic just as there can be no forgiveness for their self-justification, blasé thoughtlessness, or instinctual revulsion. Nor is ignorance a ticket to absolution. A human being knows better.

In essence, religious sanction is at the basis of popular antisemitic feeling and practice and explains how the Jews became "the Jew." This is how a scattered and multifarious collection of outcasts became a single, monolithic abstraction ulcerating in the dark substratum of the Christian imagination. The handwriting is on the wall, or rather on the desecrated tombstone. Antisemitism was in approximate remission for the last thirty or forty years of the previous century; it is now in full swing again, just as it was in the 1930s. The reviving *Kristallnacht* atmosphere permeating the world today thus makes the survival of the Jewish nation absolutely necessary, even if we cannot settle on a proper definition of the Jew. The late Pope's condemnation of Operation Defensive Shield and the censure of Israel by a synod of Protestant bishops following the Israeli military reaction to the plague of suicide bombers were wholly in line with the millennial record of Christian prejudice. So was the call of the US Presbyterian Church for sanctions against Israel in its General Assembly of July 2004, and again in February 2005, approving by a large majority the selective divestment of holdings in multinational corporations doing business in the country and likening Israel's efforts to protect its citizens to the racist policy of apartheid. It thereby demonstrated that complex of ignorance, prejudice and mendacity associated with so many NGOs and Human Rights organizations around the globe, as well as a deep sympathy with the Islamic project. As Melanie Phillips writes in *Londonistan*, "The charge that Israel is an 'apartheid' society is of course one of the Big Lies propagated by the Muslim world"—a lie that has taken hold in the West. Undeterred by reason and good sense, the Presbyterian Church's

Mideast fact-finding delegation in October 2004 went so far as to meet with Hizbullah in south Lebanon, issuing words of praise for one of the world's most vicious terrorist organizations. "We treasure the precious words of Hezbollah," the Reverend Ronald Stone, a member of the church's Advisory Committee on Social Witness Policy, was quoted as saying on Hizbullah's Al-Manar satellite network.

The Episcopalian Church then followed suit, as did the Anglican Church's Consultative Council that joined the divestment campaign in June 2005, leading to the February 2006 divestment vote of its General Synod. And the fact that the United Church of Canada has only now acknowledged the right of Israel to exist is like opening the barn door some sixty years or so after the horse was supposed to be stabled—a little late to inspire confidence in the prescience or benevolence of this confession. At this time of writing, the United Church is considering an "ethical investment plan" to divest from companies involved in building Israel's security fence or providing "products, services or technology that sustain, support or maintain the occupation"—wilfully unaware that even the term "occupation" begs the question, or that it is giving practical and moral support to a terrorist government. The Reverend Lawrence Pushee, co-chair of the Toronto Conference of the United Church of Canada's Task Force on Ethical Investment in the Middle East, has accused Israel of "disproportionate responses to any and all provocations," refers to Hizbullah as a "*so-called* 'terrorist' organization" (italics mine), frets about the "gravest concern" felt by the "Arab world," denounces Israel for being "greedy in such a nasty and murderous way that we find ourselves very sympathetic to the Palestinian complaints," and regards, not Hizbullah, Hamas, al-Qaeda, Syria, or Iran but Israel as "a menace to peace in the Middle East." Is it the Stockholm syndrome at work in a weak-willed individual bonding with the terrorist or is it just another deep antisemite and worthy member of his denomination who has found a cause? The Church did amend its position in late August 2006, extending its boycott to businesses that do not recognize the state of Israel, but retained its original provisions against firms involved in supplying materials or know-how relating to the "occupation" and the construction of the security barrier. In the same month, the World Council of Churches, which represents Protestant, Anglican, Orthodox, and other churches and tandems the Roman Catholic Church, accused Israel of unleashing "a planned operation" to destroy Lebanon in the war of summer 2006, only waiting for an opportunity. Thus the Hizbullah incursion of July 12 in which eight Israeli soldiers were killed and two abducted and the massive rocket attack on Israel's northern border on July 13 were only an Israeli pretext to carry out its felonious agenda. The Council's spokesman, Jean-Arnold de Clermont, president of the Conference of European Churches, also let Hizbullah off the hook, suggesting that Israel did not wish to see a democratic Lebanon that would outshine its own polity and that "It is the Israeli-Palestinian conflict and not the role and actions of Hizbullah that is at the heart of the present crisis." Although, one would think, if Israel had planned the war long beforehand, it would surely have done a better job of it. The sole exception to this record of ignominy appears to be the communion of Evangelical Christians in the United States that has called for the abolition of the largely Arab-staffed UNRWA, noting, correctly, that "this agency is not dealing with an even hand," and, along with its Canadian chapters, proclaiming its general support of Israel. But this is clearly a minority view—and is itself based on messianic assumptions that involve the destruction of Israel as a preliminary to the Second Coming. With such friends....

In Europe especially, with its deeply inbred antisemitism, the abscess of hatred goes on suppurating—it is precisely this that the staple Palestinian strategy to delegitimize Israel trades upon. One hears again the abhorrent "Hep, Hep" cry (*Hierosolayme est perdita*), or a variant thereof in the media and political fora, that once heralded the marauding campaigns against the Jews in Crusader times. Firebombed synagogues, hate graffiti, mob beatings, tombstone daubings, abductions and murders, suspended arms shipments, unctuous editorials decrying "state terrorism," sanctimonious condemnations by leading government officials and social activist groups, and slanted reporting have become the order of the day. It is perhaps such yellow journalism that is most damaging to Israel, owing to the instantaneous, worldwide diffusion of the televisual image. Here, once more, the BBC is especially culpable, as in a particular "news" segment dealing with the aftermath of the fighting in Jenin. The camera zooms on a solitary Palestinian grandmother sitting in a wheelchair in the middle of a large, empty field littered with wheel-defying debris while commentator Orla Guerin rues her plight. The obvious question is how a wheelchair propelled by a frail, elderly woman across a field strewn with rubble could have gotten there in the first place, and why—it can only have been deliberately planted, like a theatrical prop carried in from the wings and set centre stage for the critical scene. The play might have been called *News from Jenin,* among the BBC's finest productions in its undeviating attempt to ostracize the Jewish state.

The European polls tell a similar story. An EU poll for November 2003 reported that approximately 60 per cent of Europeans considered Israel a greater menace to world peace than Iran or North Korea, showing once again how foolishness and spite, when assiduously cultivated by our political mandarins and the media, can lead, as it did in the 1930s and 1940s, to the vilification of an entire people. A British poll conducted shortly afterward identified not Ayatollah Khameini, not Osama bin Laden, not Kim Jong-il, all of whom are threatening to use, or condoning the use of, nuclear weapons, but President George Bush as the greatest hazard to world peace, at least giving Ariel Sharon a breather. A subsequent online British survey ranked Israel as the country least deserving of international respect, as the world's least beautiful country, and as one of the world's least democratic countries—wrong on all counts, but not surprising considering the obvious ignorance of the respondents and the fact that very few if any have ever visited Israel or a history book. Not to be outdone, the great majority of respondents to a French poll in November 2004 crowned Yasser Arafat as a "hero of the resistance"; it should come as no surprise that a number of French municipalities are considering naming streets and squares after the terrorist archon. A German survey conducted in December of the same year revealed that over 50 per cent of its respondents believed that Israel was carrying out a "war of extermination" against the Palestinians when the very opposite is the declared aim of the Palestinian terrorists and their supporters. More recently, in an effort to measure and understand the growing anti-Israeli and anti-Jewish attitude in England, a Eurobarometer poll held on January 27, 2005, showed that 45 per cent of Britons and 60 per cent of those under the age of 35 had never heard of Auschwitz—by all accounts the UK is rapidly overtaking France as the foremost antisemitic country in Europe. Between fickle Gaul and perfidious Albion, what is there to choose? (Recent studies, though, have identified Spain as the most antisemitic country in Europe.) It is therefore to be expected that the

British public as well as its senior politicians protest an American transport plane with arms for Israel landing at Gatwick for refuelling, yet remain silent when the British Department of Trade and Industry issues export licences to companies shipping dirty bomb components to Iran. What is perhaps most dismaying is that the ignorance that underlies the anti-Israeli and anti-Jewish bias is so extensive and mycelial that it can only be unconsciously determined. And it is very hard to educate the unconscious.

As Bat Ye'or, author of several books on Western/Islamic relations, has brought to our attention in an article in *FrontPage Magazine* for July 27, 2004, the Venice Declaration of 1980, signed by the members of the European Community under the promptings of France, "adopted Pan-Arab conditions regarding Israel *without qualification*," including the 1949 armistice lines as Israel's proper borders (which even the dovish Abba Eban dubbed the "Auschwitz borders"), the obligation to deal exclusively with Arafat, and the refusal to underwrite a separate peace with any Arab country for the resolution of the Palestinian problem. This permitted them to "justify their ahistorical designation of Judea and Samaria *as occupied Arab land*. Ultimately, the entire European effort to delegitimize and vilify Israel hinges upon this inaccurate, disingenuous formula." The various polls and surveys are merely a public reflection of this long-standing institutional bias.

Thus it makes more sense to say that the EU, which contributed massively to Yasser Arafat's war chest and private fortune while toadying electorally to its own Muslim populations, condemning Israel for acting to ensure its right to existence as per Article 51 of the UN Charter, and softening its stance toward terrorist states has itself become one of the greatest dangers confronting international stability. By refusing to declare Hizbullah a terrorist organization, for example, the EU allows its member countries to continue transferring funds to Hizbullah and to shelter its European assets, which leads not only to the renewed possibility of war in Lebanon, but also to further unrest in the "Palestinian territories"—major cash transfusions from Hizbullah to local terror networks have been well-documented. The conclusion of the EU's anti-fraud investigation that there was "no proof" EU aid was used to finance terrorism is only another typical effort to blanch the obvious. (The stunningly inane and self-exculpatory disclaimer issued by the EU's Office Européen de lutte antifraude, regarding its support of the Palestinian Authority reads in part, "Some of the [PA's] pratices of the past—such as the payment of salaries to convicted persons or the financial aid given to families of 'martyrs' as well as the Fatah contributions by PA staff are liable to be misunderstood and so lead to allegations that the PA is supporting terrorism.") Where, then, does the money come from to fund an army of hired gunmen who have no visible means of support and are not "productive members of society," drawing their income from the PA's tumescent payroll for doing no constructive work whatsoever? Fully one-third of the Palestinian population is dependent on salaries from the Palestinian Authority, perhaps the most bloated and parasitic governing administration in the world. Nor can there be the slightest doubt that the massive and illegal arms shipment intercepted on the *Karine A* on January 3, 2002, was financed by diverted international aid money, estimated to have been in excess of $100 million. The contributions from Saudi Arabia and Iran are well documented and redirected American support also plays an important part in stoking terrorist activities, but neither are sufficient in themselves to account for the lavish expenditure required to supply the teeming Palestinian militias with arms, logistics, sustenance, housing, and salaries—not to mention the sumptuous lifestyles and offshore deposits of the upper tiers of Palestinian officials who will doubtlessly find some way of retaining their lucrative pashalics. American aid, once substantial, has drastically diminished of late and Iranian resources have, until now, been steered mainly to Hizbullah and Syria. There is no denying European participation, indirect but immense, in bankrolling the terrorist enterprise as well as subsidizing the den of thieves and terror militias that control Palestinian affairs. Europe and the Palestinian Authority entered upon a marriage made in Brussels and consummated in Ramallah, spineless appeasement snuggling up to lusty aggression. Moreover, the EU turned a blind eye to Fatah corruption and in so doing contributed significantly to the rise of Hamas, the "party of purity," as a counterweight, though a large part of the latter's share of the booty went into the purchase and smuggling of arms and explosives and the training of terrorists. And we can be confident that money will continue to flow into Palestine, through one avenue or another, despite the threat to cut off funding indefinitely if Hamas does not rewrite its Covenant. Cracks will begin to widen in the West's—and especially Europe's—resolve to boycott Hamas, owing not least to the pressure mounted by NGOs wishing to safeguard their budgets and to the persistent claim that the Palestinian people should not be made to suffer for the policies of their government. Yet, as I have pointed out, if a populace elects a terrorist administration committed to promoting regional and international destabilization, it should, rationally speaking, be isolated and condemned rather than rewarded for its freely made choice. Otherwise we should not expect the political situation to change for the better but to deteriorate even further.

I would not hesitate to venture that the EU is perhaps the most perfidious of the rogue elements in our current political equation. Indeed, European complicity has always been the case. Anti-Zionists tend to forget that Israeli Zionism is the lineal product of European antisemitism. The Middle East embroilment is of European making in more ways than one, including the pernicious play of national interests and the colonial tracing of diagrammatic rhomboids across the area, which simplify the map while complicating the political terrain. But the real issue is Jew-hatred, nothing more or less. Zionism would never have gotten off the ground if Jews had not been the victims of cruel persecution throughout the ages and ultimately of genocide in the badlands of central and eastern Europe. It is clearly not fortuitous that the EU anti-racism body (the European Monitoring Centre on Racism and Xenophobia) initially quashed a report it commissioned from the Research Institute of Berlin Technical University in which it was found that European Muslims were implicated in the alarming rise of antisemitism on the continent. The findings were considered politically incorrect by the reigning Eurocrats and were ultimately medicated to read when the report was released on March 31, 2004, "The largest group of the perpetrators of anti-semitic activities appears to be young, disaffected white Europeans." This evident distortion was partially finessed by yet another distortion authored by a parliamentary committee struck by the British government to study the rise of anti-semitism in the country. Reporting on September 6, 2006, the All-Party Parliamentary Enquiry into Anti-Semitism laid the blame for inciting hatred against Jews on a "minority of Islamic extremists," ignoring the harmful effect of the BBC, the left-wing newspapers, and prominent political figures on pervasive popular sentiment, and downplaying its own findings that detected a *threefold increase* in antisemitic acts and incidents of hate speech. In the wake of renewed terrorist activity on

British soil, it has become tentatively acceptable to acknowledge the Muslim fact—but only with reference to a convenient "minority." Both the larger Muslim community and the British public are absolved. One way or another, the travesty persists. As Denis Boyles, writing in *National Review Online*, puts it, "nihilism, anti-Semitism, and anti-Americanism are the three knee-jerk, irrational sentiments...that inform the modern intellectual life of Europe"—isms that he described as "cockroaches" for their survivability.

The Jews, however, are guilty of a far more serious charge, namely, of their blamelessness, which is another way of saying that they are held collectively responsible for Europe's demonization of itself and the unsettling knowledge of its own visceral culpability. As poet and political balladeer Wolf Biermann said in *Der Spiegel*, the twilit continent of Europe cannot forgive the Jews for what it did to them. As the old joke has it, the great Jewish crime is Auschwitz. The British, too, are answerable, from the time of their heinous betrayal of the League of Nations Mandate beginning in the 1920s and continuing until Israel achieved statehood in 1948 (and even afterward, when the British saw to the arming of the Arab militias) to this very point in time in which incitement-mosques are permitted to flourish and recruit in the very heart of London, Birmingham, and Manchester. And since Europe has gradually allowed itself to become Islamicized through a porous immigration process and a relativist approach to multiculturalism—the latter entraining a calamitous sellout of the best part of its own Enlightenment heritage—we can only expect the situation to deteriorate despite whatever half-hearted attempts at retrenchment might one day be undertaken. Europe's decline seems to have coincided as well with its continent-wide purge of the Jewish people, a significant number of the survivors emigrating to Israel and America and, of course, bringing their scientific, literary, scholarly, and entrepreneurial talents with them to the benefit of their new homes. It is a scenario that resembles—though of far greater magnitude—France's murderous campaign against the Huguenots in the seventeenth century, which led to most of the members of this industrious Protestant sect fleeing to England and Holland and so depriving France of their skills and aptitudes in the arts and crafts, science, commerce and the professions. The Revocation of the Edict of Nantes was a disaster for France and its subsequent economic decline has been reliably correlated with the loss of so integral and dynamic a part of its people. An analogous correlation may hold as well, in both the practical and intellectual domains, between contemporary Europe and the annihilation and dispersal of its Jewish population. Europe never seems to learn.

And because this is so, as the current rise in antisemitic sentiment and actions renders indisputable, Israel has become a civil imperative and remains a potential refuge for European Jews, specifically those who make their home in France and probably the United Kingdom as well. Consequently what the late Daniel Bernard, the French ambassador to Great Britain, called not long ago "a shitty little country"—conveniently ignoring the corrupt, authoritarian, and fanatical Islamic regimes lined up against the object of his spite as well as the history of European blood guilt and the vile record of Vichy France—must command our loyalty no matter how far Israel may fall from a condition of otherworldly perfection.[11] In expressing his anti-Israeli and anti-Jewish sentiments, the quintessentially French Bernard should perhaps have recalled that the ragtag Jewish uprising in the Warsaw ghetto held the German army at bay longer than the entire nation of France did.

As for Israel, we might acknowledge, as Bernard did not, that this "shitty little country" has to date produced eight Nobel Laureates (and will continue to churn them out in the coming years). This is the same country that is at the cutting edge of international medical technology, now developing among many other breakthroughs the "molecular computer" designed to detect and treat cancer at the level of the individual cell. In September 2004 two Israeli scientists were selected by the *Technology Review* of MIT as among the "Top Young Innovators" in the world in biotechnology, medicine, computing, and nanotechnology. In October of the same year, Ehud Shapiro of the Weizmann Institute received the World Technology Award for Biotechnology for his work in biomolecular computing. Also in October, Israelis Aaron Ciechanover and Avram Hersko shared the 2004 Nobel Prize in Chemistry (along with American Irwin Rose, another Jew) for their work in discovering cellular processes regulating protein degradation. In 2005 Robert Aumann shared the Nobel Prize in Economic Sciences for his work in game-theory analysis. Israeli medical researchers working in the area of molecular psychiatry have recently discovered the biomarkers (or "microarrays") that function as the signature of imminent PTSD (post-traumatic stress disorder) and are developing focused screening techniques to treat the problem before it arises. Research on D-cure (the effort to cure diabetes) is well advanced. The Technion-Israel Institute of Technology is currently breaking new ground in nanotechnology applications. In the discipline of cosmology, another Israeli, Weizmann Institute physicist Mordechai Milgrom, has developed the equations for Modified Newtonian Dynamics to account for the strange rotational behaviour of the outermost galactic stars. It was Ben Gurion University physicist David Eichler who, in a 2002 article for the *Monthly Notices of the Royal Astronomical Society*, analyzed the nature of magnetars and predicted the "giant flare" eruption of the exotic neutron star SGR 1806–20, first recorded on December 27, 2004, and still being registered by radio telescopes around the world. Israel is also an important partner in world computer technology; its Intel development centre in Haifa, having just produced an upgraded version of the Centrino chipset, is now working on the more advanced WiMax standard for wireless Internet. The Hebrew University of Jerusalem's Interdisciplinary Center for Neural Computation has come to be recognized as one of the world's primary research centres in the field of brain science. Scientists working at the same university have discovered that locusts are actuated by polarization vision that enables them to distinguish between land and sea; the application of this knowledge will lead to techniques of diversion, an inestimable boon not only to Israel but to the whole Middle East. Israeli cardiologists at the Rabin Medical Center are currently experimenting with a new heart-surgery technique aimed at creating oxygen-carrying blood vessels through gene injection, a radical innovation in the fields of genetic engineering and catheterization. Arnold Goldman's Luz International company, which builds solar electrical generating systems (SEGSs), has made Israel a world leader in solar-field construction as an alternative energy source. The list goes on. The entire international community is the beneficiary of such Israeli research results and discoveries, including the Arab world and Israel's Western detractors. All this makes it pertinent to ask a question that is generally avoided: is there a single Muslim country where anything remotely comparable is even thinkable? And, to ask a second, equally embarrassing question: can anyone seriously doubt that there is probably more innovative brilliance *pro rata*, so to speak, in tiny Israel than in any other country in the world?

Nevertheless, the anti-Israeli contagion is spreading across the Mediterranean and the Atlantic like a credal form of the West Nile virus. Not only are pro-Israeli lecturers regularly prevented or discouraged from speaking either through violent demonstrations or what is widely known as "the heckler's veto," agitation for political, scholarly, and commercial "divestment" from Israel has begun on the campuses of forty American universities, echoing the renewed Arab boycott of Israel and of companies doing business with it. A consortium of professors from the University of Toronto (and now other Canadian universities as well) also jumped on the bandwagon, circulating anti-Israeli petitions and manifestos—the contemporary intelligentsia's backward version of *Schindler's List*. And yet, I would be prepared to offer substantial odds that all these groups and institutions eager to divest from Israeli corporations, research centres and universities would be quite unwilling to dispense with the manifest benefits, scientific and medical, that flow from them. I doubt very much that the members of these organizations, finding themselves under medical duress, would be willing to extend their boycott to Israeli medicines and surgical procedures that might help them recover. At the same time, no university, or any other institution, has called for divestment from the world's truly despicable regimes: from China, from Egypt, from Russia, from Saudi Arabia, from Nigeria, from the Sudan, to name only a few. But that is the way with whited sepulchres.

As a small but growing number of people have begun to realize with dismay, our centres of higher learning, chiefly in the humanities, have become sinks of iniquity, bunkers of shoddy scholarship, bad faith, elided history, privileged ignorance, and warped political activism. A climate of thinking has come to prevail that makes it virtually impossible to teach or act outside the dominant ideological construct. This is true equally of minor hubs like the University of Waterloo, which has refused to discipline one its professors, Mohamed Elmasry, president of the Canadian Islamic Congress, for his inflammatory remarks favouring suicide bombings in Israel, and Concordia University in Montreal, which, with its 6,000-strong, riot-prone Arab student body, its pro-Palestinian internal politics, and its pusillanimous administration, is now popularly known as Gaza U (though the appellation may be plausibly contested by Toronto's York University); or of major institutions like Columbia,[12] a hotbed of doctrinaire Arabism and systemic anti-

Zionism, and the University of California at Berkeley, where campus notables like Judith Butler zealously distribute anti-Israeli agitprop and well-known authors like Irish poet Tom Paulin, notorious for urging that Jews in Samaria and Judea "be shot dead," feature as invited speakers. Duke University has also shown its colours, hosting in the name of "free speech" a Palestine Solidarity Movement conference that calls for divestment from Israel and the "right of return" while declining to condemn Palestinian suicide bombings. Not content to leave the anti-Israeli brief to the independent misjudgment of its professional staff, the University of Toronto organized an anti-Zionist hatefest, beginning February 1, 2005, under the insulting heading of "Israel Apartheid Week" and so adding to the dubious lustre of the university's reputation. The syndrome has convected in many if not most Postcolonial and Middle East studies programs across the continent, subaltern disciplines that are rarely neutral or impartial or driven by the imperatives of authentic scholarship. Their practitioners started off as *engagé* and ended up as *enragé*, and continue to fulminate against a pluralistic and democratic Israel while fawning before a tyrannical and venal Islamic polity.

We go back across the Atlantic for the latest major manifestation of such contemptible politicking, where the Association of University Teachers in the United Kingdom (AUT) passed a motion on April 22, 2005 proposing the boycott of two Israeli universities, without allowing those opposed to the motion to speak in the assembly—this is how the notions of diversity, openness, and pluralism are understood in Western academia—and without presenting the dissenting argument for the universities under attack, Haifa and Bar Ilan. (It is just another in a series of mordant ironies that the first teachers' cooperative in the world, which provided the model for later pedagogical organizations like AUT, was formed in Israel in 1903.) While the Israeli universities can boast of substantial Muslim student bodies and a hospitality to many different points of view, some of these bordering on sedition, none of the Arab universities across the Muslim world, crawling with security forces and intelligence personnel, was censured for suppressing academic freedom and enforcing political acquiescence. In fact, the text of the AUT resolution reflected the materials disseminated by various Palestinian organizations as well as the Electronic Intifada website. According to various reports, a leading proponent of the motion, speaker Sue Blackwell, draped herself in a Palestinian flag in the company of kaffiyeh-clad activists from the Palestine Solidarity Campaign distributing incendiary anti-Zionist leaflets. She then read a supporting message from the fiercely anti-Israeli revisionist historian Ilan Pappe, confirming the suspicion that what we are seeing is an especially virulent strain of academic lunacy hybridized with a highly infectious variety of antisemitism. When Blackwell bewails "centuries of oppression" of Palestinians, she is either evading the truth, whitewashing the real oppression suffered by the people at the hands of their own landlords, officials, and homegrown despots, or revealing an ignorance of Middle East affairs so prodigious as to call her qualifications as an academic spokesperson into immediate question.

The AUT tucket against Israel was seconded shortly afterward at a London rally sponsored by the British Palestine Solidarity Campaign, in which Paul Mackney, president of Britain's National Association of Teachers and Lecturers in Further and Higher Education (NATFHE), revealed his complete ignorance of the Palestinian refugee question in blaming Israel without the slightest qualification for this historical misfortune. Another participant, Andrew Birgin, went one better: "When there is real democracy, there will be no more Israel." The immitigable Sue Blackwell was also present, warning her "comrades" of the "backlash being promoted by a well-organized, well-funded pro-Israeli lobby," a variant of the standard anti-Jewish libel of press domination and economic and political control. Although AUT was ultimately forced to overturn its boycott decision as a result of sustained pressure mounted by a group of courageous professors and students, it retains considerable support in the academic community. Its advocates will continue to agitate under the banner of academic freedom, arguing, as we might expect, that resistance to their tactics and their ideology is a wanton attempt to stifle pluralism of ideas and freedom of expression, and that such opposition is nothing short of a witch hunt. Naturally, this does not prevent them from trying to stamp out the expression of views uncongenial to their own convictions—pluralism works only one way, apparently. Academic antisemitism will persist in the guise of scholarly disinterestedness, freedom of expression and political liberalism, and the influential corps of "academic skinheads" will go on marching, protesting, releasing petitions and manifestos, and organizing conferences until the scholarly world comes to its senses, if ever. In the meantime, anti-Israeli motions will certainly recur, focusing on Palestine's right to exist but refusing to affirm an equivalent right for Israel. A subsequent example of this surrender of both principle and common sense was provided by Oxford University in February 2006 in the form of Israeli Apartheid Week, hosted by the Palestinian Society and constructed around the theme of "apartheid and Zionism, divestment and resistance." And in May 2006, NATFHE carried a boycott motion similar to the original AUT resolution. The decision was rescinded several days later owing to NAFTHE's merger with its sister union and the threat of legal action, but the boycott and disinvestment obsession, whether active or dormant, continues to obtain throughout academia, as it does in churches and trade unions around the world. The latest contribution to the fray arises predictably in Ireland, where sixty-one academics sent a letter to the *Irish Times* in September 2006 urging the EU to cut ties with Israeli universities as well as targeting individual faculty members from Israel.

Another such attempt to block Israeli participation in the cultural and intellectual worlds comes from a group of British architects calling themselves Architects and Planners for Justice in Palestine (APJP), who mounted a petition to exclude Israeli architects from the Biennale Architettura exhibition in Venice in November 2006. Citing the "Palestinian tragedy of displacement and dispossession" in the war of 1948 and the continuing "destruction of their heritage," their mission statement demands the withdrawal of the Israeli entry, a collection of fifteen memorial structures titled "Life Saver: Typology of Commemoration in Israel." As with their academic peers, this parcel of architects shows absolutely no knowledge of the historical factors at work in the 1948 conflict or of the profound complexities that determine the nature of the current situation. Their brief is an expression of ignorance and prejudice and is no more than a simplification of the historical record meant to vindicate the most rudimentary forms of bias and hatred. It is painful but not surprising to learn that Israeli architect Tula Amir and her Jewish-British colleague Abe Hayeen are among the organizers of the British petition. Amir's explanation for their common stance is that the Israeli contribution justifies "Israel's wars [and] provides legitimation of the blood that has been spilled"— not, of course, Israeli blood. One can always count on a cenacle of Jewish intellectuals to collaborate with their enemies.

When they are not calling for the boycotting, disestablishment, or destruction of Israel, one of the central appeals of the liberal professoriate and of the left intelligentsia in general is to UN Resolution 242, often cited by anti-Zionists, as requiring the withdrawal of Israel's armed forces from "occupied territories." But among the various articles of the resolution, one in particular is pivotal, stipulating: "*Termination of all claims or states of belligerency and respect for and acknowledgment of the sovereignty, territorial integrity and political independence of every state in the area and their right to live in peace within secure and recognized boundaries free from threats or acts of force.*" In fact, Israel accepted the principles of Resolution 242—which specifies withdrawal to *secure* boundaries and not from *all* the captured territories—and the Palestinians did not. Very few people seem to know this, not even qualified diplomats engaged on affairs of state. This is not a question of interpretation, but is historically verifiable, as corroborated by the Palestinian National Charter, adopted in response to the resolution, which categorically denied Israel's right to exist. (Article 20 of the PLO Covenant also denies the Jewish historical relationship to the Holy Land.) Despite the media clamour and the arguments of the specialists, it is not the Israelis but the Palestinians who are in default of Resolution 242. Article (1a), specifying withdrawal, cannot be implemented if Article (1b) requiring recognition of borders and territorial security, is not accepted as well. If a treaty is not, as in civil law, *synallagmatic*, or reciprocally binding, then it is entirely perfunctory and inapplicable. Israel has proclaimed itself willing to recognize a Palestinian state, but the Palestinians have shown no serious intention of reciprocating. In addition, as legal expert Eugene V. Rostow, writing in the *American Journal of International Law*, explains in his discussion of 242, Israel was "certified by the Security Council" to remain in the captured territories and "would not be required to withdraw without a prior agreement of peace."

Similarly, Article 11 of UN Resolution 194, which stipulates that "refugees wishing to return to their homes and live at peace with their neighbours should be permitted to do so at the earliest practicable date, and that compensation should be paid for the property of those choosing not to return...," is often cited by the Palestinians and their sympathizers to reinforce their claims. But this resolution is not legally binding, does not use the word "Palestinian," and could apply equally to roughly the same number of Jews displaced from their homes in Arab countries, a fact that is never mentioned. Further, the resolution was adopted in 1948, before the Palestinian refugee count had swelled into the millions (as have, for that matter, the descendants of the Jewish refugees that Israel absorbed). It behooves us once again to remember that the Arabs and the Palestinians have refused to accept a two-state solution on four separate occasions: 1937 (the Peel Commission), 1947 (the UN partition proposal), 1967 (Resolution 242), and 2000/2001 (Camp David and Taba). Bill Clinton's last-ditch bridge proposals were also rejected by the Palestinian side of the table. As mentioned previously, the idea that the Palestinian authorities are genuinely interested in a two-state solution to the interminable conflict over rights and territory is another Western delusion. Hamas has rejected the proposal outright and Fatah was willing to enter negotiations—though without making any serious concessions—only as a prelude to the eventual conquest, in Arafat's own words, "of all of Palestine." The extent to which Fatah can be trusted post-Arafat is an open can of worms. Many writers point to the existence of Palestinian intellectuals, described as "moderates" or "pragmatists," who would be amenable to compromise. But for the time being they represent only a small sector of the Palestinian mainstream, are essentially powerless, and might be expected, when push comes to shove, to drive a far harder bargain than their champions are currently willing to contemplate. Indeed, "prominent intellectuals," as they are styled in newspaper reports, generally sided with Hizbullah and condemned those Western leaders who supported Israel in the summer 2006 war. When Alan Dershowitz, in *The Case for Peace: How the Arab-Israeli Conflict Can Be Resolved*, writes that an "important change…now seems to be occurring within some elements of the Palestinian Authority," elements that "do not see support for reasonable Palestinian aspirations as inconsistent with support for reasonable Israeli aspirations," I suspect we must be looking at two different Palestines. Or perhaps they are one and the same "entity" emitting different sets of signals. The question then becomes, Which set of signals is deceptive and which more in tune with reality?

Further aggravating the issue is the question of the border demarcations that are supposed to be reinstated. Aside from the fact that pre-1967 borders to which the Arab world and much of the international community is committed are not realistically viable and scarcely defensible, the bald truth is that *there are no pre-existent, officially recognized pre-1967 borders, only armistice lines reflecting the reality of the end-of-war situation in 1949*—and even these were not graven in treaty-stone. Clause 5(2) of the Rhodes Armistice Agreement specifies that, "In no sense are the ceasefire lines to be interpreted as political or territorial borders" and that they do not affect "the final disposition of the Palestine question." (These boundaries, known as the Armistice Demarcation Line, or Green Line, remain contested by both Israel and the invading Arab countries.) Indeed, a segment of territory on the Israeli side of the frontier, designated by the Armistice Agreement as a demilitarized zone, was illegally controlled by Syria. Current negotiations in whatever phase they happen to malinger are, as usual, negligently severed from the larger historical background. Between 1967 and 1994 when Arafat returned from Tunis under the auspices of the Oslo Accords, there was no internationally recognized legal entity in place to consult with in order to oversee and legitimize an Israeli withdrawal from the West Bank—the Madrid Conference of 1991 was in this respect an open sham with an interim Palestinian delegation, attached to the Jordanian delegation, being openly coached on site by uninvited PLO operatives—and Arafat soon proved himself an untrustworthy partner with a wholly different agenda of his own. The term "occupation" in its *current* application is itself misleading, a media red herring, since, from 1996 until well into the second intifada, 90 per cent of the Palestinian population did not live under Israeli "occupation" but under the Palestinian Authority. Facile and popular accounts like Richard Ben Cramer's *How Israel Lost: The Four Questions* must be taken *cum grano* since they shrink from placing the "occupation" fairly in the larger ecosystem of Arab and Palestinian militant hostility—Israel would certainly have preferred to have avoided the 1967 and 1973 wars and the constant threat of invasion or incursion that provoked precisely that misfortune for which Cramer and his kind take Israel to task.

Melanie Phillips rightly points out that "Israel's occupation of the West Bank and Gaza was legal because it was an action taken in self-defence against combatants who have never stopped waging war against it." Similarly, Michael I. Krauss and J. Peter Pham, in an article for *Commentary* (July-August 2006), have shown indisputably that the West Bank cannot be described as "occupied." "The British withdrawal from the territory of the Mandate resulted in a lapse or vacancy of internationally recognized sovereignty. The West Bank was, in legal jargon, *res nullius*: a thing belonging to no state." In other words, neither Jordan (which acquired the West Bank through armed aggression) nor the UN, and obviously not Turkey as the residue of the dismembered Ottoman empire, could later lay legitimate claim to the area. "In such a case," the authors continue, "sovereignty in international law may be acquired by any state in a position to assert effective and stable control without resort to unlawful means...." Since self-defence is a *legal* entitlement, Israel's defensive wars of 1967 and 1973 fulfilled precisely these internationally recognized conditions. Therefore, the notion "that Israel's presence in the territory constitutes an 'occupation' is utterly specious." These distinctions, esoteric as they may appear, are not instances of mere quibbling, paper embroidery or political nit-picking but have the full force of international law behind them and confer legitimate sanction on the Israeli presence in the territories. Very few people are aware of the provisions of international law despite making a great fuss about its applicability. But even common knowledge seems to be absent. I have observed with some amazement that many people in the ordinary walks of life who routinely condemn the Israeli "occupation" have never heard of the Six Day and Yom Kippur wars. Most are completely lacking in background information on which to base a rational political judgment. Many are not aware that, in the scoria of a repelled invasion, Israel found itself with a piece of Jordan that, as I have reiterated, Jordan subsequently wanted nothing to do with. No one seems to realize that Yasser Arafat violated every one of his Oslo pledges, including ending anti-Israel incitement, preventing terrorism, and taking concrete steps toward peace. But leave it to the journalists and the pundits, whom one might expect to know better. As Shakespeare has it in *Henry IV, Part 2*, "these villains will make the word as odious as the word 'occupy,' which was an excellent good word before it was ill sorted."

Another central appeal is to the Oslo Declaration of Principles, but this is only one more tactic of dissimulation since Oslo and its proclaimed pacific spirit had been violated so often by the Palestinians in the last decade as to have become a dead letter. For one thing, Hamas never accepted the Oslo proceedings and continued its terrorist activities unabated. For another, under the Islamic law of *Hudaibiyya*, referring to the treaty with the Quraish of Mecca abrogated by Mohammed,

Muslims are permitted to break agreements with non-Muslims, which puts in question Arafat's recognition of Israel in a letter of September 9, 1993. (Though it is important to note that for Arafat, as for every Palestinian and Arab potentate, recognition is only *de facto* and does not imply Israel's *right to the land* on which it has built its state; similarly, Iran has recognized Israel's right to exist, but not in the Holy Land—Alaska is the recommended site.) That Muslim jurists generally stipulate ten years as the maximum period of validity for pacts concluded with non-believers does not reassure. In the Islamic scriptures, treaties are only a means to ultimate victory and can be violated on a technicality when the moment is judged to be propitious. Sura 16:106 also comes into play here, articulating the concept of *taqiyya*, that is, false recantation, doublespeak, or dissimulation, provided one's "heart remains firm in the Faith"—a principle that has been freely interpreted and applied over the course of time with theological brevet. As the Prophet proclaimed in a celebrated *hadith*, "War is deceit," and instances of the broken word abound in the history of Muslim conquest, entrenching the pattern of Islamic dissimulation. Sura 8:59 reads, "If you fear treachery from any of your allies, you may retaliate by breaking off your treaty with them." But it is very easy to "fear treachery" when it becomes convenient to do so under the sway of your own ulterior aims. Another pledge made by Arafat in the same letter, the renunciation of terrorism, was cancelled less than three months later in a leaflet distributed by Arafat's Fatah movement, in which is written: "Reteach the enemy the lesson of the intifada," and Arafat's signing of a Cairo accord with Hamas in November of 1994, put paid to the entire process at its very inception. As well, Farouk Qaddumi, head of the PLO's Political Department, in a speech reported by Reuters on August 10, 1994 when Oslo was just getting underway, promised that, "The intifada will continue." Similarly, PA minister Faisal Husseini, in an interview with the Egyptian daily *Al-Arabi* on June 24, 2001, declared that the "entire land is an Islamic *waqf*" [estate, religious endowment] and referred to the Oslo Accords as a "Trojan Horse" and a "temporary procedure" in the larger "strategic" plan to destroy Israel. Arafat's real purpose was confirmed by Abdel Bari Atwan, editor of the *Al Quds* newspaper, who told the *Jerusalem Post* on November 20, 2004, that Arafat, intent on pursuing his program of "slices," had assured him that "The day will come when you will see thousands of Jews fleeing Palestine...The Oslo

Accords will help bring this about." The Palestinian dictator in his strategy of "slices" or "plan of phases" was following Tunisian president Habib Bourguiba's advice that Israel could not be erased in a frontal attack but only by bits and pieces, a plan that echoed the sermonizing of Mohammed Heikal, editor of the Egyptian newspaper *Al Ahram*, who, writing on February 25, 1971, scolded the Arabs for putting the final step before the intermediate one, that is, for aiming at "the elimination of the State of Israel itself" before effacing the traces of the Israeli military victories. Adapting method to circumstance, Arafat, a relative of the infamous Grand Mufti of Jerusalem, Haj Amin al-Husseini, merely updated the policy of Muftism into the present day. "Nothing but the sword," swore al-Husseini, "will decide the future of this country." Only, the Palestinian sword was no longer wielded to kill with a single thrust but by gradual dismemberment.

Even during the conciliatory Labour governments of Rabin, Peres, and Barak, which were willing to engage in extensive and liberal arbitration, Palestinian terrorists continued to account for Israeli civilian fatalities, often using the same weapons *that Israel had distributed among them* in its rearming of the PA police force—a move that is being repeated today as Israel collaborates in the arming of Mahmoud Abbas's Fatah. Palestinians, after all, wrote the book on terrorism. According to reports, in the year following the famous Rabin-Arafat handshake before a smiling Bill Clinton, ten separate suicide bombings claimed 125 Israeli lives. In point of fact, during the euphemistically named "peace process" between 1994 and the September 2000 terror war, several hundred Israelis lost their lives to Palestinian violence. That figure has since escalated dramatically. (One always seems to shrug off the ballooning numbers of the attendant wounded as well as the families who must live with their losses, uncountable lives blighted or destroyed.)[13]

It should be ascertainable to all that the PLO was (and is) not a genuine nationalist movement, but an organization specifically devoted to the elimination of Israel. David Pryce-Jones has shown unambiguously that it is actually "a strictly careerist grouping around a few ambitious personalities [and] an amalgamation of mercenary retinues," who have combined hatred of Israel with self-serving power politics. The title of a book by the PLO's first, Egyptian-appointed "president," Asad Shuquair, *Liberation—Not Negotiation*, tells us all we need to know. The

real Palestinian aim is not the *establishment* of Palestine but its hypothetical *liberation*, that is, the disappearance of Israel and its replacement by a Palestinian collectivity. The existence of Palestine as a state
is premised not on territorial compromise, as the road map presumes
and Western public opinion artlessly believes, but on Israel's eventual
demise, which is not a policy of state-making but of state-displacement.
This is the real reason that Arafat turned his back on Camp David,
which offered him the workable, independent state that a truly nationalist leader would have accepted or at the very least have made rational counterproposals to the offer. It is also the reason that Palestinian
peace overtures are not to be trusted. What Conor Cruise O'Brien says
of IRA tactics in *On the Eve of the Millennium* applies in equal or greater
measure to the Palestinians: "they will note how the word *peace* and the
hopes associated with it can be made to serve a terrorist cause. They
will note especially the artistry with which a conditional *suspension* of
violence can be made to supplement the violence itself and enhance its
effectiveness."

The road map in its original conception was always doomed to fail,
riddled and shredded by the Reality Principle and Palestinian double-
dealing. The international Left, however, is not deterred by such trifles
in its flagellation of Israel. Noam Chomsky, for example, in a speech
delivered at MIT in October 2001, had no compunction about blaming
Israel (and the US, of course) for allegedly "blocking a diplomatic settlement for 30 years now, still is"—this in the face of the well-known facts
about Arab uncompromisingness and Palestinian plotting available to
anyone who cares to look impartially at the events on the ground and
the data beginning to emerge from Palestinian statements of intent.[14]
Perhaps the most damaging such critique was the open letter circulated
by Nabil Amr, Arafat's former Minister of Parliamentary Affairs, in the
official PA newspaper, *al-Hayat al-Jadida*, in September 2002, accusing Arafat of provoking needless misery and setting back the cause of
Palestinian independence. (Amr was later shot for his impertinence,
suffering the amputation of a leg.)

But Palestinian mayhem is no longer exclusively an Israeli problem.
The New Saracens have now expanded their operations and joined al-
Qaeda and other terrorist conventicles, several of these jihadis having
been arrested in Brussels, Antwerp, and Milan, and more recently in
Baghdad, where they were among the foreign fighters involved in car

bombings of Iraqi civilians. The Palestinian/Israeli conflict is only one more front opened by international terror: CD-ROMs created and distributed by Hamas show Chechen and al-Qaeda fighters standing next to Hamas commanders. Indeed, it was a Palestinian scholar-jihadi, Abdullah Azzam, mentor and confidant to Osama bin Laden, who most recently articulated, in words as famous as they are macabre, the mission of contemporary Islam: "Jihad…is incumbent on all Muslims…until the Muslims recapture every place that was Islamic," including Palestine, the Philippines, parts of Africa and Central Asia, and al-Andalus (Spain). No cost is to be spared, as the reclaimed glory of Islam can only be built on a "lofty edifice [of] skulls." The method is carnage, for honour "cannot be established except on a foundation of cripples and corpses." The faith must be restored by violence to its ancient purity and hegemony—"Idolatry," asserts Koran 2: 218, "is worse than carnage." The oft-repeated intention of radical and fundamentalist Islam is to create a unified and rejuvenated Muslim Caliphate stretching along the great swath of territory from Uighur Xinjiang in China's north through the various Caucasian and mid-orient 'stans and down into the Middle East, with far-flung provinces in the Philippines and Indonesia and supplemented by the intended reconquest and annexation of designated European lands. The conflicts in Afghanistan, Iraq, and Palestine, cited by the majority of Western analysts as the cause of the current terrorist onslaught, are only pretexts for the implementation of a much larger strategic purpose. It is also disquieting to note that, according to Zacharia Zubeidi, head of the Aqsa Martyrs Brigades, al-Qaeda elements are presently working to "find a nesting place in the West Bank," and it is now known that an al-Qaeda terrorist cell, which has assumed the name of Jundallah (or, Allah's Brigades) is operating in the Gaza Strip, carrying out its first attack in the latter part of May 2005. Another al-Qaeda affiliate, the Usbat al-Ansar, operates out of south Lebanon and, as is well known, al-Zarqawi's al-Qaeda offshoot, the Tiwad and Jihad group (or Unification and Holy War) has settled in the Gaza Strip.

These facts, of course, have not restrained the international community from continuing to crosshair its Jews and to denounce the Israelis who are apparently bent on restoring a Greater Israel (*Eretz Israel ha-Shlema*) from Egypt to Iraq, another handy canard and, knowing what we know or should, another run-of-the-mill irony. Subscribing to this absurdity, Mahmoud Zahar insists that Israel should remove the two blue stripes from its flag, since in his view, the stripes signify Israel's borders "stretching from the River Euphrates to the River Nile." (The flag was designed to reflect a Jewish prayer shawl.) Similarly, Leon Wieseltier's reference in an article for the *New Republic* for January 23, 2006, to "the geographical dream of Jewish chauvinism" merely stands the issue on its head. What many commentators, political observers, and ordinary citizens have failed miserably to understand is that Israel's struggle is not about territory but about existence. They also do not see that Israel is the bridgehead proxy for Western democratic liberalism just as Hizbullah is the invasive proxy for an Iranian-style theocracy and Islamic/ Shi'ite imperial interests. Israel is fighting not only for its own survival but for the intellectual values and political traditions of the civilized West on the most volatile and perilous front today in the war against radical Islam. Those who routinely condemn Israel whenever it acts to defend itself against the terrorists in its midst and the terrorist regimes that surround it are—to speak as plainly as I can—either ignorant, bigoted, or intimidated. But whatever they are, they are also lemmings racing toward the precipice. Interestingly, prominent among these lemmings is Spain's socialist prime minister, Jose Luis Rodriguez Zapatero, who, during a rally in Alicante in July 2006 protesting the Israeli response to Hizbullah, accused Israel of using "abusive force" and, according to the Anti-Defamation League, posed for the camera wearing a kaffiyeh. In the light of the Islamist intention to recapture al-Andalus, it seems the task may already have been partially accomplished. Such Western jobbery is nothing less than political stupidity of the first order that in the course of time will find itself with much to regret when the bigger bombs start going off. Professing solidarity with their mortal enemy, Israel's detractors ought not to be astonished when some future surrogate for Hizbullah or Hamas comes loudly knocking at their own doors, as indeed they have already begun to do.

Here at home, many of us seem stone deaf. Among journalists, political figures (especially across the Left as well as in the *indépendentiste* sector of Quebec), letter-writers to the newspapers and common folk, the execrable "none is too many" syndrome of the MacKenzie King administration appears, *mutatis mutandis*, to be trembling on the verge of a comeback—certainly as regards Israel among the nations. The fact that very few of these mainspring schismatics have any first-hand knowledge of what is happening on the ground, seem blissfully unaware of the convoluted backdrop to the current impasse (including the historic presence of Jewish communicants in the region and the continued efforts at their suppression, expulsion, or extirpation), and who enjoy the safe, comfortable and liberal existences of which their newfound Islamic protégés would instantly despoil them if they could, appears not to have deterred our coddled Western gurus from pursuing so rebarbative a project. Perhaps the answer to the abstruse Koranic sura 101 is self-evident: "The Clatterer! What is the Clatterer? And what shall teach thee what is the Clatterer?"

Some of these Clatterers are out-and-out bigots; others are guilty of what political commentator George Jonas calls "pragmatic anti-Semitism," the trendy form of the pestilence taken on board by opportunistic politicos and fashionable highbrows, "just as it was in the 1930s." (Jonas comments only half-facetiously that, as antisemitism continues to grow, it may not be long before Jews are blamed for global warming.) Some are like Robert Lowell's "Serpent" in *History*, "changed from a feeble cosmopolite/to a fanatical antisemite" and others are "Chatham House" specialists who wish to influence public policy in the direction of an untutored form of gliberalism while concealing their antisemitic convictions from public scrutiny. Yet others primarily from the anti-globalist Left, influenced by the special pleading of Edward Said (and that of Said's intellectual predecessor, the Christian Arab George Antonius), have espoused the Arab cause as inherently virtuous and reasonable—these temple drums have been curiously silent of late on Arab League support for the genocidal Sudanese government.

Then there are the gullible victims of their own credulity, like *wunderkind* Naomi Klein who speaks plaintively, though not by name, of Rachel Corrie, "the 23-year-old 'human shield' whose young body was crushed by a[n Israeli] bulldozer in Gaza" where she was protesting the demolition of a terrorist's house. (Corrie, once photographed burning an American flag at a West Bank demonstration, is an apt dedicatee of Michael Moore's *Dude, Where's My Country?*, and is now the subject of a venomously anti-Israeli play co-written by *Guardian* editor Katherine Viner.) Klein (like Moore and Viner) fails to mention a number of countervailing factors, namely, that the operator of the bulldozer apparently did not see the young woman, that the International Solidarity Movement to which she belonged is funded by Hamas, and that terrorists have more than once taken sanctuary in its offices, including two Muslim suicide bombers from England posing as peace activists, one of whom soon earned his right to seventy celestial virgins by dispatching three terrestrial Israelis.[15] Rachel Corrie has become the antisemite's answer to Anne Frank, the new suffering heroine who, as the putative victim of the Jewish state, cancels out the Jewish claim to the world's sympathy and understanding. The fact that Corrie's death was both unintended and self-inflicted in the service of a dubious and ill-considered cause, and under circumstances that have been cleverly manipulated to appeal to the uninstructed "morality" of a credulous public, is a non-issue for the antisemitic Left and the anti-Israeli lobby of the Western chattering—or Clattering—classes.

Their response to the fate of Corrie's successor was equally "correct" and opportunistic. When, on August 10, 2006, twenty-four-year-old Angelo Frammartino was stabbed to death by a Palestinian Arab in East Jerusalem, the NGO he worked for, ARCI (or Active Citizenship Network), issued a statement describing the incident, not as "a terrorist attack, or a manifestation of ethnic hatred" but as "a worrying symptom of the ever-worsening socioeconomic crisis in the marginalized areas of East Jerusalem." The idiocy of this whitewash was only enhanced by the irony of a letter Frammartino had sent to an Italian newspaper several months earlier in which he regretted, among other things, "the blood of Palestinian youths from the first intifada." Naturally, such evasive scampering is to be expected in the Middle East. A group going by the name of the Palestinian Civil Society Organizations exonerated the killer by laying the blame on Israel, rehashing the usual line of "massacres against Palestinian and Lebanese civilians" and "grave human rights violations committed by the Israeli Occupation." The killer was obviously so disoriented and incensed by the Israelis that he decided to murder an Italian. These muddled equations constitute standard reasoning in the Middle East. The West has no excuse for indulging in such nonsensical rationalizations, but this does not prevent it from persisting.

One thinks as well, to cite a few rusticated examples of such Clatterers on the home front, of anti-Americans and Palestinian fellow travellers like former *Globe and Mail* columnist Heather Mallick, an überfeminist who wouldn't last a week in Gaza City. (In writing about a computer malfunction, she manages to get in a dig at the Israelis; buying a set of knickknack chickens to hang by her curtains, the onset of something like *le petit mal* has her segueing into a tirade on American chickens languishing in an Arkansas hothouse). Or the openly gay ex-NDP parliamentarian Svend Robinson, a companionable visitor to Arafat's Mukata compound, who would be quickly neutered in Ramallah should he decide to settle there. A frequent guest at and participant in Gay Pride parades from Toronto to Iqaluit, Robinson might have been aware that there are no such jubilees in Ramallah—for that he would have needed to visit Tel Aviv. Their efforts are amply seconded by parliamentary Clatterers like former MP Carolyn Parrish, no friend of Israel, who calls Americans "bastards" and grinds a George W. Bush doll beneath her boot on CBC-TV. These people would be relatively deodorized were it not for the Canadian susceptibility to the anti-Israeli and anti-American brief, but as it is their effect is no less baneful than the tendentious writing and reporting of those in the media world like Robert Fisk, Dan Rather, Chris Hedges, Tariq Ali, John Pilger, Paul William Roberts, and Orla Guerin. Robert Fisk in particular is doubtlessly the most exemplary—and among the most servile—of our liberal commentators. Dragged from his vehicle and beaten by Islamic insurgents in Afghanistan, he considered his assailants justified in their actions. Rather, Hedges, Ali, and Pilger are common-name left-liberals whose prejudices are widely known. Somewhat less profiled, Roberts trades in a subtle form of analogy-bending gratifying to literary types and has recently been taken up by PEN Canada. As for Guerin, one of the most biased, anti-Israeli reporters in the field today, who likes throwing around Zimbabwe comparisons and Grinching the Israelis for having stolen Christmas (her BBC News report for December 21, 2002, is titled "Christmas 'Stolen' from Bethlehem"), she has just received an MBE from the British government for "outstanding service to broadcasting," to go along with the London Press Club's Broadcaster of the Year Award and the News and Factual Award by Women in Film and Television UK. These are fairly typical of our contemporary breed of cognoscenti whose political convictions are demonstrably out of sync with the lifestyles they take so airily as gift-horsed—at worst, hypocrites, at best, chumps. As Peter Ackroyd has written in *The Collection*, "The trouble with those who barter in ideas...is that their ordinary intelligence tends to become deracinated in the process."

What such tabloid dilettantes have failed to understand is that the greatest threat to the liberal West today comes from the theological mutants of the desert kingdoms.[16] Even so respectable a religious scholar as Karen Armstrong in her Modern Library history of Islam errs on the side of excessive sympathy for what she regards as an inherently noble faith, exhorting the West to "cultivate a more accurate appreciation of Islam," which we are told it would be wrong to view as "the enemy of democracy and decent values." Thus it is no surprise that a terror initiator like Sheikh Ahmed Yassin, the co-founder and so-called "spiritual leader" of Hamas, who spilled a Galilee of blood before the Israelis saw to his departure, is praised for building a "welfare empire to bring the benefits of modernity to Palestinians." Armstrong is obviously ignorant of the fact that Hamas' anti-corruption and welfare programs are mainly directed to creating support for its announced mission to destroy Israel, the funds being distributed to its own militia, the families of "martyred" suicide bombers, and public institutions eventually intended to serve as recruitment centres. "Clean government" means more martyrs and "social welfare" gestates loyalty to the cause. Armstrong also seems unaware of the well-corroborated link between Hamas and al-Qaeda. Although the famous Hamas poster showing Yassin posing beside the al-Qaeda leader was circulated the year after her *Short History* appeared in a paperback edition in 2002, bin Laden's emissaries had visited Hamas in 2000 and 2001 to coordinate policy during the second intifada, giving Armstrong ample time to rectify the 2000 hardback version of the text. Nor has her scholarship uncovered the fact that the Dar-al-Arqan school in Gaza City, founded by Yassin, features texts by Sheikh Nasser bin Hamad al-Fahd promoting the use of WMD against Christians and Jews and by Sheikh Sulaiman bin Nasser al-Ulwan whose name figures on Osama's December 2001 video clip celebrating 9/11. Armstrong, like many of our liberal intellectuals, seems to process her information on a need-not-to-know basis.

There is an almost willful blindness on the part of intellectuals who, sympathetic to the values of Islam, posit an impermeable separation between the political/terrorist and social/charitable wings of such organizations as Hamas, when it should be clear to any reasonable observer that budgetary leakage is both planned and inevitable. Hamas' armed wing, Izaddin al-Kassam, is the ultimate beneficiary of just such largesse, either through covert transference of international aid money or by concomitant reduction of expenditures from its own war funds. Medical inventories may be in short supply, families may be forced to sell off their jewellery to make ends meet (though someone is obviously fluid enough to buy), and malnutrition may be a problem, as we are constantly being told. Yet the militias sport brand new uniforms and state-of-the-art weaponry and none of the armed young men we see daily in newspaper photos and TV images seems to be undernourished or wanting. Something is clearly amiss in our assessment of the situation. A new study by Matthew Levitt, *Hamas: Politics, Charity, and Terrorism in the Service of Jihad*, makes it compellingly clear that there is no firewall between the charitable and military functions of Hamas.

We should also see that the objections to Israeli policy popular in the media and intellectual domains, even in those instances where they may well be justified, are traceable to both an unwillingness to imagine the situation as unfolding at home *and* the nightmare of a rising antisemitism that has never been effectively exorcised and probably never will. Israeli mistakes—and no doubt there are many—serve as handy excuses to indulge irrational hatreds and resentments. One such "mistake," we are told, is the settlement project. We should keep in mind, however, that for Palestinian and Arab rejectionists the term "settlements" refers not just to the outlying hamlets, but ultimately to Haifa and Tel Aviv. Palestinian poet Mourid Barghouti, in his memoir *I Saw Ramallah*, refers to the settlements as "Israel itself; Israel the idea and ideology and the geography and the trick and the excuse. It is the place that is ours and that they have made theirs. The settlements are their book, their first form." Barghouti is to be commended for divulging the true nature of the Palestinian claim and the "first form" of Palestinian rhetoric and agitation. The anti-settlement campaign is only a harbinger and template of a desired future, a momentary surrogate for the dismantling of Israel itself, which is regarded as the Ultimate Settlement. The plan is: first the settlements are demolished, then the Settlement follows in turn. From the Palestinian point of view, *all* Israelis are settlers who must be resisted, harassed, and forcibly evicted. This position is shared by many Arab countries and has been explicitly adopted by the powerful Muslim Brotherhood, whose influence on the terrorist groups is a matter of record. Article 2 of the 1988 Hamas Covenant declares that it is "one of the wings of the

Muslim Brotherhood in Palestine." Even the presumably moderate Fatah movement, in its efforts to outflank Hamas and regain control of the Palestinian political scene during the June 2006 outbreak of regional hostilities, licensed its media outlets to designate the Israeli cities of Sderot and Ashkelon as "settlements." Let us not forget that the Palestinian Authority's seventeen separate militias also gave their unequivocal support to Hizbullah in its recent attack upon Israel.

Nor should we forget that the settler question is especially difficult to resolve, not only because of Palestinian intractableness, but because it is founded on a theory of historical irredentism and ancestral title that, when all the myths and fabrications have been stripped away, may well be largely justified. The settlers, of course, or at least their more radical wing, do not help their cause by agitating to restore the monarchy or claiming that the Palestinians are the incarnation of the biblical Amalekites. Here they are as blind and irrational as their Palestinian opposite numbers. But we may be thankful that radical fundamentalists make up only a tiny proportion of the Jewish commonality and do not go about issuing threats against the international community, bombing embassies, dispatching human detonators across borders, and crashing planes into office towers, whereas among the Muslims the terrorist cadres and their fundamentalist sympathizers outnumber the entire population of Israel many times over. Madmen like Asher Weisgan, who killed four Palestinians at Shilo in the West Bank (and also called for the assassination of Ariel Sharon) or celebrity-status lunatics like Baruch Goldstein and Rabbi Meir Kahane are not even remotely in the same league as fomentors and supporters of the terrorist project like Osama bin Laden, Bashar Assad, Abu Musab al-Zarqawi, Sayyed Nasrallah, Ismail Haniyeh, Khaled Mashaal, Hashemi Rafsanjani, and Mahmoud Ahmadinejad, not to mention the winner of the Nobel Peace Prize, Yasser Arafat. But the occasional Israeli fanatic will inevitably attract a disproportionate share of attention from the media and the anti-Israeli forum. This is precisely the tactic employed, to take a very recent instance, by R. T. Naylor in *Satanic Purses*, who seizes upon both Goldstein and Kahane, episodic and non-representative figures in contemporary Israeli history, and inflates them to apocalyptic proportions. Nevertheless, the actions of such individuals cannot weigh in the balance against the almost daily forays, ambushes, and mortar and rocket salvos of the intifadists.

As if to disguise what they are really up to, many of those who are anti-Israeli or anti-Zionist claim that they are not thereby anti-Jewish—and in some cases this may even be true. Conceiving Zionism as a political ideology that violates the essence of authentic Judaism, many actually declare that their real intention is to defend the heritage of Jewish thought and worship while combating antisemitism and making the world safer for Jews, seemingly unaware that in affecting to fight antisemitism they are only furthering its aims. Since in their estimation—assuming, that is, that they are being honest with themselves—the Zionist movement and the Jewish state are responsible for inflaming world opinion against Jews and are therefore the major cause of modern antisemitism, it would follow that the cure for this pathology is the suppression of Zionism and the disestablishment of Israel. This is magical thinking: get rid of what has saved the Jews from disappearing and they will, as if by some enchantment, suddenly enjoy the acceptance that has eluded them throughout recorded history. Jewish anti-Zionists represent a special case, motivated either by a tortuous disdain of Judaism or, on the contrary, labouring to preserve the religious and cultural values of the Jewish faith against its sclerotic political wing—as if the Jewish state were the enemy of Judaism and not its protector. In either case, the position is fallacious. But the argument from anti-antisemitism is paramount in this dynamic and it is a profoundly insidious one. In trying to remove what they regard as the wellspring of antisemitism, our well-intentioned anti-Zionists will have travelled two-thirds of the road toward accomplishing its purposes. With Zionism and Israel out of the way, only the Jew himself remains, shorn of all his defences except secrecy, self-effacement, concealment, subterfuge, and heedless assimilation that, as history has shown time and again, are only temporary expedients and are bound to fail.

We should not, in consequence, allow ourselves to be so readily bamboozled by the anti-Zionist brief. Many anti-Zionists who regard themselves as insightful, honourable, and "even-handed" are merely deluded—or, if they happen to be Jews, are living in a fool's paradise. Others tend to be utterly oblivious of the true nature of the morbid and primal hatred they cherish inwardly—a basic attitude that is far more endocrinological than reflective. Judging by the vehemence and toxicity of their rhetoric, which often falls back on the familiar clichés of Jewish conspiratorial intriguing, inwrought militarism, congenital invasiveness, clannishness, and media domination—this last accusation is entirely bizarre since the media are almost unfailingly anti-Israeli and anti-Zionist in their coverage—it is easy to see that many critics of Israel are unquestionably antisemitic in outlook and feeling and are merely using a political argument to camouflage a religious, racist, or ethnophobic sentiment.[17] Under the habit of the "legitimate criticism of Israel" and the querying of Zionism as a colonial movement, antisemitism has now become safe.

Plainly then, the distinction these new antisemites like to draw between antisemitism as such and anti-Zionism is only a form of maketalk intended to cloak the fundamental issue and to provide cover for vulgar ideas and beliefs. This is a very shrewd tactic and is most disconcerting not only in its vindictiveness but in its frequency. Jewish philosopher and theologian Emil Fackenheim has outlined three stages of antisemitism: "You cannot live among us as Jews," leading to forced conversions; "You cannot live among us," leading to mass deportations; and "You cannot live," leading to genocide. Amnon Rubenstein, patron of the Israeli Shinui party and author of *From Herzl to Rabin: The Changing Image of Zionism*, has added a fourth stage: "You cannot live in a state of your own," which leads to boycott, divestment, biased reporting, uncritical support of the Palestinians, and calls for the delegitimation and even the destruction of Israel among Western leftists and "liberals." It is Israel—not China, not Sudan, not North Korea, not Saudi Arabia, not Zimbabwe, not Iran, or the rest of that vast number of miscreant states that tarnish the globe—that is always the first port of call for the world's maleficent peace armadas. If this is not unqualified antisemitism, then nothing is. As Martin Luther King Jr. said at a Harvard book fair during which Zionism came under attack, "when people criticize Zionists, they really mean Jews. You're talking antisemitism."[18] According to a report released in the August 2006 issue of the *Journal of Conflict Resolution* by the Yale School of Management in collaboration with its Institute for Social and Policy Studies, the statistical link between anti-Zionism and antisemitism can no longer be denied—which should have been obvious years ago despite the disclaimers regularly circulated by covert Jew-haters.

Even the word "Zionism" now seems stained as a result of the unflagging campaign of defamation against the legitimacy of the Jewish state and its origins, a word whose first appearance in Psalms 48:2 still rings consolingly, if somewhat bitterly as well, for Jews: "Beautiful for situation, the joy of the whole earth, is mount Zion, on the sides of the north, the city of the great King"—a refrain taken up by Judaism's greatest poet, Yehuda Halevi, who wrote, "Zion, beauty's paragon, bound by love and grace,/the souls of your peers are joined to you." Halevi's "peers" are the current inhabitants of the state of Israel. *Indeed, it is not Zionism but anti-Zionism that is racist in outlook and character.* And it is most curious how few people seem to realize that the deeply emotional detestation of Zion, inscribed in the apparently dispassionate anti-Zionist platform, means the destruction of another 6 million Jews, who just happen to be Israelis. Whether suffocated by refugee influx, engulfed in a bi-national state or "driven into the sea," Israel would disappear and the fate of its people would not bear thinking about.

Of course, it must be admitted that Israel is to some extent the author of its own woes. Perhaps one of its greatest internal irritants involves the Orthodox religious parties that would like to turn a state founded along mainly secular lines into something like a Jewish mullocracy. This is a most unlikely scenario, yet it must be actively monitored, especially in the light of the justifiable resentment felt by secular Israelis toward their Haredi brethren for what they perceive as a form of parasitism on the state: disproportionate control of religious and some civil institutions, subsidized education, tax repeal, and exemption from military service. In calling for the mass defection of soldiers from the IDF, Orthodox rabbis, under the guidance of former Chief Rabbi Avraham Shapira, have raised sedition to the status of a religious duty and should be rapidly and forcefully countered by legislative authority. The militant settler wing, regardless of the validity or partial validity of its historical argument, is also a destabilizing element that must be taken firmly in hand, even at the high cost of civil unrest. Although it forms only a small minority of the more peaceable settler community that, to its credit, embraces the halachic principle of *dina d'malchuta dina* ("the law of the land is the law"), and an even smaller minority of the population in general, it is radical, committed, and prone to violence and may cause serious internal troubles. Ancient and even recent history may be for them; current history is not. Although, it must be conceded, this may change once again in the sequel to the Israel/Hizbullah war and the year-long barrage of Kassams fired from Gaza, forcing the Israelis to rethink the logic of disengagement.

Equally worrying is the marriage solemnized at the altar of unreason between the far Right and the far Left. The latter, taking its cue from Martin Buber, considers its native country as an uninvited guest in the region and agitates for the creation of a bi-national state in which Israeli Jews would shortly lose their political and civil rights, becoming a disenfranchised minority in their own land at the mercy of their ancestral enemies. On the extreme Right, the Neturei Karta anti-Zionists, who proclaim themselves the "Guardians of the City," oppose the very existence of the state of Israel as a betrayal of Jewish tradition and observance and an obstacle to the coming of the Messianic era. Members of the extreme Left Gush Shalom movement and representatives of the ultra Right Neturei Karta both attended a pro-Palestinian conference in Malaysia in March 2005, which culminated in a call for the boycott of Israeli products. Neturei Karta has since visited Iran, giving ammunition to its president by, in its own words, agreeing to "the disintegration of the Zionist entity" and, according to the Iranian news agency IRNA, praising "the 'enlightening' statements of... Mahmoud Ahmadinejad about [the denial of] the Holocaust." One wonders where these Israeli anti-Zionists, whether of the Left or of the Right, would have gone had the Zionist movement been defeated and Israel not come into being. Many would not be here to pursue their campaign to dissolve the Jewish state but would lie in European mass graves or have never even twinkled in their parents' eyes. The mind boggles.

In the larger sense, Israel's inability to implement a coherent strategic policy over the long run and the maddening and often self-defeating complexity of its rainbow political system—only two Israeli prime ministers to date have completed their terms of office—stem in part from the dishevelled nature of its social fabric. It is a country that is prone to a high incidence of absurdity, from the utterly silly quarrels between secular and Orthodox Jews over the status of married couples to Haredi *moyels* operating a pirate circumcision syndicate to the vaudeville acts that characterize its parliamentary sessions. Israel is a country in which basketball coaches have not personal trainers but personal rabbis, and in which a victory on the court is interpreted as a sign of the imminence of the messianic era. It is a country that has often fallen short of its high founding principles and, like any other nation, has its share of corrupting influences in its political administration and even in its military leadership. It is a country in which young men die at the front while old farts sell off their stock portfolios. But it is also a country, as I have been at pains to point out, that is at the forefront of the world scientific community. There is, it seems, no help for it. Israel will likely remain for some time to come a mercurial and conflicted place, torn between Orthodox and secular Jews, between town and kibbutz, between sabra and newcomer, between the older and younger generations, between Labour, Likud, Kadima, and the myriad splinter parties that wield disproportionate influence in the inevitable minority governments, between Ashkenazim and Sephardim and the various subethnicities, between diehard settlers flourishing a biblical and historical warrant for Gaza, Judea, and Samaria and public opinion at large seeking disengagement, at least until recently, between "new revisionists" and traditional loyalists, between business interests and the national welfare, between the army and the peace movement, between dedicated IDF soldiers and the jaded members of the fashionable, draft-dodging "Our Crowd" set, between religious authority and the democratic state, between feverish Hasidim and sober Mitnagdim, between eminent statesmen and cynical politicians, and, as mentioned above, between confirmed extremists on both the Right and the Left. Indeed, the Israeli Left and its cotes of ultra-doves with their hate-mongering incitement and vicious propaganda campaigns against the military and Ariel Sharon (in his pre-disengagement incarnation), along with their circumstantial adoption of Arafat's peace formula that envisioned Israel's self-destruction, constitute as great a threat to the state as the most bellicose of the settlers and the most bullheaded of the fundamentalist rabbis.

What are we to make of left-wing columnists like the popular Larry Derfner, who writes in praise of the pragmatic tractability, good sense, and loyalty of "our Arabs"—the same Arab citizens whose Jerusalem vanguard voted almost to a man and woman for Hamas in the recent elections, who cheered from the Galileean rooftops when Hizbullah missiles landed in Jewish towns, who blame Israel for the death of their own children killed by Hizbullah rockets, and whose representatives in the Knesset visit Syria, deliver inflammatory speeches, engage in unlawful consultations with representatives of Hamas, encourage the kidnapping of Israeli soldiers, and have grown increasingly militant in their hostility against the state whose benefits they share, siding openly with the Hizbullah aggressors. And what are we to make of the left-liberal, pro-Palestinian stance of major dailies like *Ha'aretz* and the Peace Now activists, who diligently work against the interests of their own country? There is far too much *Ha'aretz* in the Israeli psyche, though perhaps the nearly 4,000 rockets fired by Hizbullah at Israeli towns and cities in the summer 2006 crisis, which affected one-quarter of the population of the country, will go some way to cauterizing the pacifist infirmity. But one is sometimes tempted to speculate that if the Palestinians abandoned Israel to its own devices and allowed its revisionist professors and New Historians, its Gush Shalomites, its left-wing journalists, its Women in Black, its feeble leadership, its corrupt old-boys network, its reactionary troglodytes manning the outposts and its crustacean rabbinate to do their work in relative peace, the issue might be decided far sooner than the terrorist network could ever hope to accomplish on its own.

And yet, despite the tumultuous course of events, it may well be that the country is now perched on the cusp of its future, poised between the distant possibility of a more cohesive and unified self-definition on the one side and prolonged, internecine strife and increased social divisiveness on the other, as if enmeshed in a lurid replay of the biblical Two Kingdoms conflict. It is solemnly to be hoped that the unprovoked attack by Hizbullah, the Israeli response such as it was—far from adequate in terms of military planning but animated by the heroism of its soldiers—the resilience of its citizens under bombardment in their homes and streets, and the popular desire to return to basics and clean out the Augean stables of the contemporary political scene will generate a new and stronger sense of unity among a people marked for extermination. This is assuming that Israel does indeed have a future and that the looming conflict with Iran does not introduce an unpredictable facet or dimension to the political situation so as to render it unrecognizable in the time to come. In any case, although Israel may not and never will be Theodor Herzl's *Altneuland* (*Old New Land*), his "light unto the nations" Utopian vision of the Holy Land put forward in his 1902 novel of that title—"If you will, it is no fairy tale," he wrote—the inevitable gap between the real and the visionary should not blind us to the markedly larger gap between Israel and the surrounding Arab countries, between a small, litigious, always cantankerous, occasionally self-endangered but rather impressive democracy and an immense part of the globe sunk in both iniquity and inequality.

But it is disturbing to note that Israel itself seems to have donned a set of blinkers in order to attain the *fata Morgana* of a broad, Middle East accommodation. Israeli support of and compliance with Arafat during the Oslo period, based on the naïve and completely erroneous belief that strengthening the Palestinian dictator would enhance the prospects for peace by giving him the tools to combat his own terrorist affiliates, was probably the single greatest mistake—apart from underestimating the surrounding Arab nations prior to the 1973 war—that Israel has ever made. Yitzhak Rabin's assurance that Arafat would deal with his own extremists *bli bagatz u'betzelem* (i.e., without being hamstrung by judicial supervision) was an invitation to the meltdown that followed. Israel and its leaders do not seem to have grasped the deep psychology that allows for and enables such travesties. The "Oslo syndrome" is dissected by Kenneth Levin, in his book of that title, in which he argues that generations of inherited guilt, a feeling of responsibility for the disasters that have befallen the Jewish people, has produced something like a siege mentality, a desire to make itself small and offer amends to the world, in the hope of receiving expiation from its persecutors. This self-destructive tendency seems to have reproduced the symptoms of Battered Wife Syndrome, the attempt to mollify the tormentor by assuming liability for what has befallen the victim. But America and the international community, in bringing pressure to bear against Israel while allowing Arafat to renege systematically on his commitments, must be held equally responsible for the Oslo farce and the disintegrating hopes for a meaningful accord in the present situation. Oslo set the pattern and the favourable treatment meted out to Mahmoud Abbas—the ceremonial excess surrounding his visits to various world capitals, the sympathetic hearing he received, the enormous sums that were put at his disposal—merely perpetuated the fiasco. The terrorists will not disarm and the Palestinian Authority will give Israel next to nothing for the trauma of withdrawal and the very real political and territorial sacrifices it is willing to make. The lesson must finally be learned: there is no possibility of peace without ironclad reciprocity and unremitting scrutiny, and, as history has taught us time and again, no possibility of achieving a binding agreement with a fundamentally dictatorial regime, especially if it is clothed in democratic frippery. We need to remember that, like Hamas, Fatah has never recognized Israel's right to exist. The only advantage in having

Hamas rather than Fatah in control of the Palestinian Authority is that the imposture is harder to dissemble. It is probable that Hamas will try to acquire wider legitimacy by verbally dissociating itself from international terrorist organizations such as al-Qaeda and even more likely that the West will fall for the ploy. But this changes nothing.

My own highly personal view of this contentious issue will no doubt seem outrageous even to those readers sympathetic to my general argument in these pages. I have maintained for years that the "*Ha'aretz* take" on the situation is the epitome of tunnel vision and constitutes a clear and present danger to Israel's security. A case in point: *Ha'aretz's* political analyst, Aluf Benn, produced an op-ed article, entitled "We Need Nasrallah," placing credence in the behaviour of the Hizbullah leader as "rational," praising him for doing a good job of "maintaining quiet in the Galilee," and describing the "stable balance of deterrence on both sides of the border [as] the best possible situation." Exactly five days later Hizbullah unleashed its attack on Israel, leading to the war of July/August 2006. *Ha'aretz* and its media bedfellows have a lot of damage to undo. The Israeli Left, the various Peace coalitions, the media drift, the conciliatory administrations were and are no less a threat to the survival of the nation than its obvious enemies. Peace Now, I'm afraid, means War Later. The mainstream Israeli psyche will also have to change, away from the propensity to elect anemic and rudderless governments, to trust in an ageing and self-serving high command, and to relax over lattes in the palm-fronded cafés of Tel Aviv, toward the renewed awareness that the country has been built on the slopes of a volcano that always threatens to erupt—again.

I do not believe, despite my deepest hopes, that a permanent and guaranteed peace is probable in the area, at least for a very long time to come, if ever. I fear that Alan Dershowitz's noble program for a lasting peace, elaborated in what may be his most important book, *The Case for Peace*, is in many respects, despite its *bona fides* and its undoubted brilliance, another instance of that cheery American optimism enamoured of surfaces. After all, only one man has thus far managed to walk on water. Dershowitz's analysis of Israel-bashing and Jew-hatred among the international Left is witheringly accurate and must be carefully heeded—the Left is not so much interested in the creation of a Palestinian state as it is in the destruction of Israel—but his tendency to extend the benefit of the doubt to Palestinian claims, intentions, and aspirations is, in my view, disturbingly Pollyannish. Among the author's conditions for a resolution of hostilities, we find " a renunciation of all forms of violence" and "an undertaking by the Palestinian state to dismantle terrorist groups." There is nothing wrong with these conditions—they are admirable—except that they have been on the books since Oslo to absolutely no avail and, regrettably, the Palestinians to this very day have shown almost no intention of abiding by them. One might suggest certain other conditions on the same order of hypothetical validity that would also contribute to a lasting peace among the combatants: the renunciation of all ancestral hatreds, the total rejection of envy, resentment, and bloodlust as retrograde human emotions, the refusal to accept any form of theological imperative, and the implementation of a policy based on the belief in the fundamental goodness of one's fellow man, especially if he happens to be the enemy who has never relented in his enmity and who has violated every accord for peace within living memory. Once these provisos are accepted and signed before witnesses, peace must inevitably follow and all the conferees can hand out candy to celebrate the event.

One wonders, however, if Dershowitz would have written the same book after the Palestinian people voted a terrorist regime into power— one that refuses to recognize Israel, abjure terrorism, and honour previous agreements—and after the Hizbullah attack on Israeli soil, with the Palestinians voicing their support and the terrorist groups vowing to study and apply the methods of the Shi'ite militia. To his credit, Dershowitz admits the possibility that "someday Hamas might gain control over the Palestinian government, either by means of a coup, an election, or some such combination." But he is not particularly forthcoming on the way in which such an eventuality should be dealt with, leaving the issue unresolved in the course of his prescriptions. Dershowitz speaks of "Palestinian leaders who are actively seeking a compromise resolution to this bloody conflict," but, so far as I can see, they are not thick on the ground. The "moderate" Mahmoud Abbas in particular, in many of his public pronouncements, his refusal to disarm the terrorists, his reluctance to tackle the problem of rampant corruption, and his signing on to an inherently absurd peace proposal called the Prisoners' Document, which does not renounce terrorism and does not explicitly recognize Israel, may yet do the work of Hamas by other means.

In the state of affairs following the Hamas electoral coup and the Hizbullah war, major Israeli concessions toward a two-state destination no longer seem feasible. The much bruited road map will actually have to extend rather than contract Israel's final borders; anything less would leave Israel in an untenable position. As far back as 1967 and UN Resolution 242, it was already plain to the American Joint Chiefs of Staff (who prepared the Pentagon Map of the region), UN Ambassador Arthur Goldberg, and Undersecretary Eugene Rostow that the "minimum territory needed by Israel for defensive purposes," as specified by the map, included the Golan Heights and the mountain ridges of Judea and Samaria—considerations that the present road map does not embrace. In the current situation, it is the Palestinians who will have to make the more painful concessions, not the Israelis who have been rewarded for their withdrawal from Lebanon with a blitzkrieg of Katyushas and for their pullout from Gaza with a torrent of Kassams. Recent events have introduced a new set of "parameters" into the on again/off again negotiation process and will require the road map to be redrawn, though not to Palestinian advantage. Dershowitz, who favours the two-state solution and who understands that the mainstream churches, the European Union, most of academia, the United Nations, and the Arab world at large would all prefer to see Israel disappear, does not seem to realize that Israel, even at the risk of alienating the few allies it still has and emboldening its enemies, will have to insist far more emphatically on its rights and needs if it is to survive the two-state scenario it has itself proposed. Reality is not pleasant.

In her travel book *Where Mountains Roar*, Lesley Hazelton reports a conversation between an Israeli and Egyptian officer in the Sinai after the signing of the Camp David peace accords in 1978. The Israeli asks his interlocutor if peace is now really possible. The Egyptian replies, "peace is not possible, not in our generation.... But now we are making it possible for the next generation, giving them the framework on which to build real peace within the next twenty or thirty years." These twenty or thirty years are now up, but peace still seems a generation away. Given the more or less continuous 3,000-year history of turmoil and bloodshed in the region, and the rise of an intransigent terrorist movement in our own day, I sense that, two states or the *status quo*, peace may always be a generation away.

I would like to be proven wrong, but I am pretty well convinced that, barring the unforeseeable, Islam in its present form will never accept Judaism as a theistic co-adjutor just as the surrounding Muslim states will never truly accept Israel as a parish associate, and the terrorists are unlikely to relent in prosecuting their revanchist program. Since the day of its inception Israel has been regarded by its neighbours as a foreign "entity," a kind of infection that the body of Islamic nations has fought in every way that it could, mobilizing its immune system and releasing antibodies to counter the purported menace to its physical and political "integrity." These antibodies have so far failed in their purpose. Repeated invasions have not worked. Terrorist operations have proven ineffective. The Arab propaganda blitz that has been in high-gear since 1948 has been effective but not decisive. General Assembly resolutions are a bad joke. Security Council meetings frequently descend into the intellectual void where it is impossible to distinguish between ignorance and sheer buffoonery, as in the May 30, 2006, conclave at which the Syrian spokesman affirmed that "Israel was behind the eruption of both World War I and World War II"— Israel did not come into existence until 1948. The International Court in The Hague is a proxy institution, stuffed with political appointees and judges from autocratic nations, whose anti-Israeli judgments have only served to discredit them. The Arab League economic boycott has been parried by technological innovation and scientific breakthroughs as well as by robust entrepreneurship. The only viable alternative left, apart from a nuclear strike, with which to attack the supposed pathogen is peace. For under the trappings of peace the Islamic body can both escalade and undermine the perceived intruder, acquiring more and more territory, seeking advantageous bargaining positions, working to destabilize the political and economic infrastructure, conscripting the Israeli intellectual establishment and wooing the peace constituency, insinuating itself into the national consciousness as something inevitable, eroding communal and juridical safeguards, preparing the ground for further attacks upon Israeli soil, and ultimately weakening the country's resolve to survive. Oslo was merely the first battle in this reprimed definition of war. Even Hamas, as we have observed, is willing to "negotiate," if only on its terms.

But even where such efforts toward peace may be marginally sincere, any future warming of political relations between the Arab countries and Israel, on which Western democrats and the Israeli Left set so much store, will likely be short-lived. The terrorists will strike again, Israel will be forced to retaliate, and those Arab countries making gestures toward détente, whether notional or genuine, will close ranks with their Palestinian brethren in denouncing Israeli "aggression." We recall that Egypt and Jordan, both officially "at peace" with Israel, withdrew their ambassadors during the last intifada. Those Arab nations that initially condemned the Hizbullah attack on Israel did so not from a genuine desire for peace or a newfound solidarity with the Jewish state, but from a calculation of long-term interests—Hizbullah had made a strategic blunder—that did not prevent these same Arab nations from later lining up behind Hizbullah and helping to inflict an unfavourable and humiliating peace treaty upon Israel under the auspices of the United Nations. Israel will have to recognize, although the international community and proponents for democracy in the Arab Middle East will not, that in order to exist it may likely have to accept the distressing prospect of, at best, "low intensity" warfare in perpetuity or, at any rate, for an undetermined time to come, living in a condition of military readiness and never slackening in its defence. Further, it is a serious mistake to rely on the approval of the "international community" in the formulation of political and military policy. For in a very real sense there *is* no international community, except insofar as 150 nations are united in their hatred of Israel. And even should the worst of the violence go into remission—and this would in all probability be temporary—the crackle of skirmish fire will continue to sound in Israeli ears. The fact that Hamas outpolled Mahmoud Abbas' Fatah party by a huge disparity in the vote indicates that a significant number of Palestinians have little or no interest in repudiating terrorism or living peacefully with Israel. The terrorist movement-cum-political party will of course make minor tactical concessions along the way, but its basic charter policies regarding the existence or validity of the Jewish state are unlikely to change in any substantive way, no matter how they may be sauced for international consumption or local advantage. From the Israeli standpoint, in immediate, practical terms, the military will have to remain on alert and ahead of the game, the security fence must be completed without delay and the seam lines with any future Palestinian state kept under intensive scrutiny, the Golan Heights can under no circumstances be restored to Syria, a portion of the Jordan Valley will have to remain in Israeli hands, the far Left in its

subversive agitation must be engaged and countered by scholars, journalists, and educators just as the far Right must also be tamed by legislation and policing if necessary, Hizbullah operations in the north will
have to be met with resolution so long as a single rocket still bristles
on the frontier, and whatever piecemeal accords are franked along the
way between the belligerents will need to be closely inspected, absolutely watertight, and unbrokenly reciprocal.

This is not an overall pleasant scenario but, whether we like it or
not, it remains the price of Israel's existence. Israel's internal malaise is
more or less addressable, but the Arabs have been dedicated enemies
since 1948 (and in truth, since the seventh century and perhaps even
earlier if the reference in Psalm 83:6 to the "Ishmaelites" and the
"Hagarenes" is anything to go by) and have used every opportunity for
peace since the creation of Israel as a means of furthering their own
irrefragable program. Why this should abruptly change, as Dershowitz
believes, with the death of Yasser Arafat, dignified by the Palestinian
Authority with the title Prince of Martyrs, defies everything we know
about Arab intentions and conduct, which have been unvarying up
to now. Even a leading representative of the "young guard" in Fatah,
Jamal Shobaki, has protested that "nothing has changed since Arafat's
death." This is not to eschew the need for compromise and new initiatives, which are necessary, but to render them practicable. Nor is it to
suggest that the peace initiative should be discouraged, but rather that
Israeli concessions must be hard-wrung and expectations of definitive
success modest. You do not trade land for a sheet of paper and you
do not weaken your defences on the strength of a promissory note of
good behaviour. The menace will not vanish with another "historic"
handshake or another batch of oaths and pledges or another ceding
of real estate, but will persist in yet another "transvalued" mode. The
madness has gone so deep and endured for so long that it can no longer
be treated, only contained. It is toward this end that negotiations must
aim. To proceed otherwise is to invite catastrophe further down the
road—or the road map.

I am reluctant to say this because it would seem to put me in the
same camp as the diehard extremist—which is manifestly not my
home. My position is *not* extremist for the simple reason that I wish
heart and mind that things were different, and that I would be ready to
modify my convictions if my reading, experience, and common sense

gave me any indication to do so or if the situation seemed to offer a *founded* hope. I am not for wiping any country off the map, including virtual countries, or for starting wars of attrition, aggrandizement, or annihilation. But I am for survival, even if this means adopting unpopular points of view and being condemned for inflexibility or dismissed as a lost and benighted soul.

The response I am suggesting is, after all, not one that we regard as unacceptable or morally objectionable in everyday life. We adapt to the necessity of living under duress and adjust to the demands being made upon us, however irksome and disagreeable. We understand that it would be perilous to succumb to unfounded aspirations and pious notions by disregarding facts and embracing unrealistic options. Put simply, we often have to do what we would prefer not having to do. The life of a people is in this respect similar to the life of people. In private life, such constraints may be financial or medical, but the ultimate purpose is survival, just as it is in the realm of national existence. In the absence of miraculous bestowals, a country that intends to weather the world must face up to the hardships of the condition in which it finds itself and respond appropriately if it is to avoid disaster, even if this means having to stay on a permanent war footing. In effect, the prevalent Arab refusal to accept *genuine* co-existence with Israel should be no less surprising than the world's variable aversion to the Jew in its midst as a parvenu and outsider.

This is why the "peace process" must be approached gingerly and with levelheaded suspicion if it is not to degenerate into a war of attenuation with the advantage going to the Palestinians and their backers in Saudi Arabia, Syria, and Iran. While peace should be fostered in a pragmatic and sensible manner, a certain cautious skepticism and a disinclination to succumb to rosy anticipations and false optimism, coupled with a willingness to expect and to be prepared for the worst, are vital to Israel's long-term security. Blue diamonds are rare. The only realistic hope, if not for peace, then for the reduction of hostilities, lies not in the negotiation rite with its false starts, multiple renegings, and merely verbal commitments on the part of the Palestinian Authority or its cadet branches. It rests with the civilian population of Gaza and the West Bank, should it eventually tire of the continual round of violence and disorder called down upon it by the activities of its own militants, and finally withdraw its support from the terrorist groups, including the terrorist group it has just put in power—although here it may well be that majority public opinion will continue to victual terrorism for some time to come. We must also bear in mind that Palestinians living in Israel will naturally keep their Israeli citizenship, but the new Palestine would be effectively *judenrein*, or Jew-free (another reason why Palestine would not be a genuine democracy but a racist and apartheid state), that the terrorists will continue to threaten renewed violence if their maximal demands are not accepted, that Israel must agree to retreat to the untenable pre-1967 borders, that Hamas has refused to recognize Israel, and that Hizbullah augmented its terrorist recruitment stipend from $1000 to $20,000 per recipient, with up to $100,000 on offer for the family of any Palestinian willing to carry out a suicide attack.[19] The Palestinians reciprocated in spades, offering to join Hizbullah in Lebanon in the war against Israel.

Israel cannot afford to capitulate, not only to its self-declared enemies but to its own passionate yearning for peace. Falling backwards over the possibility of peace is a bungled negotiating paradigm, as Oslo made painfully clear—"we need to change the diskette" goes the current Hebrew slang expression, one that Israeli mediators should contemplate seriously. Any Israeli politician still hooked on Oslo represents a threat to his country. Surely it is not that difficult to see that the Palestinian negotiators, in many respects far nimbler than their Israeli counterparts, have enacted a paradoxical reversal of roles and taken a page out of the Hebrew Bible, approaching a blind, international Isaac like the smooth and wily Jacob in order to rob Esau of his blessing—an exercise that thrives on the defective awareness of the West while at the same time piggybacking on Western expedience. The new Esau must see to it that he keeps his patrimony.

The course that Israel must follow is clear. It must choose between vulnerability to seduction and the maintenance of power and defensible borders, between the placatory swoon and the unhappy rigors of *realpolitik*, in sum, between the threatening prospect of eventual disappearance and the perpetual necessity of unabating alertness. Israel will have to revive the intrepid and unshakeable spirit of the Joshua generation. Considering the lethal activities of the many Palestinian terror groups—including Tanzim and the al-Aqsa Martyrs Brigade officially belonging to the ostensibly "moderate" Fatah party—which give no sign of slackening, the electoral triumph of Hamas, the shellings and incursions of Hizbullah on the northern border, the undiminished hostility of Syria, the grafting of al-Qaeda cells in the Territories, and the ominous threat of Ayatollah Rafsanjani and Mahmoud Ahmadinejad to annihilate Israel in a nuclear attack, which cannot be dismissed as mere sabre-rattling rhetoric, the time of the generals is not over, as some Israelis not so long ago confidently affirmed, but is just beginning. It has often been pointed out that the Arabs can absorb defeat after defeat, but if Israel loses even one war, the sequel does not bear thinking. Israel must remained armed to the teeth, be ready to deploy on a moment's notice, and ensure its qualitative edge in weaponry

Israel's adversaries in the Orient and in the West would prefer to offset the technological and weapons disparity that safeguards its existence. Much is made, for example, of the fact that Israel possesses nuclear weapons whereas the Arab nations do not as yet. This "imbalance" is cited by both the Arabs and Western anti-Zionists as warrant for the development of nuclear technology in the Islamic countries to counter the supposed Israeli threat. But *everybody knows* that Israel will never initiate a first strike and that the existence of such weapons serves only as a last line of defence to avert the total destruction of the country promised by the enemy. For the Iranian leaders, as we know only too well, the nuclear option is a form of one-stop shopping to buy back the Middle East and, quite frankly, they are crazy enough to do it. In the case of Israel, nuclear weapons represent what Seymour M. Hersh, in his book of the same title, calls "the Samson Option," an analogy first suggested by Norman Podhoretz in a 1976 *Commentary* article. The temple of Dagon will come down only if Israel is blinded and in chains. It should be obvious that there is a categorical difference between a nuclear, responsible democracy and a nuclear, terror-sponsoring theocracy. Any person, group, or nation pretending otherwise is guilty of outright hypocrisy and is practising a very dangerous deception whose consequence may well be cataclysmic. In the event of a nuclear exchange, the Israelis speak only of a "second strike"—the Dolphin-class submarines purchased from Germany are intended to escape enemy "first strike" destruction on the ground. Their evident purpose is one of response, not initiation, that is to say, they are intended as a form of deterrence.

It is impossible to say how much I regret that things should be this way, but I for one would not be prepared to surrender my patrimony under the pennon of a treasured illusion. The world will not grieve if Israel is razed, divided, shrivelled, or absorbed. (One recalls the shrunken partition borders that the Peel Commission drafted, which were further emasculated by the Woodhead recommendations into two, tiny, bifurcated enclaves amounting to a small fraction of the Mandated territory, that could not have survived more than a few years at most. This was, naturally, part of the plan.)[20] Despite the pressures levied against it, overt or subtle, Israel has the potential capacity to persist in a climate of hostility, as the Jewish diaspora has for millennia. This may well be its destiny. But given its internal conflictedness, the danger of succumbing to exhaustion—being "tired of winning" is the current phrase, taken from a speech by Ehud Olmert—the siren rhetoric of its intellectuals and its desire for peace and reconciliation at a perhaps exorbitant cost, does it have the will and the foresight to preserve itself inviolate? Unhappily, the current Israeli leadership seems bent on re-enacting its own parodic version of the *Akeda*, the binding of Isaac, placing the nation on the sacrificial altar not at the divine command, but as a result of its own indecisive actions and unsound policies. One can only hope that the angel will nevertheless intervene. Prime Minister Olmert's initial response to the Hizbullah attack on Israel in July 2006, that the Israeli reaction would be proportionate but "very, very, very painful," shows that Israel would have preferred to launch adverbs rather than missiles. Thankfully, the grammar of the situation changed before it was too late, allowing for moderate Israeli gains and the punishing of the terrorist aggressor. But then Olmert's weakness and incompetence reasserted itself, the Israeli military offensive was stalled in favour of the "diplomatic process" and the usual dogs' breakfast of a UN ceasefire resolution, and a future war launched by a re-armed and reinvigorated Hizbullah and its rogue backers all but assured.

I realize that this is an unfashionably "essentialist" view that I am presenting and that many readers will find it unwelcome or inadmissible. They can only hope that Jean-Paul Sartre was right when he argued that "existence precedes essence"; however, the Middle East is the one region in the world that defeats all philosophy and where hope must be founded on practice and verification—which have always been in short supply. What has been won through generations of suffering has been won at too high a price to be traded away for ill-founded aspirations or mere diplomatic gruel. That Israel, while susceptible like any other state to error and misjudgment, has managed to survive under constant attack and threat of attack from without while fissuring inwardly in a condition of perpetual tension constitutes something of a social and political marvel. As indeed does its unprecedented creation as a modern state, as if affirming the narrative of its rebirth described in Isaiah 66:8: "Who hath heard such a thing? Who has seen such things? Shall the earth be made to bring forth in one day? Or shall a nation be born at once? For as soon as Zion travailed, she brought forth her children." For on a single day, May 14, 1948, Israel appeared on the international stage as a functional nation with its formative institutions intact, even though these institutions have been and are still subject to enormous pressure externally as well as internally. In the light of so unique an event, one does wish this brave but fractious country, somehow holding together in the *balagan* ("disorder," "shambles") of its daily life, could finally get its act together and, just as important, never again underestimate the real intentions of its adversary. One may propose the figure of poet Haim Gouri, war hero, patriot, political critic of both the Left and the Right, upholder of human rights, and lyric virtuoso, as one of the living symbols of national reconciliation. "It's better," Gouri writes, "to live with complex contradictions than to castrate your identity." And who knows, perhaps one day Israelis will become what some of them like to believe they are, *am ehad*, one people. The issue remains, if not open, then at least ajar. "What is Israel," asks poet Robyn Sarah, "but a collection of shards with a mandate to become a pot?" But also, considering the fracas that is Jewish identity, "perhaps," she speculates, "it is better to live as a whole shard than a cracked pot." That Israel is filled with crackpots is beyond contesting.

At the same time, even those censurers of Israeli policy who seem untainted by antisemitism do not appear to realize that in levying a gross and unshaded condemnation of the country—generally, simplifications lifted out of context—they are collaborating with those, both closet Jew-haters and outright enemies, who envision and pursue the total reprobation of the Jewish state.[21] Any problematic episode seems to do if it serves to highlight whatever might be interpreted as unfavourable to Israel and its reputation among its supporters as a nation founded on the concept of morality. Some of these ostensibly neutral critics, to take one well-known example, have seized upon the Rudolf

Kastner affair as proof of Israeli skullduggery. Kastner, a political colleague of Prime Minister David Ben-Gurion and an official in the Ministry of Commerce and Industry, was accused by a certain Malchiel Greenwald, a Holocaust survivor, of collaborating with the Nazis in Hungary where Kastner was a high official in the *Judenrat*, or Jewish Agency. Greenwald was then sued in turn by the Israeli government for slander. The case did not go well for the administration and Kastner, who had become a political liability, was found mysteriously murdered while the trial was underway, with the blame falling on right-wing militants. The evidence against Kastner and the conduct of the government in concealing his activities was persuasive and Kastner's removal may well have been orchestrated by the Mossad to avoid further embarrassment, as Ben Hecht tried to show in his 1961 account, *Perfidy*. But the point is that this unsavoury episode in Israeli history—which it is only fair to say was never conclusively established, however high the probability—functions in the arguments of Israel's detractors as *prima facie* evidence not of Kastner's but of Israel's guilt. (A former literary acquaintance, the author of sundry books dealing with the Middle East, who is anti-Zionist but claims not to be antisemitic, has used this incident in personal correspondence with me to lay bare Israel's depravity.) Despite the fact that all states have engaged and continue to engage in such iniquitous practices, that in the larger scheme it is no more than an obscure blip, and that it was, after all, *an Israeli court that discountenanced its own government*, the event is regarded as a clear sign of a uniquely Israeli baseness of motive and deed that must therefore call the character of the nation into question. The level of exaggeration is both unmistakable and obscene and brings not so much Israel's as its accusers' integrity into doubt.

In a similar vein, Barry Chamish has put forward a conspiracy theory in *Who Murdered Yitzhak Rabin* that reflects discreditably on Israeli political life, implicating the Shin Bet and high-ranking officials in the assassination of the Israeli prime minister. In Chamish's view, the presumed assassin, Yigal Amir, was either the fall guy, a dupe, or a co-conspirator in an elaborate plot and subsequent cover-up carried out by the pro-Oslo fraternity that suspected Rabin of being about to renege on the "peace process." Chamish assembles a host of incriminating facts in support of his thesis that are strongly persuasive until one remembers that "facts" may be tweaked in any of a number of different ways or may be generated by an even more shadowy group of conspirators to frame yet another set of hypothetical plotters, as conspiracy theories tend by nature to constitute their own food chain. While I have little respect for the intelligence of Israel's professional Oslovians, I doubt they would be so foolish as to leave Amir alive, any more than Lee Harvey Oswald and Jack Ruby were—or would have been—permitted to survive in the dubious postlude to the Kennedy assassination, whatever the truth behind that terrible event. But what is most objectionable is the wilful blackening of Israel's public reputation under circumstances that remain at this time highly ambiguous.

One is troubled, to take yet another example, by the work of an otherwise erudite and conscientious scholar like Malise Ruthven, who in the last chapter of A Fury for God (in every other respect an estimable book), clearly shows his hand, treating the Arab League's offer in March 2002 of recognition for Israel, in exchange for withdrawal from the Territories, as fully trustworthy. (The League's convention soon disintegrated into a Levantine morass of factional infighting and is now busy protecting the Sudanese regime from outside intervention in its genocidal war against its animist and Christian minorities and its own black Muslims.) He then suggests that the terrorist organizations might well mitigate their avowed intention to liquidate Israel in exchange for political and territorial concessions although many of these terrorist groups have announced that they will settle for nothing less than the complete obliteration of the country, however they manage to achieve their aim. Were he actually living in Israel or in any country struggling for its survival against implacable suicidals, he might swiftly reconsider. Apart from this, the three no's of the Arab Khartoum summit of September 1, 1967—no recognition, no negotiations, no peace with Israel—are still *effectively* in place. (Only four nations of the twenty-two-member Arab League have diplomatic ties with Israel: Jordan, Egypt, Turkey, and Mauritania.) Further, Ruthven believes that Iran is "moving slowly toward secularism and democracy," despite all the evidence to the contrary as the mullocracy tightens its grip and seeks the acquisition of nuclear weapons. His conclusion that the "relatively open democracy which now exists in Iran" should be left to its own devices is more than a little contestable under the circumstances, given Iran's declared intention to destroy Israel by nuclear holocaust.

He next equates the "violations in the Israeli-occupied territories" with the policies of Saudi Arabia, anticipates Michael Ignatieff's argument in *The Lesser Evil* that the West should foster democracy in the Islamic countries *even if this should produce "hard-line Islamist rule,"* takes a run at President Bush and his entourage for their "neo-conservative's arrogant bombast," blames Ariel Sharon's visit to the Temple Mount for triggering the second intifada—Sharon was not in office at the time—when it has been known for some time that Israeli ministers had made frequent excursions to the site, that prior consultations had been held with the PA to clear Sharon's visit, and that the intifada had been long in the planning. He then asserts that the Palestinians should be awarded sovereignty "over what remains of their homeland." Note the sly formulation. While this last proposal would appear to be acceptable in principle, the phrasing begs the question and reveals a concealed agenda, for it assumes that the *rest of the land at issue is also Palestinian homeland unfairly wrested from its rightful owners*—a hornet's nest that has yet to be smoked. As I have contended throughout, and as Joan Peters has indisputably shown in her sedulously researched *From Time Immemorial*, the case for Israel is far stronger than the case for Palestine, especially if we recall that the British census reports during the Mandatory period were regularly falsified to create the impression of a massive and indigenous Palestinian presence that did not exist, that the *whole of Palestine*, both what is now Israel and what is now Jordan, was originally intended by the League of Nations as an indivisible Jewish homeland and that the Jewish state was officially recognized by the United Nations.

Ruthven's hatred of Israel (allied with his contempt for the United States), breaking out in the concluding section of his book, cuts short the historical perspective, and simply shoots down his seemingly nonpartisan approach, ruining an otherwise fine effort. Like the terrorists he is analyzing, he is unable to control his rage and his affidavit suffers for it. The important point, however, is that ostensibly decent and competent scholars like Ruthven must become more self-aware if they are to avoid unconscious prejudice passing itself off as good faith or speculative detachment. It is not, to quote William Butler Yeats, that "the best lack all conviction," but that even the best are perhaps little better than the worst in the harm that impressive credentials can wreak if they are not lived up to.

When we proceed to consider the diverse forms of antisemitism at work in the world, perhaps the most tenacious and resistant variety is the unconscious antisemitism of those who proclaim they have no personal stake in the matter, who speak movingly of respecting Arab dignity and honour and argue reasonably about Israeli unreasonableness, who are given to romanticizing the flowing robes and checkered head scarves of the desert nomads and the plangent intonations of the muezzin's call to prayer, who draw back in fastidious horror at "pushy" Jewish claims of precedence or sovereignty or the historical right of self-defence, and most of whom know just enough about the intricacies of the Middle East—information gathered primarily from uncontextualized and often unfairly tilted newspaper and TV reporting—to validate their detestation of all things Jewish and Israeli while keeping their philoMuslim sentiments unimpaired. But their knowledge stops precisely at the point where anything in excess of that paucity would force them to reevaluate their proprietary attitudes and to recognize the depth of their prejudice. A little knowledge is a comforting thing in that it both reinforces the illusion of sobriety and preserves the unconscious from painful scrutiny. For beneath the veneer of prudence and rationality swirls a libidinal delirium.

This reflex of "unconscious antisemitism" is extremely common and we come across it everywhere, even among staid and temperate historians who seem overly willing to credit the testimony of others without sufficient analysis, or are quick to put a pejorative slant on "documentary evidence." I remember the astonishment I felt when reading John Harvey's history of the Plantagenets. A professional historian, a defender of the political concept of monarchy and a man presumably without a religious axe to grind, Harvey had no problem referring to the Jewish community in medieval England as an "alien body" responsible for causing "economic hardship" and possibly implicated in "a series of most sinister crimes committed against Christian children, including murder...." Trading in the most dubious allegations, his prosaic assurance remains unruffled. "Whatever we may think of the evidence in favour of 'ritual murder,'" he continues, "a number of instances of mysterious child-murder undoubtedly did occur in twelfth- and thirteenth-century England." He concludes by writing in "vindication of English justice," that is, of the decision "to remove the whole Jewish community," and cites Chaucer's Prioress as well as a collection of "exquisite folk-songs."

Here is an old wives' tale that has been given a modern cast with the renewed focus on the supposed intrigues of "the Jewish lobby" and especially on the behaviour of contemporary Israel. A telling example is Alexandre Trudeau's documentary *The Fence*, released in September 2004, which does for the Palestinian cause what Michael Moore's *Fahrenheit 9/11* and John Sayle's *Silver City* do for the Democratic Party, but far more subtly because the filmmaker's intentions are, presumably, opaque even to himself. Trudeau vividly presents the troubled and violent lives of Palestinians without overt or sufficiently expository reference to the terrorist movement that is directly responsible for their immediate condition and sympathetically interviews al-Aqsa Martyrs Brigades chieftain Zacharia Zubeidi, staging him as a husband and father and focusing on the gunpowder stains on his face but not the blood on his hands. He boldly taunts Israeli border guards who now have to deal with another Western political tourist who believes he is somehow exempt and inviolable, slams the numerous checkpoints in the West Bank for causing hardship and humiliation among ordinary Palestinians, but again without considering the bombs in baby carriages, handbags, and school satchels being smuggled across the border to blow up Israeli civilians, and shows an Israeli youngster playing sniper video games—a killer in the making—as if Canadian and American children were strangers to Sega, PlayStation, Xbox, and GameCube and Palestinian youths were not firing real Kalashnikovs in the streets. Finally, he flogs the construction of the security fence that divides the two peoples and further alienates them from one another without acknowledging that the *real* builder of the fence is the second intifada (or what has been called the Arafada), that is, Yasser Arafat along with Hamas, Tanzim, al-Aqsa, and the rest of the terrorist mafia. Nor does Trudeau consider that the greatest impediment to the completion of the fence emanates from within Israel itself, that is, from the decisions of the Israeli High Court of Justice that habitually rules against the proposed route and agrees to hear protest petitions in such numbers as to slow down the entire process, thus abetting the incursions of the suicide bombers. Many Israelis believe that lives might have been spared if the Court had acted more responsibly in the midst of what is nothing less than an undeclared war, but Trudeau sees fit to bypass entirely the costly impartiality of the Israeli judiciary. As propaganda, the film is extraordinarily effective; as a documentary, it is a maudlin sham that brilliantly cloaks its underlying motives not only from the viewer but possibly from the filmmaker's own cinematic eye.[22]

Another such example is Ted Conover's article in the *Atlantic* (March 2006), entitled *The Checkpoint*, which is only slightly more shaded. While acknowledging, more or less in passing, that there is such a thing as a terrorist threat, his sympathies clearly align with the suffering Palestinians for whom the checkpoints are "frustrating, humiliating, and anger-provoking." "Checkpoints can be brutal," he grieves, seemingly unaware that the brutality card has been long overplayed in the Western press. Brutality is inevitable in abnormal situations, but the more unfortunate incidents he documents are primarily just that— incidents. In the midst of a terror war, checkpoints are as necessary as customs controls in peacetime. While he does mention the episode in which a Palestinian teenager was ordered to lift his shirt, only to reveal "a vest wired with explosives," the accompanying photo shows instead a Palestinian youngster lifting his shirt to reveal—a bare midriff. "You see what we have to put up with," says one of his interlocutors. But neither Conover nor his new acquaintance do *see*. For what the Palestinians "have to put up with" is self-inflicted: disarm the terrorists, recognize that the wars of 1967 and 1973 were monumental blunders, reject the legacy of Yasser Arafat, and what they will then "have to put up with" is not the Israelis but only Arab governance. But this is not all. Conover also, rather conveniently, skims over the fact that anti-civilian brutality is a mainstay of the other side where it has acquired the status of formal policy and deliberate practice. Then there is the ambulance business. Although Hamas and Islamic Jihad, as he well knows, have used ambulances as assault vehicles and personnel carriers, Conover mourns the "cruel…indignities [of] hours-long detention of ambulances carrying Palestinian patients." Worse, an injured man is made to leave an ambulance to be frisked in greater security; that he may be concealing explosives under his bandages does not seem to occur to our reporter, nor that it is precisely such Palestinian tactics that have led to such "brutalities." And there is more. For Conover, the security fence that saves Israeli lives is a "symbol of…restriction," as it is for Trudeau. The "occupation" is taken at face value and the issue of "encroach[ment] on

Palestinian land" is hoisted completely out of its ambiguous historical habitat with the result that the concept of "Palestinian land" has been accepted without analysis, becoming the opium of the uninformed. There is a crippling absence of logic in such journalistic performances, as if there were no clear connection between Israeli punitive actions and the almost daily incursions of the terrorist intifada—*as if, that is, the Palestinians were not, in reality, the victims of their own terrorist militias.* Conover may be, according to his credits, "a distinguished writer-in-residence at New York University," but he is distinguished only by the acerbic subtlety of his anti-Israeli bias masking itself as egalitarian sensitivity.

The Israeli response to the second intifada was certainly harsh and disruptive, as indeed it had to be considering that, with its small population, the proportionate trauma caused by the terrorist offensive is far higher in Israel than in the United States or Russia. The math is not hard to do. In relative numerical terms, the number of Israeli civilians murdered by the terrorists during the second intifada alone would be roughly equivalent to 50,000 Americans. The number of injured and maimed would swell to 300,000. This is something we do not like to think about; rather, Israeli defensive operations have spawned a veritable industry of censors and detractors. These critics of Israel are often not in possession of the relevant facts, which is the best way of supporting an untenable argument. They seem unaware, for example, that in the pre-Oslo period when Israel was in control of the territories, there were neither checkpoints nor curfews and Palestinians enjoyed freedom of movement and goods; it was post-Oslo, when Arafat reigned over the autonomous territories placed under his disposition, that there was a vertiginous spike in terrorist activities and Draconian Israeli defensive tactics became necessary. Further, when it comes to Israel, such critics rarely pause to reflect how difficult it is for a people to proceed with equanimity and unstinting compassion when the "background radiation" of that people's collective life consists of the prospect of always-imminent extermination, a people who, apart from the quislings in their midst, have never forgotten what happened in the Treblinka of Jehovah's eye. The predominant Israeli attitude is best summed up in the oft-recited poem of Yiddish poet Mordecai Gebirtig who, after the pogrom in the Polish town of Przytyk in 1936, wrote his widely anthologized *"Undzer Shtetl Brendt"* ("Our Town Is Burning"), the concluding stanza of which reads:

> *Brothers, don't stand by calmly*
> *with folded arms.*
> *Don't stand by, brothers, put out the fire—*
> *our town is burning.*

And should such a disaster actually come to pass one day, should the "town" burn to the ground, what will these carpers say then in extenuation? Whoops, we goofed? Or maybe, Never Again? Though, more likely, just as 9/11 is blamed on "American arrogance" by left-wing and "liberal" apologists for Islamic terror, the dissolution of Israel would be regarded by these same indoctrinated dupes as self-engendered. (Of course, if Israel continues to give away land and enter into one-way agreements with the Palestinians, there might then be a moiety of truth to this absurdity.) This state of affairs is perhaps most depressing in the case of invertebrate Jews in influential media posts, such as *Globe and Mail* columnist Rick Salutin, ideological heir of Israel-bashing I. F. Stone and of Robert Silvers and Jacob Epstein of the *New York Review of Books*; or Tony Judt, a historian with pretensions, who, in his articles for the *New York Review of Books*, the *Nation*, and the *New Republic*, has contended that Israel must cease to exist—it is, in his words, an "anachronism." (A collaborator of Edward Said's, Judt pontificates, as did Said, from a New York university soapbox where he is free to indulge his hatred, not only of Israel, but of America as well.) These are people who casually court disaster in the remorseless anti-Israeli (and *pro forma* anti-American) posture they affect. At home in a latter-day Iberian delusion—if one recalls the eventual fate of the Spanish conversos—they have far more to brood about than their Gentile compatriots. Their only consolation in the ever-possible event of a resurgent and maniacal anti-Jewish national movement or devastating terrorist attack is that, like the Jewish Councils in Nazi Europe, they would be among the last to go, once their revisionist services were no longer needed by the *shahids* they have invited into the house. Nor is the indifference of the assimilated Jew to the fate of Israel any less damaging than the heteroclite zeal of his brasher colleagues. As George Steiner wrote in *Language and Silence*, "If Israel were to be destroyed, no Jew would escape unscathed. The shock of failure, the need and harrying of those seeking refuge, would reach out to implicate even the most indifferent, the most anti-Zionist." For, he continues, "In a crisis of resentment or exclusion, even the more assimilated would be driven back to our ancient legacy of fear." And so would the apostate and the revisionist. It is the very fact of the existence of the Jewish state, a country that has so far beaten all the odds and lives on the cutting edge of military, scientific, and intellectual achievement, that empowers the Jew in the Diaspora, which is precisely why the antisemite must now seek to vilify and delegitimize the national guarantor of the Jew's value, dignity, confidence, and stature in the world. The new antisemite pretends that it is not the Jew he objects to, but the Zionist or the Israeli, for he knows that with Israel out of the picture, the Jew is once again a universal mendicant, reverting to "type" as an object of condescension, derision, humiliation, or worse.

Caveat Judaeus! One Jew's warp is another Jew's weft, with no way out of the tapestry. There is a passage in Amos Oz's recent *A Tale of Love and Darkness* that makes this running together of distinctions painfully clear. Referring to the Nazi cleansing operations in the Polish town of Rovno, he writes, "the Germans opened fire and slaughtered on the edge of pits, in two days, some twenty-five thousand souls...well-to-do and proletarian, pious, assimilated, and baptized, communal leaders, synagogue functionaries, peddlers and drawers of water, Communists and Zionists, intellectuals, artists, and village idiots, and some four thousand babies." The message is that we're all incriminated. Warm Jews, lukewarm Jews, and cold Jews are equally at risk. At the end of the day, the antisemite never stopped to take their temperature.

4

But, after all this, the problem of definition remains. Complicating matters is the fact that many Jews see their identity as that of the sacrificial lamb, embracing the slaughterhouse. As Amotz Asa-El points out in his "Letter to a Palestinian Colleague" (*Jerusalem Post*, December 30, 2004), there is "a suicidal side to us Jews: big time," having submitted collectively over the millennia to the dream of survival without a nation and an army, relying only on the preservation of Judaism's spiritual

heritage and the Lord's generosity. In the current political environment, one thinks of the New Historians who have sold their birthright
for scholastic perquisites and career status among their postmodern
peers, the Israeli peaceniks suing their own government over the legal-
ity of the security fence meant to defend them, dishonest thinkers like
Buber and Scholem who wrote their books and prospered in the sanctuary afforded them by the country whose founding principles they
opposed, the ideologues of the far left who grovel for Palestinian absolution from the mortal sin of Israel's existence and seek to deconstruct
the Jewish state, academics like Harvard's Herbert Kelman and the
Peres Center for Peace's Ron Pundak who remain under the mesmeric
trance of a "two-track diplomacy" that does not take Palestinian recre-
ancy and terrorist intransigence into serious consideration, Israeli cabinet ministers like Yosef Lapid who irresponsibly brings up Holocaust
comparisons with regard to defensive operations in the Gaza Strip and
Meretz Chairman Yossi Beilin still operating under the necromantic
spell of Oslo, and writers like Aharon Appelfeld who place their trust
in weakness and solitude. One thinks, retrospectively, even of Hannah
Arendt who resisted the formation of a Jewish state and defended her
former lover Martin Heidegger, a philosopher who never recanted
his belief in Nazism; and of the influential president of the Hebrew
University, Judah Magnes, who campaigned tirelessly against the idea
of a sovereign Jewish power and a national homeland for the dispossessed even as millions of Jews were being exterminated during the
War and deported and interned during the peace.

Broadly speaking, it is hard to suppress the suspicion that many
Jews, both in the assimilationist diaspora and among left-wing Israelis,
are simply tired of being Jews, weary of history, of having constantly to
defend their traditional ways of life as well as having to fight for their
very existence. They have had enough and wish for nothing more than
to become an unremarked (and unremarkable) part of the societies in
which they live or to dissolve the Jewish state, which their parents and
grandparents laboured at such cost to create, into an obliterating sea
of Arabism. Like Achilles in his tent, they have retired from the battle;
but unlike Achilles, they have no intention of emerging. It's as if a kind
of senescence, the slumping defeatism of old age, has finally overtaken
them. Recently I read an open letter to the *Globe and Mail*, signed by
members of the Shalom-Salaam Jewish-Arab "dialogue group" in

Montreal, casting shame on Prime Minister Stephen Harper for his pro-Israeli stand in the Israel/Hizbullah conflict, insisting on the disproportionality of the Israeli response, omitting or distorting the facts, denying that Israel was fighting in self-defence, and denouncing the Jewish state for its "policy of aggression" and for perpetrating "a brutal occupation." Signatories with names like Lippman, Shaffer, Block, and Yarosky, whose knowledge of their own political history and of the real forces at work in the always-active volcano of the Middle East seems vacuous or factititous, have turned themselves into the potential victims of the next social purge, whatever form it might take. These are Jews who have been emptied of substance and who have, in a way, anticipated the extinction that much of the world, whether secretly or openly, desires for them. Here we see the kind of thinking that sets in when one grows exhausted by history and abdicates the struggle for survival, dignity, and cultural vigour.

One might also reflect upon that mournful specimen, the bumbling, well-meaning, naive—naive regardless of educational or professional qualification—and overly self-confident Jew, often with pretensions of grandeur, who is as much a danger to his people in his dealings with the adversary as the latter himself is. Sir Herbert Samuel, First British High Commissioner in Palestine, springs immediately to mind. A supporter of pan-Arabism and the main figure in the political cretinism that led to the installation of Haj Amin al-Husseini, Jew-hater and Nazi collaborator, as Grand Mufti of Jerusalem, Samuel was an easy mark for duplicitous British officials working from within the Secretariat, who helped appoint the Mufti under fraudulent circumstances. Perhaps the chief contemporary exemplar is Shimon Peres, who began his career as a Ben-Gurionite and helped develop Israel's military infrastructure, but went on to become a believer in the Utopian dream of a *Pax Arabica*. Following in the pseudo-mystical footsteps of Martin Buber, who saw the Holy Land as a temple "for all peoples," and seduced by what he calls the "shining example" of Western Europe, Peres argues in *The New Middle East* for the evolution of the state of Israel from a "particularist nationalism" that has become "irrelevant" toward "the ultranational development of regional communities." That the prospect of an Arab-Israeli federation erected on the fantasy of an "ultranationalist identity" is a surefire formula for self-destruction troubles neither his ardour nor his eloquence, nor does Peres seem to have noticed that

Arafat's second intifada and the "particularist" intentions of the suicide bombers have made such ideas "irrelevant." Peres is a specimen of that breed of eternal Jewish optimist who would have said in the 1930s that it should be possible to come to some kind of arrangement with the Nazis.

Then comes the vanguard of Israel's secessionary professors, those "jackal counterfeits" (in Oswald Spengler's phrase) protected by the principle of academic freedom and drawing their salaries from the public treasury, who vigorously pursue their campaign to delegitimize the country and the institutions that nourish them. Taking not just a page but whole volumes out of Arab curriculum and methodology, they do not shy from putting themselves and their country in the line of fire, very much like their left-liberal counterparts in the West capering in ideological amusement parks defended by those whom they misprize. Thus Moshe Zimmerman, head of the German Studies Department at Hebrew University, compares Hebron Youth to Hitler Youth, the IDF to the Waffen SS, and the Bible to *Mein Kampf*. Neve Gordon, from the Political Science Department at the same university, is convinced that Israel is a fascist country whose policies do not materially differ from the acts of Palestinian terrorists and that Israel is guilty of crimes against humanity; his visit of encouragement to Yasser Arafat during Operation Defensive Shield, in company with the anti-Zionist Ta'ayush group, should have come as no surprise. Though a less prolific defamer of his country, his colleague Ze'ev Sternhell promotes "armed resistance" among the Palestinian terror squads. That such "armed resistance" translates as carnage visited upon a civilian population does not appear to vex the good professor unduly. Ran Hacohen, professor of Comparative Literature at Tel Aviv University, condemns Israel for "fulfilling Hitler's dream." Lev Grinberg, who directs the Humphries Institute for Social Research at Ben Gurion University, writes in European newspapers about Israeli "state terrorism" and comes to the defence of terrorist kingpin Sheikh Ahmed Yassin. Oren Yiftachel, professor of Geography at the same university, claims that Israel is not so much a democracy as an "ethnocracy," views Israeli citizenship as an "illusion," and presses for the revocation of Israel's Law of Return. Binyamin Beit Hallahmi, professor of Psychology at the University of Haifa, accuses all Israelis of original sin. Similarly, Meron Benvenisti of Beersheba University wonders if there is not "some 'original sin' that lies at the foundation of the Zionist enterprise" and describes the IDF operating against terrorists and arms smugglers as an army of "Israeli attackers" actuated by "a primitive desire for vengeance and uninhibited militancy." This, as it turns out, is the same army that takes unnecessary casualties in trying to avoid civilian fatalities and that allows Professor Benvenisti to enjoy the luxury of original sin in a country whose founding principles he disputes. Aharon Shabtai, professor of Greek Culture at Tel Aviv University, is an acclaimed poet who suffers eloquently for the Palestinians, scorches the IDF as an army of snipers and "idiotic soldiers of lead," and compares Israelis to "members of the master race"; in his last book of poems (2003), Shabtai accused Israel of murdering Muhammad al-Dura, but has not yet seen fit to publish a retraction in the light of the exonerating evidence that has surfaced in recent years, making it more than likely that the affair was a well-coordinated hoax. Haifa University graduate student Teddy Katz, a protégé of Ilan Pappe, after admitting in court to having falsified evidence for his Master's thesis alleging that the Alexandroni Brigade had massacred hundreds of Arabs during the War of Independence, continues to merchandise the same gallimaufry of lies as he addresses university audiences around the world. The list goes on and on. With such Jews, who needs Arabs?

Working in the spirit of the German-Jewish emancipationist thinkers and teachers to wrest Jewish education away from its traditional moorings in Jewish history and faith, Israel's revisionist intellectuals have betrayed the principles that honour and reason, as well as self-interest, would have required them to defend. That they are also in violation of the State Education Law passed in 1953 seems to be a matter of no importance to them. Such contemporary "prophets," preaching to the multitudes from lectern and editorial page, unwittingly confirm the utterance of the Talmudic sage Rabbi Yohanan, who said in the tractate *Bava Batra* that when the Temple was destroyed, prophecy was taken from the prophets and given to fools and children. As with so many of their colleagues among the Israeli *anshei ruah* (men of the spirit, the cultural magnates), the consummation of their ideology is a severing of ties to the Jewish past and the abandonment of a Jewish future, which, in the context of the actual world, is tantamount to self-slaughter. The meld of cowardice and stupidity evinced by such intellectual and pedagogical luminaries, who hold the educational future in their custody, constitutes perhaps the greatest danger imaginable to the survival of the Jewish state. And their efforts are countersigned by many of the current generation of Israel's political rulers, who behave as if they were writing on the Western Wall, with reference to their own nation, the dread phrase from the book of Daniel: MENE, MENE, TEKEL, UPHARSIN. Observing the disarray in the political and intellectual life of the nation, I am put in mind of Pieter Bruegel's allegorical masterpiece, *The Parable of the Blind*, based on *Matthew* 15:14: "If the blind lead the blind, both shall fall into the ditch." In Bruegel's painting there are six stumbling figures, whom I am tempted to update and name: the "peace movement," the media, the Revisionist professors, the Orthodox anti-Zionists, the literati, and the Barak-like politicians, all of whom have put out their own eyes. There can be no question that, for the most part, Israel's media and academic elite, abetted by many of its politicians, rabbis, agitators, and literary and artistic stars, are actively soliciting for the enemy, a condition bordering on madness. They have not only buried their heads in the sand, they have notched them in the guillotine.

One can't help but wonder whether two millennia of appalling immolation have somehow produced a sacerdotal love of extinction, a death wish so potent that it may finally resist analysis. Perhaps Anthony Hecht is close to the truth when he writes, in his chilling poem "More Light! More Light!"—an ironic twist on Goethe's dying words—from *The Hard Hours*, "Much casual death had drained away their souls." But, whatever the reason, this is definitely a strain in the Jewish "character"—to be, in the words of the prophet Isaiah, "a light unto the nations," but a darkness unto itself—that would be reprehensible were it not so pitiful. Jews would be far better off going to school with Ze'ev Jabotinsky who, in his famous "Iron Wall," article of 1923, argued that one cannot make concessions except from a position of recognized and undoubted strength. The security fence now being erected (which Jerusalem mayor Uri Lupoliansky has justifiably named "the fence of life") is a tangible instance of this Iron Wall, but Israeli policy must follow suit as well if future negotiations are ever to bear fruit.[23] Israel will also need a solid anti-missile wall—the Patriot, the Nautilus, the Arrow, the Spyder—no less than a human wall of competent politicians and incorruptible commanders behind which it can live in relative security. What Israel does not need is another ninth of Av on which to mourn the ruins of its sacred places, another broken wall of remembrance to pray before. What Israel does not need is another murky conclusion to a war of aggression against its sovereign territory, as in the summer of 2006.

Meanwhile, the Gentile and Islamic worlds keep heaping it on. Jews are variously attacked as impenitent Zionists, as colonial expansionists, as displacers of indigenous peoples, as members of a sinister cabal dedicated to world domination, as a dark chthonic race reminiscent of H. G. Wells' Morlocks or as an effete society of cultural elitists resembling Wells' Eloi, as proto-communists (the book of Amos) as well as revolutionary Bolsheviks, as directors of American neocon foreign policy, as a guileful sect of economic conspirators and capitalist entrepreneurs, as a ragtag collection of peregrine undesirables akin to the gypsies, as a treacherous and terrorist-sponsoring people responsible for abominations like the 9/11 attack on the US perpetrated under the sign of Islam—what Abraham Foxman in *Never Again* dubs "the latest version of the Big Lie," though, as he points out, many Jews and even some Israelis died in the inferno—,as the accursed conscience of civilized man with its relentless and unrealizable demands ("Conscience is a Jewish invention," wrote Hitler in *Mein Kampf*), as a historical fossil whose day in the sun passed eons ago (according to the authority of Arnold Toynbee), as a tribe of sophisticated cosmopolitans sapping the natural energies of a victimized humanity or as a primitive band of lipid parasites feeding off the body politic, or as the devil's own spawn given to the practice of horrendous rites from the paschal devouring of children to the art of skeptical inquiry that must be resisted by every means at the world's disposal from unmitigated violence to professional divestment. The GPS device has not yet been invented that can help the Jew track his position in the cruelly whimsical and metamorphic world he inhabits.

Thus, if Judaism is not denounced for creating the "slave morality" of the Christian West, as in Nietzsche's *On The Genealogy of Morals*, then it is blamed for inspiring Western "arrogance," traced back to the notion of Chosenness, as in Toynbee's *A Study of History*. Abasement or hubris, it matters little since, as applied to the Jew, the rules of logic are set aside and opposites do not cancel but reinforce one another. Here is perhaps the single instance in our experience where the law of non-contradiction does not hold. But in the actual world we live in, opposites do indeed cancel out. If reason X cancels reason Y, then what remains is no reason at all. What this batch of self-negating causal explanations for hatred of the Jew tells us is that, when the equation has been properly factored, there is absolutely *zero* reason left to justify this mishmash of clichéd abominations. When all is not yet said and not quite done, what stays constant in this shifting landscape of chimeras is the deprivation of a people's right to survive and prosper without being subject to a perpetual calvary.[24] But where amongst these many and conflicting pseudo-identities does the Jew reside?

For its presumptive bearer, Jewish identity is made up of so many competing and irreconcilable elements that the appellation "Jew" seems more of a misnomer than what philosopher Saul Kripke, in *Naming and Necessity*, has called a "rigid designator" or a "universal quantifier." The term "Jew" designates not so much a single entity or a "being for itself" as, on the one hand, a crowd of conflicting social and religious self-manifestations and, on the other, the world's need for prejudicial and contradictory reductions. To quote Kripke again, one might say that the Jew, whether from the world's perspective or his own, is the victim of the universal "tendency to demand purely qualitative descriptions of counterfactual situations." Nevertheless, the identity issue remains as crucial for the Jew as does his problematic status in the world. James Parkes in *Whose Land?* points to "the perpetual paradox of Judaism, a particularism which fenced in a particular discipline of life for a single people, and an ethical monotheism of universal significance"—is the Jew for himself or for others? Rabbi Hillel's most famous saying, recorded in the *Pirkei Avot*, a tractate of the *Mishnah*, underlines the dilemma: "If I am not for myself, then who will be for me? And if I am only for myself, then what am I? And if not now, when?" Jewish communicants seem unable to decide.

The conundrum has been given a modern cast by French psychoanalyst Daniel Sibony, who argues in his latest book, *L'énigme antisémite*, that the Jew is reproached and persecuted as the bearer of an unstable identity, trapped between a divine message and a faulty transmission, for both of which he is made equally responsible. He suffers an "identité barrée," locked between the ideal and the real and oscillating between various identity possibilities, which epitomizes the deep insecurity, the inability to settle upon a single, coherent way of life and to find psychic wholeness, experienced by "modern man," the identity-deficit native to humanity as a whole. The resurgence of antisemitism today may thus be traced to the anguish and crisis of identity engendered by the cultural and spiritual dislocations of modernity, which are then projected upon the Jew. The argument is compelling and yet perhaps too rarefied and evanescent to be harnessed to material indices—it may or may not be so.

A. B. Yehoshua develops a similar hypothesis in an essay for the Israeli journal *2000*, entitled *An Attempt to Comprehend the Root of Antisemitism*. Here he accounts for this "psychosis of humanity" as a mental deformation produced by what he conceives as the virtual, flexible, and fluid elements of Jewish identity as it is transferred from country to country, igniting the Gentile's anxiety respecting his own lack of clear self-definition. For Yehoshua, this is "the root" of antisemitism, which is "structural and not a matter of content." It is the imaginative element in the process of Jewish identity-configuration that stimulates a counter-imagination in the Gentile. If I understand Yehoshua aright, the Jew is thus both recoiled from and regarded with a deadly fascination as the bearer of the unbearable, a kind of universal Loki-figure, trickster and shape-shifter, carrier of the free-floating possibilities of identity change who "activate[s] imagination to crystallize identity." The Lord may be One, but the Jew is not. It is this very undecidability, this protean slipperiness and elasticity, that makes the Jew a threat. At the same time, we might add, it is also this perceived amorphousness or multiplexity that accounts for the need to reduce the "Jewish nature" to a single, definitive attribute as the inabsorbable alien in our midst, very much like Tolkien's Gollum, the figure of greed and disruption. (The name derives from the Hebrew *golem* or *g-l-m*, an "unshaped form.") The paradox of giving form to the stubbornly formless is only apparent. Reductiveness is a defence against intolerable plurality. It follows that the Jew kindles in the tinder of the Gentile sensibility a flame of hatred and fear, along with a grudging enthrallment, for challenging by his presence the psychic ductility of his Other.

Analogously, when it comes to the question of Islamic hostility in particular, Yehoshua in *The Liberated Bride* has his protagonist, an Israeli orientalist, argue that the "problematic indeterminacy of Jewish identity undermines the old stability of the Arab world that slumbered peacefully for centuries in the desert" (which, incidentally, it didn't), thus depriving the Arab of a single, reified Jewish correlate or metatype *against which to establish his own sense of cultural unity and coherence.* According to this thesis, the poor Jew's fractured self inspires the intensified enmity of the Arab world by failing to provide a fixed, homogeneous target—an interesting idea supported by the perceived Muslim need to refer to a politically striated, internally divided and racially and ethnically polychromatic Israel as *the* "Zionist entity." But the Yehoshuan hypothesis is nevertheless theoretically provisional in once again making the Jew, however subtly, responsible by self-diffraction for the irrational hatred of the Jewish Other's Other—the Arab who steps into the biblical sandals of the Christian or even of the pre-Christian pagan. But from whatever angle we view the matter, the Jew's fate, it seems, is to be a Jew if he is a Jew, to be a Jew if he decides he isn't a Jew or does not see himself as a Jew, to be a Jew even if his identity is irremediably fractured, or to be a Jew even if he is only one of innumerable "specifications" in an inchoate and indefinable category of human beings frequently in conflict with and within themselves. There is no operation known to man that can transform a Jew into a non-Jew; even gender, I sometimes think, is a more malleable category of being. One can always undergo a sex-change, but one cannot successfully unJew oneself.

This imposition of an artificial identity, however, is not to be confused with the notion of the Jew as scapegoat, as per certain copper-bottomed theories of popular psychology. Even more sophisticated elucidations of the scapegoat psychology, such as that of philosopher René Girard, who in his essays on the subject develops the notion of "mimetic victimage"—the violence *between groups* in a given society is resolved by projecting it upon a third party that is then expelled—do not entirely account for the antisemitic prepossession. The function of the scapegoat, as derived from Leviticus 16, implies consciousness or intent on the part of the community that exiles or sacrifices its proxy. For the community's collective sins are *deliberately* transferred to a chosen vehicle that, by being cast out, relieves the community of its accumulated guilt. But the scapegoating of the Jew emerges from the cisterns of the unconscious. Girard, be it said, credits the operative effect of the unconscious, but in his theory the unconscious functions selectively at certain "ritual" intervals when a social group experiences internal dissension, which is then externalized upon a convenient "Other." The phenomenon, however, would appear to be more fundamental, affecting the individual in the very germ of his being—neuronally, as it were. Those who condemn the Jew do so for unconscious reasons that cannot be explained simply, or only, by ritual mimesis—that is, in Girard's language, when "an object becomes the focus of mimetic rivalry between two or more antagonists"—and are always masked beneath mere ostensibilities, that conflicting array of social and economic factors generally adduced to explain or justify Jew-hatred. The Jew is not a scapegoat, in the proper acceptation of the term (or even in its ritual distillation), but is, at least plausibly, humanity's unacknowledged, interior surrogate, the image and reflection that cannot and must not be recognized, the "inner self" systematically repressed and banished from the circle of awareness. From this perspective, as Ernst Simmel suggested in *Anti-Semitism: A Social Disease*, the Jew is everyone else's bad conscience that, as usual, is confined to the realm of the infrared. Why this should be the case—if it is the case—is a conundrum that can never be satisfactorily plumbed. Perhaps, as some have thought, the Jew is dimly understood as the living incarnation of a moral imperative—the Freudian superego—that is deeply resented because it cannot be fulfilled; or, alternately, feared as the avatar of a long tradition of questioning, distrust, and irony that arouses the abrasion of self-doubt and the rasp of self-contempt. Saul Bellow reflects in *To Jerusalem and Back*, "Jews do, it is well known, make inordinate demands upon themselves and upon one another. Upon the world, too. I occasionally wonder whether that is why the world is so uncomfortable with them." The Jewish mind is humanity's hairshirt, the irritant worn beneath the daily apparel. Or to phrase it differently, if somewhat conjecturally, *the Jew is the Gentile's unconscious*.[25]

Such a noetic intimacy, welding him to the very soul of man, is no consolation for the Jew, who must also struggle to find his own individual psychic balance among the jumble of personal, social, religious, and historical factors, pertaining to his elusive selfhood, that buffet him endlessly. To put it in everyday terms: if he is an orthodox Haredi, he must look with disdain and disbelief at his recusant brothers whose temporal world-view clashes with his own. If he is an eremitically inclined ascetic, he must demur in horror from his younger, urbanized co-religionists revelling in the cafés and nightclubs of Tel Aviv-Sodom and Haifa-Gomorrah, reaping their bloody reward of nails and rivets. If he is a member of the Leftist camp, he must at times feel a certain schizoid unease at the conformity of his political position with that of the Palestinian who would dispossess him of his birthright. If he is a right-wing patriot, he must wonder who the real opponent he is fighting against happens to be, the terrorist firing mortar shells and detonating suicide bombs or the Jewish peacenik protesting against his own army's defensive maneuvers to ensure his safety. And if he is, quite simply, a devout and unworldly lover of God, he must occasionally reflect upon the old saying, which begins in ideal Hebrew and ends in realistic Yiddish: *You chose us from among all the nations—what did You have against us?*

The assimilated diasporite is a special case. Even if he couldn't care less about Israel or his own defining tradition and history and retains only a vestigial sense of being a Jew, he must at some level of the unconscious indistinctly realize that the psychological nose job is no less artificial and futile than the proverbial physiological one. Though he may be utterly aloof to politics and wish only to be allowed to live a private and insular life, to distract himself with quotidian issues, as if what playwright and essayist David Mamet endearingly calls "preholocaust attention" were still possible, he cannot evade the excommunicatory fusillade of the print and electronic media, the intensification of anti-Jewish propaganda, the calumny of the chattering classes, and the violence in the Middle East in which, whether he likes it or not, he is profoundly implicated and which he must struggle to understand. These are issues he must labour to come to terms with, to grasp in all their complexity, if he is not to find himself at sea in the face of the criticism and tribulation he must naturally expect. Professions of ignorance or disclaimers of responsibility are always useless. And if he (or she) is a Jew married to a non-Jew—or vice versa—it would be folly to assume that one or another partner is not in some degree potentially compromised. That, too, is a splinter in the soul. Can a more self-divided and fissiparous people be found anywhere in the world today? This is perhaps the most pressing question: How does the Jew, who must also contain in little all these competing dimensions of identity, commitment and disavowal within his own psychic economy, accord with himself? Or as Nietzsche would have put it, Where does he locate his "ipsissimosity"? There are, in effect, many different Jewries in play along a brassy diapason from reciprocal antipathy to passionate debate to cool indifference to actual self-hatred rather than anything like a single people gathered around the same patrimonial tentpole, and this variety is reflected in the soul of the individual Jew who is in some sense always at war with himself, even when under apparent sedation.

The Jewish people lives on the fault lines of history, initiating or undergoing a constant series of collective transitions: from slavery to freedom, from paganism to monotheism, from a priest-oriented faith to a text-centred dispensation, from nationhood to dispersal and from dispersal back to nationhood. This sense of passage and realignment is carried by one of the etymologies of the word "Hebrew," namely *'abar* (passed over), whence *'eber*, ("one who passes through"), and is reinforced by another derivation from the Aramaic, *'ibri*, (one from the other side). In the twentieth century, perhaps the greatest divide was that between the profane and the sacred, with Jews, on the one hand, contributing massively to vast anti-religious movements such as revolutionary socialism and communism and, on the other, re-establishing strong Orthodox communities bent on the preservation of halachic Judaism. The dilemma for the individual Jew preoccupied with what distinguishes him from other people, whether on his own count or on theirs, may be perceived to an important extent as a function of the shifts and displacements of the amorphous collectivity to which he willy-nilly belongs. Thus when he looks inwardly to determine where he abides, he finds only a welter of different addresses.

Although I, personally, did not celebrate a bar mitzvah, married outside the faith, happen to drive a Volkswagen, and, more to the point, was never subject to the attentions of suicide bombers or cashiered by the Academy, when I think it over I see I am a Jew predominantly because as a child I was routinely beaten and insulted for being one. A mere trifle, of course, compared to some of the horror stories from the "old country": a grandfather bludgeoned to death over his bible and an aunt cut to pieces in the street, victims of that universal form of entertainment, the pogrom. Nothing compared to what the Zionist settlers in the Holy Land had to endure or the present inhabitants of Israel are made to suffer. But the bond is there. And I am a Jew, too, because, like all Jews, I have been socially gibbeted for that indelible and arcane entelechy, the default setting of my identity. I have often had to embarrass people in public—even "nice" people, as in Elia Kazan's 1947 film *Gentleman's Agreement* that lanced the hypocrisy putrefying beneath the veneer of decency—by declaring my hidden credentials after they had relieved themselves of anti-Jewish slurs, sentiments, and off-hand remarks. But they would have found me out anyway in the course of time.

And although I am not an Israeli and remain selectively critical of certain Israeli policies—including the misguided, neo-Oslovian efforts of the Sharon/Peres administration in cajoling the Palestinians in the direction of superficial reforms while having left the PLO and the terrorist infrastructure still in place, a position that hopefully seems to be changing—I acknowledge that, for all its problems as an embattled country, for all its falling short of an unattainable ideal, and for all its bickering contradictions and divisive anomalies, Israel is still engaged in the historic struggle to restore the four cubits of the law, and that the struggle is unremitting. Israel is both the scene and the mirror in which the battle for the Jewish soul may be observed in process. In truth, a plenary history of both personal and collective suffering and isolation makes an excellent mixing bowl for selfhood no matter how amorphous a body the Jewish people may happen to be and no matter how problematic the concept of selfhood remains. The paradox is ineludible, but so is the feeling of complex singularity, a presentiment that persists even when it is screened from consciousness. Paul Celan told us what it is to be a Jew, although many of us would prefer to stop our ears and pretend otherwise, as if the "Death Fugue" were only a poetic composition:

> Black milk of daybreak we drink you at night
> we drink in the morning at noon we drink you at sundown
> we drink and we drink you[26]

Nevertheless, I sometimes ask myself what I have to do with this querulous and often self-injurious people. When I consider the mutual suspicion, infighting, divisiveness, and exploitation that dominates its historical existence and its social life, and the absurd conflict between its various religious denominations that has led to centuries-long acrimony and occasionally bloodshed; the belief in some quarters that the Holocaust was either deserved or self-inflicted and the hostility between Zionist and diaspora Jews prior to the formation of the state of Israel that might well have derailed the project; the long indifference of American Jewry to the fate of their co-religionists trapped in the prison house of Nazi Europe and the fact that American Jews are among the most generous contributors to Palestinian "charities," like those French Jews at the time of the Dreyfus trial who donated to Catholic charities to mollify those who hated them; the current practice of Israeli manpower companies that cheat their own Ethiopian immigrants of salary and benefits, the government-sanctioned monopolies, the cronyism of political managers and the crushing bureaucracy of both the unions and the administration; the post-Zionist judiciary that energetically undermines the *esprit de corps* that keeps that country together; the activities of Israeli leftists who work as *agents provocateurs* in collaboration with Palestinian farmers with a view to expelling Jews from legally owned property in Judea and Samaria; the printing by the left-wing newspaper *Ha'aretz* of a large notice, placed by the "Courage to Refuse" movement, advocating that Israeli soldiers refuse to follow orders—this in a country under daily attack from Palestinian rocket fire and subject to Hizbullah raids and bombings—and of another large ad by the Peace Now movement advocating the return of the Golan to Syria and taking terrorist-sheltering and Hizbullah arms supplier Bashar Hassad's peace overtures as trustable; the efforts of the Jewish American Left, through such organizations as the American Friends for Peace Now, the Israel Policy Forum, and the Religious Action Center of Reform Judaism, sponsored by Jewish plutocrats like George Soros and Peter Lewis, to scuttle a congressional bill to isolate Hamas; the similar efforts of the Jewish British Left, through such organizations as the Israeli Committee Against House Demolitions, whose director, Jeff Halper, has joined other anti-Israeli groups, including the Campaign Against Arms Trade and the Palestinian Solidarity Campaign to lobby for an arms embargo against Israel—their publications do not mention the use of Syrian and Iranian arms by Hizbullah and falsely place the blame for the 2006 war, as well as the situation in Gaza, squarely on Israel; the movement among many Israeli and diaspora writers, thinkers, and peace activists to purge the country of its Jewish character and create a purely national entity in its stead, which would eliminate the very reason for the existence of Israel and once again place the Jewish people at the world's disposal; the parallel movement to sink even Israeli secular nationality into a joint federation with the Palestinians and Arab countries, as if resurrecting Felix Warburg's daft vision of Palestine as a "second Switzerland," which would have

the effect of rubbing Israel off the map; the policy of an elected government to transfer El Al cargo contracts to Alitalia, thereby reducing both
the airline's profit margin and jeopardizing military shipments in times
of need; the gradual dwindling of the qualities of pluck, fortitude, and
audacity that nerved the state in its perilous hours; and the oblivious-
ness of many Jews, especially in the diaspora, to the prophets, philosophers, sages, and poets who constitute the crown and quintessence of
Jewish culture—seeing all this and more, I am ready to throw up my
hands in despair and, like those whom I am critical of, do everything in
my power to reject, discount, or delaminate my heritage. Here are the
Pharisees, there the Sadducees, on the peripheries we find the Zealots,
all at one another's throats and all equally contemned by the Essenes.
Only the names seem to have changed. And yet, even as I watch this
people dance around their various golden calves—whether their naïve
vision of a false peace, their belief in the biblical mission of the Jews at
the expense of the nation itself, or, conversely, their disastrous flirtation
with the debilitating principles of the post-Zionist Left, their venera-
tion of foreign ideologies, their investment in the idol of immediate
gain, their adoption of "Canaanite" mores—and baffled as I may be by
discord when there should be harmony, factiousness when there should
be purpose, civic self-suspicion when there should be communal self-
affirmation, obtuseness when there should be intelligence, servility
when there should be daring, among a people living always near to the
abyss, I cannot bring myself to "disengage." Somehow, *ahavat Israel*—
the love of Israel, both the land and its people—endures.

It finally comes down to this. If I am a Jew, it is because I would
be ashamed of not being one, of reneging on a commitment I don't
quite understand, of defrauding that part of the self that is innocent.
I may well be, in Isaac Deutscher's telling phrase, a "non-Jewish Jew,"
yet all that misery is a kind of epical subsidy, even if one's civic account
has been debited as the price of one's existence. I am a Jew out of a
sense of defiance. One becomes proud of not knuckling under even
if one is unclear exactly what one is standing up for. I readily admit
that my devotion is flawed, that the *daf yomi* calendar—the seven-and-
one-half-year, leaf-a-day Talmudic reading cycle—is not for me, that
Reform Judaism strikes me as humdrum as Orthodox Judaism appears
to me needlessly recondite, but I patch into the Prophets, the Talmudic
sages, Maimonides, and Spinoza, each in their different ways having

something of value and continuing relevance to say, and each in their own way, however at odds with one another, inscribing what I have come to regard as the muniments of the tribe. The medieval poet and mystic Abraham Abulafia, in one of his few extant poems, expressed this sense of the textual recovery of the broken self, of the soul by the spirit, that is part of the Jewish experience: "And YDWD said to me: 'Know that your soul's name is blood, and ink is the name of your Spirit.'" My identity as a Jew, however obscure, is somehow involved not only with blood but with ink, with the major writings of the great Jewish minds.

As for the cover of assimilation or *marrano* cosmetics, we should be aware by now that it just doesn't work—a Jew will always be winkled out when the forces ranged against him so intend, irrespective of who he is or isn't. In fact, as French-Jewish philosopher Alain Finkielkraut has persuasively argued in an essay entitled "The Jew and the Israelite," it is precisely the urge to assimilation that the Gentile world holds against Jews, the hidden Yidden, even those whose "will to integration" leads them to become antisemites themselves. Assimilation is an example of "historical irony attaining a tragic perfection," for it was the very "will to integration that was really the crime." In the last analysis, the effort to melt into the mainstream, the desire for respectability and approval, the depilation of the vestigial past, is nothing less than "a bad bargain with emancipation," a mortal affront to the Gentile sensibility, which culminates one way or another in disdain, hatred, ostracism—or worse. The Jew seeks the Holy Grail of acceptance, thinks he may actually have found it, and discovers he has been handed a chamberpot.

This is the message of the book of Esther (and its associated Purim festival), which cautions Jews that the attempt to blend in is always idle, that even a place at court is no safeguard against antisemitic malice and that Jewish identity, however inscrutable or contested, cannot be forsworn. This is true of today's "court Jews" as well, that cabal of journalists, editors, professors, authors, and pamphleteers who fulminate against their own while maintaining their ostensibly privileged status in the corridors of preference. For the Jew, paradoxically, asserting his or her identity—whether that be one's communal allegiance or that which the world has constructed for us—is no worse and perhaps an even better survival strategy than abjuring it. One recalls how the philosopher Moses Hess, formerly a passionate assimilationist, was shocked into reality by the Damascus riots of 1840 and became what we might call a proto-Zionist. Similarly, Theodor Herzl, founder of the Zionist movement and author of the epochal *The Jewish State* (1896), was himself a staunch assimilationist until he visited France and saw with his own eyes the locust swarm of mindless and deep-seated hatreds let loose by the Dreyfus trial. The conclusion he came to, however painful and against the grain, changed the course of his people's history and cannot be controverted by the dejudaicized Jew who still wishes to preserve his sense of reality and ultimately to survive.

For whether he accepts his "identity" or not, he is like the angel in the Walter Benjamin parable, *Agesilaus Santander*, based in part on the Paul Klee watercolour *Angelus Novus* and in part on the Jewish tradition of the personal angel of each human being, who represents the latter's secret self and whose true name and nature is yet to be discovered. This is the angel who dwells in things one no longer has, is blown backward into the future, who wishes to experience "the having again," and who "can hope for the new in no way except on the way of the return home, when he takes a new human being along with him." The title of this extraordinary short tale, echoing the name of the redoubtable Spartan king, is an almost perfect anagram for "Der Angelus Satanas." The "satanic" angel who puts man to the test is also the angel with whom Jacob wrestled and from whom he received his transfigured name: Israel. The journey back, the narrator testifies, is the journey "whence I came." It makes no difference whether this flight out of historical dereliction into the retrieved future, which is also the resurrected past and the paternal home, is revolutionary or messianic or "merely" self-preservative. It remains both a necessity and a necessary possibility.[27]

Despite the unease and resistance the notion may produce, assimilation is for many Jews only a protracted stage on the journey to exile, pariah-hood or, as history has confirmed is always a hideous possibility, the concentration camp. Its lesson, repeated over the generations, is that assimilated Jews, their children, or their grandchildren, will one day, in one way or another, feel the lash of the antisemite. One cannot deny that the Jew has been the object of a 2,000-year terror campaign that reached its apogee in the *Shoah* and that still continues to fester, both in the Christian West and the Islamic East. Joan Peters was probably right when she pointed out that such knowledge "required an awareness too painful to bear—that flight for Jews was inexorable…and that any haven other than Israel was only transient." American Jews, in particular, who think they are safe should read the recent report, issued as a Faculty Working Paper, written by J. Mearsheimer and Stephen Walt of the Kennedy School of Government at Harvard University, that accuses Israel of being a torture state, of not being a genuine democracy, and of not being a reliable partner of the US. But its salvos are not directed solely toward Israel. It then proceeds to attack influential American Jews like Paul Wolfowitz, David Wurmser, and Douglas Feith for orchestrating the American involvement in Iraq and purports to show how the American Israel Public Affairs Committee "manipulates the media" and "polices academia." What is most disturbing is that this lying and bigoted report, which has since resurfaced in the *London Review of Books* under the title "The Israel Lobby," has the authority of a great American university behind it and, equally distressing, is surely only the first of such blatant propaganda documents to come from heretofore unimpeachable sources. Indeed, Michael Massing has recently followed suit with another rancorous screed in the *New York Review of Books* (dated May 11 and June 8, 2006) in which he declares that the Jewish lobby in the United States is using the war on terror to "expand[ ] its mission." While critical of some aspects of the original paper, Massing concludes that "on their central point—the power of the Israel lobby and the negative effect it has on US policy—Mearsheimer and Walt are entirely correct." Nor can he refrain from stressing—here it comes again—the Jewish money nexus, citing some very dubious word-of-mouth sources, accusing American-Jewish power of ensuring that the "strain on the Oslo accords was intense" and contributing to the failure of the road map, making exaggerated claims (what the Jewish lobby wants is "a powerful Israel free to occupy the territory it chooses"), focusing on the Jewish neocon presence, providing a long list of explicitly Jewish names guilty of the crime of supporting Israel, and generally downplaying Palestinian terror. *Alea ajacta est.* Perhaps American Jews should begin to take comfort in Itzhak Shamir's pledge to the Jewish communities in America, made at the time Israel was evacuating Falasha Jews out of Ethiopia: "and some day, we'll come for you."

Jews should never delude themselves into the belief that they can "put down roots." Ahasuerus, the legendary Wandering One, lives inside every Jew, either as a memory or a premonition—or the content of repressed consciousness. This is one of the central meanings of the important holiday of Sukkot, or the Feast of Booths: to remind Jews that they are still in exile, still crossing the Sinai in the biblical years of wandering wherever they may have chosen to settle in the present. Even Israel is not guaranteed, although there Jews have the option of defending themselves and the hope of establishing their presence in the world, transforming themselves, as in the Heinrich Heine poem from *Hebrew Melodies*, from "the butt of mocking city Arabs" into "Prince Israel."[28] And transforming themselves, too, in much the same way that the Zionist settlers terraformed what had been an Ottoman *khirbet* (wasteland) into a land of flourishing fields and gardens. ("We will spread a rug of gardens at your feet," wrote the much-loved Zionist poet Natan Alterman.) And yet, ironically, now that nearly 6 million Jews are concentrated in one place, they are vulnerable to destruction, to use the ominous words of the Iranian president, "by a single storm." There may be no escaping the pincers—Babylonian captivity and Roman conquest, Nazi gas chambers and Islamofascist nukes—unless the vise itself is taken apart. The odds are not encouraging. Hizbullah leader Hassan Nasrallah has recently trumpeted his joy over the concentration and ingathering of Jews in one place.

In the summation of Moritz Goldstein from his controversial 1912 essay, *The German-Jewish Parnassus*, "We can easily reduce our detractors to absurdity and show them their hostility is groundless. But what does this prove? That their hatred is *real*. When every slander has been rebutted, every misconception cleared up, every false opinion about us overcome, intolerance itself will remain finally irrefutable." The same conviction was expressed by the Zionist ambassador and first president of Israel Chaim Weizmann toward the end of his life: hatred of Jews "is a sort of disease that spreads according to its own laws.... I believe the only fundamental cause of anti-Semitism...is that the Jew exists." The much-maligned Jewish scholar Leo Strauss concurred. "There is no solution to the Jewish problem," he wrote in *Jewish Philosophy and the Crisis of Modernity*. We should not expect the world to deal with its Jews from a rational or ethical standpoint. "This hatred," writes David Mamet in *The Wicked Son*, "is unreasonable"; the predicament is that "one cannot reason a lunatic, or a congeries of the same, out of their delusion, for the delusion is the absence of reason." Consequently, "this persecution is inevitable and constant (now waxing, now waning, but inevitable)...." In treating of what has been called the world's "longest hatred," Eva Hoffman put it simply in *Lost in Translation*: "Anti-Semitism is a darkness of the mind...rather than a deviation from moral principles." These are only a few of the voices crying in this particular wilderness.

To which I add my own. Antisemitism, I suspect, will be with us until the end of days or the last Jew; it is only a question of relative malignancies. As we have seen, it may go by many new names—anti-Zionism, moral equivalency, even-handedness, the much ballyhooed but too-often fraudulent "legitimate" criticism of Israel—but whatever name it goes by, it remains only another form of Judeophobic resilement. Many contemporary historians tend to treat antisemitism as a contingent phenomenon that can be largely explained by local or background factors, by political, social, and economic trends, or by cultural, time-bound, or period frames. Antisemitism, regarded from this vantage, is neither fixed nor absolute, but is rather a post-biblical interlude of long duration that, under the right set of empirical circumstances, would eventually recede and cease to trouble, remembered only as a grim and sanguinary aberration. This is plainly a more discreet, scholarly, differentiated, and socially acceptable way of proceeding. Many writers even go so far as to argue that the Holocaust is not a unique or singular historical event, but a particularly murderous instance of the moral barbarism common to humanity as a whole. In one sense, this is certainly true, but in another, equally important sense, it misses the point. The Holocaust is unique inasmuch as it is always liable to happen again *to the same group of chosen victims* who remain unrehabilitated in the imagination of mankind, despite the "averaging out" effect of assimilation or the establishment of a legitimate homeland. *The Holocaust is repeatable*, and herein lies its singularity. The Jew remains vulnerable to the unthinkable, potentially or actually, no matter where he may happen to be, in America, England, France—or Israel.

The thinkers and statesmen mentioned above would not concur with the effort to explain away the persistence of Jew-hatred by socio-economic factors or reduce the Holocaust to a local and temporal expression of a generalized human tendency and so trivialize it as only one holocaust among many. To the contrary, they regard antisemitism as something that appears in its uncanny perseverance to transcend history itself, as something that bears a metaphysical or ontological stamp and assumes the quality of a radical singularity. On the level of "gut feeling," I sense that they are right, unpopular and even simplistic as such a view might be received by both professional historians and laymen. As Daniel Goldhagen wrote in *Hitler's Willing Executioners: Ordinary Germans and the Holocaust*, "the call for complexity is sometimes the refuge of those who find certain conclusions unpalatable."

Though it may be discordant to say this, it is fair to assume that the Jew is a victim not like other victims. Melanie Phillips proposes that Jews are the only minority that does not receive preferential treatment because Leftist analysis has ordained that Jews are part of the power network. I am convinced it goes much deeper than that. I would suggest rather that the Jew is the chosen outlet for the phobia of resentment for the human condition and the insecurity of the impoverished self. Antisemitism will not disappear because it is *needed*. The Jew is made responsible for the inescapable distress of being human along the entire spectrum from the empirical to the ontological—an excuse for failure, a means of false absolution and a convenient repository of all we are unwilling to acknowledge about ourselves. For the Jew seems *permanently* inscribed in the cultural and historical annals of the human race as the archetypal, residual, and invariant Other, unlike the Black, the Arab, the indigene, the gypsy, the sexual "transgressive," the social deviant, the minority political or ethnic group, or the victim of colonization, all of whom are in the process of gradually being reintegrated into the category of the normative. Alain Finkielkraut argues that the need to remember the Holocaust, so that we may never have to relive it, has turned Jews into super-victims who, according to the new antisemites, have monopolized Memory at the expense of other groups of victims now claiming their share of international attention through violent acts and hate speech, mainly against Jews who ironically become victims of their own memory. This thesis may be so as far as it goes, but what we need to see is that the new antisemitism is merely an adaptable and transient variant of the old, that the larger context firedogs the post-colonial and "humanitarian" ideologies of the day, and that the Jew persists *essentially* as a heterodox and immiscible figure, humanity's everlasting trespasser. Antisemitism is not a question of power, territory, economic resources or any other historically "valid" reason that may spring to mind. Its ghoulish persistence must be traced to a rictus in the human soul.

Jew-hatred is of course manifested in history but its supervening animus, as I have pointed out, behaves as if it were outside or beyond history, accounting for its felt status as something permanent and indissoluble. As Israeli novelist Aharon Megged writes, "What so clearly distinguishes Jewish history from the history of any other nation is that the forces that 'in every generation have risen against us to annihilate us,' as it is said in the Passover Haggadah, were ahistorical forces: an irrational, timeless hatred" in which "history becomes biology." The Yiddish poet Foiglman, from Megged's eponymous novel, sums up the bitter, inescapable truth: "We are the lepers of the world, from time immemorial to eternity." This is perhaps another way of saying that the motivational psychology that powers antisemitism, the veiled principle governing the virtual tattooing of an entire people for estrangement, discrimination, exclusion, and worse, resists displacement or transference despite the passing of millennia.[29] For it endures undiminished as a kind of psychic throwback although its *experiential* causes or reasons have been thoroughly understood, its perverse illogicality laid bare, its mythic character long exposed, and its various embodiments readily espied. The "Jew" seems here to stay as long as he stays here. That, after all, is in the nature of the unconscious. He is thus graven in the human imagination as the perpetual outsider, the landed immigrant whose citizenship papers are constantly deferred or, should they be issued, may be instantly revoked. To quote David Mamet again from *The Wicked Son*, "the majority culture has 'allowed' you a provisional membership, provided that you *never* pursue your proclivities…your very nature has been indicted as loathsome, and that which presents itself as an indulgence is, thus, a vicious expression of loathing." It is as if the Jew is the casualty of a supra-historical decree or a law of nature that establishes him within history as the primordial vagabond among men. Even at best, even if he has been zoned for only furtive apartheid,[30] his standing is always uncertain—or rather, only too certain. Unlike history's other collective victims, he remains eternally Iscariot. The prophecy of Balaam resounds to this day: "The people shall dwell alone, and shall not be reckoned among the nations." The antisemite and the fearful Jew will regard such an argument with distaste, dismissing it as both an exaggeration and a form of narcissism. This is to be expected since the antisemite cannot acknowledge the irrational nature of his hatred and the fearful Jew is reluctant to surrender the presumptive safety of his illusions. But in the long run, no reparation or repatriation is possible.[31]

If there is any doubt about this, merely consider the investments of anterior prejudice and assumption in the presumably *indicative* use of language. A word like "Jew" comes loaded with connotative baggage, unlike "Christian" or "Muslim" or "Buddhist." Say it out loud to yourself: "*Jew*"—and it should become immediately evident that it does not merely signify a faith or a member of that faith, but implies something unsavoury, obnoxious, repugnant. The implications sink into the language like contaminants into the soil. The same is true for many other languages as well. Even in Mandarin Chinese, the written word for "Jew" ("yu-tai") is composed of a combination of strokes suggesting a monkey, and its connotation is that of miserliness. (These characters were devised by Christian missionaries in the nineteenth century.) It is the one religious designator in common use that is not value-neutral, in the same way, as we have seen, that "Zionist," a perfectly lovely word with a rich and evocative biblical pedigree, has taken on the odium of the unhallowed. The "Zionist" label merely allows for the condemnation of the Jews not as bearers of an ethnic or racial particularity, but as the perpetrators of a colonialist political movement, and is nothing more than a clever linguistic strawberry. Ostensibly descriptive speech works in this case to reinforce a persistent residue of formulaic antipathy. Antisemitism has gone so deep that it is fixed within normative linguistic usage and resists all attempts at decorous circumlocution. Periphrasis only points up that which is being self-consciously avoided. A "person of Jewish ancestry," a man or woman of "Hebrew descent," is still a "Jew," perhaps even more so. The term "Israeli," the latest in a sequence of verbal pentacles, is now acquiring the same rancid fetor as its cognates.

Of course, antisemitism is also like a wave phenomenon, subsiding for a time and seeming to grow quiescent or even fade from sight only to surge up again and engulf large parts of the world like an ideological tsunami. Earlier I referred to it, somewhat metaphorically, as functioning the way a gene does. But at the present time, to adopt the language of biologist Richard Dawkins, we might say that antisemitism is well on the way to becoming a malefic, twenty-first century "meme," defined as a "self-replicating entity" or a "unit of cultural transmission" that propagates from brain to brain via a process of imitation. Dawkins' colleague, N. K. Humphrey, adds that a meme may colonize the brain, "turning it into a vehicle for the meme's propagation in just the way that a virus may parasitize the genetic mechanism of a host cell." What is most troubling is that, to quote Dawkins again, the cultural environment or "meme pool" may come to have "the attributes of an evolutionary stable set, which new memes find it hard to invade." While it is true that "Nothing is more lethal for certain kinds of meme than a tendency to look for evidence," Dawkins concedes that the "Memes for blind faith have their own ruthless ways of propagating themselves," one of the most effective of which is the "unconscious expedient of discouraging rational inquiry." Unfortunately, rational inquiry is not a human strong suit in dealing with matters of dogged faith in a treasured idea or cemented prejudice or in the human tendency to defend an ardent conviction in the teeth of the evidence against it, and memes tend to reproduce automatically. Antisemitism, regarded as a cultural meme (or meme set), selected millennia ago and multiplying exponentially, will not easily be dislodged and will probably remain with us as a blind replicator *in seculae seculorum*. This meme more than satisfies the conditions that, according to Dawkins, make for survival value: longevity, fecundity, and copying-fidelity.[32]

Still, the question I keep revisiting refuses to go on pension. Who or what *is* a Jew? Can the denomination be expanded to include the animal creation as well? Can there be, for example, such a thing as a "Jewish dog"? Certainly the taxi driver in my home town who jumped the sidewalk to run over our cocker spaniel thought so, since this was the reason he gave for his act of social cleansing. One thinks of the famous Cossack inscription placarded to four fresh corpses, mentioned by André Schwarz-Bart in *The Last of the Just*: TWO JEWS TWO DOGS ALL FOUR OF THE SAME RELIGION.[33] The theory is that the Jew is a universal pollutant, a blight upon the cosmos itself, and that everything he touches is defiled or profaned (though, oddly enough, Jewish property has never been regarded as befouled by association as far as acts of confiscation and sequestering are concerned).

The question grows more vexed when we move upward to the transcendent dimension. The "Jewish God," while acknowledged as Creator and, perhaps more saliently, as the Father of the Saviour, is nevertheless denigrated as the purveyor of an inflexible justice or, variously, as subject to capricious and irascible shifts of mood, that is, as ultimately unlovable, arbitrary, and distressingly fallible. Carl Jung's *Answer to Job*, for instance, which construes the advent of the Christ as the Lord's attempt to make restitution for the harrowing of Job by suffering belatedly in the Person of his Son, is built on the pervasive notion that this God behaves no differently from many of the captious and autocratic patriarchs and prophets. The Jewish God is in some sense understood by the Christian as the emanation of a martial band of invasive nomads which have obstinately denied the true God, the God of mercy and compassion, and which persists in the worship of a theological idol, a superannuated Deity, a reflection of its own overbearing and churlish character. The flow of derivation is thus surreptitiously reversed. A Jew is one who creates an eidolon, who corrupts even the Divine in projecting his own doubtful image upon the heavens in the form of a chosen God. This is "what" he is.

For the purposes of our inquiry, however, we may dispense with the objective or pseudo-objective "what" and stick with the subjective "who," with the mystery of essence and identity. Reflecting upon my own circumstance, I have come to realize that I was a Jew, both *ab ovo* and *in potentia*, even as I learned to deny my heritage during the years when I found the question entirely irrelevant to my existence. I see now that I shared many of the doubts and hesitations, even the "racial" allergies, that we find in the great Russian poet Osip Mandelstam, who fled from the perceived stigma of lower-class Ashkenazi life and converted from Judaism to Christianity. In his quasi-autobiography, *The Noise of Time*, he derides almost everything Jewish, sneering at Yiddish as "anything in the world, but not a language," describing his experience in the synagogue as a "heavy stupor," wincing at Orthodox Jewish women "with an abundance of false hair showing under their kerchiefs," recoiling from overcoated old men "full of philoprogeneity," deploring his own great-grandfather's supposed avarice who "must have had just exactly enough to last him till the day of his death, since he did not leave a kopeck behind," and shuddering at Jewish homes where "diapers hung from the lines, and piano scales would gasp for breath," among many other such abhorrences. But I have understood, however tardily, that this is a deep and self-conflicted aversion the Jew must labour to surmount if he is ever to become whole. What one dislikes in the Jew is only what one dislikes in other people but makes the Jew the repository of, especially if the caviler is a Jew in revolt from his suspected "essence"—which may be ultimately nothing but a tribal or ethnic reminiscence. Or perhaps, in this peculiar case, René Girard is right, at least in part: "mimetic rivalry tends toward reciprocity" and the self-hating Jew becomes "the imitator of his own imitator," reproducing the Levitical expulsion. This expulsion can take many forms, however. It can appear as a rejection of the ethnic community, leading to assimilation or conversion, as with Mandelstam and so many others; it may express itself as a vociferous repudiation of Zionism and the Jewish state; or it can manifest as a process of psychological antisepsis in which the self-loathing Jew tries to expunge the effigy with which he has come to identify. In this latter case, having internalized the image of the caricature-Jew, he turns upon himself in an effort to expel what he now regards as his distinguishing features in order to be accepted as "normal," as something other than the freak of human nature he suspects or actually believes he is. But in evicting a false replica, he at the same time paradoxically eradicates his own dignity, his sense of who he really is or might be, and his pride in communal accomplishment, arranging for his expulsion from history in an act of wholesale ingratiation with the other he wishes to become.

Although I once shared Mandelstam's asperities, I have come to realize that I was still a Jew when I disparaged Yiddish as a plebian excuse for a language, refused to observe our defining holidays, and took up the Palestinian cause as a sign of my presumptive disinterestedness—before I gave myself the trouble to study the issue more closely and arrive at conclusions more in agreement with reality. I was a Jew when I inveighed against the hardening of the arteries associated with shtetl piety or halachic orthodoxy and felt a vicarious shame and embarrassment for the sallow and asthenic physical specimens of the Hasidic communities with whom I had nothing in common and whom I could not help looking down on—as if I were an involuntary member of the Mitnagdim, the diehard opponents of Hasidism. I was still a Jew when for a time I rashly accepted the arguments of our intellectual clerisy that in the name of the "community of mankind" sold out its cultural dower to the enemies of civilization—who, it turns out, were and are resolutely anti-Jewish. I was always a Jew, whether retroactively or embryonically, even when I had no idea what it meant to be one, and remain a Jew, though unable to say with assurance whether Jewishness can be reduced to a matter of belief, ethnicity, genetics, illusion, duty, allegiance, or cultural attitude. Something in me insisted on keeping the faith I did not practice and could not fathom, on perpetuating, however leadenly, a venerable tradition as if there reposed invisibly on my bookshelves a copy of the holograph Aleppo Codex, a bible written in Tiberias and preserved by the tenth-century Jewish colony in Aleppo against all the vicissitudes of time and tumult, which I consulted without knowing it. And I was a Jew, as I have now come to realize, because the world would never let me conclude otherwise. Today, in the midst of the renewed outbreak of antisemitism across the world, I have come to sympathize with Freud's affirmation in a speech delivered on the occasion of his seventieth birthday to the B'nai Brith Lodge in Vienna, "I myself was a Jew, and it always seemed to me not only shameful but downright senseless to deny it." And I have come consciously to accept Emil Fackenheim's "614th Commandment," which he added to the 613 *mitzvot* or Commandments contained in the Pentateuch, of not giving Hitler a posthumous victory. This injunction has become my *Shamash* candle, the "helper candle" used to light the Hanukkah menorah in memory of the miracle of endurance.

"One cannot reestablish a link with a tradition that has been lost," argues Jean Améry in *At The Mind's Limits*, "No one can become what he cannot find in his memories." But if one's memories are filled both with what one has renounced as a component of one's formative experience and what has been inflicted on one even for that which has been renounced, then the "dialectical process of self-realization," the teleology of self, is not obstructed but reconfirmed and resumed, whether in nostalgia, resentment, perplexity, or affliction. As Heine said, "Judaism is a family tragedy." Alberto Manguel, in a wistful meditation entitled "On Being Jewish," recalls having been taunted as a young boy by a schoolmate, "Hey, Jew, so your father likes money." Years later he asks himself, "Did the epithet hurled at me insultingly…grant me citizenship in that ancient, beleaguered, questioning, stubborn, wise people? Was I—am I—part of Them? Am I a Jew? Who am I?"[34]

That is the question. And that question is particularly complex for those who have not experienced the historical and ongoing trauma of the "condition" and for whom being a Jew is to some extent constructing an identity or playing the role of spectator. However we construe the matter, a Jew cannot be absent from the world, cannot avoid sharing in an identity *the world has constructed for him*. In effect, then, however else he may regard himself, *a Jew is the incarnation of an imposed destiny*. And that destiny, to rewrite a sentence from novelist Matt Cohen, is to be an exile from everywhere.[35] The Jew will always be reviled—or at best, regarded with suspicion—even if he repudiates his God, disowns his faith, annuls his law, rejects his biblical chosenness, refuses to say *kinot* (the traditional prayers of mourning), exits the synagogue before the *maftir* has done reading, assimilates or converts, or undergoes an extreme makeover, and, like Kurt Tucholsky, Noam Chomsky, Israel Shahak, Alfred Lilienthal, Michael Neumann, Norman Finkelstein, William Blum, Ilan Pappe, Howard Zinn, Tony Judt, George Soros, and the pitiable Charles Enderlin among that ever-expanding census of anti-Zionist, Jew-baiting, non-Jewish Jews, turns upon his own people with the sophistry and malice of the sworn antisemite.[36] Ironically, if Arthur Koestler was right when he wrote in *Arrow in the Blue* that "self-hatred is the Jewish form of patriotism," then these Jewish self-haters are as Jewish as those whom they detest for being so, even though they have joined the colony of those whom Alan Dershowitz has called the "antitruth zealots." (I remind my readers that, for many Jews, condemnation of Israel—not criticism, condemnation—is only a way of making the psychically oblique look morally perpendicular.) And yet the enigma remains: how to explain such stygian depths of self-hatred. The famous passages from Jeremiah 12 leap out at us once again with a sharp, contemporary relevance, "I have forsaken mine house, I have left mine heritage…it crieth out against me: therefore have I hated it." These are the Jews who despise Israel for making them feel like Jews. These are the Jews who detest other Jews and Judaism itself, as Sander Gilman suggests in *Jewish Self-Hatred: Anti-Semitism and the Hidden Language of the Jews*, for motivating their societies to single them out as aliens and pariahs and calling into question the validity of their assimilative passion.

The Jewishness of the Jew is unsubtractable—his denials are always futile against the social and psychological categories, based on his scriptures and his historical existence, that have been created for him. And, to reiterate, this is so whether he is a secular Israeli sabra or a non-juring assimilationist. What Steven Aschheim says in *In Times of Crisis* about the "feeling of utter isolation and vulnerability" permeating the

Jewish psyche in the weeks before the 1967 war should be brought to mind today: "The predicament of the Jewish state and the powerless Diaspora were no longer regarded as antithetical; Jewish fate was existentially and politically one." This is as true today as it was at the time of the Six-Day War. Should Israel go under, no Jew anywhere else in the world would be immune from the growing menace of a renewed Holocaust. *Israel and the exilic community share the same future.* If the Jew does not feel threatened in a world that cannot be trusted, then he is little more than an amnesiac fugitive from that world, a truant from reality, no matter how he chooses to define or redefine himself and no matter where he invests his citizenship. He may not adhere to the old Talmudic aphorism, *kol Yisrael arevim zeh bazeh* (all Jews are responsible for one another) or the Yiddish saying, *Ganz Ashkenaz iz eyn shtot* (All Ashkenaz is one town), but he cannot reasonably deny that all Jews are involved with one another, even if the choice is not of his own choosing. "Every Jew," said the originator of the Hasidic movement, the Rabbi Baal Shem Tov, "is a limb of the Divine Presence," another way of proposing that every Jew is related to every other Jew. However the individual communicant may feel about the Baal Shem Tov's pronouncement, the world is not slow to impose a targeted sameness upon a dispersed and variegated community.

This is not to imply that a Jew cannot define himself with respect to his traditions, the events of his summative chronicles, or the principles of his faith, but these traditions, events, and principles can be interpreted in many different and conflicting ways or even jettisoned lock, stock, and barrel—and yet the Jew will paradoxically *survive* in the world's estimation as what we might call a delimited being. This remains the case whether the Jew is honoured as the founder of monotheism and the concept of universal law or excoriated as Satan's minion and the murderer of Christ, whether improbably extolled as a blessing to mankind or rabidly denounced as a curse on the human race. Of course, it is the latter designation that inevitably and always occludes the former and motivates the brutal rituals of social and cultural exorcism that, as much as anything else, including the prescription toward endogamy, have made the Jew who he is.[37]

For better or for worse, the Jew lives in time and not in eternity and his self-definition in the sphere of the everyday is of little account in the estimation of the rest of humanity. Jewish thinkers like Leo Strauss and Franz Rosenzweig argued that Jews could not be defined by a common history of exclusion and degradation or merely by a common heritage or community of mind. Rather, they believed that Jewishness, if it is to be genuine, is constituted on a foundation of divine revelation, on the principle of a divine gift. Still, in the practical realm of human relations and social formations, it is not some divine imprint, invisible essence, or mystical quiddity, the vague hypostasis of something called "Jewishness" that makes the Jew. Neither is it a cluster of somatic idiosyncrasies that presumably exemplify that esoteric inwardness. The presumed external marks of Jewishness—accent, physique, forms of expression—are most likely hereditary or reproducible traits stemming from an East European, long-ghettoized "community of blood," transmitted through physical, linguistic, and cultural channels. (James Parkes tracks facial characteristics back to a Hittite origin, shared by a wide variety of originally Middle Eastern peoples through a process of racial miscegenation.) Maghrebian Jews, however, do not exhibit these features, at least not to the same degree—Philip Hitti, for example, argues in his great *History* that the "prominent nose" is not a Semitic feature at all, tracing, like Parkes, the famous proboscis to a Hittite-Hurrian origin, acquired through intermarriage. (Though Hitti, whose name may also indicate a Hittite origin, seems to think the Hebrews are not quite semitic.) Many Russian Jews are startlingly "Aryan" in appearance—my grandmother was blond-haired and blue-eyed. And first- and second-generation Israeli sabras often seem to come from a different genetic stock altogether. As Amos Oz describes them in *A Tale of Love and Darkness*, "These were different genes. A mutation." Nevertheless, the exclusionary hypothesis remains in place and establishes the Jew's identity *for the world* as if he were a member of a single genetic phylum, an act of definition that impinges on his very existence irrespective of religious, cultural, or bodily factors, even when they are not in evidence.

Does this mean that there is no such thing as Judaism *per se*? Yes and no. If Judaism is to be authentic it must surely be accepted as a faith complete with its laws, rituals, observances, and sacred texts that structure the conduct of everyday life and worship, as they have done continuously from the return of Ezra with the text of the Law from Babylon to the Holy Land in 458 BCE and the later doctrinal reforms to the normative consolidation of the faith between the second and sixth centuries to the present time. In this sense Judaism is a rabbinical faith of which Orthodoxy may well be its only legitimate expression. Though it makes me uncomfortable to say this, it can be argued that to be a Jew *authentically* is to be an Orthodox Jew and to ground one's life on the norms, rites, and prescriptions of the Torah and the Talmud. Absent these foundational texts and what is left on which to establish a hereditary community? But only a minority of world Jewry perceives itself from this strict perspective. For the majority of Jews who still see themselves as Jews—for example, those who subscribe to the Reform or Reconstructionist movement, those who have taken up residence in Conservative Judaism, which is basically an uneasy compromise between Orthodoxy and Reform, and those who have more or less integrated into the mainstream of their host countries without entirely rejecting their genealogy, satisfied with a kind of pick-and-choose, *à la carte* Judaism—the content of the faith is diluted so that only a varying modicum of its traditional nucleus and classical form is preserved, enough to impart a distinctive coloration to one's practice and to assuage a guilty conscience. For such cambered adherents, enjoying what sociologist Herbert Gans called "symbolic ethnicity," Judaism is not so much a religion as a way of life, a set of cultural folkways that gives a certain cohesion to life, provides for the glue of social memory, and unites one with a historic *demos* that generates a feeling of depth and meaning. This is not Judaism as religion, then, but Judaism as culture. But when we turn to the secular Israeli, the non-consenting sabra of the kibbutz, the marketplace, the university, and the army, we find that Judaism is neither religion nor culture so much as it is a political construct embodied in a state that furnishes the institutional and territorial means of existence. Here Judaism morphs into what we might call Israelism, the faith displaced as nation and imposing unity, however precarious, for the purposes of both civil life and military defence.

Reviewing the big picture, we might say that Orthodoxy represents the spiritual avionics of the faith intended to enable the Jewish spirit to coordinate explicitly with the Divine. As loath as we may be to admit this, Orthodoxy would be cutting-edge Judaism; moreover, its biblical rootedness and legalistic carapace have kept the religion alive and the sense of peoplehood intact for millennia in the wilderness of the *Galut* (exile) when it would have been so much easier to accept the religion of the surrounding peoples. Reform, from the standpoint of integral Judaism, is backsliding, and outright secularism a contradiction if not a betrayal. And yet, in the context of contemporary life, Orthodoxy is a theological atavism, unbending, sterile and endogenous, ill-adapted to the complexities of experience and the imperative of survival in an inimical world bristling with high-tech weaponry, sophisticated techniques of cyber warfare, and an imprecatory media dragonnade of international scope. "Ghetto orthodoxy," writes James Parkes in *A History of the Jewish People*, "has not shared the experience of emancipation and of western technical and political advances, and it has no understanding of the moral problems of a modern and independent state." In contrast, the Reform and secularist persuasions represent efforts to adjust, however incongruously, to the demands of social and political reality, but at the cost of real bewilderment about what conjoins them with quintessential Judaism, that is, with the theological substratum of the faith dating from the time of Ezra to the second century CE when the patriarch Judah the Prince produced the codification of interpretations, judgments, and laws known as the Mishnah. Unencumbered by Mishnah, the Jew is better able to adapt to the social and political world in which he must function although he may practice certain rituals, mumble certain phrases, send his children to educational camps, and contribute generously to the United Jewish Appeal. But is he still a Jew in his own interior ophthalmology? Can one be a Jew without believing in the Jewish God, without a thorough immersion in the Torah and the Talmud, and without a genuine sense of historic continuity? "We recognize our historic identity," wrote Theodor Herzl, "only by the faith of our fathers."

This brings us to the related question of what sort of Jew one can be while agitating for the complete secularization or political disestablishment of Israel, a nation conceived as the ancestral homeland of the Jewish *yishuv*, the legitimate, enduring and verifiable centre of its very existence and the vital node of its spiritual life. Is it possible to cease regarding oneself as a citizen—or a potential citizen *in absentia*—of a Jewish state without forfeiting the historic connection that binds the Jew to what counts as his communal and national identity *as a people*? This matter is far more immediate and compelling for the Israeli than the diaspora Jew, but it cannot be dissociated from the problem of Jewish self-definition any more than it can be separated from the issue of continued Jewish existence in a fickle and treacherous world. Can there be any reasonable doubt that the Jewish character of the state as well as its geopolitical integrity must be maintained if it is not to become a contradiction in terms, a state in which Jews would find themselves as vulnerable to the menace of antisemitic prejudice and brutal suppression as anywhere else in the world? Those Jews opposed to the idea and existence of their own state, especially the fellowship of revisionist Israeli intellectuals, have, as it seems to me and to cite from an Alterman poem, allowed their hearts to grow dark in a room, without the stars they have abandoned outside. The concept of a *totally* secular Jewish state has no meaning, just as the proposal for a bi-national union with an Arab Palestine has no political validity in the framework of Jewish history and the trauma of dispersal, insecurity, and, ultimately, of genocide. David Ben-Gurion was surely right when he wrote in a memorandum to the United Nations in 1947 that, "A Jewish minority in an Arab state, even with the most ideal paper guarantee, would mean the final extinction of Jewish hope." The real question—and the only question that makes any sense—is the extent to which the governance and the day-to-day life of the country are to submit to religious authority. Israel as a *mainly* secular country with a strong religious component and a positive Jewish flavour is an eminently feasible proposition. Certain rules of custom and conduct and various legislative enactments, such as the Sabbath moratorium and military exemptions, may plausibly be modified or repealed while, for example, the Jewish culture-and-value-oriented educational curriculum and the Law of Return remain on the books. The issue cannot be skirted. A commitment to an acknowledged Jewish state, however diluted, and the very meaning of the words that conclude the Passover seder's chronology of hope, *L'shana ha'ba-ah b'Yerushalyim* (Next year in Jerusalem), are central to the debate that swirls around the puzzle of Jewish identity and the desideratum of Jewish survival—even if Jerusalem may one day become an international city.

For Judaism means both a faith and a nation, as is clear from its founding moment in Genesis 12 when the Lord commanded Abraham to "get thee...unto a land that I will show thee," promising to make of his servant "a great nation." This is not to say that one must necessarily believe in the actual existence of the Lord as propounded in the scriptures, but rather that, in the mental universe of authentic Judaism, faith and nation are conceptually inseparable and exist in a relation of historical symmetry, if not of psychic fusion. The nation is the political expression of the faith and the faith is the basis of the body politic—though neither is the isomorphic equivalent of the other. Of course, nation and land are obviously not synonymous since the Jewish people has survived as a nation through millennia of dispersion, thanks to the moveable synagogue of the sacred texts, but owing as well to the perpetual aspiration for and promise of a return to the very land itself—"next year in Jerusalem."[38] It is legitimate to ask how long a deterritorialized identity may be expected to endure when it cannot be successfully reterritorialized in an exilic "homeland." In the long historical run, the diasporation of the self is not a viable project where exclusionary resentment or ethnic hatred remain as cultural determinants or social reflexes. Land is a form of anchorage, the means by which a more substantial degree of stability, consolidation, self-preservation, and intelligibility may be achieved. This is why Israel is necessary for the Jew, whether he has made aliyah or is content to wait upon events, whether he treads on Israeli soil or plants a tree in its ground for the future. Thus, faith, nation, and land come together as one in a spiritual, political, and geographical unity that constitutes the *adat b'nai yisrael*—the assembly of the Jewish people—whose cohesion ultimately requires all three terms of a covenant that is both temporal and perduring. What Psalm 122 sings of Jerusalem—"Jerusalem is builded as a city that is compact together"—is equally true of Israel. We might say that faith, nation, and land form the three points of the vertical triangle of the Star of David, chosen as the symbol of modern Israel and represented on its flag.

But there is a second, interlocking triangle that comprises the Star of David whose meaning we may try to fathom, if only as an explanatory metaphor. We can begin by considering another form of commitment that we may call humanistic Judaism, involving the consciousness of one's incompleteness in the face of Divine perfection, conjugated with both the responsibility to strive toward achieving it and the inevitable sense of failure and humility stemming from so incommensurable a pilgrimmage. The inner conviction that animates this belief is that the Jew must struggle to "repair" the world—the Kabbalistic notion of *tikkun*[39]—through his deeds and thoughts, which implies a constant vigilance towards himself and others. But this type of Judaism, a way of relating to mankind learned from eons of wandering, persecution, and spiritual reflection, has much in common with Buddhism and early Christian heretical movements. It is a sacramental philosophy of living shared by many who do not profess the Jewish faith and that, while deriving for the humanistic Jew its essential character and impetus from Jewish history, has come in the course of time to assume the form of an autonomous morality, a system of values available to any thinking person. It is not *necessarily* associated with Judaism as a dogma, a communion, or a social canopy of *moeurs* and behaviours although Jews of a philosophical bent embrace this redemptive ethos as the heart of their faith. The Kabbalistic Tu B'shvat feast, which concludes in the celebration of the *briya*, or the world of creation, in order to bring its participants closer to goodness, is paralleled in many of the world's religions.

Notwithstanding its wide distribution among other faiths and belief-systems, this ethical or humanistic commitment is an integral part of the Jewish experience and is closely associated with two other, rather obvious structural factors in the psychological makeup of the Jew, at least in the realm of the ideal. First, the Jew is betrothed to a sense of history as the culmination of personal memory: the long tradition of an ancestral homeland to which the return was always envisioned, the recollection of exile and suffering, of rejection and displacement, and the binding power of his sacred, exegetical, and narrative texts have become part of his mnemonic fabric, the interior Haggadah or story to which he is wedded regardless of infidelity, casual indifference, or glacial apathy. The injunction to remember is inscribed in the eighth chapter of Deuteronomy as a test of Jewishness, "to prove thee"; forgetting entails dereliction, what we might term a chrono-sectomy. Communal history and personal memory unite in Jewish consciousness in a sort of nuptial compact, a perfecting of the oneness of the two dimensions of outer and inner time. What happened in the worldly past continues to happen in the psychic present and external history is domesticated as personal existence. We see this tendency in the poetry of Judaism's greatest modern poet, Chaim Nachman Bialik, which brings together as one the two domains of personal and national identity, of private life and historical event. The Jew, in other words, is bound to his chronicle, as the great Russian scholar Nicolai Berdyaev pointed out when he wrote in *The Meaning of History* of "the absolutely peculiar tie existing between the Jews and the 'historical,' and their extraordinarily intense feeling for history." True, the transition from the collective to the personal has been disrupted in the secular diaspora and, to a significant extent, in Israeli consciousness as well, but it nevertheless constitutes the essence of Jewish memory in its ideal and covenantal form.

Additionally, the self is understood as an autonomous agent that is frequently at loggerheads with the divine injunction that speaks from the centre of the Jewish faith. Abraham may follow the Lord's command, yet does not hesitate to haggle—"intercede" is the word in the King James—with the Transcendent over the fate of a city. Moses reasons with God on the mountain of Sinai, "and the Lord repented." Job resists and queries the exactions of his God, searching for the meaning of his trials and emerging from his contest with Yahweh the moral victor, however subdued by inimitable power. The *individual* strain of questing and questioning, of a kind of sanctified dissatisfaction, is thus equally at the centre of the very self formed by *collective* tradition, leading to that impulse toward stubborn independence—though also, it must be admitted, toward waywardness—that even the Hebrew scripture disparages as "stiffnecked." Once again, I stress that these are ideal components of the Jewish psyche, but they are also the archetypes for the construction of a durable and distinctive sensibility. Projecting the Star of David as a heuristic device, we might then say that morality, history, and self constitute the three points of the inverted triangle that intersects its vertical cognate—with faith and self at their mirrored apices, morality subtending nation, and history complementing land.[40]

These different aspects of Judaism, across the entire compass of the spiritual, intellectual, historical, civil, and political domains, are often in conflict with one another and would appear in many cases to be mutually inhospitable. And when one considers that each of these branches, estates, or gradations is itself a multiplicity of competing practices and convictions, that there are several varieties of Orthodoxy along a continuum from Modern to Ultra, descending from the ancient battle between the flexible rulings of Rabbi Hillel and the dogmatic strictness of his Talmudic rival Rabbi Shammai, different degrees of Reform, assorted levels of assimilation, diverse modes and intensities of humanistic ethics springing from the Jewish experience but by no means confined to it (and not infrequently in collision with the more restrictive forms of religious observance), backslidings and fallings away from the meaning of the six-pointed star along every one of its apices, and a wide spectrum of political loyalties and convictions among ordinary Israelis and secular diasporites that often leads to misunderstanding and hostility between those whose collective existence continues to be threatened, one may reasonably ask what mysterious agent holds all these incompatible elements together.

The answer I have suggested is that the inside is held together by the outside, that the kaleidoscope is shaken by an external hand to create a pattern or a semblance of pattern, that an identity is projected upon the Jew by a world for whom the distinctions I have listed above are of no importance whatsoever. As Herzl wrote in *The Jewish State*, the Jews were "one people—our enemies have made us one." Persecution is the crucial factor in selecting for one form of self-understanding over many others that contend for prominence in the individual psyche as well as in the communal totality—the self we tend to experience most intimately and profoundly is the persecuted self, no matter how strenuously we may seek to deny it. I am not the first to remark that without antisemitism in its global dimensions, Judaism as a body of belief and conduct, however diversified, could conceivably fragment, weaken, blur, grow denatured, and ultimately transform itself into something unrecognizable, leaving, perhaps, only a fundamentalist remnant. And even this is far from certain, for should the ghetto mentality and the deep sense of quarantine no longer apply, the traditional garb, ceremonials, sacraments, and usages might well follow into desuetude. And yet, one may plausibly suspect that Judaism will never entirely disappear if only because the world needs its sacrificial Other. In the event of a second and more thorough Holocaust, a token will be left behind, another Adam and another Eve, to repopulate the dominion of the unconscious. In the meantime and doubtlessly for the long hereafter, the Jew remains the Jew chiefly because the world has decided the question for him.

Such is the common and unavoidable Jewish experience, "much as," in the pungent phrasing of Peter Gay in his *Weimar Culture*, "some Germans later discovered themselves to be Jews because the Nazi government told them that that is what they were." From a somewhat different angle, this is the Jew whom Alain Finkielkraut, reflecting on his experience in France, calls, in his book of that title, "*le juif imaginaire,*" the Jew whose Judaism, even when professed, is without specific content.[41] George Jonas remarks in *Beethoven's Mask*, that "My own Jewishness was not defined by dietary laws, Friday candles, or Hebrew phrases in a prayer book. It was defined by a yellow star sewn to my lapel by my mother, in my native Budapest, as required by Nazi law...." Historian Eric Hobsbawm, himself a non-Jewish Jew, an unrepentant communist and a stinging critic of Israel, frankly acknowledged the problem. Writing in his memoir *Interesting Times* of his formative years in Vienna, he comments, "Though entirely unobservant, we nevertheless knew that we were, and could not get away from, being Jews."[42] The Jew's "identity" is preordained for him no matter how hard he tries to "get away" from it.

And yet, the issue remains ambiguous, for there is something in the Jew that also accepts the ascription of identity from without, however indefinable that may be, whether as a corollary of inner conviction or as an expression of his lack of such. There are times, of course, when the Jew is forced to go into hiding or seeks to camouflage his Jewishness, but these maneuvers do not conceal the heart of the matter. Why is it so difficult for many Jews to surrender their troubled sense of destiny or—what amounts to the other horn of the dilemma—why do those who wish to escape their heritage often insist so vehemently on their apostasy? Why, on the one hand, does the Jew cling so tenaciously to his besieged and problematic selfhood or, at the other extreme, repudiate his origin and community with such righteous and over-protesting clamour? Why this constant calling attention to oneself, whether as a believer or a renegade? Why does one Jew loudly celebrate *aliyah* to Israel and another Jew conspicuously advertise his desire to see Israel disappear? These questions are perhaps not as baffling as they might seem. For in the depths of his spirit, the Jew knows he cannot bargain away a more than 2,000-year history of exile and suffering without losing himself, and suspects conversely that he is always unsafe no matter what lengths he is willing to go to and what sacrifices he is prepared to make to reject his Jewishness and thereby ward off the world's animosity. The Jew remains a Jew because he cannot validly discard nearly eighty generations of quasi-nucleic substance that creates a feeling of collective belonging, even if he cannot say with assurance precisely what he belongs to, and because, at some level of consciousness, he intuits that the world will not tolerate indefinitely the ruses of self-evasion he is tempted to embrace. Thus on the one hand his emphatic affirmation and on the other his redoubled disavowal. There is no sidestepping the almost innate presentiment of exclusivity. Whether chosen by God as His people or chosen by the world as its perpetual outsider, *the Jew is still chosen*. There is a strange complicity of awareness between the inside and the outside—neither will nor can forget what it means to be a Jew.

In the last analysis, the Jew becomes who he is as a function of who he is not and never will be, and has no legitimate alternative but to accept and even assert his peculiar uniqueness. Amin Maalouf may be correct when he writes in *In the Name of Identity* that the word "identity" is "treacherous" and a "false friend," nudging us in the direction of a "single affiliation," toward all that is "narrow, exclusive, bigoted, simplistic." The individual should have the right to profess the multiple and often contradictory aspects of his composite selfhood and should be free to refuse a megalithic commitment to only one determinant. But in the case of the Jew, it is the world that insists on his reductive and unassimilable identity, permitting him no escape from what Maalouf regards as the trap of single affiliation. He has, as a result, no real choice but to bravely assert his being-as-a-Jew, not as a metaphysical essence, a nostalgic reminiscence, or an ambiguous badge of honour, but as a historic identification with a suffering and uprooted people in whose temporal body he inescapably subsists beyond his limited and contingent self. As Alain Finkielkraut wrote with respect to his quest for an authentic selfhood, Judaism was "no longer a kind of identity but a kind of transcendence," a parabola traced by the individual's journey toward a spiritual and historic commonality whose basic values remain paramount, however honoured in the breach: study and education, marital stability, the centrality of the family, the moderate use of stimulants, deference toward elders, the rule of hospitality, ethical probity, respect for law and justice, aid to the poor, the reluctance to proselytize or impose one's faith upon others, and, not least, a daily conversation with Divinity. And such a panoply of values cannot justly be said to constitute a "trap" of "single affiliation." Nor can the seven Noachide Laws, as laid out in the Talmud and the Maimonides Code and which anchor Jewish (but also Gentile) moral existence, be considered as a diminishment or constraint.[43]

It follows that the elusiveness of a metaphysical identity-core does not preclude the possibility of acceding to a historical option, of voluntary self-identification as a Jew in one's own as well as the world's eyes. Freud himself, in the Preface to the Hebrew translation of *Totem and Taboo*, claimed that he was Jewish "in its very essence" although admitting that he "could not now express that essence clearly in words." Identity (or essence) may elude definition—or, if we agree with Maalouf, may even in certain cases be contra-indicated—but *identification*, as a matter both of conscience and of public disclosure, is a definable act. For the Jew, it is also a necessary one. It is how he becomes a moral being at no one's expense except his own, and how he finally becomes himself. Assenting to that which he may not be capable of fully understanding but cannot successfully shed or repress, the Jew must embark upon the continuing quest to retrieve his past, to unmake his ignorance, to rediscover his courage and his self-respect, to experience consciously and even welcome his imprescriptible distinctiveness and his integrity, to be able to say with pride and conviction "I am a Jew" even if he is perpetually in search of the material and signifying content of that statement. Perhaps that, too, is what it means to be a Jew. There is nothing else he can do if he is to avoid becoming either a nullity or a simpleton. He cannot refute his difference and he cannot pretend that his catchment books, the Bible and the Talmud, had never been written, even if he does not subscribe to all of their laws and tenets. Nor can he ever escape from under another set of definitive texts, *Mein Kampf* and *The Protocols of the Elders of Zion*, that will continue to circulate and to clinch his "identity" for much of the world. He may construe himself otherwise from his kinfolk, he may find himself at odds with some of their customs, beliefs, and practices, he may feel no tribal or religious consanguinity, he may deny a racial affiliation, but on the moral, historical, and existential planes of his being he is nevertheless bound to them inextricably. His "substance" is both inwardly and outwardly determined—it is both earned from within and learned from without. And this means that for the foreseeable future, no divorce is possible. Judaism is like a dysfunctional marriage that lasts.

But whatever personal stance he adopts toward his heritage, the Jew will remain the stranger, the intruder, the outlander, the one who does not fit in. And there is no reliable way to pretend otherwise, nothing really to hide behind; he will always be given away, whether by his habits and expressions, or by his physical features, or by his consecrations, or by his conspicuous attempts to slough his ancestry, or by a visitor from the past, or by an inadvertent slip, not to mention his very name.[44] Nonetheless, his exclusion constitutes the warrant of the uniqueness he must ultimately affirm.[45] For just as being hated for no good reason becomes in the long course of time a potent reason for being hated, so alienation becomes a kind of shared "identity," and persecution, the family home. It is an unalterable law of life that one becomes what one has suffered, and derives from unmerited cruelty and scorn a sense of dignity and worth one can never betray without betraying oneself—the real sin of Judas.

Afterword

Although my purpose in this duograph was to elaborate a set of general ideas that are both internally related and conceptually independent of the turbulent and often contradictory flux of daily affairs, I have tried to keep abreast of recent developments in the geopolitical world, especially with respect to the Middle East, but also with the political and ideological tensions that bedevil the West as it wrestles fitfully and ineffectually to preserve its moral centre and come to terms with the threat posed by Islamic fundamentalism. This effort to stay *au courant* by addressing the details of the moment, as well as the fact that much of this book was composed between 2002 and mid-2006, may account for the dated feel of certain aspects of the text that, by the time of publication, might well have been superseded by events and by articles and studies that will have appeared in the interim. Though much will have happened in the interval between the *now* of script and the *then* of print, it is my hope that the presaging function of the text will not have been unduly impaired.

With regard to the Israeli-Palestinian conflict in particular: by the time this book appears, circumstances may have changed dramatically since events can turn on a shekel, a rial, a piaster, or a dinar in the region. Indeed, anyone who undertakes to write about the caldera that is the Middle East is liable to extreme embarrassment before the ink dries and the lava hardens. A difficult peace may finally have been established, in which case I will have been proven wrong in my apprehensions and parts of the second essay might be discarded. At the other extreme, a third intifada and even an organized, widespread military campaign may be about to begin or already underway, and Israel will have mobilized for a protracted siege, reoccupying portions of Gaza and the West Bank and an expanded buffer strip in southern Lebanon. Or it may be just business as usual: the terrorists pursuing their program of violent infiltrations and provocations, the Palestinian Authority, or whatever political group or terrorist coalition may be exercising its powers, speaking out of both sides of its mouth, the Arab nations and Iran maintaining their drumbeat of hostile propaganda, and the Israelis trying to cope with misguided international censure, the sterility and bias of most media analysis, European fecklessness, their own dissidents and revisionists, state commissions and upheavals in government, and the staccato of shooting, bombing, and rocket attacks against their civilian communities. While recognizing the possibility that a troubled and laborious peace initiative may have borne some fruit, I strongly suspect that one of the latter two alternatives is far more probable. We should not forget that for the Palestinians terror has become a veritable cottage industry. It is what they do best. Nor can we dismiss the possibility of a greater regional conflict, given the ongoing militarization of the Sinai by the Egyptian army, the insurgency in Iraq and Afghanistan, the funding and exportation of "revolutionary" activity by the Saudis, the perennial meddling of Syria as a sponsor of terrorism, Hizbullah continuing to ply its trade in Lebanon even under the noses of an international peacekeeping or monitoring force, and especially the labile state of affairs in Iran that may erupt at any moment.

But there is a larger framework in which the events, topics, and ideas I have discussed in this book must be situated. I recall those ringing lines from Thomas Lovell Beddoes' Gothic tragedy, *Death's Jest-Book*: "Now see you how this dragon-egg of ours/Swells with its ripening plot?" It seems evident to me that a great civilization is on the point of foundering, subject to its inner contradictions and no longer able to contain its destructive antinomies or isolate its axial enemies. Suffering from a kind of historical glaucoma, liable to insularity of judgment, and crippled by immediacy, we have traded long-term survival and haleness for short-term profit and respite. We now find ourselves placed in the unique position of watching what spookily resembles a civilization in its death-throes, the disintegration of a way of life and an underlying system of values whose bearers no longer seem willing to endure the sacrifices or maintain the hard discipline of moral and intellectual clarity needed for its continuance. The almost daily capitulations of our intellectuals, opinion-makers, and political leaders to the invasive forces of what is nothing less than a global jihad must be seen for what they are, portents of imminent collapse. The populace at large merrily goes along for the ride, profoundly unaware of the looming destination. It is in its way a perversely exhilarating spectacle: not many get to see in their lifetime a civilization coming to pieces before their very eyes, like a star going supernova. But it is also, and principally, a tragic spectacle, for this is the detritus we leave our children.

And yet, this is not the worst of it, for the disintegration of a civilization takes time—Conor Cruise O'Brien generously gives us until the third century of our millennium—but time is what we may no longer have. Pakistan, as we know, is only a bullet away from morphing into a nuclear, Islamofascist regime. And then there is Iran. If it makes good on its intention to wipe Israel off the map by nuclear holocaust, as Ayatollah Hashemi Rafsanjani threatened in 2001 and President Mahmoud Ahmadinejad reiterated in 2006, this dragon-egg of ours may well hatch with the progeny of Armaggedon. Rafsanjani is cruelly mistaken when he boasts that the Islamic bomb "would not leave anything in Israel, but the same thing would just produce damage in the Muslim world." He seems quite willing to absorb "thirty or forty million martyrs," unaware that the casualty count may well exceed his estimates. World leaders are equally delusional in believing that a mixed package of economic incentives and sanctions will influence the Iranians to moderate their ambitions, or that mutual deterrence remains a workable paradigm. Iran has just declared the nuclear issue a closed file although European heads of state are still pressing for more discussions. The Iranians appear to mean what they say and the entire world may come to rue its policy of appeasement and its condition of intellectual dormancy. We have seen in the past what the wages of appeasement are. It is now common knowledge that had the liberal West acted in 1936, Germany's small, under-equipped army would have been defeated, Hitler would have fallen from power, and six years of global devastation and 55 million deaths would have been averted. Once again, the weakness and inertia of the Western response to an undoubted menace may issue in unimaginable disaster. We should remember that in a sermon delivered in a central Teheran mosque on October 16, 2006, Ahmadinejad claimed to have enjoyed direct contact with God, who assured him that Iran would triumph. Ahmadinejad is also on record as anticipating the pending arrival of the Hidden Imam, who will usher in the End of Days in blood and thunder and whose divine timetable can be hastened by human intervention. He should be taken at his word.

In refusing to act before we reach the point of no return, the West is guilty of the most irresponsible form of brinkmanship, hoping perhaps for a spontaneous uprising among the Iranian masses and the overthrow of the mullahs. But this is not a likely scenario. It would certainly be opposed by the European nations. Iran's projected switch to the euro as an oil transaction currency, rejecting the American dollar and boosting the European economy, ensures that Europe will do little to offend the Iranian leadership. Nor can we rely on the foresight of the non-Western members of the Security Council: China needs the oil for its booming industrial base and Russia profits obscenely from arms trafficking, which means, quite simply, money in the pocket but a ruinous investment portfolio. Since the Iranians have no intention of relenting in their quest for nuclear enrichment, a pre-emptive raid upon their operational sites and facilities appears to be the only solution to our common predicament. For what we must keep in mind is that in the event of an Iranian nuclear strike, Israel cannot be expected to go quietly. Never again. As Eric Hoffer wrote in the *Los Angeles Times* in 1968, "As it goes with Israel, so it will go with all of us. Should Israel perish, the holocaust will be upon us." Those of us who think we are immune to the aftermath in virtue of distance from the scene of detonation would be in for a mortal surprise. The Middle East is not simply a metaphorical "tinder box" that could explode into a regional conflict, leading to geopolitical realignments and a spike in oil prices. It is, in effect, a gigantic oil field ready to burst into thermonuclear flames. Should this happen, none of us will be spared.

It is hard not to feel like Samuel Taylor Coleridge's protagonist in his great poem *Kubla Khan*: "And 'mid this tumult Kubla heard from far/ Ancestral voices prophesying war." I do not inhabit Coleridge's visionary world and, unlike the poet, I have not taken laudanum in the act of composition. I do not wish to pass myself off as a purveyor of doomsday scenarios or a Cassandra *manquée*. I have no prophetic pretensions. I can only say what I see, and write in the hope of a miracle.

Acknowledgements

Many people have contributed over the years in helping me order my ideas and clarify my feelings regarding the issues I address in this book. These benefactors are too numerous to list them all by name but I would like to take this opportunity to mention in particular my editor at *Books in Canada*, Olga Stein, and my publishers, Malcolm Lester, David Mason, and Wesley Begg, who have been enthusiastic supporters of this project throughout its various stages. I am also grateful to Andrea Knight for her diligent copy editing. I would like to thank my friend, Eric Ormsby, former chair of the Department of Islamic Studies at McGill University, as well as my translator Yolande Amzallag, who have graciously placed their knowledge of Islamic theology and Jewish thought at my disposal. Conversations with Israeli novelist A. B. Yehoshua stimulated further reflection and led to certain late adjustments in the text, though in a direction confirming my own position rather than his; nevertheless, his "intervention" was much appreciated. My wife, Karin, has assumed the often unenviable role of literary conscience, research assistant, and patient confidante.

I am equally indebted to the work of innumerable writers in the field, though again I can mention here only a few from among an ever-expanding bibliography. Elie Kedourie's *The Chatham House Version and Other Middle Eastern Studies* is probably the definitive text in the discipline, deconstructing what the author describes as the "meliorism of western liberals, the activist categories and the hopeful concepts of their political science" which have done so much harm—and continue to do so—in our relations with the Arab Middle East. Kedourie's first-hand experience of violence and dislocation, together with his encyclopedic erudition, make him the doyen of Middle East specialists, on whose work the best recent scholarship in the subject is in varying degrees dependent. His crisp, unsentimental approach, his mastery of detail, and vast conceptual sweep have set (and raised) the bar for all subsequent writing on this most complex of issues. Samuel Huntington's *The Clash of Civilizations* remains, as the French say, *incontournable* despite the resistance it has provoked in intellectual circles of late; his argument seems essentially correct and the evidence he presents in support of it cannot be conscientiously disregarded. Joan Peters' *From Time Immemorial* served as an indispensable reference manual and detailed summary of the British Mandatory period in Palestine. No one who genuinely wishes to understand the present situation in the Middle East can afford to neglect this work, however impressionistic it may read in part and however contested it may be in anti-Zionist quarters. (That it has been attacked by revisionist writers like Norman Finkelstein and Noam Chomsky only serves to recommend it.) The Reverend James Parkes' *Whose Land: A History of the Peoples of Palestine* develops one of the most balanced accounts of the Middle East in the literature, and especially the history of its settlement patterns over the millennia, which has grounded my research into the subject. Bernard Lewis' various works on the march of Islam are standard reading, as is Albert Hourani's *A History of the Arab Peoples.* The latter, however, presents a jam-packed and rather disorganized canvas that may lead to a certain amount of confusion, and is rather weak on perspective. Perhaps the best book on the subject, from the standpoint of relative impartiality, coherence, and comprehensiveness, is Philip Hitti's *History of the Arabs* (and its later distillation *The Arabs: A Short History*), although Hitti mistakenly regards Zionism as an "adjunct" of the British Mandate and the resounding peroration of his work, that the "Arabic-speaking peoples have...taken their place among the forward-marching democratic societies of the world and promise to make further contributions to the progress of mankind," betokens a lover's hope rather than a historian's sobriety. H. J. Simson's 1937 study, *British Rule, and Rebellion*, speaks volumes about our own political world. His analysis of the functioning of militant organizations, the rise of fake charities or "subscription lists" to divert funds to guerrilla operations, the use of crowds to provoke "incidents," and the Western folly of giving self-government to people who have had little or no "practice under supervision" could have been written this morning. Further, his isolation of the category of "sub-war," as distinct from civil and international war as well as from riots and uprisings, in which "every effort is made to use force under cover of the Government which is being attacked" while casting the onus on Government "of proving…the illegality of each act, as if each were a disconnected deed done by some disgruntled individual," and his concern over the failure of the judiciary to react to the threat of subversion by its insisting "on the usual procedure, the usual laws of evidence, and the usual proofs" in dangerously unusual situations, reads today as second-sighted. The occasional lectures and articles of Albert Camus, collected under the title *Actuelles III* and translated as *Resistance, Rebellion, and Death*, should be obligatory reading for anyone with a political conscience. To be sure, there is at times a genial innocence about Camus' belief in the power of reason to effect changes in human sensibility, but his castigation of "a political society where the will to be lucid and intellectual independence are becoming rarer and rarer" is very much to the point today. Though writing in the 1950s, often about specific issues and events, his analysis and admonitions remain timely and prescient. "The great tragedies of history," he reminds us, "often fascinate men with approaching horror. Paralyzed, they cannot make up their minds to do anything but wait. So they wait, and one day the Gorgon devours them."

I would direct the interested reader to the philosophical ruminations of Eric Voegelin, in particular his *The New Science of Politics*, which furnishes a profound analysis of the ideological misconceptions that vitiate the political thought and practice of the West's governing elites; and to Bat Ye'or's *Eurabia: The Euro-Arab Axis*, which sets the record straight on the European sellout of its Enlightenment heritage. Robert D. Kaplan's *The Coming Anarchy* is prerequisite to understanding the turbulent age in which we are now living, as are the various works of Kaplan's mentor, military historian Martin Van Creveld, in particular *The Transformation of War* and *The Rise and Decline of the State*. (Kaplan's *The Arabists* also provides valuable insight into the American and British ambassadorial love affair with the Arab world.) David Pryce-Jones' *The Closed Circle: An Interpretation of the Arabs* should, in my estimation, be read by every Western diplomat engaging with the Arab world as a primer for this most sensitive and explosive question in current international relations. Pryce-Jones focuses on what he calls the "power-challenge," "shame-honour ranking," and "money-favour" ethos of Arab culture, "basing [it]self upon the call of Islam," in which perpetual plotting, endemic prevarication, systematic corruption, cunning and deviousness, inwrought conspiracy, tribal alliances, and institutional violence nullify the concepts of fair negotiation and treaty obligation, putting Western diplomacy at a constant disadvantage. The historical vise, with its twin jaws of culture and faith, has clamped too tightly on the Muslim individual to permit a convincing redescription of identity. Similarly, the Western invention of the democratic state, with its balance of powers and tradition of parliamentary debate, cannot flourish where the "concept of loyal opposition is evidently too strange to be credible." (Pryce-Jones' book, incidentally, is not to be confused with Jonathan Coe's latest novel, also titled *The Closed Circle*, which is more critical of the West, and Britain in particular, in the current political crisis than of the Islamic terrorists. Coe adopts the usual line that the terrorists have been provoked by the war in Iraq.) I should also mention Jacques Barzun's *From Dawn to Decadence* and Theodore Dalrymple's *Our Culture, What's Left of It*, each of which furnishes a rich source of both information and tested wisdom. Two more excellent books belong on the first shelf of initial study: Lee Harris' *Civilization and its Enemies* and Paul Berman's *Terror and Liberalism*.

With regard to Jewish/Israeli issues: Yoram Hazony's *The Jewish State: The Struggle for Israel's Soul*, with its titular evocation of Theodor Herzl's founding Zionist pamphlet, tackles the complexity of the Middle East from another angle, showing how the Jews are, as often as not, their own worst enemies. Hazony has no sympathy to spare for those Jewish intellectuals who are eager to surrender the claim to national entitlement for the hookah bubble of integration into a "bi-national" state with an Arab majority. Though Hazony is regarded with suspicion and condescension by the Israeli Left, he is, in my view, among the most brilliant exponents of reason engaging in the current debate. Alain Finkielkraut's *The Imaginary Jew*, though dealing in part with aspects of the "Jewish question" debated in the France of the 1970s, remains a seminal text and continues to speak to the present day. I find much in common with Finkielkraut, whose experience of an antisemitism masking as anti-Zionism and whose initial ambiguities regarding his allegiance to the Jewish community resemble mine in many ways. My book also shares many ideas and some documentation with Alan Dershowitz's lambent *The Case for Peace: How the Arab-Israeli Conflict Can Be Resolved*, although I take a certain exception to the Arcadian nature of some of his working assumptions.

I wish to acknowledge a ruefully ambiguous relation to five other books. I came to Robert Spencer's *Islam Unveiled* rather late in the day, as I was revising my text, and discovered that our position on Islam (though not on Christianity) was almost identical and that we had sourced much of the same literature on the subject. The same holds in part for Sam Harris's *The End of Faith*, which I read shortly after coming across Spencer. Harris's contention, echoing Huntington's, that "our problem is with Islam itself, and not merely with 'terrorism' " is one of the kernel arguments around which my book was conceived and built. As Harris puts it, and I cannot agree more fully, "the evil that has finally reached our shores is not merely the evil of terrorism. It is the evil of religious faith at the moment of its political ascendancy.... Western leaders who insist that our conflict is not with Islam are mistaken." These leaders would need an introductory course in the Islamic scriptures and an at least proximate grounding in Arab history from the seventh century to the present moment if they are to govern sensibly; otherwise, ignorant of the intentions and methods of the forces that confront them, they will be at a loss to formulate the most effective policies, to resist the blandishments of a spurious diplomacy, and to serve as guardians of the trust that has been vested in them. As it is, the majority of our leaders spend their time in office truckling to the enemy and kissing the hem of the *galabieh* rather than showing the backbone one would expect of strong and principled statesmen. Claire Berlinski's *Menace in Europe*, a probing analysis of Europe's interior corrosion and the mythic nature of its pervasive anti-Americanism, is a testament that should figure prominently on the political curriculum. Berlinski writes with verve and panache, carrying the reader to a sobering and logically rigorous conclusion. Bruce Bawer's *While Europe Slept* is a stunning condemnation of Europe's wholesale prostration to its Islamic fifth column: on a number of occasions, we have referenced the same articles and events to support our arguments, but such overlap is no doubt inevitable. With its wealth of detailed information and its no-holds-barred style, it is a book that I cannot recommend highly enough. The same is true of Melanie Phillips' harrowing and thoroughly depressing *Londonistan*, which has laid bare the utter foolishness at the heart of Western appeasement of its Islamic minority populations and the imminent loss of America's chief ally, Britain, in the struggle against the craftiest of enemies. But the contestatory impulse is obviously in the air, which is one of the few encouraging signs in today's consensus-ridden, intellectually decadent, morally inverted, and politically correct world.

It seems that Spencer, Harris, Berlinski, Bawer, Phillips, and myself have arrived independently at similar conclusions in the War against Error. We concur that, with respect to the House of Islam and its profound, tenacious, and theologically inspired hatred of the West and everything the West stands for, as well as the West's refusal or inability to collect its forces and assemble once again at Plataea, the popular Telus advertising slogan—"The Future is Friendly"—has it all wrong. The future is definitely not friendly.

Notes

Part I

1 The Islamic commentary is scarcely worth mentioning as it is entirely foreseeable and almost without exception interpretively primitive, a discourse
that could use a heavy dose of caustic to rid it of ideological and rhetorical
grunge. To take just one instance from a blizzard of such intellectually dismaying materials, Tarek Ghanem, a Cairo freelancer writing in IslamOn-
line, seems to think that Houellebecq, a "Stalinist, xenophobic, nihilist,
chauvinist," is also a Nobel Laureate, which, judging from his tone, barely
constitutes an improvement. As we proceed, we learn many other fascinating things; for example, that Salman Rushdie is doubtlessly implicated in
triggering "a cold-blooded wave of hatred in literature [which] targeted
Islam and Muslims," that Trinidad-born V. S. Naipaul, a "travel writer living in the darkness of post-modern ignorance," loathes "his own country,
India," that Americans and Germans form separate races, that the Jews
have intentionally created an "anti-semitic platform" in order, apparently, to
defuse anti-Israeli criticism, that poor Daniel Pipes is trapped in "an Orientalist paradigm," is afflicted with an "ideological sickness," and is a writer of
hoaxes that are "custom-made to fit his former job as 'an advisor' to the US
State Department" (which, as we know, is consistently pro-Arab), and so
on and on. What is most chastening is that Ghanem's screed is comparatively abstinent. Of course, it must be admitted that such incompetent and
deceitful rebuttals are much to be preferred over the standard reaction of
Islamic clerical authority, which is to declare a fatwa.

2 It might be pointed out that Michel and his similitudes are also the premise
and platform for Edward Said and his tribe of like-minded postcolonial
candle holders, the latter thriving on the indifference of the former. Said,
himself not a Muslim but a self-proclaimed Christian Palestinian—although it now turns out that, like Yasser Arafat (who claimed to be from
East Jerusalem), he was an Egyptian—is the Pied Piper of our current
Orientalists and postcolonial brahmans, a public figure whose intellectual
respectability and personal charisma made him a very effective evangelist
for the movement in all its frowning provincialism. Ibn Warraq in a long,

closely reasoned critique for the Institute for the Secularisation of Islamic Society has convincingly shown that Said's major work, *Orientalism*, is a veritable tissue of fabrications, misconceptions, internal contradictions, damaging omissions, historical blind spots, false attributions, and extremely shabby scholarship, all amounting to what Warraq calls a form of "intellectual terrorism." Robert Irwin's demolition of Said's "labyrinth of false turns, *trompe l'oeil* perspectives and cul-de-sacs" is no less devastating. In *For Lust of Knowing*, Irwin writes that "the distortion of subject matter in *Orientalism* is so fundamental that to accept its broad framework as something to work with and then correct would be merely to waste one's time." Said's book, he continues, "seems to me to be a work of malignant charlatanry in which it is hard to distinguish honest mistakes from wilful misrepresentation."

Apart from Warraq, Irwin, Bernard Lewis, Kanan Makiya, Martin Kramer, and, most recently, a seemingly repentant Christopher Hitchins, very few thinkers have had the audacity or the courage to call Said's bluff. Why did no one challenge him when he expressed doubt that Saddam Hussein had gassed the Kurdish village of Halabja, an attested fact that only diehard revisionists can question? Why have we so capriciously accepted his accusation that the West has worked with prefab stereotypes of the Orient without investigating how the Orient has assembled an equally illusory straw man of its presumed Western oppressor? Does the production of convenient figments operate only in one direction? And why, for that matter, have we waited so long to explode Said's self-perpetuated myth of origins—or to savour the piquant fact that he was born in a Jewish hospital in Jerusalem where his parents rightly evaluated the odds of a safe delivery? I might also mention that Said's articles in the Egyptian newspaper *Al-Ahram*, while occasionally critical of his hosts, were frequently little more than propaganda exercises for the Islamic cause. See in particular his installment in Issue No. 625, 2003. One thinks, *mutatis mutandis*, of Jean Genet's *The Screens*, whose protagonist, an Algerian Arab named Said, has made both a career and an art form of mendacity.

In lionizing a hypocrite like Edward Said, popular novelists such as Ahdaf Soueif and debatable scholars such as Rashid Khalidi—Khalidi has recently come under fire for apparently plagiarizing an article by K. J. Asali—and their peers and colleagues do not advance the cause of truth and understanding, but play to the intellectual bleachers while larking in culturally vetted stereotypes and adding ever more entries to the pseudodoxia epidemica. The tendency to rely on clichés, unreflected truisms, popular beliefs, and what Francis Bacon called "Idols of the Theatre"—faults arising from received systems of thought—should be seen for what it is, a form of intellectual prosthesis that spares critic, novelist, or scholar from having to examine issues independently, outside the dispensary of commonplace assumptions. When it comes to fictional representations, a truer if glancing picture of Said than the poster images we have been showered with may be found in A. B. Yehoshua's *The Liberated Bride* which goes part way to offsetting Soueif's bathetic surrogate figure in *The Map of Love*.

3 No less a public personality than Abdulrahman al-Rashed, general manager of Al-Arabiya television, has made this quite clear. Commenting in the pan-Arab *Asharq Al-Awsat* newspaper on the bloodbath caused by Chechen and Arab guerrillas in Beslan in southern Russia, in which hundreds of children were slaughtered, Rashed entitled his column: "The Painful Truth: All the World Terrorists are Muslims." In a rare gesture in the Muslim world, although he cannot bring himself to mention Israel by name in his list of victimized countries, he admits that "Our terrorist sons are the end-product of a corrupted culture." He was seconded recently by Syrian university professor Mundir Badr Haloum writing in the Lebanese daily, *Al-Safir*: "Muslims produce terrorism, succour it, and praise it." But very few of the Muslim literati are willing to look truth in the eye. Even the great Syrian poet, Nizar Qabbani, in his bitter and, for Arabs, embarrassing 1995 poem "When Will They Announce the Death of the Arabs" (*Mata Yulinun Wafat al Arab*) condemned his co-religionists not for their violence and irrationality but for their weakness. The tenth-century Abbasid poet, Abu al-Ma'arri, whose renegade flights of poetic fancy are as pertinent today as they were in his time, should be accorded a prominent place on the Islamic syllabus and brought to the attention of Muslim intellectuals (and many of their Western colleagues and supporters), especially the verse that reads:

> *I directed my concerns*
> *To God; I failed to ask*
> *If an eclipse might fall.*
> *Many ignorant men*
> *Save themselves from this death,*
> *While thinkers hasten to it.*

In the West, it is only now, with the publication of the report of the National Commission on Terrorist Attacks Upon the United States finally breaking the shackles of political correctness, that the devil has been officially called by its name. It is not some sort of generic terrorism we are dealing with. It is "Islamist terrorism." But that is not enough. As Commission Chair Thomas H. Kean and Vice Chair Lee H. Hamilton write in the Preface to the *Report*, "We hope our report will encourage our fellow citizens to study, reflect—and act."

4 In what sense can an intrinsically autocratic faith make room for a moderate alternative? How does a lay electorate determine who has been chosen
by God to articulate His will? In the words of Kanan Makiya in *Cruelty
and Silence*, a democratic polity depends upon "the absolute isolation of all
matters of belief from entitlement and obligation in public life." But where
there is no separation between Church and State, what meaning can words
like "moderate" or "representative government" possibly have? Or to put it
in other terms: is a genuine Islamic democracy even conceivable? Sheema
Khan, chair of the Council on American-Islamic Relations, poses the latter
question in an article for the *Globe and Mail* (September 12, 2003). She decides that an Islamic democracy is indeed a workable proposition, despite
admitting that polls have shown an overwhelming majority of Muslims
"rejected the idea that Islam should tolerate diverse interpretations" and
favoured "a greater role for religious leaders." How this antinomy can be
resolved must escape a rational inquirer. The locution "Islamic democracy"
makes no more sense, whether as a concept or a slogan, than the "Islamic
socialism" of Nasser's Egypt or the "Ba'ath socialism" of Assad's Syria or
Saddam's Iraq.

One would have thought that by this time the vacuous and baneful
notion of professional orientalists like John L. Esposito and Richard Bul-
liet—one a former president of the Middle East Studies Association and
the other a quondam director of the Middle East Institute at Columbia
University—that Islam represents a different sort of democracy than what
they regard as the product of "Western hegemonic discourse" would have
been decisively repudiated. What can a "different sort of democracy" possibly entail? A system of oligarchic potentates? A rota of infallible clerics? A
clashing discord of extended families or tribal warlords? A one-off election
whose results cannot be undone in subsequent elections since there would
be no subsequent elections? Not all the principles and ideals that govern
human relations can be subject to that fashionable postmodern dissol-
vent, "the indeterminacy of truth," as if there were one sort of truth for the
Western world and another sort of truth for the Islamic world, or to put it
plainly, as if a lie were not a lie.

In any event, when it comes to democratically inspired revolt or opposition, the fact is there is no tradition of civil disobedience or genuine political dissidence in the Arab world. The prevailing attitude may be illustrated
in the words of the twelfth-century Islamic scholar Al-Razali, "Better 100
years of tyranny than one year of social upheaval." This is why Iraq with
its Sunni core and Shi'ite majority can scarcely be expected to mutate into
a truly responsible democratic state and why even Turkey, a presumed
beacon nation, will always remain potentially unstable. Turkey has recently

attempted to pass a law criminalizing adultery in order, according to Prime Minister Recep Tayyip Erdogan, to preserve "human honour," and EU market commissioner Fritz Bolkestein has warned that, with a Muslim population of 70 million, Turkey's accession to the EU is only one more step in the eventual Islamization of Europe. The fact that *Mein Kampf* has become a bestseller in the country is equally worrying. As Iranian author and editor of the Paris-based *Politique Internationale* Amir Taheri has acutely argued with relation to Turkey, the great mistake of the nation's prime ministers from Menderes in the 1950s to Erdogan today lay in "assuming that the Islamist ideology could be exercised in moderation." Taheri concludes his analysis of the conditions underlying the recent terrorist attacks in Turkey by warning its current leaders that "anyone who mixes politics and religion risks having that mix explode in his face" (*National Post*, November 27, 2003). For a sense of what to expect in the future, Turkey's premier novelist Orhan Pamuk furnishes a rather disturbing speculum in his most recent novel, *Snow*.

Islam, despite its dynastic segmentations, is a totalist faith that treats religion, society and state as a single entity, recognizing no distinction between civil law and canon law. It is for this reason that one of the most demagogic and eloquent of modern Islamic scholars, Said Qutb, condemned Kemal Atatürk, who abolished the Caliphate in 1924. The realms of the divine and the empirical cannot be sundered from one another. "Political and religious objectives," writes Bernard Lewis in *The Arabs in History*, "were never really distinct in Muhammad's mind or in the minds of his, or for that matter our, contemporaries...[R]eligion alone could provide the cohesive power for a state among Arabs to whom the whole concept of political authority was foreign and repugnant." One does not vote for God. What we must finally understand is that in Islam, the religious scripture will eventually and always trump the political card. When American Secretary of State Condoleezza Rice told the Sciences Politiques Institute in Paris on February 9, 2005, that "there is no inherent conflict between Islam and democracy," she was, I'm afraid, merely acting in character.

5 The celebrated sura 5:32, often cited by Muslims to emphasize the peaceful nature of Islam, states that anyone who kills another human being "should be regarded as though he had killed all mankind." Yet the same verse introduces an exception—"except as punishment for murder or other wicked crimes"—leaving the definition of "wicked crimes" open to interpretation. Further, the very next verse appears to revoke its predecessor: "Those that make war against Allah and His apostle and spread disorders in the land shall be put to death or crucified or have their hands and feet cut off...." The notion of spreading disorders is also open to interpretation and readily

results in the killing of "another human being." Consider as well the notorious Sword verse (Koran 9:5): "Slay the polytheists wherever you find them, and take them, and confine them, and lay in wait for them at every place of ambush." The sentence seems partially commuted in the Tribute verse (Koran 9:29) in which certain unbelievers may remain unmolested if "they pay the tribute out of hand and have been humbled" (what is meant by "out of hand" or "humbled" has never been satisfactorily explained and still causes dispute) and in the so-called No Compulsion sura (Koran 2:256) where we read, "No compulsion is there in religion." But such conciliatory ukases are regularly scanted and overturned in practice. The Islamic authorities are extremely loath to activate what is known as the "abrogation" or "revocation" process to void or amend the Sword sura by the Tribute or No Compulsion verses. In contemporary Islam, the opposite is the more probable sequence, as in the "proof-texting" of the Muslim Brotherhood and other radical organizations. Proof-texting, however, is not cherry-picking. What is stated in the Koran is what is stated in the Koran and the Koran is infallible. Contradictions are explained away by the principle of *Naskh* in which the later Medinese section of the Koran may override the earlier and more tolerant Meccan portion of the text. Indeed, the number of Koranic verses enjoining violence is almost beyond counting. Even the practice of beheading hostages adopted by the various terrorist groups in Iraq is justified by sura 47:4, which reads, "When you meet the unbelievers in the battlefield, strike off their heads." Those who argue, like former RCMP anti-terror specialist Tom Quiggan (*National Post*, June 3, 2006), that "poisonous jihadist messages…bear little resemblance to the actual message of Islam" quite frankly do not know what they are talking about. And as far as the oft-admired principle of *Ijtihad* goes—the process of making legal decisions by independent interpretation of the sources of the law with a view toward revocation—the practice itself pertained only to the *mujtahid*, or accredited scholar of Islamic law, and became largely moribund in the tenth century.

6 Fallaci's legions are curiously reminiscent of the "rage-infected" swarms in the 2002 Danny Boyle post-apocalyptic genre film, *28 Days Later*, which passes elliptical commentary on current events. As Boyle said in a *RES Columns* interview, "You can't quite trust your usual sense of judgment about perception, depth and distance when dealing with the infected." It would be comforting to dismiss these Fallacian-type "zombies" as horror-flick absurdities fouled by a killer virus that soon runs its lunar course were they not so prodigiously lethal in the real world. The 2004 genre satire, *Shaun of the Dead*, directed by Edgar Wright, adopts a somewhat different tack. Here the zombies uncannily resemble their victims so that the distinction between the infected and the noninfected is moot. Wright's point is that the

consumer society we live in now has become so stupefied and trivialized by
its own excesses that both individual alertness and collective intelligence
have all but disappeared.

7 Ibn Warraq's name is pseudonymous as several fatwas have been issued
against him. The name derives from the great skeptical rationalist, Al-War-
raq, who died in exile in the early tenth century. "Ibn Warraq" means "son
of Warraq"; "Warraq" itself is Arabic for "bookseller."

8 One can only be amazed at the gloating tone affected by the majority of our
liberal professors, journalists, editorialists, and newscasters whenever they
comment or report on an American reversal of fortune in Iraq (or anywhere else). This is the *Iliad* with a twist. The war against terrorism takes a
back seat to the war of the West against itself and the Trojan horse standing
at the portals has been built and placed there by the very people who are
presently under attack. The self-righteousness on display here is as evident
as it is distressing. Even the International Red Cross—the same Red Cross
that remained silent when it learned of the Nazi extermination camps in
1942—now claims to have long been aware of prisoner abuses in American-
administered Iraqi jails. Why it did not step forward and sound the alarm
when it presumably uncovered the scandal several months before it became
common knowledge seems somewhat baffling. And why it did not protest
when Saddam Hussein executed 4,000 inmates of the Abu Ghraib prison
(known to Iraqis as Saddam's "torture central") in 1984 and 100 in a single
day in 1999 remains a mystery. No, it's not nice, but detention scandals
happen in wartime. With respect to America, this is an anomaly; with
respect to the Arab nations typically clamouring against American perfidy,
it is the normal course of events. "Why is it," wonders Democratic Senator
Zell Miller, "that there's more indignation over a photo of a prisoner with
underwear on his head than over the video of a young American with no
head at all?"

But what is most bewildering is the philistine tendency among Western
journalists and pundits and the so-called "peace constituency" to impugn
the motives and attack the bona fides of the one power or coalition in the
world that has moved, at considerable risk, to protect both itself and them.
It is the good faith of these very agencies that should be put under scrutiny:
the CBS news service and its star anchor Dan Rather relying on forged
documents to implicate the American president, Amnesty International
with its habitually inflated figures and its refusal to distinguish between
democratic nations and totalitarian regimes in documenting violations
of human rights—as if the latter were not 100 per cent culpable, the *Daily
Mirror* publishing fake photos of prison atrocities and thus putting its own
country's soldiers in peril, the *Boston Globe* admitting that its photos of US

troops sexually assaulting Iraqi women were counterfeit, the CBC having to retract its claim of Israeli involvement at Abu Ghraib as well as having to apologize for showing video footage of American helicopter fire, dug out of its archives, with no bearing on or connection to Abu Ghraib, *Newsweek* being forced to disclaim an unsubstantiated article in which American soldiers were falsely reported to have flushed a copy of the Koran down the toilet at Guantánamo Bay, which led to riots throughout the Muslim world and resulted in seventeen deaths and hundreds of injured, etc., etc. (In this latter instance, one recalls the old Koran-shredding ploy, reported by H. J. Simson, used by the Arabs to incriminate British officers during the Palestinian rebellion of 1936.)

But all this is small potatoes compared to the political behaviour of the European Union. For, as Bernard Lewis has pointed out in *The Crisis of Islam*, it is the European Union that has come to replace first Nazi Germany, then the Soviet Union, as the patron of the Muslim world in their mutual campaign against the perceived threat represented by the United States. The irony here, as Robert Kagan argues in *Of Paradise and Power*, is that Europe is permitted to roister in its post-historical, geopolitical paradise only because America "remains stuck in history…leaving most of the benefits to others." Europe is now living to a worrisome extent in a political fantasyland as it proceeds to decouple from America, the only power capable of defending it in its state of military weakness and mental unpreparedness— even from conflicts in its own backyard, as in Serbia and Kosovo. The same applies to the military option that may be the only way to solve the Iranian crisis. Addressing the United States, Europe whispers, "You do it! You do it!" And should the Americans (or the Israelis) actually take matters in hand and launch a pre-emptive strike, Europe will exclaim, "They did it! They did it!" In effect, Europe would prefer to lounge in a state of sepia nostalgia for what never was and never can be than to act in any decisive way. But the continental naifs dreaming their Kantian dream of perpetual peace, as Kagan says, "cannot long survive unless the United States does use its power in the dangerous Hobbesian world that still flourishes outside Europe." Kagan neglects to mention that the Hobbesian bacillus in its Islamic metamorphosis has already percolated into the European body politic.

9 Michel's briefly voiced and hopeful belief that materialism will eventually conquer fanaticism calls to mind Benjamin Barber's contention in *Jihad vs. McWorld*, but carries little conviction and quickly disappears within the larger theoretical economy of the novel. Even Houellebecq's own passing observation that Islam will eventually be undermined by capitalism reads more like a throwaway remark than a weighed pronouncement.

10 It is certainly fitting that Houellebecq penned a critical study of H. P.

Lovecraft (*Contre le monde, contre la vie*, not easy to find but well worth the search), this opulent supplier of (in Lovecraft's own phrase) "cosmic horror," creator of the unhinged Yemenese poet Abdul Alhazred and his diabolical book the *Necronomicon*, and logothete of the dread being Cthulhu the centre of whose cult "lay amid the pathless desert of Arabia." For the scene unfolding before our eyes today might have emerged dripping from the master's imagination. We might say, adopting Lovecraft's terminology, that what we are beginning to experience is not only terror but *horror*, whose "basic element" he identified as "any mysterious and irresistible march toward a doom." From this perspective, Houellebecq is Lovecraft transposed from the realm of the fantastic to the world as we are coming to know it, with the important difference that Lovecraft entertained racist and supremacist convictions while Houellebecq, whose horror of Islam is social, political, and theological, does not. But they are at one in their sense of premonition as, each in his own way, they record the emergence of destructive and inhuman powers. Indeed, observing the gathering forces of a renascent Islam, Houellebecq might have been thinking of Lovecraft's nebulous "sky-spawn" in *The Call of Cthulhu*, which, briefly scattered by its quarry, begins to recombine in its original form. *Platform's* silurid probably owes something as well to Lovecraft's flooded monstrosities, "about five feet long; with crustaceous bodies bearing vast pairs of dorsal fins," from *The Whisperer in Darkness*. "The evolution of the modern world has made Lovecraftian phobias ever more present," comments Houellebecq.

11 For Voegelin, the modern intellectual is the reincarnation of the early Gnostic, who interprets the order of concrete society (or the *cosmion*) as an *eschaton* (or heavenly city), who seeks to replace the civil order with a civil theology, and for whom the "nonrecognition of reality is the first principle." In Voegelin's view, "Gnostic politics is self-defeating in the sense that measures which are intended to establish peace increase the disturbances that will lead to war." Voegelin was writing in the early 1950s, yet the force of his argument must be acknowledged. It was the dream world of the Gnostic politicians that "used a victory deliberately for the purpose of creating a power vacuum to its own disadvantage," that put the Soviet army on the Elbe, surrendered China to the Communists and "in addition demobilized our own army." Phenomena of this magnitude, he continues, "cannot be explained by ignorance and stupidity. These policies were pursued as a matter of principle, on the basis of Gnostic dream assumptions about the nature of man, about a mysterious evolution of mankind toward peace and world order, about the possibility of establishing an international order in the abstract without relation to the structure of the field of existential forces...." He concludes that these policies, principles, and assumptions

"seem to show that the contact with reality is at least badly damaged and that the pathological substitution of the dream world is fairly effective." A similar idea is developed by Eva Hoffman in her memoir *Lost in Translation*, where, borrowing Alan Tate's word, she speculates that her American peers and colleagues suffer from a form of "angelism"—"a desire to be more immaculate beings, avatars of pure ideas…so they can ricochet from one vision of utopia to another." She expands on this notion as the ability to think "privileged thoughts…thoughts that cost nothing and that weren't produced by the labor of their own experience."

12 Aristotle's thesis in the *Politics* has, to my mind, never been bettered. Although he argues against the unifying state of the *Republic*—and would to this extent eschew the overriding concept of patriotism—he saw the polis not as dispensable or constricting, but as balanced by the powers of other, smaller interstitial communities. For decentralists, group memberships are essential to both the development of the individual and allegiance to the larger community of the patria. Although they must be prevented from growing hypertrophic and all-determining, as in the Muslim world, communal and associational ties are necessary in order to avoid the homogenization and ultimately the tyranny of the unitary, absolute community. One thinks of Edmund Burke, who wrote in *Reflections on the Revolution in France*, "To be attached to the subdivision, to love the little platoon we belong to in society, is the first principle (the germ, as it were) of public affections." Similarly, Milan Kundera, in *The Book of Laughter and Forgetting*, warns against "the age-old dream of a world where everybody would live in harmony, united by a single common will and faith…. Once the dream of paradise starts to turn into reality, however, here and there people begin to crop up who stand in its way, and so the rulers of paradise must build a little gulag on the side of Eden. In the course of time this gulag grows ever bigger…while the adjoining paradise gets ever smaller." Though admitting, presumably with Diogenes, that "local and national forms of political organization" need not be abolished, the main thrust of Nussbaum's thesis clearly envisions the pasturing out of patriotic feeling as narrow, demoralizing, potentially jingoistic, and passé. (Here the philosophical community is on the same page as the literary avant-garde. American poet Jorie Graham has also embraced the flagless condition of political being. "Time of the flags is long past—how/strange—a Flag!" she writes in her recent and tumescent hymn to herself, *Overlord*.)

The paradox is that Nussbaum, a recognized authority on Aristotle, has served up an argument that, for all its apparent open-mindedness, is really a form of mystical monism that has more in common with centralist thinkers like Plato, Hobbes, and Marx than with pluralists like Aristotle,

Proudhon, and de Tocqueville, whom she might logically be expected to favour. Nussbaum has substituted loyalty to a country with loyalty to an Idea, the most monolithic Leviathan of them all.

The Nussbaums of the world were captured perfectly by Henry James in the character of Eustache Poupin from *The Princess Casamassima*: "a theorist and an optimist and a visionary…he believed that the day was to come when all the nations of the earth would abolish their frontiers and armies and custom-houses, and embrace on both cheeks, and cover the globe with boulevards…where the human family would sit, in groups, at little tables, according to affinities, drinking coffee…and listening to the music of the spheres." Such people, James has his protagonist think, are "in a state of chronic spiritual inflammation." This is not to say that we do not from time to time detect signs of intelligence in play—and often of considerable astuteness in the working out of an argument, however divorced from reality—but as James comments, "what is the use of intelligence if you haven't got a backbone." To cite from Robert Kaplan's *The Coming Anarchy*, the efforts of our public intellectuals would be far more effective in the long run if they sought "to grapple with how the world actually works, rather than to describe a better world that may never be." Margaret Thatcher was on to something when she said that "the facts of life are conservative."

13 Ignatieff proceeded to exacerbate the mischief in his keynote address to the Banff Television Festival in June 2004, in which he defined terrorism in Clausewitzian terms as "politics by other means." These are "disgraceful, illegitimate means," he conceded, but nevertheless "means that serve the needs and aspirations of people." Which brings up an obvious question: what needs and aspirations of which people were being served by the slaughter of September 11, 2001? The sandstone dwellers of Yemen? The gun-toting tribesmen of North and South Waziristan? The fanatic misogynists of the Wahabbi peninsula? The metastasizing cells of cateran guerrillas? The Palestinians who danced in the streets and handed out candy in the days after 9/11 to celebrate the death of defenceless innocents? Somehow I doubt it. And since he mentioned as well the Palestinian-trained Red Brigades and the Baader Meinhoff cadre of the 1970s and 1980s, may we not also inquire what particular stratum of the population their adoption of terrorist methods might imaginably have benefitted?

Rather than engage in such unanchored speculation, Ignatieff might have been better advised to consult Amir Taheri's *Holy Terror: Inside the World of Islamic Terrorism* or the research findings of Rohan Gunaratna, author of *Inside Al Qaeda*. Gunaratna has shown that in the decade 1993–2003, 86 per cent of suspected and committed terrorists were Muslims and the rest were mainly converts to Islam. It is also disturbing that Ignatieff buys into the contemporary cliché that the Islamist terrorists murder and maim from political and economic desperation, forgetting that the terrorists who brought down the Twin Towers hailed mainly from privileged backgrounds and that Osama bin Laden never lacked for money. Ignatieff is one of the more respectable and intelligent members of the Solonic comity; he is undone not by irrational anger or a prior political allegiance, but by the boy-scout ingenuousness of the well-tempered citizen. Nevertheless, that he should reveal himself as so lazy a thinker and so credulous an observer speaks volumes about the competence of the constituency of which he forms a part. It is precisely the effete and pixilated cultural milieu built up, defended, and populated by the Nussbaums and Ignatieffs of the intellectual world, strangely eager for Herostratic honours, that Houellebecq is contesting in the only way that seems to garner public attention: with a profane, indecorous and knuckle-duster directness that does not pull its punches.

14 Canada is particularly liable. In this country a convicted Palestinian terrorist, Mahmoud Mohammad Issa Mohammad, can feasibly protest his deportation order because he would forfeit his Canadian health care benefits. Similarly, members of the pro-Taliban, Osama-friendly Khadr terrorist family have been permitted to resettle in Canada from Pakistan on the grounds that they are Canadian citizens and that the youngest son, wounded in a firefight in Afghanistan against our American allies, requires medical treatment.

But this is not all. The Canadian Minister of Immigration in the former Liberal government went on record safeguarding the privacy rights of fifty-five suspected war criminals, wanted for crimes against humanity, who have skipped their deportation hearings and have conveniently disappeared. According to the then Minister, "the government must act carefully to ensure that the Privacy Act is not violated." The presumption of innocence and the rights of due process clearly take precedence over public safety, even in the case of known murderers and armed militants. (It is no accident that Canada with its 36,000 missing deportees has come to be regarded by many political analysts as a harbour for the terrorist enterprise.) But there should be no doubt that defeating what *Daily Telegraph* correspondent Janet Daley, rightly or wrongly, calls the "mystical nihilism" of the new terrorists "is going to take all the organised energy and commitment that the rich, decadent West can muster." For the right to live, as she soundly argues, is the single entitlement "on which all other rights are predicated. There are no civil liberties in the grave." One thinks of Spinoza's proposition from the *Ethics*: "The endeavour after self-preservation is the essence itself of a thing. If, therefore, any virtue could be conceived prior to this of self-preservation, the essence itself of the thing would be conceived as prior to itself, which (as self-evident) is absurd"; and of poet George Szirtes' apt lines: "Nor can survival/Brook a rival." I am very much afraid that in the current situation nothing short of *lex talionis* will suffice, accompanied by a pre-emptive resoluteness that leaves no doubt about the Western will to survive. As Roger Kimball observes in *Tenured Radicals*, "Civilization is not a gift; it is an achievement—a fragile achievement that needs constantly to be shored up and defended from besiegers inside and out." And in prosecuting such a defence, eudemonistic legislation must sometimes give way to the uncompromised application of force.

15 Aron's main concern was the intellectual's relation to Communism and not to Islam—the book was published in 1955. But his peroration still holds good. "The intellectual who sets some store by the just and reasonable organisation of society will not be content to stand on the side-lines, to put his signature at the bottom of every manifesto against every injustice. Although he will endeavour to appeal to the conscience of all parties, he will take his stand in favour of the one which appears to offer humanity the best chance...." Aron goes on to underscore the importance of humility and of remaining aware of both "the arguments of the adversary" and "the faults of [one's] own side," but the intellectual must nevertheless refuse "to surrender his soul to an abstract ideal of humanity, a tyrannical party, and an absurd scholasticism." He must "doubt all the models and utopias" if he wishes to "abolish fanaticism." For fanaticism is the real enemy. "We can admire the sombre grandeur of these armies of believers. We can admire their devotion, their discipline and self-sacrifice," yet "such fanaticism is not for us."

16 The nature of "history" has changed since 9/11, but our liberal intellectuals, in allowing themselves to be carried by the momentum of the past, are merely acting out the aphorism of Houellebecq's poetic contemporary, Michel Devrient, who wrote, "Aller dans le sens de l'histoire, c'est comme prétendre se laisser guider par son vélo dans les Pays-Bas." (To go with the flow of history is like pretending your bicycle is what's steering you through the Low Countries.) In essence, our left-leaning oracles have been unable to extricate themselves from Viet Nam, which has become their own conceptual quagmire. Although the global situation has changed dramatically since the 1960s and 1970s, they insist on seeing the American response to international terrorism under the sign of Vietnam, prescinding from what is no longer relevant to what is no longer the same. Their anti-war stance was justified then; now it is at best irrelevant and at worst inexcusable. 9/11 was no Bay of Tonkin. And despite what columnists like the *Guardian*'s Sidney Blumenthal seem to think as they proceed to denature language and deform reality, Guantánamo Bay is no Soviet gulag, Fallujah

is no Stalingrad, and the American president is no fascist. "This shows the elite's lack of a sense of reality," writes Hannah Arendt proleptically in *The Origins of Totalitarianism*, and then goes on to anatomize and deplore the "alliance between the intellectual elite and the mob." For the "learned" have the crowd with them in the dissemination and acceptance of such nonsense and indeed have become not only the people's ephorate, but part of the crowd themselves. The personal fastidiousness of the elite seems to require the popular mudbath.

17 A representative instance of this doddering attitude to the major challenge of our time was provided in John Doyle's review of the BBC documentary for the *Globe and Mail* of April 22, 2005. Doyle had nothing but praise for the series, which he described as a "devastating analysis of contemporary politics." In the course of his panegyric, we find him referring to Said Qutb, the most important member of the Muslim Brotherhood and the chief mover of Islamic jihad that has brought so much bloodshed upon us, as simply an "Egyptian educator." In the same breath, he endorses the attack on Leo Strauss, considered as largely responsible for the neoconservative nightmare from which we are presumably suffering. (Strauss' influence has been grossly exaggerated and it is by no means clear that he can be dismissed as a fundamentalist crank.) The battle lines are clearly drawn: Qutb the Islamic educator, Strauss the mentor of neocon villains like Donald Rumsfeld and Paul Wolfowitz. The Islamic threat, we are meant to understand, is really a neoconservative conspiracy. Doyle's unshaded dithyramb for the British production functions as a popular litmus of contemporary opinion. Nor does Doyle seem to realize that the leftist BBC of today is in many ways the successor of the rightist BBC of the 1930s, whose director at the time, John Reith, held the fascist dictators in high esteem. The chirality is immaterial—the BBC generally backs the enemy.

18 See former Canadian Minister of Foreign Affairs, Bill Graham, writing in the *Globe and Mail* for May 14, 2004. Graham contended that terrorists have exploited Islam as a "pretext for violence," that "unwarranted suspicion" has been cast "on hundreds of millions of peaceful Muslims around the globe," that, as the leader blazons, "Now is the time to reach out to the Muslim world," and that, in effect, multiculti Canada can serve as a beacon for "like-minded progressives in Muslim countries." Such cliché-driven naivety—or is it simply electoral politics at work—on the part of a Minister of the Crown to whom we entrust our defence is, to say the least, rather disturbing.

Of course, we should not forget which country Graham speaks for— a country in which Muslim voters are assiduously catered to, which until very recently has consistently supported anti-Israel resolutions brought forward by the Islamic bloc in the UN, which played a conspicuous part in the shameful and misnamed Durban World Conference Against Racism, and in which a study just completed by Government Policy Consultants for the Canadian Council for Israel and Jewish Advocacy finds that 42 per cent of Canadians do not know that Israel is a democratic state and that a large majority believes that Israel does not enjoy freedom of speech.

19 As the guerrilla protagonist Willie Chandran of V. S. Naipaul's latest novel, *Magic Seeds*, remarks, "I know enough now, to understand that life can never be simplified like that, and that there will be the same little trap or flaw in that dream of simplicity...." In point of fact, Naipaul's *Among The Believers* spelled out for us in 1981 (and his follow-up volume *Beyond Belief* in 1998) the very trap, flaw, or simplifying dream we are trying to come to grips with now.

20 A restatement of the words of the patron of modern Islamism, Said Maududi: "Islam wants the whole earth and is not content itself with only a part of it. It wants and needs the entire inhabited world." Zahar's pledge was reiterated by Yasser Arafat on July 29, 2004, when he assured a Fatah assembly in Ramallah that the struggle would continue until "our children raise the Palestinian flag on the walls, minarets and churches of Jerusalem." Perhaps we should be grateful that he left out the world.

21 This caveat applies equally to the United Nations, which seems to be growing increasingly irrelevant; indeed, it is not only irrelevant, it is hazardous. It was under its supervision, we recall, that the Pyongyang government was allowed to remove enough plutonium to build half a dozen nuclear bombs.

22 A group of Ontario Muslims has been lobbying to establish a judicial tribunal implementing *sharia* law to resolve civil and marital disputes. Though the effort was eventually stymied, there is clearly much sympathy for their petition among provincial officials, the electorate at large, and some of our major national newspapers, like the *Globe and Mail*, which in its editorial policy does not seem unduly alarmed at the danger of family *sharia*. Government and party officials in Ontario and in other parts of the country—with the laudable exception of the General Assembly of the province of Quebec which voted decisively and immediately against the implementation of *sharia*—seem to have absolutely no idea what Islamic law entails. In their desire to save on administrative costs for domestic legal proceedings, they considered for some time empowering a concept of law that acknowledges only the Divine as supreme authority on all matters civil and religious and that recognizes only the Prophet Mohammed, his successors, and sanctioned interpreters as competent, by direct revelation or privileged access, to interpret and express it. More recently, the Metropolitan Airports Commission in Minneapolis-St. Paul has vetted a system

that allows Muslim cab drivers to refuse passengers carrying alcohol. As
Daniel Pipes comments, "Why stop with alcohol? Muslim taxi drivers in
several countries already balk at allowing seeing-eye dogs in their cars.
Future demands could include not transporting women with exposed arms
or hair, homosexuals, and unmarried couples." Pipes quotes the wife of the
former head of the Minnesota Chapter of the Muslim American Society,
with which the airport commission has consulted in arriving at a *modus
vivendi*, who explains that the goal of the Islamic organization is "to educate
everyone about Islam and to follow the teachings of Islam with the hope of
establishing an Islamic state."

When one looks at how *sharïa* is applied in Muslim countries, the only
sane reaction is apprehension: rape victims stoned to death for the crime
of having been raped, children of divorced parents given over exclusively
to male custody, young women students condemned to die in a burning
building for not being properly attired in their haste to escape. But *sharïa*
is defended by many enlightened and zealous Canadians under the ensign
of "religious pluralism." Islamic family arbitration panels would be only a
first step toward ever greater demands in the service of a tribal, patriarchal,
and outmoded system of authoritarian law that, unlike other faith-based
dispensations, leans toward the institution of extreme sanctions. Let us not
discount the theory of small beginnings. Lenny Bruce quips about a devout
Catholic serving time for murder. How does one get from there to here?
Finally he understands. "It begins with bingo in the Catholic Church." In
today's world, it begins with a judgment in the Islamic mosque.

23 These ballot assumptions are advanced by Natan Sharansky in *The Case
for Democracy: The Power of Freedom to Overcome Tyranny and Terror*, an
important book that has clearly influenced the thinking of the White
House. But while Sharansky's general argument—that it is only freedom
that makes peace and human rights possible and that the primary challenge for the West is finding the moral clarity to see evil where it actually
lives—is impeccable, his belief that the Islamic peoples are readily susceptible to the lure of liberal democratic principles seems overly optimistic.
Sharansky's formative experience is with a secular dictatorship and transferring his principles and convictions to the political behaviour of Islamic
states, insofar as these are political entities, would seem on the face of it to
be sound. But as *Jerusalem Post* columnist Jonathan Rosenblum has pointed
out, Sharansky's belief that "a long list of democracies that were once
thought incapable of freedom is not proof that Arab society can rise to the
challenge." It is moot whether the reform of the Islamic state will lead to
peace and mutual understanding unless the Islamic faith also undergoes a
thorough reformation.

24 See as well the recent discussions for a nuclear deal, spearheaded by France, Germany, and Britain with tacit Russian support—countries too distracted by the venalities of the moment and too muffled in their councils by diplomatic insulation to identify and pursue their long-term interests—that would have provided Iran with light-water reactor fuel that could be used to produce bomb material within nine weeks although International Atomic Energy Agency inspectors visited Iran only every quarter year. The Europeans continue to "negotiate" with Iran when it is obvious that the country has long embarked on a nuclear enrichment program toward the day when it will announce a *fait accompli*. (In point of fact, Iran has no nuclear power stations and consequently has no need of enriched uranium for fuel.) At the moment of writing, Britain is opening a branch of the Standard Charter Bank in the Iranian free-trade zone on the island of Kish to accompany the Iran-Europe Commercial Bank, owned jointly by Iranian and German investors, and Britain's Department of Trade and Industry has given export licences to firms that deliver dirty bomb components, like radioactive caesium 137, americium-berylium, and zirconium silicate, to Iran; Russia is setting up a Russian-Iranian trade council and supplying Iran with nuclear fuel for the Russian-built nuclear plant in Bushehr, as well as with missiles to defend it; China continues to furnish Iran with advanced weapons technology; and France is involved in an array of ventures in the country, including tourism, culture, telecommunications, and industrial management, not to mention the light-water reactor fuel deal in tandem with Britain and Germany. At the same time, the UN Human Rights Commission, meeting in Geneva in April 2005, refused to cite Iran as, along with Sudan, the worst violator of human rights in the world. What all this means is that, apart from the US, the entire veto-wielding UN Security Council is actively involved in fostering ties with Iran and/or abetting its nuclear program, despite the recent intention to refer the country to its authority.

25 The more advanced of our left-wing "democratic" agitators (who belong increasingly in scare quotes) have been influenced by the Italian social philosopher Antonio Gramsci's well-known hegemonic thesis, which prescribed the gradual infiltration and control of social and political institutions and cultural groups acting from the margins to ensure beneficial social change. These thinkers were supposed to have roughly the same effect in the pragmatic sphere that Gramsci in his *Prison Notebooks* allotted to stage directions in theatrical works, "contribut[ing] to the representation of the characters [which] limit the actor's freedom of choice and lead to a more concrete description of the character." For some of his adherents, this "limit" is worth pursuing in the interest of social welfare in the context of anarchic capitalistic aggrandizement; for others, it has come to represent a

confinement and a brake on individual growth, persuading them to move toward the Right, like developing characters eschewing the stage directions that would restrict their freedom of thought and action. But for the majority of the liberal-left constituency, this issue never arises, as they appear to think and act more or less by rote, like hackneyed method actors repeating their roles rather than inventive playwrights living into their evolving dramatic characters.

26 As Hannah Arendt wrote to Karl Jaspers in a letter of August 17, 1946, with reference to the Nazis, "This guilt, in contrast to all criminal guilt, oversteps and shatters any and all legal systems." The application of this remark to the present moment is self-evident.

27 Confronting these "source nations" means, as well, checking the credentials of those influential officials appointed to monitor their activities. One notes that Mohammed ElBareidi, director general of the International Atomic Energy Agency, somehow neglected to specifically mention, in his tabled reports on the Iranian nuclear program, the suspicious Parchin test site southeast of Teheran, an omission that led the US delegation to the Agency's board to accuse the IAEA of keeping silent on so critical a question. The same applies to the facility at Lavasin. The IAEA also watered down a crucial report released on November 26, 2004, that originally indicated that Iran had acquired "huge amounts" of the nuclear initiator beryllium "from a number of nations." The beryllium mysteriously disappeared from the document. It is also troubling to learn that the IAEA was aware of Iran's nuclear ambitions throughout the 1990s, but chose to do nothing about the mounting crisis. Equally disturbing, ElBareidi swiftly acceded to the recent Iranian demand that the IAEA drop Belgian inspector Chris Charlier whose investigations were proving embarrassing to the Iranian regime— Charlier has also been denied access to the relevant documents. It is, of course, ElBareidi who should have been cashiered. The world is paying for its negligence as Iran has now arrived at the technological step to producing "enrichment cascades"—the point of nuclear no return.

28 Movies can be a valid form of adventitious or incidental commentary on current events, but their influence can also be baleful, apart from the more deliberate propaganda efforts like Michael Moore's *Fahrenheit 9/11*. (Moore, the unshaven, baseball-capped "man of the people," enjoying a lavish New York lifestyle and marketing pseudo-documentaries that selectively tweak the data, is probably the most visible deputy of the humbuggery of the New Left.) We now know that Hollywood-made films have become source texts and instruction manuals for al-Qaeda and related terrorist groups. *Blackhawk Down* is an obvious example. Malise Ruthven has pointed to the role that *Executive Decision* may have played in 9/11. Rambo has become

a popular *shahid* role model, down to the trademark bandanna. But even farces and comedies are not to be scouted. Take a piece of harmless puffery like *The Pink Panther Strikes Again*, in which the mad, former Chief-Inspector Dreyfus(!), seeking revenge on his nemesis Inspector Clouseau, commandeers a death-ray type of weapon that can make buildings disappear. His chosen target is the United Nations Building in New York, which is duly vaporized, dematerializing from the top down to its foundations. In the background the camera pans on the Twin Towers. Meanwhile, the villain complains that he would prefer to see mayhem and tangled metal in the heart of the metropolis.

29 Many of the so-called "camel corps" of fifty-two former British ambassadors who circulated a petition condemning the Middle East policies of Tony Blair and George Bush were exposed in the *Daily Telegraph* as having lucrative consulting and business ties with various Islamic enterprises. They are the more sophisticated successors of the infamous "fag brigade" of British Middle East Colonial Office types and diplomats who proliferated in the 1930s and 1940s, the sterile progeny of T. E. Lawrence. It is also an open secret that many former American ambassadors and envoys to Saudi Arabia remain, in one way or another, on the Saudi payroll. Some of the prominent names among high-ranking American political figures who have gone to work for the Saudis include former vice president Spiro Agnew, former senators William Fulbright, Charles Percy, and Edmund Muskie, and former Reagan aide Michael Deaver. Former president Jimmy Carter's Atlanta Carter Center is lavishly funded by Arab donors, including the United Arab Emirates, Oman, Kuwait, Morocco, Jordan and especially, once again, Saudi Arabia. Carter's friendship with Yasser Arafat and his antipathy towards Israel are well known. Carter also staffed the already anti-Zionist US State Department (aka Foggy Bottom) with pro-Islamic graduates from the Middle Eastern Studies departments of American universities and continues to this day to lobby against Israeli interests.

30 Even modern cosmology seems to concur. As Charles Seife points out in *Alpha and Omega: The Search for the Beginning and End of the Universe*, since life and consciousness run on energy, and the supply of energy in any finite system is constantly decreasing, "civilization slows down more and more, thinking less and less, until it ceases entirely.... Some would say the process has already started." Seife does not indicate whether cosmologists mean civilization in general or a given civilization in the course of its particular trajectory, or both—but if each civilization is considered as a finite system containing a discrete amount of "thought energy," we might argue that what we call "Western civilization" is fast approaching a state of entropic dispersion. It certainly appears to be "thinking less and less."

31 It is important not to misread the signs or to expect victory to flow from misguided assumptions. Houellebecq, educated in the French classical system, would surely have known the passage from Book XII of the *Aeneid* concerning the flight of birds that falsely augured victory for the Latins but led instead to inglorious defeat. More pertinent, perhaps, is Hitchcock's *The Birds*, in which most of the characters cannot—or refuse to—recognize the avian peril closing in on them, preferring to rationalize away the danger as accidental, impossible, or merely temporary.

32 See Alan Cullison's ominous essay, "Inside Al-Qaeda's Hard Drive," in the *Atlantic* for September 2004.

33 This talk, delivered to the International Advisory Board of "a large multi-national corporation," may be found on a multitude of different websites, and should be perused in its entirety. Harari has recently published an expansion of this talk in book form, entitled *A View from the Eye of the Storm: Terror and Reason in the Middle East*, which is essential reading. "It has been pointed out long ago that idealism increases in direct proportion to the distance from the danger," he writes, "but now the danger is everywhere."

34 The same applies to the International Criminal Court that, in the logic of the situation, would now have to impeach George Bush, Tony Blair, Ariel Sharon, John Howard, and several other democratic heads of state as war criminals and move to reinstate the Taliban in Afghanistan and Saddam Hussein in Iraq. One may also wonder why Slobodan Milosevic was not flanked in the prisoner's dock by the leaders of the NATO countries since the war against Serbia did not receive official UN sanction and was therefore manifestly illegal, that is, a criminal act. The conventions by which the ICC operates are clearly obsolete.

35 Broadly speaking, the crucial problem for the West is that the Muslim world is plunged in an ignorance so profound and extensive that genuine dialogue may well be impossible. As Khaled Fouad Allam, author of the just-released *Letter to a Suicide Bomber*, has said, "the Muslim world is submerged in an intellectual night." He believes, however, that "it's possible to emerge from it." Yet how is one to treat with a world-historical civilization that has translated fewer books in the vast span of time from the ninth century to the present day than modern Spain alone translates in any given year—the approximate estimate is 100,000—or whose book sales among a population of approximately a billion and a half are so low they do not figure on the statistical radar. How is one to come to terms with a cultural domain that interprets the killer tsunami of December 2004 either as an act of divine retribution for Western "fornicators" cavorting on the beaches of Asia or as the aftermath of nuclear tests conducted jointly by the United States, India, and Israel?

36 "Only a god can save us now," said Martin Heidegger in his last interview, the only one of the philosopher's utterances that continues to resonate. This despite the fact that by his embracing of the Nazi racial ideology and his subsequent refusal to renounce his commitment to a totalitarian political faith, he contributed significantly to the very condition that he so eloquently lamented and that, in another guise, continues to afflict us into the present moment.

37 Houellebecq's Thailand sequence was especially prescient. On April 9, 2004, the British Foreign Office issued a travel advisory warning tourists to stay away from southern Thailand owing to terrorist activity in Narathiwat, Yala, and Pattani, scenes of several recent bomb attacks. Thanks to the Islamist terrorists, it is becoming increasingly dangerous to travel, to have babies, to visit places of worship and learning, or to pursue the daily course of normal life anywhere in the world, as the train bombing in Madrid in March 2004, the downing of two airliners and the Beslan slaughter in Russia in September of the same year, the London commuter bombings in July 2005, and the Heathrow airline plot in August 2006 have made abundantly clear.

38 The popular conceit of Dutch open-mindedness and generous forbearance needs to be revisited, if the national sport can be said to serve as a barometer of the racial climate. Rival soccer fans of the Ajax Amsterdam team, which represents a city with a long Jewish history, regularly chant antisemitic slogans at games, two of the most frequent being "there goes the Ajax train to Auschwitz" and "Hamas, Hamas, the Jews to the gas." At a match in Rotterdam, the team bus was surrounded by fans performing the Heil Hitler salute—the same fans who came up with the hissing sibilant to suggest the gas chambers. According to press reports, this issue has become the latest test case for Dutch tolerance.

39 Immigration is very much an issue, not only because of raw numbers, but because, as Robert Spencer has written in *Europolitica* for September 20, 2004, echoing Houellebecq's concern, "one cannot by any means screen out the jihadists from the moderate Muslims, and the moderates are not helping identify the jihadists either."

40 Fables have an odd and unexpected way of turning into ironic facts and those who propagated and believed the slander about perfidious Jews may soon have reason to rue the truth about radical Muslims. This threat, especially to the United States, should not be downplayed. Gilles Kepel's counter-intuitive argument in *Jihad: The Trail of Political Islam* that 9/11 marks not the next stage in the ongoing ferocity of Islamist terror but the point from which it has begun to decline is in the context of the present far more debatable than not. Kepel is not alone in his belief that the epidemic

of violence and destruction we are experiencing today is a sign of Islam in decay rather than ascent, a prolonged spasm of valediction to the world. But for Houellebecq, the indications are far more premonitory of impending disaster, and many of the political and historical thinkers I have cited in text would emphatically concur. Nor is Osama's power and influence on the wane; it continues strong throughout a world in which it is estimated that 100,000 al-Qaeda trained operatives are on the loose. Osama should not be underrated but rather acknowledged for what he is: a modern incarnation of the eleventh-century Ismaili Grand Master Hasani Sabbah, the "Old Man of the Mountain," who, having convinced his band of fanatical suicide Assassins (*Hashishim*) of their reward in heaven, sent them forth from his inaccessible fastnesses to sow terror among his enemies. See also Bernard Lewis, *The Assassins*.

41 This is a position that has been argued by internationally-renowned ethicist Margaret Somerville, author of *The Ethical Canary*, who has no problem with gay unions but vigorously opposes gay marriage, on the grounds that children require both a mother and a father for optimal development. Somerville was recently awarded an honorary doctorate by Ryerson University, but following obstreperous protests by student unions and gay organizations which accused Somerville of hate speech and compared her stand to those of the Nazis and KKK, the university moderated its support, claiming prior ignorance of her views. The intellectual cowardice evinced by the awards committee is entirely consistent with the prevailing, chicken-hearted strain of political correctness to be found in most university administrations today.

42 This, as we have seen, was in part the burden of André Gide's thesis in *The Immoralist*, published in 1902, and indeed, in Compton Mackenzie's 1956 successor novel *Thin Ice*, in which the story's protagonist, Henry Fortescue (a lesser version of both Michels), pursues his homoerotic pleasures in the hinterlands of Morocco.

43 "Desire itself becomes the death instinct, latency… that actually produces a desiring-machine that is at the same time social and technical." See Gilles Deleuze and Felix Guattari, *Anti-Oedipus*. This thesis has been carefully worked out by Houellebecq's slightly older contemporary and a likely influence on his work, the acclaimed sociologist Gilles Lipovetsky who, in his major book, *L'Etre du vide: Essai sur l'individualisme contemporain* (1983), examined "the beginning of a postmodern culture…that was satisfied merely to democratize hedonist logic," a culture that made men both indifferent and non-different and, moving away from the communal project and the protestant work ethic, "gave rise to liberation, pleasure, and sex." (Cited and discussed in Luc Ferry and Alain Renaut in their 1985/1990 study, *French*

Philosophy of the Sixties: An Essay on Antihumanism.) Lipovetsky, it should be noted, adopts a somewhat more ambiguous perspective than Houellebecq, on the one hand deploring the ontological vacuum of modern capitalist society while, on the other, extolling the practice of narcissism as a healthy consummation of democratic principles. The brief for narcissism is developed more robustly in his 1994 *The Empire of Fashion: Dressing Modern Democracy*, the only one of his books to be translated into English. It is here that Lipovetsky and Houellebecq decisively part company. "There are certain solitudes which seem without cure," writes Houellebecq in his first book of poems, *The Pursuit of Happiness* (*La poursuite du bonheur*).

44 Quoted in Fred A. Reed, *Anatolia Junction*. Nursi dedicated himself to reviving a slumbering and decadent Islamic world, projecting a vision of hope for the future. His writings, in some ways, prefigure the themes addressed by Tariq Ramadan. Nursi believed that, in the course of time, Christianity, "following the Qur'an...will unite with Islam." For Ramadan, Islam will, amoeba-like, absorb the West.

Part II

1 See Israel Finkelstein and Neil Asher Silberman, *The Bible Unearthed: Archaeology's New Vision of Ancient Israel and Its Sacred Texts*, for the evidence supporting the 1200 BCE date and population percentages during the Babylonian exile. Finkelstein is director of the Sonia and Marco Nadler Institute of Archaeology at Tel Aviv University; Silberman is director of historical interpretation for the Ename Center for Public Archaeology and Heritage Presentation in Belgium. The Edomite material has been researched by an archeological team led by Russell Adams of McMaster University, Thomas Levy of the University of California at San Diego, and Mohammad Najjar of the Jordanian Department of Antiquities, working at a dig at Khirbat en-Nahas in southern Jordan.

2 Interestingly, no such revisionist historiography has appeared in the Arab world since, for one thing, the pertinent documents have not yet been declassified nor are likely to be at any time in the foreseeable future, and, for another, such archival digging would be the kiss of death for any Muslim researcher. As for the Jewish "New Historians," whose writings are widely disseminated in the Arab world, they must accept responsibility for giving aid, comfort, and reams of tainted material to their avowed enemies. (One of the most vile and discriminatory books ever published on the subject of Israel, Roger Garaudy's *The Founding Myths of Israeli Politics*, owes much to these Jewish revisionists.) Karsh has shown convincingly that these "New

Historians" have shamelessly manipulated the documentary evidence, misquoting frequently and rewriting sources, subordinating their integrity as scholars "to expedience and fashion." Karsh, who has written many books dealing with Israel and the Arab nations, makes for indispensable reading. His findings are exhaustively researched and he has no political or ideological brief to skew his conclusions; indeed he is an avid supporter of the movement for the creation of an independent Palestinian state. His conclusions are scrupulously supported by the research of Meyrav Wurmser, director of the Center for Middle East Studies at the Hudson Institute in Washington, DC. See in particular her article on the Institute's Internet homepage for September 19, 2001, entitled "Made-Up Massacre," in which she cites Haifa University graduate student Teddi Katz and his defender, New Historian Ilan Pappe, for manufacturing evidence and fudging facts in their effort to indict Israel in the so-called Tantura "ethnic cleansing" near Haifa in 1948, now discredited as a hoax. Yoram Hazony, who directs the Shalem Center for social thought and public policy in Jerusalem, has written a major work that deconstructs the illusions and deliriums of the anti-Zionist Jewish professoriate. *The Jewish State: The Struggle for Israel's Soul* traces the subversive effect of the largely German-Jewish intellectual circle at the Hebrew University which has done so much to educate Israeli youth away from the belief in a sustainable Jewish state. Hazony singles out Martin Buber as the chief corrupting influence, showing how the philosopher strove to build "a Jewish intellectual leadership in Palestine that would see as its mission the dissolution of the idea of the Jewish state in the minds of the Jews." I would also bring to the reader's attention another important volume on the "truth subject," Mitchell Bard's thorough and compendious *Myths and Facts* which provides a circumstantial point-by-point account of the tangle of untruths and half-truths that have turned the fashionable historiography of the Middle East into a propaganda exercise.

Coming back to the New Historians, their express mandate is to "reconstruct" the past, following the infectious maxim of theoretical relativist E. H. Carr who, reversing the methodological precept of the eminent economic historian Sir George Clark, defined the study and writing of history as a "hard core of interpretation surrounded by a pulp of disputable facts." Only, they do not regard their "facts" as disputable in the least, despite their tendency to play broken telephone with source materials in order to shore up both a preconceived thesis and a professional bias. In the larger intellectual context, these New Historians constitute the Israeli wing of the postmodern antihumanist movement, taking their cue from the genealogical studies of Michel Foucault, whose relation to the documentary archive was notoriously supercilious and who openly advocated the partisan, perspectival writing of history as opposed to the presumably unattainable objective of traditional historiography. Foucault himself was influenced by Nietzsche's pivotal tenet from *The Genealogy of Morals* that "there are no facts, only interpretation," a maxim that is obviously intended to be taken as a fact. The ruling principle such revisionist thinkers espouse, namely, the relativity of all truth claims, applies to everything, apparently, but their own insights and pronouncements.

3   It is worth noting that the 1976 Canadian World Atlas, issued three years after the last major attack against Israel, still maps the West Bank as part of Jordan. But of course, Jordan wants nothing to do with another couple of million restive Palestinians agitating within its borders for independence or the destabilization and overthrow of the Hashemite state, as in the days of Yasser Arafat's Black September guerrilla movement that wreaked havoc in the country in the early 1970s.

To complicate matters, it might also be argued that Jordan has no substantive claim to the West Bank, having annexed it by military force in 1948–1949. And to complicate matters even further, the so-called London Agreement of 1987 between Jordan's King Hussein and Israeli Minister of Foreign Affairs Shimon Peres, which would have provided for Palestinian elections *without PLO participation*, leading to an international conference to confirm the results, was rendered null and void because the two principals interpreted the results differently and because Peres had apparently failed to consult Prime Minister Yitzhak Shamir. Peres claimed that he had informed Shamir of the negotiations; Shamir denied this. Perhaps more to the point, it should be obvious that Arafat would surely not have consented to being sidelined and would have reacted from his Tunis headquarters in his characteristic manner by fomenting yet another violent uprising in Gaza and the West Bank, as indeed happened in 1987 during the first intifada, which, although spontaneous in its origins, the PLO supported and ultimately coordinated from afar. Where the responsibility lies for the failure of the agreement will probably never be satisfactorily determined, but even if Israel is implicated in this tortuous affair, Jordan remains a key player in the game. To complicate matters ever further, it may be argued that West Bank Palestinians are still *de facto* citizens of Jordan.

4   It is true that the next Koranic verse allows for the possibility of peace, but *that* peace in real terms hinges on the "right of return" that, according to Arafat (and his successors), is a non-negotiable condition and would, of course, mean the disappearance of the Jewish state. It is important to note that Israel's Law of Return, which grants special status to Jews in the diaspora, should not be confused with the Palestinian insistence on the "right of return." The former is predicated on the founding of a nation in a

legitimate decision-making forum and is meant to redress 2,000 years of exile, dispersion and suffering as well as to ensure against another Holocaust; the latter is a doubtful concept that ignores the salient facts of the matter, including the vicissitudes and displacements of war, the results of deliberate policy on the part of the Arab nations to create a weapon against Israel, the forcible expulsion of Jews from Arab territories, and the ineluctable fact that *the overwhelming majority of Palestinian claimants have no historical title to the land in question.*

5 Everybody lies, and official institutions at the national level are built on the lie. But there is a difference. Truth may well be a rare commodity but it can nevertheless be found from time to time in both private and public life. It is only when the lie becomes the very air an individual or a collective breathes and *the intrinsic condition of their psychic equilibrium* that catastrophe becomes inevitable. Hannah Arendt made a similar point, in her study of Adolf Eichmann and the banality of evil, with regard to the Germany she knew: "it is sometimes difficult not to believe that mendacity has become an integral part of the German national character."

Until it is understood in the West that the Palestinians live by and in the lie as the Arab nations, steeped in a world of virtual politics, live by and in a climate of hatred, resentment, systematic betrayal, and pandemic dissimulation, no headway can be made in trying to effect a *lasting* Middle East peace accord. True, there are a small number of gallant individuals in the Muslim community who may be regarded as exceptions to the rule, who have "given the lie" to the babes and sucklings in the West who wring their hands over "root causes"—Kanan Makiya, Irshad Manji, Ibn Warraq, Ayaan Hirsi Ali, and Amir Taheri, heirs each in his or her own way of the great and atypical fourteenth-century Arab historical thinker Ibn Khaldun, come immediately to mind—but the Rule of the Lie remains the rule, uniform and unchangeable. The minim of brave thinkers who have struggled to bring clarity and candour into the sinister machinations of Arab disinformation have either been marginalized, expelled from the tribe, fatwa'd, or assassinated by the *Mukhaberat* (Arab Secret Services) in order to keep the fictitious narrative intact.

Merely track the Arab/Palestinian/Muslim record of public discourse from the atrocity stories of rape and massacre at the village of Deir Yassin, in which a regrettable but problematic event was inflated beyond any semblance to what actually happened ("We have to say this," admitted Palestinian commander Hussein Khalidi to Hazam Nusseibi of the Palestinian Broadcasting Service in a moment of internal confidence, "so the Arab armies will come to liberate Palestine from the Jews"); to Palestinian cabinet minister and senior negotiator Saeb Erekat's similar canard about a massacre at Jenin, later refuted by a UN fact-finding commission (Erekat, possibly the most polished and oleaginous liar in the entire Palestinian entourage of spin doctors, just can't help himself, calling an IDF operation in Beit Lahiya in the northern Gaza Strip against rocket launching crews in which eight Palestinians were killed, a "massacre"); to the Palestinian fable that the Jabaliya explosion causing twenty-one fatalities was the result of an IDF missile strike when witness reports showed that Hamas activists had accidentally set off explosives at the rally; to the stories put into circulation in the Arab/Palestinian press holding the Mossad responsible for the tragedy of 9/11; to the Palestinian denial of any implication in the *Karin A* episode; to Iranian TV accusing Israel of spreading AIDS in the Arab world and Egyptian TV dramatizing *The Protocols of the Elders of Zion* for a mass audience; to the Saudi government putting the blame for a recent spate of terrorist attacks against resident Westerners on Israeli covert operations; to Yasser Arafat's deploring the ravages of the suicide bombers in the Western media while at the same time praising and inciting these very same murderers in the Arabic media; to the grotesque fabrication surrounding the death of young Muhammad al-Dura for which the Israelis were held accountable, as they were for the Al-Soudanyia beach tragedy in Gaza caused by Hamas mine emplacements; to the shameless whopper put about by the Palestinian Authority that the teenage suicide bombers dispatched to blow themselves up at Israeli checkpoints and supermarkets were actually recruited by the Israelis for propaganda purposes; to Palestinian UN observer Nasser al-Kidwa including the name of the Palestinian teenager Hassan Jamil Za'anin, murdered by the Aqsa Brigades for trying to prevent his family property from being used as a Kassam missile site, on a list of "martyrs" submitted to the world body; to the episode on August 9, 2006, in Gaza involving the death of a five-year-old girl, which was blamed on an Israeli military strike, although on August 10 the news emerged that she had fallen from a swing; to the PA allegation that Israel is dumping poisoned candies (an old tactic: as the British Royal Commission of 1936 states, the Arabs accused the British of "dropping poisoned sweets from aeroplanes"), "carcinogenic juices," and radioactive substances on the Palestinian market as well as releasing hordes of wild pigs to destroy the fields around Palestinian villages and using landfills in the Territories for disposal of toxic wastes; to the fact that whenever a mortar shell or a bomb being prepared for launch against Israel explodes prematurely in a Palestinian home or enclave causing injuries or death, it is almost always Israeli tank fire that is blamed, even if no IDF units are operating in the area; to almost every public statement issued by the Palestinian Authority—and we may eventually come to understand what we are up against, a terminal case of collective tardive dyskinesia.

Even so reputable a historian as Albert Hourani in his *A History of the Arab Peoples* plays fast and loose with the facts, claiming that Jews possessed "a large proportion of the most productive areas" of war-torn Palestine—which is simply untrue—and then asserting that they were mainly urbanized—which is not only contradictory, but also patently false. But what is yet more distressing is the gauzy fairy-tale atmosphere of his account of the 1947–1949 war in which the skein of cause and effect is almost entirely passed over while the invading Arab armies are described as merely responding to an indigenous conflict. No mention is made of the *effendi* class who actually sold the land—largely uncultivable—to the Jewish settlers and then settled in comfort in large urban centres in Lebanon, Syria, and Egypt. No mention of the ongoing presence of Jews in the Holy Land from early biblical times and throughout the centuries up to the present moment of conflict. No mention of the Egyptian representative to the armistice talks in the wake of the 1947–1949 war who casually informed a British journalist that, "We don't care if all the refugees will die. There are more than enough Arabs around"—which neatly epitomizes the attitude of the invading powers who were less concerned with the restoration of Palestine than with the annexation of the entire region and the consequent obliteration of the new-born Jewish state. Of the vast number of Jews living in Arab countries who were driven from their homes and their property confiscated, all we are told is that these ancient communities "virtually ceased to exist" and that they "moved mainly to Israel." Here the reality of violence and expropriation is serenely scrubbed out in the implication of voluntary abandonment. Hourani's studiously unimpassioned style and summary evasiveness is perhaps the most effective and damaging way of lying of them all.

6   I have applied my stopwatch to the TV screen and the results are grimly conclusive. Dead and wounded Palestinian children luridly receive three to four times as much media exposure as dead and wounded Israeli children. Ululating Palestinian women are featured twice in the same news segment, the camera zooming lovingly on those exotic and contorted visages; a grieving Israeli mother is caught briefly in the camera's catalectic glance. Another report devotes nearly two minutes to the Israeli army's mistaken shooting of several Palestinian civilians and concludes with a twelve-second commentary on an Israeli couple deliberately killed by terrorists on the same day. A demolished house in Nablus garners a one-minute TV clip; a blown-up bus in Jerusalem with many dead and injured, eighteen seconds. (Only those scenes in which Palestinians are shown in a negative light are expurgated or suppressed: although many clips and stories have been selectively rerun over the last few years, I have yet to see a retransmission of the Palestinian jubilee celebrating 9/11.) The same applies to newspaper

coverage where not only space but heart-wrenching photos are intended to draw sympathy for the Palestinians. Let a Palestinian teenager be killed in a firefight between Israeli soldiers and Palestinian terrorists and he or she is blazoned in the world press, which is always quick to feature a photo-op funeral; but seventeen-year-old Ella Abukasis, rendered brain-dead by a Kassam rocket attack on Sderot on January 15, 2005, and taken off life-support on January 21, disappears into the archives. On the one occasion I am aware of when a newspaper (the *Globe and Mail*) reproduced a graphic photo of the victims of a mangled Israeli bus, readers wrote outraged letters to the editor vehemently protesting the absence of propriety.

Sometimes, the anti-Israeli media spin is far more subtle. On July 23, 2006, in the second week of the Israel/Hizbullah war, the UN Undersecretary General for Humanitarian Affairs, Jan Egeland, called the Israeli offensive a "violation of international law," but on July 24 he condemned Hizbullah for its "cowardly blending among women and children"; in its reporting of these statements, the CBC reversed the order of rhetorical precedence, beginning with Egeland's later remarks and concluding with his earlier denunciation of Israel, for what is last said remains longer in the mind—a well-known device in classical rhetoric, the manipulation of *kairos*, or "timing."

The same ethos is also at work in the public lecture forum where anti-Israeli speakers are regularly accorded time and respect, while pro-Israeli advocates are often deprived of their civil rights and privileges. No one to my knowledge has yet disrupted an address by Noam Chomsky or indeed prevented a Palestinian speaker from conveying his or her message. Leila Shahid, a paid propagandist for the Palestinians, is received with high honours at a conference held at the Université du Québec à Montréal. Hannan Ashwari, among the most sinuous of Palestinian contortionists, is everywhere welcomed with open arms. Palestinian (and Hizbullah) flacks are invariably treated as reputable authorities. But former Israeli Prime Minister Benjamin Netanyahu is, in effect, chased from the podium at Montreal's Concordia University by a violent pro-Palestinian mob—and the sponsoring organization, Hillel, chastised for inviting him to this venue. More recently, former Israeli Prime minister Ehud Barak, despite his dovish credentials, was denied the right to speak at the downtown campus of the university, a decision praised by Palestinian student representatives. It comes as no surprise that the alleged ringleader of the plot to blow up the Holland Tunnel, Assam Hammoud, is a graduate of Concordia. Middle East scholar Daniel Pipes, one of the very few reasonable and erudite capacities in the field, is rudely cautioned by police to avoid incitement prior to his lecture at York University while those who would silence him go unreprimanded. Two years later, Pipes is once again subjected to verbal harassment by a gang of eighty professors and graduate students at the University of Toronto, where he was invited to speak, accusing him of sowing "hate, prejudice and fear-mongering." Pipes' scholarship is careful, balanced, and *verifiable*—his great sin in the current academic environment.

7 The liberal-Democratic campaign against the American president regarding this point entered the realm of pure slander. A certain Dr. Joseph Price, in a prominently featured letter to the *Atlantic* (October 2004) commenting on an earlier article by James Fallows (July/August 2004) that dealt with George W. Bush's presumably diminishing rhetorical skills, proffers the diagnosis of "presenile dementia." This theme was also developed by Justin Frank in his 2004 book entitled *Bush on the Couch: Inside the Mind of the President*. Similarly, the infamous Lyndon LaRouche disseminates a webcast (October 6, 2004) with the heading, "The Number One Issue in the Presidential Debates Is George W. Bush's Mental Illness." Extrapolating from Frank, LaRouche lists among the infirmities from which Bush apparently suffers: "an omnipotence complex; paranoia; an Oedipal Complex; sadism…"and so on. Bush is further accused of seeing the world in rigid black-and-white (as if, after 9/11 and the gathering Islamic threat, it were still possible to shuffle about in non-dichotomous grey). Bush's so-called deficiencies are then falsely reified as "diagnosed mental disorders." The moral crudity of these allegations should be seen as a logical development of the vulgar and reflexive crusade of the intellectual Left against an incumbent president. (Of course, LaRouche has also claimed that the Queen of England heads an international drug smuggling racket.)

8 Although a BBC news report on the night of the attack stressed the unfortunate nature of this event, its correspondent mentioned in passing that there had been a series of prior provocations on both sides. What he did not mention was that the Israeli provocations consisted of a right-wing settler threatening a Palestinian woman and another group of settlers raising a rather harmless fuss on the outskirts of a Gazan village; the Palestinian provocations comprised a running spate of almost daily terrorist attempts to attack Israeli military and civilian targets, mortar and rocket barrages on Israeli towns and settlements even in the midst of the ceasefire pact, roadside bombs, and, ultimately, the Tel Aviv blast on Saturday, February 25, 2005. Nor did he see fit to mention that this was the sixth suicide bombing in that quarter of Tel Aviv since the start of the second intifada. The correspondent then went on to indicate that negotiations had stalled for several years owing to the Israeli refusal to deal with Yasser Arafat; he pointedly neglected to explain the reason and the context—the second intifada, Arafat's "million martyr" campaign, his praising of the suicide bombers, and his call for "rivers of blood" in the Arabic media.

9 As columnist Caroline Glick wrote in the *Jerusalem Post* for February 4, 2005, "So, here we are again, at the dawn of a new peace process which will bring no peace; will legitimize terrorists and the authoritarian regimes that support them; will weaken Israel's democratic institutions while endangering its citizenry; and will engender scorn for America and faith in Israel's eventual destruction in the hearts of millions of people who today waver between support for freedom and support for terror." With Arafat behind us and Abbas and Mashaal before us, neither of the latter two willing to dismantle the terrorist networks, and considering the US State Department's unfounded exhilaration with the Palestinian people, if not always their leaders, as well as Europe's irrational antipathy against Israel, I strongly suspect that Glick's warnings will prove truthful.

10 Many of these Jewish refugees, after much suffering, eventually found their way to Israel and, like their Palestinian counterparts, were fruitful and multiplied. They now constitute about half the current population of the country. The irony here, as Paul Berman points out in *Terror and Liberalism*, is that these Jews of Middle Eastern provenance are "routinely reviled, by anti-Zionists everywhere, as European colonists." A further irony is that these displaced Jews cannot seek the redress that the Palestinians claim for themselves. Their properties are lost and no compensation of any sort is forthcoming, neither from the Arabs nor from the Europeans.

11 Bernard was formerly the official spokesman for the Quai d'Orsay, the French foreign ministry, into whose centennial antisemitic tradition, from Louis Herbette to Louis Massignon to Claude Cheysson (of "My condemnation of Zionism is absolute" fame) he fit quite seamlessly. It should be admitted, however, that such "diplomatic" remarks are probably no more damaging in the long run than the more "scholarly" utterance of a Palestinian apologist like Edward Said whose intellectual respectability both masked and facilitated a more dubious agenda, especially in his contributions to the Cairo newspaper *Al-Ahram*, which are replete with anti-Israeli lies and fabulations. The only nation that can compete with Israel in degree of heinousness is the nation in which he flourished as a tenured professor, honoured thinker, and prominent citizen, the United States. Ibn Warraq's paper on intellectual terrorism published by the Institute for the Secularisation of Islamic Society, which outed Said's "historical howlers" and "intellectual dishonesty," is a debunking that has been long overdue. See also Martin Kramer's *Ivory Towers on Sand* for a superb exposé of Said's spurious apologetics.

Be that as it may, such Said-like thinking has become epidemic among the intellectual emir class. The fact that the Muslim Middle East currently has little to offer the world except lessons in state repression and religious fanaticism and the efficient distribution of bloody, indiscriminate killing techniques seems to have escaped these luminaries almost completely.

A dynamic and pluralistic Israel, the only functioning democracy in the region and one in which all shades of debate and opinion are not only permitted but encouraged, remains, of course, an affront to such discerning sensibilities. One can perhaps excuse Greece's celebrated composer and national hero Mikis Theodorakis' outrageous remarks about Israel—"this small nation is the root of evil"—as the maunderings of advanced senility or cosseted ignorance, but what is one to make, for instance, of the influential libel of a Nobelized writer like José Saramago denouncing the Jews for perpetrating an equivalent Holocaust on the West Bank, thereby showing that literary genius can go hand in hand with moral regression and plain stupidity? (Saramago would have been right at home in the Lisbon of 1373, 1449, and 1482 during the bloody anti-Jewish riots there.) Or of *Harper's* correspondent Chris Hedges, an ideological descendant of Walter Duranty, who claims to have witnessed Israeli soldiers enticing Palestinian children into an enclosed space and mowing them down for sport—perhaps he was viewing doctored Palestinian videos? Or of the CBC's Jerusalem correspondent Neil Macdonald whose unabated anti-Israeli slant has further tarnished the reputation of the national broadcaster—he has been reassigned to Washington where his innuendoes are now directed against the Americans? Or of a sensitive and imaginative novelist like Louis de Bernières claiming, with what can only be described as opprobrious naiveté, that "Israel has been adopting tactics reminiscent of the Nazis?" Or of UN special envoy Lakhdar Brahmini violating the principle of neutrality by anathematizing Israel as a "poison" and boasting that he has never shaken a Jewish hand (unlike interim Iraqi prime minister Ayad Allawi, who shook the hand of Israeli Foreign Minister Silvan Shalom at the United Nations—and was immediately castigated by Hizbullah, which called the gesture "disgraceful" and an "affront" to the Islamic world)? Or of a distinguished scientist like Richard Dawkins adding his name to the divestment campaign? (I can only hope this is another Richard Dawkins whose name appeared on the divestment petition or that it is an error.) Or of French Foreign Minister Philippe Douste-Blazy who, during the summer 2006 Mideast war, lauded Iran for playing "a stabilizing role in the region," showing that France is either completely out of touch with reality or, more likely, playing its usual cynical and destabilizing role on the world political stage to the detriment of Israel?

But there is nothing sadder than the involuted spectacle presented by the Jew whose self-soiling will not buy him absolution when the world's tribunal is convened. A recent example of this mephitic species at work is furnished by Haim Bresheeth, an Israeli academic at the University of East London, who in a demonstrably one-sided anti-Israeli conference sponsored by the School of Oriental and African Studies at the University of London on December 5, 2004, claimed that in comparison with South African apartheid, "Israel is much worse." Bresheeth gladly joined ranks with fellow conferees and infusorial antisemites like Palestinian Solidarity Campaign UK representative Betty Hunter, who proclaimed that "our aim is to make Israel a pariah state"; Palestinian political analyst Omar Barghouti, who equated the IDF with the Nazi army; and the scurrilous Tom Paulin, who said of Jewish immigrants to Israel, "I feel nothing but hate for them." But Bresheeth has lots of Jewish company. Renowned symphony conductor Daniel Barenboim was a far better friend to Edward Said than he is to the state of Israel; judging from his performances in the political forum he must surely qualify as an honorary Palestinian. Trent University philosophy professor Michael Neumann stated on an Internet website, "I am not interested in the truth, or justice, or understanding, or anything else, except so far as it serves my purpose"—which is "to help the Palestinians." He then amplifies his convictions: "If it means encouraging vicious, racist antisemitism, or the destruction of the state of Israel, I still don't care." The *New York Times'* Sulzberger family, who suppressed almost all reference to the Holocaust during the most cataclysmic period in Jewish history and persists in a policy of isolating Israel, merits nothing but shame and disgrace. (The younger Sulzberger has made much of his Episcopalian conversion.) Harold Pinter, another prominent Jewish intellectual, a playwright of some talent and a poet of none, has outspokenly supported the Palestinians and was one of the signatories to the British campaign to boycott Israeli businesses. Of Norman Finkelstein, student and acolyte of Noam Chomsky (the same Chomsky whose political acumen is perhaps best characterized by his still-unrepudiated support for Pol Pot's homicidal Khmer Rouge regime) and one of the most perfervid of Jewish Jew-haters, the less said the better. I have far more respect for that self-hating Austrian Jew, Otto Weininger, author of *Sex and Character*, who had the courage to take his self-loathing to its logical conclusion, committing suicide at the age of twenty-three.

Jew-haters, both Jewish and Gentile, should never forget that Israel, for all its internal struggles and contradictions, is fighting for its very survival against an ancestral enemy that has long refused to recognize its existence and that has embraced the worst excesses of (real) Nazi propaganda in its campaign of lies, defamation, and ceaseless violence. The following passage from a poem by Natan Yonatan well expresses the Israeli hope to reclaim the Negev, both geographically and spiritually, in the face of such barren and irrational ferocity.

> *May God preserve the places and the names*
> *May he some meager strength reserve*
> *To complete the map within the light.*

The "map within the light" is not the so-far chimerical "road map to peace" that has mesmerized the international community. For the Muslim, the "road map" may have a different traditional connotation as well, namely that of the *Sirat*, or "the road," referring to the bridge across the fires of hell over which the righteous will pass and from which the unrighteous will fall. In the Islamic mindset, there can be little doubt who are the righteous and who the unrighteous or how the concept of *Sirat* may be applied to the current situation. The "road map" is the Arab/Palestinian means of trying to ensure that Israel becomes the victim of the *Sirat*. Eventually there may be two states in the disputed area, despite what David Horovitz in *Still Life with Bombers* has pithily described as a dialectic of "murderous Palestinian plotting and fierce Israeli countermeasures." But the fact of the matter is that Israel will never be fully secure and Palestine will probably never be even remotely self-sustaining.

12 Referring to the current troubles at Columbia, the *New York Times* headline for March 31, 2005, reads, "Columbia Panel Clears Professors of Anti-Semitism." What was not reported was that the university worked out an arrangement with the *Times* that gave the newspaper exclusive rights to the panel's findings if it agreed not to solicit comments from those Jewish students intimidated and censured by their Arab and pro-Arab professors.

13 The words of the 10th/11th century Jewish poet Joseph ibn Abithur carry an eerie foreboding into the present context of the slaughter of the innocent in the towns and cities of Israel. In his "Lament on the Devastation of the Land of Israel," he writes:

> *Weep for the blind who wander on,*
> *Defiled, through the land of Zion,*
> *With the blood of pregnant women,*
> *The blood of the aged and young children.*

14 See *The Anti Chomsky Reader*, edited by Peter Collier and David Horowitz, for a rigorously documented account of Chomsky's character, scholarship, methods of persuasion, and propaganda exploits. This book should be read by anyone who is still impressed by Chomsky's artfully constructed persona

as a civil libertarian and as America's leading dissident. A wealth of sources
and documentary "addresses" are furnished in minute detail and can be
easily verified by those who stubbornly refuse to challenge the factitious
reputation of their idol, if they are willing to take a little time. A significant
number of Chomsky's own sources are provided as well, both in the body of
the text and the notes, an essential addition since many of these sources are
often not fully referenced, are cleverly decontextualized or subtly recontex-
tualized when they are not simply misquoted or abridged, or are so obscure
and of such dubious origin as to be almost impossible to find without a
guide. Assembled and explicated here for readerly convenience, what contributor Paul Bogdanor calls the "hallmarks of his intellectual repertoire:
massive falsification of facts, evidence, sources and statistics, conducted in
the service of a bigoted and extremist ideological agenda" can no longer
be ignored. As another contributor to the volume, Werner Cohn, asserts
(and explicitly shows), "one of Chomsky's chief rhetorical techniques is to
misrepresent the writings of others." What is no less troubling is Chomsky's
obvious reluctance to reconsider those of his sources who have gone on to
revise or repudiate their earlier conclusions. The shoddy scholarship alone
should have alerted any attentive reader to the bad faith of this unscrupulous ideologue. The wonder is that so few have bothered to check the facts.

15 For Naomi Klein, see *Arts & Opinion On-Line Magazine*, Vol. 2, No. 4, 2003.
For details on the International Solidarity Movement, see the *Jerusalem Post*
for April 12, 2003, and the *New York Times* for May 4, 2003. These matters
are also discussed in Alan Dershowitz's *The Case for Israel*. Dershowitz wryly
observes that these sensitives "have never offered to serve as shields protecting Israeli citizens against Palestinian terrorism" and concludes, "The
media should stop referring to these people as peace activists and should
call them what they are: active supporters and facilitators of Palestinian
terrorism." Denis Boyles (mentioned in text) remarks on this score that for
most of the European press, there may be a war on terrorism, but fortunately there are no terrorists; there are only resistance fighters. (Or what are
variously called "militants" or "activists.")

The media, we might add, should also cease referring to the Jewish state
as a torture haven when it is very likely the most humane and enlightened
of all embattled countries. Those who condemn Israel for such nefarious
practices gloss right over the obvious: that when Muslim political detainees
in the United States are to be "worked over," they are sent not to Israel but
to Egypt and Syria, where torture is routine procedure. Iran is especially
notable in this regard, cited even by the anti-Israeli Human Rights Watch
as among the world's worst torture states, and condemned in the memoir of Grand Ayatollah Hossein-Ali Montazeri, who refers to "crimes…

committed in the prisons of the Islamic Republic in the name of Islam the like of which was never seen in the Shah's evil regime." And what happened to William Sampson in Saudi Arabia is normal procedure, whereas the Israeli High Court has passed binding legislation making it illegal to exert even mild "pressure tactics" to extract information from terrorists. The rulings of the Court are followed to the letter, even when they are detrimental to Israeli security.

16 Israel, as has been often noted, is the West's eastern front and is exposed to the gravest danger, as it has been since ancient times. "They have said," reads Psalm 83, "Come, and let us cut them off from being a nation; that the name of Israel may be no more in remembrance"—the Bible's way of saying, "Come, let us wipe them off the map." But should Israel be "cut off from being a nation," the devastation would not stop there.

17 "You can't even blow up Jews these days without being labelled an anti-Semite," quips filmographer Barry Oringer in an article for Pacific News Service entitled "Terrorism Chic and the Brain-Dead Left." As Michael Coren, of *Mere Christian* fame, put it in a troubled reflection on the Mel Gibson movie *The Passion of the Christ*, "try being even partly Jewish and see what anti-Semitic e-mails look like. Anti-Semitism in the guise of anti-Zionism is once again flowing like some malignant disease through the sickly bloodstream of modernity." The anti-Jewish bias, it should be said, is often far more subtly peddled than it is in the Gospel according to Mel. See for example the Montreal French-language daily *Le Devoir* for November 1/2, 2003, which bannered as its lead front page article the abominable fact that the Centraide charity organization disbursed $1 million to the United Jewish Appeal, described as "un organisme plusieurs fois millionnaire." It also points out that the UJA has "notamment pour mission de soutenir Israël." As the president of Centraide affirmed in a CBC radio interview shortly afterward, the Centraide subvention to the UJA is allocated proportionately and is not redirected to Israel. The article purports to be objective, but one wonders how many of the newspaper's readers will ask themselves why this minor irrelevance with its air of an exposé—apart from the fact that it is intentionally misleading—should receive pride of place anyway, dominating the front page and eclipsing important world events. The circumstance of donation, in itself not shameful, has been presented so as to give a very wrong impression. The article feeds two birds with one seed: it lets by implication the terrorist-funding Islamic charities off the hook while reinforcing the cultural stereotype of the Shylockian Jew.

Even presumably respectable organizations are contaminated by evident bias. The *British Medical Journal*, for example, has got into the act, publishing an opinion piece in its October 16, 2004, issue that accuses the Israeli army of regularly shooting children, claims that the "pro-Israel lobby" is "morally corrupt," and condemns the separation barrier while making only passing reference to the suicide bombers with no mention of the identity of the victims. The *Library Journal*, too, consistently recommends to over 100,000 library directors publications that favour the Palestinian narrative—books such as Ilan Pappe's fiercely anti-Israeli *A History of Modern Palestine: One Land, Two Peoples* or the unabashedly pro-Palestinian *Of New Intifada: Resisting Israel's Apartheid*, which includes a Foreword by Noam Chomsky, while typically downplaying a biography of Yasser Arafat by perhaps the most reputable and competent scholar in the field, Efraim Karsh, as insufficiently complex.

We should not deceive ourselves into believing that "it can't happen here." Sinclair Lewis's 1935 novel of that title should have put paid to so myopic and self-pampering a notion long ago. Rather we should believe with Jean Améry that "the dramaturgy of antisemitism continues to exist. A new mass extermination of Jews cannot be ruled out as a possibility."

18 Quoted in Dennis Prager and Joseph Telushkin, *Why The Jews?* The authors point out what cannot be doubted: "The contention that anti-Zionists are not enemies of Jews, despite the advocacy of policies that would lead to the mass murder of Jews, is, to put it as generously as possible, disingenuous.... Given, then, that if anti-Zionism realized its goal, another Jewish holocaust would take place, attempts to draw distinctions between anti-Zionism and antisemitism are simply meant to fool the naïve." All that has happened, according to these authors, is "only a change in rhetoric." Anti-Zionism, they claim, "is unique in only one way: it is the first form of Jew-hatred to deny that it hates the Jews."

19 It should be evident that there will never be anything resembling even a faltering peace in the region until Hizbullah, the single most destabilizing and fanatical element in the Middle East warscape, with its grid of Iranian-supplied rockets primed at Israel's northern border, is disarmed and dispersed. For without Hizbullah (and its Iranian backers), the terrorist nexus would be deprived of its senior patron and its primary source of funding and *matériel*.

20 Israel's need for clear, defensible borders may also be understood as an extension of the kosher laws articulated in Leviticus. As anthropologist Mary Douglas has explained in *Purity and Danger*, kosher categories are based on the concept of wholeness, intactness, and appropriateness. Animals that jump categories or mix characteristics are considered unclean. Dietary prohibitions have to do with preventing "boundary violations," a cultural wall erected to resist impurity and the threat of chaos. In the same way, though far more significantly, a clearly demarcated set of physical borders

are required in order to preserve the nation intact, to forestall the intrusion of that which would disrupt the physical integrity of the state.

21 A recent example of such intellectual frivolity is provided by Jacques Derrida who, in an interview with *Le Monde* for August 18, 2004, fashionably referred to "la politique désastreuse et suicidaire d'Israël." To use a word like "suicidaire" to qualify the policies of a nation riddled with suicide bombers is not only in bad taste, but bespeaks a turn of mind captivated by its own discursive formulations at the expense of any serious purchase on the real world or of the felt need for moral substance. Derrida, we recall, himself a Jew, was an unswerving defender of Nazi collaborator Paul de Man.

22 Trudeau is also lauded for his previous film, *Embedded in Baghdad*, documenting the experience of an Iraqi family during the American-led invasion. He is piquantly described by the film's TV sponsor, Bell Globalmedia, as having "spent 40 days and 40 nights in Iraq." It is reassuring to recall that Noah also spent forty days and forty nights under that which fell from the skies, that Moses took the same amount of time in receiving the tablets, and that the Son of God fasted not a moment less. Trudeau's qualifications are impeccable.

23 The notion of the "wall," like that of the "road" (see note 11), has a profound theological resonance, this being the Middle East. Ibn Warraq directs us to Koran 7:44, which mentions the wall separating paradise from hell, as well as to the Jewish midrash in which Rabbi Acha describes this wall as being of so narrow a span that people can see from one side into the other. The wall that divides the saved from the damned is thin as a veil but is nevertheless unbreachable and will remain always in place. In practical terms, the Islamic "wall" is social, political, and theological, and has universal import; the Israeli "wall" is local and is intended to prevent suicide bombings and to create a defensible buffer zone.

24 The Jew is also caught between the various denominations of his own faith. There is a Jewish joke that underlines the problem. An Orthodox and a Reform rabbi find themselves seated side by side at a religious conference. In the process of getting to know one another, the Orthodox rabbi recounts that he has recently officiated at a bar mitzvah in which he was informed that the celebrant received the gift of a Harley. Puzzled, he asks his Reform neighbour, "But what is a Harley?" "It's a motorcycle," comes the reply, "but what's a bar mitzvah?" And as I continue to ask, what is a Jew?

25 The concept of the unconscious is as murky as it gets, whether we consider it as a cistern of buried instincts, appetites, and desires (Freud), an inventory of symbolic archetypes (Jung), or as a ghostly semiotic structured like a language (Lacan). Nevertheless, if we regard the unconscious as a repository of hidden refusals, as a light eclipsed by shame or even as a form of

shuttered contrition whose sign has been reversed, it makes some sense to define the Jew as the Gentile's latent and undisclosed, interior Other. To apply the words of Peter Gay from *The Naked Heart*, in which he discusses the nature of mental repression, we might say that the Jew inspires the "ideals and fears, incentives and threats [that] help to shape the self as much as the instinctual urges that spring from profoundly buried inner reservoirs." The issue must always remain somewhat obscure since the Jew may be regarded equally as the bearer of the id or libido (the Song of Solomon) and the representative of the superego (the book of Job), both troubling texts for Christian hermeneutics.

26 The most famous passage from this poem, "Death is a master from Germany," is echoed by Khaled Fouad Allam, author of *Letter to a Suicide Bomber*, who refers to the radical Islamic clerics as "the masters of horror."

27 The angel, writes Benjamin, which is also the Shekhina (the feminine form of the Divinity), flies backward into the future "which he knows so well that he traverses it without turning around and without letting the one he has chosen out of view." Elizabeth Bishop uses a similar trope in one of her best poems, "The Man-Moth," which, though intended differently, offers as good an image or topos of the Jew as can be found in modern literature. This, as I say, was clearly not her intention, but symbols are mutable by nature.

> *The Man-Moth always seats himself facing the wrong way*
> *and the train starts at once at its full, terrible speed,*
> *without a shift of gears or a gradation of any sort.*
> *He cannot tell the rate at which he travels backwards.*

But the poem must be read in its entirety. I think as well of a poem by Robyn Sarah entitled "Here/There," which reads in part:

> *Get thee forth and Get thee back*
> *are the beginnings of two stories*
> *good for a lifetime,*
> *as wandering*
> *is only wandering*
> *in relation to somewhere left behind*
> *or yet to find.*

28 As Rabbi Ariel Bar Tzadok proclaimed in *Yeshivat Benei N'vi'im Online*, "My son, I pray G-d, will learn Torah and learn Martial Arts." The rabbi is probably familiar with Yiddish poet Abraham Sutzkever's lines from a poem about casting leaden type into bullets: "Jewish bravery once hidden

in words/Must now strike back with shot." Similarly, poet Irving Layton writes in a Maccabeean poem dedicated to his sons, after mentioning "The wandering Jew: the suffering Jew/The despoiled Jew: the beaten Jew," the Jew burned, gassed, humiliated, and helpless:

> *Be none of these, my sons*
> *My sons, be none of these*
> *Be gunners in the Israeli Air Force*

Thus Agesilaus Santander or the Man-Moth, in his latest agonistic incarnation, is now an IAF pilot, flying the right way.

29 It seems especially difficult to explain how intelligent, educated, or ethical individuals could harbour antisemitic feelings, but perhaps the answer is really quite simple. We are all, to put it crudely, potentially bloodthirsty brutes, killers from the egg, but some of us possess a conscience and can discipline the turmoil within. But since the Jew is almost universally proscribed as the perennial enemy of mankind and is therefore seen to deserve the vicious treatment handed out to him, the antisemite can put his conscience at rest or, better, convince himself that conscience demands a cleansing ruthlessness vis-à-vis a world defiled by the Jew. Thus the antisemite is able to release his intrinsic savagery and violent impulses without succumbing to remorse, shame, or guilt. He may even, if he thinks about it, persuade himself that he is acting for the benefit of humanity. Antisemitism might be described as a socially approved form of sociopathic behaviour.

30 "Apartheid" as wielded by anti-Israelis and antisemites is an ambiguous if not disingenuous concept. Jews will not be permitted to settle in Gaza or the West Bank once the new state of Palestine has been established, and are excluded by law in Saudi Arabia, Jordan, and other Arab countries. If this is not apartheid, then the concept has no meaning whatsoever.

31 German-Jewish historian George Mosse has claimed to the contrary that, "It's the same as the stereotype of all outsiders: sexual deviants, gypsies, the permanently insane, people who have hereditary diseases. They all look alike. They are absolute lookalikes. And, of course these are all the people Hitler wanted to exterminate and whom he did exterminate. They all look the opposite of the middle-class, self-controlled idea of beauty, energy, all of this sort of thing." (Quoted in Steven E. Aschheim, *In Times of Crisis*.) Victims are victims; it is only a question of degree. And not only are the victims franchised out, even the victimizers are subsumed under the lemma of all humanity. Aschheim comments approvingly that the "stage has not only become European-wide, but the central categories rendered appear far more a matter of class than of nations." But the relativizing of the deeds

of the perpetrators, no more than the convenable democratization of their victims, does not in any way dilute the "category" of the "Jew," who remains the eternal refugee, mankind's "racial" quarry. This, as they say, is written in stone. Mosse's gypsies, madmen, infirm, and gays (Mosse was himself homosexual) are now recognized, at least in the West, as part of the human family. But the Jew is a historical desideratum. As George Steiner wrote in *Language and Silence*, "the Jew in a gentile nation sits near the door"—even if, I might add, he mistakenly believes that his chair has finally been placed next to the hearth.

32 See Richard Dawkins, *The Selfish Gene* and, to a lesser extent, *The Blind Watchmaker*. Respecting the tyranny exercised by the meme, Dawkins ends his discussion of the subject in *The Selfish Gene* on "a note of qualified hope," since human beings "can rebel against the tyranny of the selfish replicators." "We have the power," Dawkins asserts, "to defy the selfish genes of our birth and, if necessary, the selfish memes of our indoctrination. We can even discuss ways of deliberately cultivating and nurturing pure, disinterested altruism—something that has no place in nature, something that has never existed before in the whole history of the world." Perhaps. But two millennia of memetic stubbornness in the case of the antisemitism replicator does not reassure. It is not even a question of genetic advantage. For, as Dawkins also postulates, "All that is necessary is that the brain should be *capable* of imitation: memes will then evolve that exploit the capability to the full." Both the Christian West and the Islamic Orient furnish the antisemitism meme with a fertile and hospitable environment for reproduction.

33 In the Heine poem from *Hebrew Melodies* mentioned earlier in text (entitled "Princess Sabbath"), the Jew has been changed by a witch's spell into "the likeness of a dog" who "noses/Through life's filthy mire and sweepings." On the Sabbath he is briefly transformed into a Prince, but soon comes the "evil hour" in which he once more

> *Seems to feel the icy fingers*
> *Of a witch upon his heart;*
> *Shudders, fearful of the canine*
> *Metamorphosis that awaits him.*

34 The mercantile image of the Jew was established in the Gospel of John in which Judas is identified as the apostle's manciple and the carrier of the money bag. See verse 12:6: "This he said, not that he cared for the poor; but because he was a thief, and had the bag, and bare what was put therein"; and 13:29: "For some of them thought, because Judas had the bag, that Jesus said unto him, Buy those things that we have need of against the feast..." The image of the Jew as bagman has remained with us to the present day.

35 Cohen writes in *Typing: A Life in 26 Keys* that a Jew is an exile from nowhere, a striking phrase that is not quite right. Franz Kafka was closer to the truth when he described himself in his *Diaries* as living in a condition of multiple exile: as a German speaker from the surrounding Czech majority, as a Jew from the German enclave itself, and as a secular Jew from the heart of his own religion. One thinks also of the political philosopher Leo Strauss, an exile to the US from Weimar Germany, who found, at the very least, an academic home among a like-minded group of scholars and students, adapting the "philosopher-king" theory of intellectual authority that has generated so much controversy in recent years. His theoretical position served him reasonably well as a refuge of the mind though it has now, some years after his death, come under attack for what its critics identify as its dogmatism, elitism, and secretiveness. (See Shadia Drury, *Leo Strauss and the American Right*.) Strauss is also taken to task for his paranoia and Machiavellianism as well as his "crackpot ideology" which "purported to discover hidden meanings in the works of the great philosophers by relying on numerology and encoded silences." (See Daniel J. Flynn, *Intellectual Morons: How Ideology Makes Smart People Fall For Stupid Ideas*.) Strauss, however, can also be understood as a deeply exilic thinker, that is, as one who carried the notion of inner exile into the very texts he was explicating. The text becomes a kind of sheltering environment into which the mind, especially the Jewish mind, emigrates and finds succour, often dissembling its identity. Jews may thus be regarded as a "people of the book" in at least two senses: the text is not only a portable homeland, but a "place" where verbal camouflage is always possible.

It is only fair to note in this connection that the great Jewish scholar Eliezer Berkovits opposed the vision of Jewish thinkers like Hermann Cohen and Franz Rosenzweig who argued that the condition of exile was proper to the Jew since it allowed for the dissemination of Jewish moral teachings among the *goyim* (nations). Berkovits came out strongly for the establishment of a Jewish state precisely to combat the exilic status of the Jew, stressing that national sovereignty was essential to the development of an ethical and creative community. "Only by the creation of such a Jewish environment," he wrote in *Towards Historic Judaism* in 1943, "can we give back to Torah the great partnership of life which alone is capable of freeing Judaism from its present exilic rigidity, and create the circumstances in which evolution will again be possible."

36 Charles Enderlin, France-2's Middle Eastern correspondent, who is deeply involved in the al-Dura libel that helped kick-start the second intifada, is not only Jewish but holds Israeli citizenship as well. Enderlin was not present at the Netzarim shootout but justified his reportage by saying that "the

image corresponded to the reality of the situation." The cameraman who filmed the event and who then passed the footage to Enderlin, Talal Abu Rahma, later retracted his testimony implicating the Israelis. This did not prevent Palestinian poet Mahmoud Darwish from not revising his *Requiem for Muhammad al-Dura*, a piece of versified hogwash that has circulated throughout the Arab world and continues to resonate. "Mohammad," Darwish writes, "hunters are gunning down angels, and the only witness/is a camera's eye..."

Enderlin's vetting of this image (not to mention his suspicious insistence that portions of the film were too painful to reveal, enabling him to bury the outtakes) renders him complicit in what has become a worldwide campaign of disinformation. France TV is now fighting to clear its name in court, suing neither the *Atlantic Monthly* nor the German forensic team that established the case against it, but a certain Phillipe Karsenty, director of a Paris-based analysis firm called Media-Ratings, who aired his grievance on his web site. The nature of the suit does not inspire confidence in the plaintiff. In a partial reprise of the Dreyfus scandal, the French Court of First Instance, *despite the recommendation of the public prosecutor that it rule in Karsenty's favour*, convicted the defendant of libelling France 2 TV and Charles Enderlin. Karsenty has vowed to continue the fight. For the harm that Enderlin has done to both Israel and the truth is incalculable. Indeed, his immediate influence on events is perhaps even more destructive than Chomsky's or Finkelstein's, owing to the power and ubiquity of the television image. (For a convincing refutation of France 2 TV's claims, see www. seconddraft.org.)

37 There is no doubt that Jews, especially in the Pale, have also been exclusionary and xenophobic, but this social and religious dynamic owes as much if not more to the severe restrictions and persecutions to which Jews have been subjected over the centuries. The ghetto responds by reconceiving itself as a gated community. Those who are condemned to live in the precincts of hell will often, if the afflicted community is literate and founded in a sustaining scripture, reimagine hell as the vestibule of heaven from which their persecutors have been excluded. See Jacob Katz, *Exclusiveness and Tolerance*, an exacting study of Jewish/Gentile relations in the medieval and modern worlds.

38 "Next year in East Jerusalem" might well be the Palestinian slogan. But as we have seen, in the successive frameworks of millennial Jewish settlement, Ottoman hegemony and Jordanian sovereignty, *Palestinian* titlehood in the region is far less historically persuasive than Israel's and far more politically debatable than Jordan's.

39 The concept of *tikkun olam*, the repairing or perfecting of the world and the attaining of spiritual freedom, is a basic principle of Jewish mysticism

and owes much to the thought of the sixteenth-century Kabbalist Isaac Luria, who taught that the work of retrieval proceeds through the exercise of kindness, ethical presence, prayer, love, and meditation. The goal is the evolution and spiritualization of the whole of creation and as such bears an obvious affinity, though not necessarily an absolute equivalence, with the teachings of other faiths. The practice of Kabbalah is now a fringe phenomenon, but its humanistic distillate marrows the bones of Ezekiel's valley, the world as we know it.

40 The star, of course, is a well-known pagan symbol adapted to the political allegory represented by the national flag. It is widely believed, for example, that Turkey's five-pointed star alludes to the five pillars of Islam, Jordan's seven-pointed star to the first seven verses of the Koran, and so on. The true meaning of the Star of David remains obscure. In Hebrew, it is the *Magen David*, or Shield of David, attesting to King David's reliance upon the Lord in his various wars. One might speculate that the intersecting triangles refer to the uniting of the two kingdoms of Judah and Israel under David. In Kabbalah, it represents the duality of man and the opposing directions of salvation and perdition. Some exegetes refer to the interlocking back-triangles that reinforce the strength of the battle shield, a technology presumably developed during the Bar Kochbah revolt against the Romans in 132–135 CE. My own explanation obviously owes something to fancy, something to the back-hexagonal pattern used to support my argument.

41 Finkielkraut, who has been an outspoken critic of left-leaning, anti-racist organizations that practice a covert antisemitism under the guise of anti-Zionism, has recently been arraigned in a French court on grounds of defamation. The suit, which is flawed by misquotation, misattribution, unfounded allegations, and gross exaggeration, was brought by Le mouvement contre le racisme et pour l'amitié des peuples (the Movement Against Racism and for Friendship Among Peoples), or Mrap. In his preliminary rebuttal, the philosopher lessoned the plaintiff that "l'ennemi auquel vous aurez affaire, ce n'est plus votre contraire, le racisme, c'est votre double, votre caricature, votre contrefaçon monstreuse" (the enemy you are engaging, racism, is not your opposite, it's your double, your caricature, your monstrous counterfeit). He singles out the notorious Durban World Conference and its *gangue raciste* for having borrowed "ce nouvel idiome immaculé, idiome de l'antiracisme" (this new immaculate idiom, the idiom of antiracism). It was, of course, the Durban Conference that accelerated the BDS (Boycott, Divestment, Sanctions) campaign against Israel.

42 Despite the occasional insight to be found scattered here and there in his memoir, Hobsbawm goes so far as to accuse Israel, along with India and Italy, as harbouring in their governments "the heirs of fascism or parties

inspired by fascism," which goes to show how creaky and partisan his
thinking can be. Himself an heir and supporter of the most vicious and
durable totalitarian ideology of the twentieth century, this loyal Marxist
proudly proclaims that he was never a Zionist and derogates the "project
of a Jewish nation state," opining that Theodor Herzl "would have done
better to stay with the *Neue Freie Presse* as its star columnist." Hobsbawm
was one of those lucky European Jews who were spared the Nazi concentration camps, and whose intellectual lives were neither compromised nor cut
short by the Bolshevik regime to which so many gave their allegiance. I find
it difficult not to get personal about this. When I compare, for example, the
heroic and lucid example of a man like Natan Sharansky, a democrat, dissident and Jew who spent nine years in a Soviet prison and who insists on
the need to preserve the rare faculty of "moral clarity," with the narcissistic
humbug of a coddled Western historian like Hobsbawm, also a Jew, who
has nothing to say about the Holocaust, whose own good fortune seems to
have escaped his encyclopedic attention, and who retains into old age his
commitment to a failed and brutal ideology, I am, quite frankly, appalled.
There can be no excuse for such a prodigy of bad faith. But Hobsbawm is
no mere anomaly. The darling of the radical Left and a widely acknowledged authority in his field, he continues to exert a noxious effect on contemporary political thought.

43 The seven Noachide Laws, or *Brit Noah*, are:
    1. Do not murder.
    2. Do not steal.
    3. Do not worship false gods.
    4. Do not be licentious.
    5. Do not eat a limb removed from a live animal.
    6. Do not curse God.
    7. Set up courts and bring offenders to justice.

44 Names, of course, can always be changed. My own surname, "Solway," is
Scottish, bestowed upon my grandparents by an immigration officer who
stumbled over the Russian "Solovetchik." But the name is usually a dead
giveaway. In this context, I am amused by yet another episode in the career
of London's mayor, Ken Livingstone, who was recently cleared of the charge
of antisemitism regarding certain defamatory remarks he made at the
expense of two Jewish real estate developers, David and Simon Reuben. The
Greater London Authority Standards Committee accepted his defence that
he did not know the two men were Jewish. *David and Simon Reuben*?

45 We may note that the destiny of exclusion is as true of the assimilated
Jew in his adopted country as it is of the Jewish state in the Arab Middle
East. The Jew, whether individually, collectively, or nationally, remains
the perpetual outsider.